Defining
New Yorker
Humor

Defining

New Yorker

Humor

Judith Yaross Lee

University Press of Mississippi
Jackson

For use of the *New Yorker* illustrations, permission from *The New Yorker* is gratefully acknowledged. Material from the Alan Dunn and Mary Petty papers and the Gluyas Williams papers is used by permission of Syracuse University Library, Department of Special Collections. Material from the E. B. White collection is used by permission of the Division of Rare and Manuscript Collections, Cornell University Library, and Mrs. Allene White. Material from the Frank Sullivan collection is used by permission of the Division of Rare and Manuscript Collections, Cornell University Library. Material from *The New Yorker* Records is used by permission of the Manuscripts and Archives Division, The New York Public Library, Astor, Lenox and Tilden Foundations. Material from *Life Magazine* Records is used by permission of the Manuscripts and Archives Division, The New York Public Library, Astor, Lenox and Tilden Foundations.

www.upress.state.ms.us

08 07 06 05 04 03 02 01 00   4 3 2 1

∞

Library of Congress Cataloging-in-Publication Data

Lee, Judith Yaross, 1949–
  Defining New Yorker humor / Judith Yaross Lee.
    p. cm.— (Studies in popular culture)
  Includes bibliographical references (p.) and index.
  ISBN 1-57806-197-0 (cloth : alk. paper) — ISBN 1-57806-198-9 (paper : alk. paper)
  1. American wit and humor—New York (State)—New York—History and criticism. 2. American wit and humor—20th centu-ry—History and criticism. 3. Popular culture—United States— History—20th century. 4. New Yorker (New York, N.Y.: 1925)—History. I. Title. II. Studies in popular culture (Jackson, Miss.)
  PS438 .L44 2000
  051'.09747'1—dc21   99-048347

British Library Cataloging-in-Publication Data available

This one's for Marya
with love

When you deal with humorists, you deal with dynamite.
Harold W. Ross to E. B. White [Summer 1936]

Contents

Acknowledgments

I have acquired a drawerful of debts from this book, and my name appears on the title page because of help from many quarters.

New Yorkers repeatedly welcomed me back over five years of research and writing. Deep thanks go to Susan and Paul Levy and Robert and Jean Ashton for their friendship and hospitality and for their willingness to listen to long tales of adventures in the archives. The return of James, Catherine, and Ted Conmy to New York brought more friends into the project; I wish I could share it with Susan and Chris too. To Phyllis and Gerald Spielman and the late James R. Slater, my gratitude for befriending and entertaining a tired researcher. I owe much to Kathleen and Terence Malley, quintessential New Yorkers, who first asked me, "Do you read the poetry in the *New Yorker*?" This book got its start when Victoria Brand asked, "Will your next book be on *New Yorker* humor?"

I was fortunate to receive expert assistance with the *New Yorker* Records from the staff of the Rare Books and Manuscripts Division of the New York Public Library, especially Mary B. Bowling, William Stingone, Richard Salvato, Melanie Yolles, Laura O'Keefe, John Stinson, Valerie Wingfield, and Angie Sierra. I owe similar thanks to Lucy B. Burgess of Rare and Manuscript Collections, Kroch Library at Cornell University, which holds papers of E. B. White, Frank Sullivan, and other *New Yorker* writers; and to Carolyn Davis of Special Collections at Syracuse University Library, whose marvelous cartoon collections include the archives of *New Yorker* artists Alan Dunn, his wife Mary Petty, Gluyas Williams, and Isidore Klein.

Ohioans in my home base contributed in many ways. Matthew Smith, research assistant extraordinaire, helped me build a bibliographical database of sixteen thousand items. Karen Sue Manderick brought expert secretarial and managerial assistance to the data entry. Research assistants Kim Jones, Alexis Chaboudy, and Hilton Villet ferreted out biographical details; Emily Morris dug up Thurber's old work on the *Columbus Dispatch*. Special thanks to librarians at Alden Library from top to bottom. George Bain and Sheppard Black of Special Collections helped with *Judge*. Microforms staff Ted Foster and Jeff Ferrier and their neighbors in the South East Asia Collection Chau Hoang, Lucy Conn, Judy Connick, Cheryl Cannady, and Lian The-Mulliner provided moral and technical support for two years of *sitzfleischarbeiten*. Reference librarians Sharon Huge, Tim Smith, Nancy Rue, Karen Williams, and Bob Politello tracked down fugitive sources. Graphics specialists Richard Innis and Peggy Sattler of Alden Library's Instructional Media and Technology Services digitized and beautified ancient cartoon images.

Several grants supported work on this book. Funding for bibliographic and archival research came from the Ohio University Research Council and the Ohio University School of Interpersonal Communication (InCo). I am grateful on many counts to Sue DeWine, director of the School of Interpersonal Communication, for her unequivocal support of scholarship. In addition, I am grateful to my InCo colleagues, especially rhetoric faculty members David Descutner, Raymie McKerrow, and Roger Aden, for carrying my teaching responsibilities while I was on faculty fellowship leave to write this book. For the luxury of those nine months for reading, writing, and thinking, I thank Ohio University, particularly Provost Sharon Brehm, and Dean Kathy Krendl of the College of Communication.

From the community of scholars, I owe special thanks to conference organizers and session chairs who allowed me to benefit from sharing work in progress with colleagues near and far. M. Thomas Inge encouraged me to start this project; David Sloane and Linda Bergmann read early versions of chapter 1. As the manuscript took shape I benefited from the insights of series editor Nancy Walker of Vanderbilt University, whose tact is a match for her scholarship, and the patience of Seetha Srinivasan, director of the University Press of Mississippi, whose good faith I hope to gratify.

As this project ends, I am aware how much it owes to my parents Lillian and Irving Yaross, who provided art, literature, and jokes to enjoy, and the education and values to appreciate them. My husband Joseph Slade and our children Joe and Marya make family life as rich and full as I ever wished, and I'm grateful that I can have my work and love them too.

Defining
New Yorker
Humor

Introduction

Why a Scholarly History of the New Yorker?

Of course, it is my carefully arrived at and calmly studied opinion that the New Yorker *is the best magazine in the world.*

James Thurber to E. B. White [1938]

"The early history of New York is obscured in myth," observed a writer identified only as "Sawdust" in "The Story of Manhattankind" in the first issue of the *New Yorker*, dated February 21, 1925; "and to separate the purely historical from the purely hysterical is no easy task" (6). The same must be said of the early history of the magazine itself. The purely historical (if such a thing exists) was largely obscured until the *New Yorker* archives opened to scholars in 1994, although Dale Kramer conscientiously sifted through evidence and interviewed most of the principals for *Ross and the "New Yorker"* (1951). The hysterical—pure and otherwise—dominates the anecdotes that have stood as history in the memoirs of those present at the start. The most notable of these is James Thurber's *The Years with Ross* (1959), but others have had almost as much influence: Jane Grant's *Ross, the "New Yorker," and Me* (1968), Margaret Case Harriman's *The Vicious Circle: The Story of the Algonquin Round Table* (1951), and Brendan Gill's *Here at the "New Yorker"* (1975). An enduring myth presents founding editor Harold W. Ross as an inept but lucky guy—a classic American comic hero of the type that Hamlin Hill and Walter Blair compared to the Greek *eiron* (as opposed to his braggart opponent, the *alazon*) in their *America's Humor: From Poor Richard to Doonesbury* (1978). Indeed, the image of Ross's eccentric ineptitude has so persisted that Thomas Kunkel's revisionist biography, the first study to test anec-

3

dote and memoir against archival evidence, acknowledged in its title the myth that the book dispels: *Genius in Disguise* (1995). No less an authority than the *New Yorker* itself confirms that Kunkel got it right. Even the title of Charles Mc-Grath's review, "The Ross Years," in the seventieth anniversary issue, quietly revises Thurber's title, and thereby his assessment, in supporting Kunkel's account (McGrath).

Like so many other dimensions of the magazine, the myth originates with Ross himself. Indeed, the earliest recitation of the magazine's comic history appeared in the magazine's first issue, where a column of miscellaneous notes entitled "Of All Things" ended by detailing the tribulations of starting a new magazine. Here in the first issue, before the arrival of Robert Benchley, E. B. White, James Thurber, or S. J. Perelman—the writers historically credited with

Editorial Sanctums as the Magazine Readers Picture Them

Two years before the *New Yorker*'s debut, this cartoon by its art editor found humor in readers' confusion between editors and their magazines—a confusion not altogether comic in reconstructing the *New Yorker*'s early years. Rea Irvin, *Life*, 9/6/23:18–19.

defining *New Yorker* humor—is the first avatar of the *New Yorker*'s Little Man, a variation on Mark Twain's pose of the comic Sufferer (a posture of inferiority for comic ridicule [Gerber]), in the guise of a novice editor daunted by one Jumbo Jr. Not an elephant but a telephone switchboard, Jumbo is an apparatus so simple that "a child can operate" it (2/21/25:2), but our editor cannot, as he discovers soon after his secretary escapes Jumbo's ringing and buzzing for a hastily arranged marriage. Undaunted, our hero confidently wrests Jumbo's operating manual from the telephone company, only to discover that the instructions "pertain to . . . a deceased cousin of the incumbent," but he perseveres, subdues the beast, and after sundry workmen quit the premises, finally manages to put together the magazine before us. "This does not leave you unshaken, of course," he concedes in conclusion, "and at this point your doctor advises a couple of weeks' rest" (2).

This anecdote would be notable as one of the most successful bits of humor in the first issue even if it didn't anticipate "the dementia praecox field" (Benchley's phrase) that became the *New Yorker*'s comic trademark: tales of neurotic little men driven insane by jumbo women and modern life—especially things technical or commercial. Nearly ten years passed before Benchley's "All Aboard for Dementia Praecox" invited readers of the "March of Events Page" in the New York *American* to join him in neurotic bliss (6/18/34:n.p.), but nervous breakdowns specifically defined "*New Yorker* Humor" from 1937, when Mark Twain's literary executor Bernard DeVoto declared White, Thurber, Benchley, and other *New Yorker* writers "the true and most flourishing successors of the southwestern school [of American humor]" (DeVoto 20). The tale of Jumbo Jr., though generally unknown, reveals how history and hysteria have blended in the study of *New Yorker* humor. Following Benchley and DeVoto's lead, historians have conflated the *New Yorker* of the thirties, when scholarship in American humor and literature began, and the *New Yorker* of the twenties, when the magazine first took shape. On the hysterical side, the story of Jumbo Jr. became the template for histories of the magazine even as the anecdote's details receded from view. Ross's reputation as the incompetent leader of a madcap organization and the *New Yorker*'s reputation for "undisguised misogyny" (as Thomas Grant put it, 157, 167 n.1) begin here, in the inaugural issue, in jest. Like the unhuntable Big Bear of Arkansas in T. B. Thorpe's 1841 tall yarn, Jumbo Jr. leaves the hero embarrassed and unsatisfied by his unexpected success.

As a comic version of what rhetoricians call the "modesty trope," a conventional disclaimer to preempt criticism, the saga of editorial travail succeeds. (But just to be sure, the next paragraph insists, "THE NEW YORKER asks consideration for its first number.") Signed only "*The New Yorker*," the column spoke for founding editor Harold W. Ross, even if he didn't write it himself. But he probably did. He had just two other editorial employees at the time, Tyler (Tip) Bliss and Philip Wylie, neither of whom had reason to pose as the *New Yorker*'s founder. Who else would describe "the first things you do in starting a magazine, after you have got the notion to do it . . ." (2/21/25:1)? Moreover, the column concludes with statements of editorial practice and purpose that Ross drafted in a 1924 letter to members of the proposed advisory board,[1] which eventually included Ralph Barton, Marc Connelly, Rea Irvin, George S. Kaufman, Alice Duer Miller, Dorothy Parker, and Alexander Woollcott. (Benchley's contracts prevented his participation, but the title of his 1921 book *Of All Things* headed a *New Yorker* column.) As the magazine grew and prospered, staff members enjoyed characterizing Ross as nearly disabled by his intensity. The November 6, 1926, parody issue ran away with this theme,[2] but as the staff's birthday gift to Ross, the issue also shows that the ribbing, whatever its origin in truth, had become an inside joke providing fun for everyone as their collective achievements grew.

Consider, for example, Lois Long's version in her "Tables for Two" column in the second anniversary issue, February 19, 1927. Because Long didn't arrive on the scene until Charles Baskerville resigned as the nightlife correspondent (his last review ran 7/11/25), she glosses over the telephone story in favor of other incidents, but her story presents the three main strands of what became the *New Yorker*'s official myth: an eccentric editorial leader, a disorganized and unreliable staff, unexpected success rewarding creative chaos in the absence of an editorial plan. With melodramatic tone, Long described "those dear dead days when a group of talented young people struggled for the success of a little known weekly" as a time that was "very gay, very haphazard, and very appalling to an efficiency expert." This staff was, she explained, virtuosic in how to dance the Charleston but "completely ignorant of how to use the telephone, even if the distracted operator had ever been able to find any of us." The editor's "greatest delight," moreover, "was to move the desks about prankishly in the dead of night. The result was that you could easily spend an entire morning which you might have spent—God forbid—in honest labor, running up and downstairs in the elevators looking for your office" (2/19/27:76). In those days, she claimed, her business consisted of roller-skating back and forth to her assistant's office at the opposite end of the floor or finding her typewriter installed in the second floor ladies' room, and staff meetings consisted of a daily craps game followed by dinner. "Nobody then had ever heard of an editorial policy. We made them up as we went along. We used to rummage busily along the row of packing boxes that comprised our files to look for stuff left over for the next issue, and we never found a thing. So we made that up, too." And already in 1927 the *New Yorker* myth held that the magazine was better in this disorganized golden age than in the present. "We don't have half as much imagination now as then. We make mistakes, which we blame on the printer, but we aren't very whimsical" (2/19/27:77). Long's second-anniversary account, a cousin to Ross's inaugural anecdote, set the pattern for hysterical histories to come.

Despite its origins in this tradition of comic suffering, Thurber's memoir has stood for forty years as *the* eyewitness report of the early days despite his arrival on staff two weeks after the magazine published Long's declaration that the golden age had passed. Jane Grant of the *New York Times* did witness central events in *New Yorker* history before she and Ross divorced in 1929, and as a shareholder she remained privy to behind-the-scenes politicking thereafter, but her memoir shares Thurber's tendency to lionize the reporter. Ralph McAllister Ingersoll, who joined the magazine eighteen months before Thurber but left in 1930 to become founding editor of *Fortune,* furthered Thurber's version of the tale; long after the fact, he praised Thurber to his biographer for editorial and staff work enabling "the Whites and me to grasp that we had adopted Ross's mission. . . . We saw our jobs as building an organization so strong that Ross couldn't break it with his eccentricities" (Kinney 344). These examples should remind us that memoirs and biographies dispense rewards and punishments as well as recount experiences. Brendan Gill acknowledged as much when he declared that he wanted *Here at the New Yorker* to let Ilonka Karasz know, at long last, that he admired her art (209)—but not when he scorned "Ross's never-ending and never very successful attempt to educate himself" two pages before a comment about his joining another writer "in an attempt to get back at Ross for his rough handling of our well-wrought prose" (14). While finishing *The Years with Ross* in the summer of 1958, Thurber treated the Whites to four single-spaced pages of invective on Ross's stinginess, with examples going back thirty years.[3] E. B. White, noting that Thurber's book prompted "much sorrow and pain around the shop," confided to a friend that he and Katharine saw it as retribution, "a sly exercise in denigration, beautifully concealed in words of sweetness and love."[4] *New Yorker* mythology sidelines Ross as tit for tat.

There he stands, pulling his wild hair and ranting, "I'm surrounded by women and children. We have no manpower or ingenuity" (Thurber, *Years* 3). Not that Thurber made up the story; Ingersoll put those words in Ross's mouth in his 1934 *Fortune* report, which also declared Ross "definitely an anti-feminist" who resented Katharine Sergeant Angell (Ingersoll, "*New Yorker*" 88). By 1984 not even humor scholars questioned Sanford Pinsker's assertion that "Harold W. Ross was the unlikeliest of candidates to found a magazine that would place the best modern American humorists between slick covers and draft the manifesto under which the *New Yorker* would prosper" (Pinsker 191). Ross's credentials of "high-school dropout and wastrel newspaperman, Aspen and Salt Lake City" also dismayed Earl Rovitt (551). Indeed, they typified nineteenth-century editors, not the newly educated professionals of twentieth-century journalism. Until Thomas Kunkel sought editorial evidence in the magazine's archives, Ross's genius remained well disguised.

Had E. B. White and Katharine Sergeant [Angell] White, his wife, put *their* version of the magazine's history on record, however, they would have cast Ross as its hero. Both arrived at the magazine before Thurber, Angell shortly after Ingersoll in 1925, and maintained positions near the center of action and power. As late as 1975, in a draft letter to Helen Thurber, Katharine White disputed what she called Thurber's "insistence that Ross was an illiterate clown": "He was one of the most literate men I've known. He wrote awfully well himself and he was a wonderful editor. His notes weren't nearly as crazy as Jim said they were because Ross always modestly said they were just suggestions, and the editors he trusted were permitted to throw out any of his notes without even asking him."[5] E. B. White saw Ross similarly. White's notes for a never-written history of the *New Yorker* concede that Ross "lacked every qualification they demanded (accommodating nature, educational-literary background, a way with contributers) and possessed every trait they disparaged."[6] But they also point out two reasons that he succeeded nonetheless. First, he "simply decided that you can't find talent unless you examine everything that comes in—every picture, every manuscript."[7] More important, "He was a genius at encouraging people."[8]

Katharine and E. B. White's views remain buried in their personal papers, where only a few scholars have seen them. But together with the magazine's archival records, they remind us that for twenty-five years Ross *was*—as he signed the story of his battle with Jumbo Jr.—the *New Yorker.* Ross hired Ingersoll, Angell, White, and Thurber (in that order), envisioned their mission, fostered their talents, and sustained the organization after they moved on—all the while allowing them to believe that its success hinged on their work alone. Today this accomplishment would rank him high among entrepreneurial and managerial savants, regardless of his interpersonal and administrative quirks. These continue to make delightful stories, as in Dan Pinck's 1987 reminiscences of his days as a *New Yorker* office boy nearly forty years earlier (Pinck), but they point up what *New Yorker* writer Charles McGrath has called the "common failing of *New Yorker* historiography—the tendency to reduce everyone, and every event, to colorful anecdotes" (180). The impulse is understandable, because the 1920s still glitter with the talents and energy of the magazine's early stars, including James Thurber and E. B. White among the writers and Peter Arno and Helen E. Hokinson among the artists. But it also reflects a sense that real historical work is irrelevant, if not downright churlish—a job for spoilsports.

Nonetheless, the magazine's importance to American popular culture, to America's comic traditions, and to the public who reads it means that the *New Yorker*'s history matters. A month after Ross's death, W. H. Auden announced, "the 'New Yorker' is the best comic magazine in existence." More recently, Russell Baker declared Ross's magazine "For two generations . . . the home office of American humor" (Baker 107). Indeed, Sanford Pinsker had the right idea, though the wrong date, in claiming that "February 25, 1925—when the first issue of the *New Yorker* . . . rolled off the presses—is the date when the 'character' of American humor changed" (Pinsker 192); the first issue carried Saturday's date, February 21, but probably hit newsstands on Tuesday the seventeenth, certainly no later than Thursday the nineteenth.[9]

In any event, that character is the subject of this book, which aims not to recycle stories but to reclaim, rediscover, and reimagine the early *New Yorker*. And to ask one central question: How does a magazine construct and communicate—that is, define—its distinctive personality?

In the seventy-five years since its founding, the *New Yorker*'s view of the world has become so well known, particularly as rendered by Saul Steinberg, that the magazine has achieved a cultural stature disproportionate to its original conception as a weekly humor magazine for an elite local audience. The small staff of full-time journalists and editors whom Ross assembled late in 1924 cultivated contributors who could articulate his vision: letter after letter in the editorial archives exhorts contributions from established writers and artists, and reports with unfailing kindness on the fate of unsolicited cartoons, poetry, and comic prose in the "slush pile." Week after week they made decisions about acceptance, rejection, revision, layout, future ideas, and contractual relationships—decisions that defined the *New Yorker* and its sense of humor. As a result, the *New Yorker* succeeded in formulating and communicating its comic vision despite the exigencies of the early years. To be sure, these difficulties included a wobbly financial base and an eccentric cast of characters, whose exits and entrances belong more to the world of a French farce than a successful American enterprise. (A case in point: when Ross asked Dorothy Parker, who wrote book reviews from 1927 to 1929 under the pseudonym "Constant Reader," why she was at a speakeasy instead of the office at midafternoon, she apparently replied, "Someone was using the pencil.") But by the end of the 1920s, when businesses all around them foundered and failed, the *New Yorker* continued going strong. It had defined itself and redefined American humor as urban and urbane: the magazine's artists and writers transformed nineteenth-century traditions of charac-

ter, dialect, and situation into materials appropriate to a mass market of educated, sophisticated consumers. For these readers, more interested in Picasso's
Paris than Will Rogers's Oklahoma, the *New Yorker* forged new links between
visual and verbal wit.

The *New Yorker* concluded its first five years as the most vigorous voice in
American print humor. By 1951 John O'Hara could claim, "Practically all present-
day writing that rises or attempts to rise above the standards of *Field & Stream*
(one of my favorite magazines, by the way) or the L. L. Bean catalog (my favorite
catalog, by the way) is influenced to some degree by *The New Yorker* in style, attitude, or both" (3). It survived and grew during the Great Depression, when
older comic magazines collapsed, despite the flow of capital and audiences to
newer, nonprint mass media: the "talkies" that drew Benchley, Parker, and the
Marx Brothers to Hollywood and the radio comedies like *Amos 'n Andy* that revived such staples of lower-class entertainment as dialect humor and minstrelsy
routines.

The *New Yorker*'s success stems in part from Ross's seizing upon niche, or target, marketing at just the right time: when urban newspapers were consolidat-
ing and advertising was acquiring statistical mechanisms for segmenting
consumer markets. The *New Yorker* was the first modern city magazine to target
the affluent, educated audience lately described as DINKs: dual income, no kids.
The market niche that Ross targeted in 1925 accounts today for 6.2 percent of
all American consumer magazines published (Magazine Publishers of America
[MPA] and Kanner 12). Given this combination of economic and editorial leadership, it's no surprise that the *New Yorker* now ranks among America's oldest
and most distinguished magazines. Its changes in leadership are front-page
news; its special cartoon issue was the subject of a television news feature where
no one disputed Tina Brown's description of *New Yorker* cartoons as "a sort of national treasure" (ABC News).

Not surprisingly, either, books on the *New Yorker* constitute a small publishing industry. The magazine itself collects cartoons into *New Yorker Albums* at
regular intervals and periodically offers omnibus collections of the collections as
well. Tina Brown capitalized on the staying power of *New Yorker* writers by publishing anthologies of its fiction, and even brought out a "talking book," *The
"New Yorker" Out Loud* (1998). Memoirs by longtime contributors such as E. J.
Kahn (*About "The New Yorker" and Me,* 1979), Janet Flanner (*Paris Was Yesterday,*
1972), and Philip Hamburger (*Friends Talking in the Night,* 1999) vie with such
beautiful coffee-table books as Lee Lorenz's *Art of the "New Yorker," 1925–1995*

(1995) and *The Complete Book of Covers from "The New Yorker," 1925–1989* (1989), with an introduction by John Updike. Biographies of central figures in the saga appear steadily—in 1995 alone, two books on Thurber, Harrison Kinney's *James Thurber: His Life and Times* and Neil A. Grauer's *Remember Laughter: A Life of James Thurber,* as well as Kunkel's volume on Ross.

But in all the years that Eustace Tilley has scrutinized a single butterfly through his monocle on the cover of the *New Yorker* no one has done the same to the magazine. Most books tracing the magazine's past take a long view and shortcuts. Dale Kramer took on the whole twenty-five-year story when he wrote *Ross and "The New Yorker"* in 1950. So did Thurber in *The Years with Ross* (1959). As the magazine has aged, the early years become a smaller slice of history, giving increasing emphasis to the details that repetition has declared essential to the tale. Moreover, virtually all discussions of the *New Yorker* leap from the first year to the 1930s, as in the special number of *Studies in American Humor* in Spring 1984. Emphasis on the 1930s partly reflects the history of humor studies, which in the midthirties first claimed a place in the academy on a disciplinary spectrum midway between folklore and literature. By this time, the magazine had reached a rich and mature form, spawned a few imitators (including the *Brooklynite* across the bridge and the *Boulevardier* in Paris), and choked the humor competition, a process abetted by the depression. A fledgling group of city magazines was also growing (Moon 11–12). Glossing over the twenties, however, skips the process by which the *New Yorker* developed its sense of humor. Indeed, by 1930, Ralph Ingersoll claimed, "the excitement of its creation was over" (Ingersoll, *Point* 243–44).

The opening of the *New Yorker* archives and development of specialized bibliographic computer software now make it possible to organize and identify the comic contents of the magazine's first years, and to contextualize the early development of the magazine and its humor within the publishing enterprise that gave them life. The task is formidable—even for the first five years. The *New Yorker's* comic contents for volumes 1–5 exceed 15,000 items: 261 covers, 3,000 cartoons, 3,000 "Talk" items, 4,000 prose pieces, 2,500 illustrations, 500 caricatures, 1,700 poems, and 2,300 newsbreaks. (Multiply those numbers by *at least* 5 to approximate the contents published during Ross's twenty-five years as editor; then triple that product to estimate contents published in the seventy-five years since the 1925 founding.) Much of this humor was effectively lost unless the author or an anthology reprinted it, because neither an annual index nor even a weekly listing identified the magazine's contents until 1969. Work that did get reprinted—usually by the most famous writers and artists—rendered the remaining contents even less visible while skewing the record of what *New Yorker* humor was.

Cartoons reprinted in the various *New Yorker Albums,* which began appearing in 1928, were chosen according to criteria specific to book publication, including whether an artist had other plans for publication and how successfully a drawing would survive separation from the pages of the magazine. Indeed, in the case of the first Album, Ross allowed the publisher, Doubleday, Doran and Co., to choose the drawings, claiming that the *New Yorker* staff knew them too well to do the job.[10] In any case, albums aimed to make money for artists and the magazine, and to publicize their efforts, not to provide a representative sample of the *New Yorker's* comic art. By contrast, the complete contents of the magazine, together with the extant editorial record—2,566 file boxes of rejection and acceptance letters, internal memos, and requests for revisions—define *New Yorker* humor.

In their absence our understanding is distorted. Bernard DeVoto's assertion that New Yorker humorists represent the heirs to the legacy of Mark Twain and southwestern humor appeared in a three-page review in the *Saturday Review of Literature* of Walter Blair's landmark anthology *Native American Humor* (1937). DeVoto contrasted modern and nineteenth-century humor with an acknowledgment that his descriptions "generalize too sweepingly," but his focus on the *New Yorker* prose writers most familiar to his own readers in the midthirties has kept the focus there and then, and no one has subsequently traced the emergence of New Yorker humor in other genres, such as verse, nor analyzed relations among its various visual and verbal types. Instead, scholarly studies of *New Yorker* humor have focused on either the magazine's comic contributions across a long time frame, as in Walter Blair and Hamlin Hill's *America's Humor* (1978) and Jesse Bier's *Rise and Fall of American Humor* (1968), or the contributions of individual writers in the context of their reprinted collected works, as in the special issue of *Studies in American Humor* (Spring 1984). Both procedures privilege well-known, much reprinted male writers of prose over the more ephemeral but more varied contents of the weekly magazine—including verse, caricatures, and uncollected work by women. Consequently, even though the editors of the *New Yorker* produced a magazine, scholars have studied books. And scholarly writers have tended to pay more attention to other writers than to the comic art for which the magazine is best known. No one has written a biography of cartoonist Peter Arno or art director Rea Irvin; the focus of art historians on painting, prints, and sculpture has likewise shunted even such prolific art contributors as Barbara Shermund, Ilonka Karasz, Alice Harvey, Alan Dunn, Gardner Rea, and Alfred Frueh into historical mist.

Or into mists of error. For example, Betty Swords commits two mistakes in claiming that "Mary Petty made extremely rare appearances in *The New Yorker* after she married Whitney Darrow, Jr., . . . But she did 'appear' on the cover when she painted the cartoons of her color-blind husband" (73). Swords first confuses Mary Petty, an artist who painted her own *New Yorker* covers, with Perry Barlow's wife, Dorothy Hope Smith, who (according to John Updike's official history of *New Yorker* covers) did help her color-blind husband with his covers (*New Yorker* Magazine vi); Swords also confuses Darrow with Alan Dunn, the *New Yorker* cartoonist whom Petty married in 1927 and who was an unfailing promoter of his wife's art throughout her life. In fact most of Petty's art— and all of her *New Yorker* work—appeared often after she married Dunn. Other errors, corrected throughout this volume, reflect the recycling of stories from one memoir to the next and the habit of relying on reprints.

Defining New Yorker *Humor* focuses on the visual and verbal humor published in the *New Yorker* during its first five years. Readers looking for a theory of humor or a study of its psychological and sociocultural dimensions will find this book disappointingly concerned more with trees and thickets than with forests. It is frankly historical and textual in orientation, documentary and rhetorical in method, on the assumption that text is the product of the editorial process and rhetoric the means by which texts, creators, and audiences interact. I aim to trace the history of the magazine's early graphic and verbal humor, describe its characteristics, and identify its contributions to American comic culture.

A magazine can publish only what editors receive or write themselves. I therefore treat magazine publishing as an interpersonal process resulting in a series of concrete products, that is, individual *New Yorker* numbers, as well as the imaginary spectrum created from these individual points on the line, the magazine. As a result, I have set my sights on the magazine and its contents and regard its people and editorial practices as the means to those ends. Editorial practices exist, of course, in various degrees of manifestation: some articulated in official correspondence, others implied by manuscript alterations, revision requests, and rejection letters, still others expressed via editorial choice. What the editors bought and rejected and how they worked with the material they chose are matters of rhetoric: the available means (to paraphrase Aristotle) for communicating with their readers, consumers of the magazine's contents. Editors chose and honed their acquisitions by category. Review, service, and fact departments operated separately from "The Talk of the Town." Purchases of poetry, prose (fiction or casual essays), and art reflected distinct criteria and selection processes. These individual modes of *New Yorker* humor developed separately even as they shared the magazine's overall life.

Most *New Yorker* contributors specialized in a single mode—verse or caricatures or idea drawings or fiction—and editors cultivated them accordingly. Though editors' correspondence with both authors and artists demonstrates openness to comic experiments of all kinds, in the main Angell's staff and the art committee encouraged each contributor to submit variations on successful efforts. This conservative practice promoted coherence among items from many hands, but it also allowed editors to mentor humorists on what the magazine would like well enough to buy. Individual chapters of *Defining* New Yorker *Humor*, therefore, trace the trends of each humor genre in turn. And within each genre, I trace how individual humorists both adapted to and helped shape the *New Yorker's* comic style.

The magazine's contents reflect particulars of time, place, and experience—among the editors as individuals and members of an organization, as well as among artists and writers making personal choices about what kind of work to produce and how best to profit from it. Some of those choices, I presume, indicate perceptions about what editors will buy and what readers will enjoy. Thus each issue of a magazine negotiates many interests, some of them compromised and many inconsistent with a developmental or evolutionary approach to history, with its assumptions that everything gets better as time goes on. Nonetheless, whether it's a restaurant or a magazine, a new organization that offers a succession of individual products on which the whole operation will thrive or fail necessarily refines its procedures and output; the alternative is to continually reinvent both the wheel and the road, an effort too exhausting to sustain. The endurance of the *New Yorker* for nearly seventy-five years, one-third of them under the founding editor, testifies to its success in finding and applying workable formulas. In conceptualizing this history as a process by which editors and contributors defined *New Yorker* humor, I consider the refinement process as a progressive assurance about what was appropriate to the magazine and its audience, yet always a compromise between what was appropriate and what was available. In this regard, it's noteworthy that rejection letters to authors and artists often spoke euphemistically of regret that the material wasn't "available" for publication.[11] Editors do the best with what they get. *New Yorker* editors have done their best in their own particular ways.

A magazine cannot survive without balancing novelty and familiarity; each is-

sue must be new enough to warrant attention by readers and payment by advertisers yet familiar enough to be part of a continuous expression of editorial identity. Considering the difficulty of other entertainment media in meeting these
goals—weekly comedies and dramas on television rarely last more than a few seasons—the endurance of the *New Yorker* is extraordinary. To a certain degree, the
New Yorker met that challenge by changing its identity from a local humorous
weekly with an aversion to politics to a national publication with a much more
serious public role. The issue devoted solely to John Hersey's *Hiroshima* (8/31/46)
is as far from the slapstick of the early *New Yorker* as one can imagine.

In the 1950s and '60s the magazine gave less weight to comic commentary
on contemporary life (real and imagined) and more to politicized journalism.
Hannah Arendt's *Banality of Evil,* Rachel Carson's *Silent Spring,* James Baldwin's
The Fire Next Time all debuted in its pages. These demonstrations of social awareness and responsibility, perhaps a correction to the *New Yorker's* much-criticized
silence on suffering during the Great Depression, highlighted the editorial
choices of William Shawn, who began writing for "Talk" in 1929, joined the
staff in 1933, and rose to managing editor in 1939. Ross credited Shawn with
"the idea of how to publish" *Hiroshima*;[12] six years later, Katharine White admired Shawn's first year as editor, telling Frank Sullivan, "I think he has done a
remarkable job, for that was about the worst spot any man ever had to step
into—to follow Ross."[13] Following Ross's death on December 6, 1951, Shawn
became the *New Yorker's* second editor on January 21, 1952, shortly before the
magazine's twenty-sixth birthday, and he reigned for thirty-five years, ten more
than Ross, until February 13, 1987.

Shawn presided over a period of tremendous editorial and financial success.
Even the *Wall Street Journal* could not quite believe it. Statistics told the tale: in
1958 the *New Yorker* ranked first among American consumer magazines in ad
lineage, and its 10 percent profit (percentage of sales after taxes) stood well ahead
of the 2.7 percent industry average (Rutledge and Bart 1). Ingersoll divulged
numbers in his 1961 memoir: circulation 415,000, twelve million dollars in advertising, a little less than the stock valuation of F-R Publishing (167). In explaining the phenomenon for business professionals in "Urbanity, Inc.," the
Journal rewrote Shawn into the Ross myth for a new generation of readers. Its
headline, "How The *New Yorker* Wins Business Success Despite Air of Disdain,"
led into discussions of "Unorthodox Economics," a "Combative Individualist,"
and Facetious Advice" to suggest that the *New Yorker* succeeded by virtue of eccentricity, not excellence (Rutledge and Bart 1). Insiders joined outsiders like

the *Journal* in conflating Shawn with Ross. Brendan Gill implied in his "Comment" for the seventieth anniversary issue that Shawn's genius was to introduce major changes with "a stealth that made them *seem* minor" (2/20–27/95:12). He also adopted Ross's traditions as his own. Well into the informal 1980s Shawn sustained the intraoffice courtliness by which Ross always wrote to "Mr. Thurber," "Miss Long," "Mrs. Angell," "Mr. Fleischmann," and other members of the organization. During Shawn's tenure, the practice became evidence of his personal modesty and dignity, and the respectful admiration of his staff (Mahon 101; Rutledge and Bart 6), while Ross's use of the practice was forgotten.

Longtime *New Yorker* watchers found Shawn's ouster by S. I. Newhouse even more stunning than his purchase of the magazine for $168 million two years earlier. The purchase prompted Gigi Mahon's exposé of takeover politics, *The Last Days of "The New Yorker"* (1988). But critics had charged the magazine with having lost its sense of humor ever since Lois Long's 1927 anniversary piece, a trend continued in the *Wall Street Journal*'s 1958 report that "the magazine plainly has fallen into the formula approach" (Rutledge and Bart 6). In 1983, however, Ben Bagdikian claimed that Shawn had set the magazine on a downward course when he published Jonathan Schell's "Reporter at Large" piece on Ben Suc village, Vietnam, in the issue of July 15, 1967. By making the magazine a vocal opponent of American engagement in Southeast Asia, Bagdikian argued, Shawn began attracting "the wrong kind of readers" while alienating the *New Yorker*'s core audience, the affluent elite supporting the war (Bagdikian, "Wrong Kind" 52–53).

At least one longtime art contributor also detected a shift in the late 1960s, though he characterized the wrong readers differently. "The *New Yorker* is acting more and more like it doesn't really need us," Warren Chappell wrote fellow artist Alan Dunn, June 20, 1968. "Instead it's sending secret messages to some nasty little elite that is impossible to recognize! The atmosphere has changed to such a degree!" But he couldn't identify the source of the change, and asked Dunn, "Tell us just how basic the editorial shift has been—is it ownership or editorial?"[14] Two years later, he blamed Shawn for replacing frivolity with an inflated and misguided social responsibility:

> The *New Yorker* is trying to invent a new Eustace Tilley. No more sniffing butterflies . . . they want the symbol to be *concerned—of course*—but I seem to detect a willful scheme to intellectualize the *Common Man* by making his head seem more important than the facts can support. We sent money in to keep the magazine coming so we can

see you, John Updike, & Brendan Gill. But they* do know how to *bug us,* God help
'em.

(*the editors . . . what slobs!)[15]

By 1971, Chappell had a diagnosis. After Dunn's wife, Mary Petty, suffered a
hideous mugging, which she survived for five years without recovering mentally,
Chappell complained that the magazine had lost the local focus that once defined it. "It is shocking," he exclaimed, "that the *New Yorker* can run more lineage attacking the failures of American social and economic policy than it will
print [on] the beasts who stalk the streets of Manhattan and prey upon the weak
and helpless."[16]

Whatever the source of its decline in the late '60s and early '70s, the *New
Yorker* recovered enough affluent readers and ad pages by 1981 for Bagdikian to
use it as an example in *The Media Monopoly* (1983). That book demonstrates how
conglomerate ownership and advertising practices join forces in American mass
media in a hegemonic process that sells out the masses for elite interests. In
1982 Josephine Hendin objected, similarly, that "the controlled surface of the
magazine feeds our hunger for order, and assures us of our membership in an
elite of the self-possessed" even when topics should evoke outrage or despair. But
despite the internal coherence as business and editorial shared a single agenda,
the magazine began to lose advertisers again. In 1985, when the *New Yorker*
passed to Newhouse's Advance Publications, ad pages stood at 3,150 annually
(Pogrebin, "Year" 6). They continued to decline, bringing Newhouse losses of
$100 million despite the appointment of a new president, Steve Florio
(1985–94), and a new editor, Robert Gottlieb (1987–92). Analysts declared the
New Yorker "editorially tired" (Pogrebin, "Year" 1, 6).

As with so much of the magazine, however, Katharine White diagnosed the
problem long before anyone else. In 1957 she complained to her husband's old
college friend Howard Cushman that "everything is getting too long."[17] In her
view, solutions lay in humor and risk taking. She defended Donald Barthelme's
"Snow White," despite its profanity, not only because she admired his "gifts"
but also because she believed that the magazine "needs and must seek out" such
"an experimentalist and a modern with a sense of satire and humor . . . if it is to
keep up its tradition of innovation."[18] In this sense, Tina Brown, who replaced
Robert Gottlieb in September 1992, truly succeeded Harold Ross as the editor
who sought to make money with an irreverent comic survey of the New York scene.

Brown left the *New Yorker* in July of 1998, after six years on the job, having reduced annual deficits from $30 million to $11 million (Pogrebin, "Staff" C1, 6) and having persuaded the *Village Voice*, at least, that she had "revived the years with Ross" by giving contemporary moneyed readers a flattering view of themselves (Carson 48–48). Newhouse delighted longtime readers and staff members by naming staff writer David Remnick as her successor; Roger Angell, whose roots at the magazine go back to his childhood (his mother was Katharine Sergeant Angell), praised Remnick as "good looking and articulate and scholarly . . . [and] a good guy"—a choice so apt as to be "highly suspect" (Pogrebin, "Staff" C6). For all the flap about her violation of the magazine's hallowed traditions, however, Brown made no secret that she looked to the *New Yorker* of the 1920s for insight and inspiration. In a *New York Times* interview (which the reporter hoped would bring comfort to "distressed readers"), she explained, "Basically, my whole thrust has been to go back to Ross's magazine":

> It gave a writerly, newsy, interesting, intriguing feel to the contents rather than having contents that were overpresented on a plate. . . . It was contents you had to squirrel around amongst to find things to be enchanted by and surprised by and amused by. "Fancy this being here?" was the sort of response that you had to it. That's really all gone from The New Yorker, largely because the length of the articles really grew and grew and because they really ate into the space that Ross had allocated for the really short material. (Carmody B1, 4)

After six months on the job, Brown remained certain that the early *New Yorker* represented the magazine's essence: "full of mischief, lots of wit, and covers bursting with life" (Warren 2).

This is the *New Yorker* humor defined genre by genre, writer and artist, from 1925 to 1930.

CHAPTER 1

Old and New, Borrowed and Blue

The New Yorker in Context

When I started this magazine I had an incredible run of luck, as I look back on it, and the magazine is really a whim of God's. . . . This magazine found more top writers and artists in its first year than it has in any five year period since and, as a matter of fact, the few that were dug up at the start are still better than anyone that has come along since. It{'}s amazing. That's the word for it.

Harold W. Ross to E. B. White, 1943

Harold W. Ross had seven years' experience editing large-circulation weeklies when the *New Yorker's* first issue came out six weeks late, three days before its publication date of February 21, 1925. Claims to ignorance and luck notwith-standing, the high-school dropout from Utah succeeded in establishing the so-phisticated magazine "not edited for the old lady in Dubuque" because he saw and seized opportunity, earning professionals' respect in the process. First came *Stars and Stripes,* the official newspaper of the American Expeditionary Forces (A.E.F.) in France. Competing for readers with the Paris edition of the *New York Herald, Stars and Stripes* targeted a well-defined, homogeneous audience with hu-morous cartoons, prose, and news items in seventy-one weekly issues from Feb-ruary 8, 1918, to June 13, 1919 (Cornebise 208). Ross joined the profitable weekly soon after it began and became managing editor in November (Kunkel 48, 61); ten years later he made its humorous attitude the *New Yorker's* trade-mark. In the meantime he capitalized on the network of contributors and other contacts acquired through *Stars and Stripes*, connections that put him near the center of New York's booming postwar media industry. After publishing some spin-off books with his wartime colleagues, Ross spent the next five years in editorial positions at two other national magazines, the *American Legion Weekly* and *Judge*. There, within New York's journalistic circles, he developed the know-how and connections on which the fledgling *New Yorker* drew. As he pressed forward with his plans for a magazine specializing in local humor for a sophisticated audience, Ross exploited changes in the economic structures of publishing and the demographics of American society, allowing the *New Yorker* to thrive as other American magazines failed.

Networks Old and New

Ross had limited journalistic prospects as an itinerant newspaperman before the war. Buoyed by having covered the Leo Frank trial for the *Atlanta Journal* in the spring and eager to break in at the *New York Times* or another Manhattan daily, Ross failed to penetrate New York publishing circles in 1913 when he was twenty years old. He settled for work as a stringer for the *Brooklyn Eagle* and *Hudson Observer* (Hoboken, New Jersey) until early in 1914, when he left New York on his father's invitation to take over the family demolition and scrap business in Salt Lake City, Utah. He abandoned that too before the year was out, seeking newspaper work in San Francisco. There he remained as a reporter for the *Call,* Mark Twain's old newspaper, until he enlisted in the Army railway regiment, the Eighteenth Engineers, soon after the U.S. declared war in 1917 (Kunkel 30–44). On the basis of his previous editorial experience (as an eighteen-year-old he ran the small daily *Marysville (California) Appeal* for two months in 1911 after its editor died), he served briefly as the second editor of the Eighteenth Engineers' regimental publication, the *Spiker* (Kunkel 31–32, 46). After several frustrating months digging ditches and trying to stay warm in officers' training camp, and having his requests for transfer to the new A.E.F. weekly magazine ignored, Private Ross presented himself and his typewriter to the editorial staff of *Stars and Stripes* (Kunkel 48).

There he gained his first significant experience as an editor and proved his capacity for editorial entrepreneurship. While his reasons for leaving the *Appeal* remain unknown, his success as managing editor of *Stars and Stripes* is unquestionable. Ross rose to the position after the armistice, elected by his colleagues when they ousted the current editor, Captain Guy T. Viskniskki (Kunkel

61). Under Ross's management, the magazine closed with a profit of $700,000 (duly returned to Congress, although the editors sought to spend it on French war orphans [Kunkel 64–65]), and his leadership prompted his major to nominate him for a Distinguished Service Medal (Cornebise 16), though as a private he was ineligible. Still further evidence of ability lies in the projects, all profitable, that Ross and his former colleagues undertook after the war. One example is *Yank Talk,* a joke book. Ross collected jokes from the files at *Stars and Stripes:* the Red Cross alone bought fifty thousand copies, prompting a sequel, *More Yank Talk,* immediately after (Kramer, *Ross* 33–34).

Despite this history of success, Ross's achievements have received primarily comic treatment—both then and now. If he went AWOL in the process, as Dale Kramer claimed (*Ross* 20), the story relies entirely on Ross's word. The crime eluded his commanding officers, and Cornebise's authorized history of *Stars and Stripes* says nothing on the subject (though the military would want to downplay it). *Vanity Fair,* naming Ross to its 1927 Hall of Fame, twitted him good-naturedly for his earlier success by noting that "after the mutiny on *The Stars and Stripes,* during the war, he was the private elected by the other mutineers to edit that rebellious A.E.F. weekly" (Amory and Bradlee 139). In this mode, one historian after the next discounted his achievements at *Stars and Stripes* (Ingersoll 75, Gill 22, Kunkel 48), until Thomas Kunkel noted that the experience made Ross "intimately familiar with the production, personnel, and advertising demands of a big publication" and enabled him to "see the possibilities of some unfamiliar journalistic forms" (Kunkel 62). Thurber's latest biographer, Harrison Kinney, goes so far as to claim that Ross became editor of *Stars and Stripes* "by force of personality," as if financial and editorial success played no part. In this context it's no wonder that Thomas Kunkel called his biography of Ross, the first to praise his editorial talents, *Genius in Disguise.* Ross's prewar publishing experience, which followed a familiar nineteenth-century path of tramp journalism and self-education, proved insufficient for the professional demands of even early twentieth-century urban journalism, as demonstrated by New York editors' disinterest in hiring him. By the end of his tour with *Stars and Stripes,* however, Ross was ready to become a New York editor himself.

Assisting him in this process were his *Stars and Stripes* colleagues. New York journalists themselves, many belonged to the Algonquin Round Table, the elite group of wits usually credited with providing talent for the early *New Yorker.* Among the most influential was Captain Franklin Pierce Adams, the famous "F. P. A." of the *New York Mail* and *Tribune* before the war, and the *New York World* after. Another was Sergeant Alexander Woollcott, the New York theater critic and man-about-town, who allowed his name to grace the *New Yorker*'s first masthead and contributed the occasional "Profile" biographical sketch until the end of volume 4, when he finally agreed to write a regular feature, "Shouts and Murmurs" (2/16/29), its title borrowed from his 1922 book. (Tina Brown revived the department title for humorous essays in the 1990s.) More New York newspaper connections came through First Lieutenant Grantland Rice, *Tribune* sports columnist until 1930 (Cornebise xi, 22). Leading the magazine contacts was Tyler "Tip" Bliss, who wrote the *Stars's* humor column "Dizzy Sector" (Cornebise 189, n. 41), published in *Life* and *Judge* after the war and became one of Ross's first *New Yorker* staff members. (The others, Jane Grant recalled, were secretary Helen Mears, an old western buddy Roy Kirk, public relations specialist Philip Wylie, and art editor Rea Irvin [208–9].)

These French connections led directly to the *New Yorker,* despite its myopic focus on the hometown scene. On arriving in New York after the war, Ross and three other *Stars and Stripes* staffers jointly discharged on April 30, 1919— Woollcott, Private Cyrus LeRoy Baldridge, and Private John T. Winterich— jointly founded *The Home Sector: A Weekly for the New Civilian Conducted by the former Council of the Stars and Stripes,* a weekly running from September 20, 1919, to April 17, 1920, published by Butterick Company (Cornebise 35, 173). The *Home Sector* folded when the staff—suffering through weak advertising revenues and a printers' strike that cost eight issues (Kramer, *Ross* 36)—decided to move over to the *American Legion Weekly,* with Winterich continuing as editor through its conversion into *American Legion Monthly* until 1938 (Cornebise 173, 178). Located in the same building were the editorial offices of *Judge,* a national humorous weekly directed toward a middle-class readership. Ross moved to *Judge* in 1924, when the *American Legion Monthly* bought an interest in it (Kunkel 90), and thence to the *New Yorker.*

In fact, *Stars and Stripes* led to so many overlapping personal and professional connections ultimately beneficial to the *New Yorker* that E. B. White's 1928 criticism of New York as less like a city than "like an alumni reunion" hardly seems hyperbolic ("Open Letter: To the Department of Correction" 8/4/28:21–22). Civilian writer Heywood Broun, who wrote *The AEF: With General Pershing and the American Forces* (1918) and *Our Army at the Front* (1918), became a *New Yorker* contributor, friend, and (once back in the United States) roommate to Ross and his wife, Jane Grant. Ross and Grant had met through Woollcott; she was close friends with Broun's wife, Ruth Hale. A reporter for the *New York Times,* Grant used her own professional network to publicize the fledgling *New Yorker* in the *Times* and elsewhere; such publicity helped the magazine survive beyond their marriage, which ended in 1929.

Funding for the *New Yorker* came via the former wartime buddies and their friends who made up the Thanatopsis Literary and Inside Straight Poker Club, a group of New York publishers, writers, and their friends constituting the nocturnal auxiliary to the famous lunchtime assemblage at the Algonquin Hotel. Thanatopsis poker games attracted a diverse crowd, and introduced Ross to Raoul Fleischmann (nicknamed "Royal Flushman"), who had become a millionaire through his family yeast and baking business and found Ross's publishing plans an appealing gamble. Late in 1924, Fleischmann contributed $50,000 in startup funds—twice the $25,000 put up by Ross and Grant—followed by more than ten times as much to keep the *New Yorker* afloat: $190,000 for the first year, $360,000 for the second and third (Kramer, *Ross* 74, n. 1). Fleischmann also provided other necessities: an office at 25 West Forty-fifth Street, around the corner from the Algonquin (Kunkel 92–93), and a long-term advertising contract for full pages extolling the medicinal value of Fleischmann's Yeast.

The Algonquin and Thanatopsis groups themselves participated in a larger, national phenomenon of peer social networks that brought other contributors to the *New Yorker* and gave it the flavor of an alumni reunion. Sociologist Paula Fass has suggested that youth values began dominating American culture in the 1920s because of the shift from a family-based culture to what she calls the "peer society." Whereas previous generations of children were nurtured by families and socialized into multigenerational value systems, Fass notes, the generation maturing in the 1920s grew up in an environment dominated by peers, whose values achieved dominance through peer pressure. By the 1920s children from middle- and lower-class backgrounds, not only the wealthy, spent their days in age-based classrooms rather than the factories or farms where their counterparts of the late 1800s had worked alongside adults. Schools intensified age segregation by dividing themselves into elementary, middle, and high schools. College enrollments tripled between 1900 and 1930 (Fass 407, n.3), extending the influence of school pressures for peer conformity well into young adulthood and establishing the college set as the new American social standard (Fass 119–35, 407 n.3). As middle-class magazines such as *Atlantic* and *New Republic* sided with their dismayed elders (Fass 17–29), the field opened for a youth-oriented consumer magazine like the *New Yorker*. In the pages of the *New Yorker,* affluent, college-educated, young urbanites displaced Huckleberry Finn and other adolescent hicks—not to mention the Widow Bedott and her fellow cracker-barrel philosophers—as the heroes and voices of American humor. The comic insecurities of the *New Yorker's* Little Man express this shift away from a humor based on rustic wisdom.

As a cultural development, the peer culture explains at least three aspects of the *New Yorker.* From a historical perspective, it first of all clarifies the social and economic accuracy of Ross's infamous sneer at the old lady in Dubuque in favor of this highly visible, potent generation of reader-consumers. Second, from the editorial perspective, the peer culture identified the magazine's subject matter: a comic mirror to their lives. Third, from a practical standpoint, the peer culture constituted the *New Yorker's* circle of writers, artists, editors, and friends, each of whom belonged to other networks that together gave the magazine a balance between continuity and diversity. This balance may seem uncomplicated in retrospect, but during the first five years it involved juggling contents of 261 individual issues, each containing a handful of "Talk of the Town" pieces, a dozen cartoons, a few caricatures and other illustrations, a couple of fiction and fact pieces (including a "profile" personality article), half a dozen poems, reviews of books, movies, plays, art exhibits, shopping opportunities, and musical recordings (shellac and piano roll)—some 16,000 editorial items in all. The peer culture unified this abundant variety.

Overlapping circles of interpersonal connections helped unify tone and viewpoint. The most famous of these is the Algonquin Round Table, which originated (Dorothy Herrmann claims) in a 1919 feud: theatrical press agent John Peter Toohey, angry at Alexander Woollcott for not promoting Toohey's client Eugene O'Neill, gave a party at the Algonquin ostensibly in Woollcott's honor but in fact to berate him, and thus started a tradition (17–18). The Algonquin Circle gave Ross access to publishing talent and potential contributors in addition to his wartime colleagues now installed in key roles at major New York newspapers; regulars included *Vanity Fair* staff members Robert Benchley, Dorothy Parker, and Robert Sherwood, Broadway figures George S. Kaufman, Marc Connelly, and Herman Manckiewicz, writers Donald Ogden Stewart and Edna Ferber, editor Art Samuels of *Harper's Bazaar,* and artist Neysa McMein (O'Connor 102–3). The group's notorious wit led Margaret Case Harriman, daughter of the Algonquin Hotel's manager, to call them "The Vicious Circle" (Harriman). All became early *New Yorker* contributors, many of them drawing their colleagues into the fold.

Staff of the *New York World,* in particular, found the *New Yorker* ideal for moonlighting. The first five years drew on submissions from well-known columnists such as Frank Sullivan, F. P. A., Alexander Woollcott, and Heywood Broun as well as lesser-known writers such as Finley Peter Dunne and Herbert Asbury. Cartoonists Milt Gross and Rollin Kirby contributed occasionally, whereas Carl Rose and Al Frueh became mainstays. Another group, including Baird Leonard and Howard Baker Cushman, came from the *Morning Telegraph*.

Closer to Fass's conception of the peer society, a second circle reflected alumni groups. The Ivy League predominated. Tip Bliss (Ross's wartime colleague and original *New Yorker* employee) led the list of Harvard alumni: Heywood Broun (who graduated with Walter Lippmann in the class of 1910), Fillmore Hyde (class of 1915), Robert Benchley, Robert E. Sherwood, and Gluyas Williams.[1] When Benchley roomed with Donald Ogden Stewart in 1924, he drew the Yale alumni network into the *New Yorker* circle—including writer Fairfax Downey, managing editor Ralph Ingersoll, and artist Reginald Marsh.[2] Cornell alumni included not only Frank Sullivan (class of '14) but also E. B. White and Howard Baker Cushman, two friends from the class of 1921; a third classmate, Gustave Stubbs Lobrano, succeeded Katharine White as the *New Yorker*'s fiction editor in 1938.[3] Former Cornell *Widow* editor Charles Baskerville[4] wrote and illustrated the *New Yorker*'s first nightlife department.

New Yorker contributors who migrated from the hinterlands also seem to have found the magazine through peer connections. Ross knew artist John Held Jr. not only from their collaboration at *Judge* but also because they were children together in Salt Lake City. Roommates Helen Hokinson and Alice Harvey led the contingent of *New Yorker* artists trained at the Art Institute of Chicago—including Garrett Price and Perry Barlow.[5] A more unlikely network originating in Columbus, Ohio, shows how the *New Yorker* benefited from overlapping school and professional networks. Donald Ogden Stewart did not join other Algonquinites in contributing to the *New Yorker* until 1927, when Benchley and Parker told him about the wonderful material Ross was publishing by a new writer named James Thurber—whom Stewart already knew from junior high school; the two had met up again in 1923 when Thurber interviewed Stewart, triumphant from the success of his *Parody Outline of History,* for the *Columbus Dispatch.*[6] The Ohio connection probably also includes Gardner Rea, who like Thurber worked on the humor magazine at Ohio State University in 1913–14.[7] The *New Yorker* grew as overlapping personal and professional networks reinforced each other.

The details of these connections underscore a key difference between *New*

Yorker humor and its predecessors. In contrast to the limited formal schooling enjoyed by American humorists of previous generations, when even lawyers were apprenticed and self-educated, this group of writers and artists graduated from college. The cultural shifts at work in the peer culture of the 1920s reshaped one strand of American humor to become not only urbanized but also educated. And in the *New Yorker,* this strand targeted a narrower market.

But not quite as narrow as might appear. The low profile of the *New Yorker*'s women contributors today makes their networks difficult to reconstruct, but they had penetrated major New York publications and were quite visible in their day. Their networks also overlapped with men's. Gilbert Seldes praised versifier Baird Leonard's daily column for the *Telegraph* as superior to F. P. A.'s. Lois Long moved from *Vanity Fair* to take on the *New Yorker*'s nightlife and shopping columns. Ross's wife, Jane Grant, who wrote for the *New York Times,* helped found the feminist Lucy Stone League in 1921 along with Ruth Hale (O'Connor 73), who married *World* columnist Heywood Broun. Long also belonged to the league. Ralph Ingersoll became managing editor in June 1925 after an introduction from another of Grant's friends, F. P. A.'s wife, Minna Adams (Grant 228). Grant's correspondence with her wartime friend Janet Flanner, another Lucy Stone cofounder, metamorphosed into *New Yorker*'s biweekly "Letter from Paris" (Lorenz 38). Flanner's own friends abroad included the expatriate habitués of Sylvia Beach's Shakespeare and Company bookstore, though Djuna Barnes and F. Scott Fitzgerald were among the few who published in the early *New Yorker.* Writer Ann Honeycutt, a close friend of Frank Sullivan and James Thurber, began contributing in 1929. Contributor Herbert Asbury's sister-in-law Emily Hahn first wrote for the magazine in 1929 and continued through the 1980s. And this list does not include such well-known connections as artists Mary Petty and Alan Dunn, married in 1927, or the July 1925 suggestion from Fillmore Hyde that his summertime neighbor Katharine Sergeant Angell apply for a job as a manuscript reader (Davis 55).

The networks' origins in the ivy leagues, local journalism, and social relations—bastions closed to persons of color—explain why the otherwise trendy *New Yorker* barely broke into Harlem or published the work of the new voices arising there. Contributors' lives were expected to mirror readers': no blacks or rubes needed apply.

These peer networks also explain why the *New Yorker* appeared to publish only from a small group of contributors when in fact the staff faithfully slogged through the editorial slush pile of unsolicited stories, poems, cartoons, and

"Talk" ideas. Despite its growing population, New York was (and in many ways remains) a small town. Consequently, the declaration in Ross's prospectus that the magazine would feature small-town gossip drew on a very real fact of New York life: like small-town Americans, New Yorkers live and work and play in overlapping circles of acquaintance.

Borrowed Ideas and Innovations

Intensifying the small-town quality of these peer networks were developments in New York media. Consolidation among newspapers and staff exchanges among magazines pressed publishers to distinguish their product from others. The growth of advertising especially squeezed membership- and subscription-supported magazines such as *American Legion Weekly* and *Judge* in 1924, as Ross began seriously planning the *New Yorker*. With their large circulation but limited advertising, humor magazines presented a special challenge, which the *New Yorker* soon addressed through targeted editorial and marketing strategies. The germ of this idea probably came from *College Humor*. The durability and success of America's general circulation humor magazines, *Life* and *Judge*, also provided examples and object lessons, as did *Vanity Fair*, which offered highbrow material to upscale readers. By 1930 the *New Yorker* shared a substantial number of writers and artists with its predecessors, but the newest magazine outperformed them all.

Judge satisfied American readers for more than half a century before the *New Yorker* and then the depression came along. Surviving from 1881 to 1939, it not only outlived the *American Punch* (1879–81), *Puck* (1877–1918), *Life* (1883–1936), the *Smart Set* (1900–1930), and a host of the lesser-known humor magazines (Sloane), but also absorbed *Leslie's Weekly* (1855–1922), America's oldest national illustrated weekly. As early as 1921, the general slump among national weekly magazines in the twenties drove Leslie's, a giant among nineteenth-century mass-market publishers, to offer combined subscriptions to *Leslie's Weekly, Film Fun*, and *Judge; Judge* and *Leslie's* merged in December, 1922, and subscriptions ran just five dollars a year for both. Three years later the same five dollars would buy a year of the *New Yorker* or *Life*, both much livelier weeklies, though *Judge* limped along until 1937.

The target marketing that eventually sustained the *New Yorker* made general circulation weeklies less profitable. *Judge*'s strength lay in its broad appeal—precisely the opposite of the *New Yorker*'s niche marketing. A house ad on the inside front cover for June 16, 1923, claimed circulation of more than 200,000 copies weekly (*Judge* 6/16/23), a figure translating into a million dollars annually at five dollars per year or fifteen cents for a single newsstand copy. A close look at individual issues of *Judge* suggests that circulation revenue kept the magazine relatively independent of advertising. Of each 32-page issue, *Judge* typically sold only one of the covers—the outside back page—to advertisers, reserving the other two glossy pages for house ads, contest announcements, and the like. By contrast, ad pages in the *New Yorker* hovered at eight per issue until November of the first year, and by the issue of September 12, 1925, three full-page ads preceded "Talk" and three more concluded the back of the book. Subscription income gave *Judge* independence from seasonal shifts in advertising revenue, thus maintaining stable size and contents: every issue contained thirty-two pages of cartoons and text.

Financial stability may have made *Judge*'s editors wary of change, but it attracted notable contributors. George Jean Nathan, co-editor of *American Mercury* with H. L. Mencken, wrote the weekly theater reviews. Artist John Held Jr. had a weekly cartoon page, as did Ralph Barton, in a preview of his regular theater caricature department for the early *New Yorker*. Held and Barton also drew for *Life* and *Vanity Fair;* they brought their reputations as well as artwork to the *New Yorker*. Corey Ford made an early appearance in *Judge* as a student at Columbia in the College Wits issue of May 12, 1923; his "Philosophies of a College Fellow: Is Love Physical or Spiritual?" appeared just below a cartoon by S. J. Perelman, then at Brown (5/12/23:24); Chester Gould, who later created *Dick Tracy,* represented Northwestern in the same issue. Gardner Rea, W. J. Enright, Clive Weed, Paul Reilly, R. B. Fuller, Alice Duer Miller—these freelancers may not have sent *Judge* their best work, and they apparently fought with editors over payment,[8] but they continued to publish in it. By exemplifying how not to treat contributors, *Judge* also paved the way for the extreme graciousness with which *New Yorker* editors dealt with artists and writers.

Historians have treated *Judge* mainly as an object lesson in Ross's editorial education because his unhappiness there led him to found the *New Yorker*. *Judge* also has a bad reputation among *New Yorker* partisans because its contents and format began a steep decline in 1924 and 1925, the time when the two magazines are most often compared. They have taken *Judge* to task for enclosing little jokes in iconic outlines; these FunnyBones (bone shapes), Lizzie Labels (auto license shapes), and Epilaughs (tombstones) *were* stale even in 1924, but they entered the magazine in the issue of August 9, 1924—just after Ross left.

1. **Alexander Vishnevsky**, as Boris Godunoff in "Tsar Fyodor"; 2. **Nikolai Alexandroff**, as the Actor in "The Lower Depths"; 3. **Vassily Luzhsky**, as Butler Firce in "The Cherry Orchard"; 4. **Leonid M. Leonidoff**, as Dmitry in "The Brothers Karamazoff"; 5. **Olga Knipper-Tchekhova**, as Masha in "The Three Sisters"; 6. **Constantin Stanislavsky**, as Shabelsky in "Ivanoff"; 7. **Alla Tarasova**, as Grushenka in "The Brothers Karamazoff"; 8. **Maria Uspenskaya**, as Charlotta in "The Cherry Orchard"; 9. **Vera Pashennaya**, as Olga in "The Three Sisters"; 10. **Vassily Katchaloff**, as Dr. Stockmann in "An Enemy of the People"; 11. **Ivan Moskvin**, as Luka in "The Lower Depths"; 12. **Nikolai Podgorny**, as Trofimoff in "The Cherry Orchard"; 13. **Lydia Korenieva**, as Irina in "The Three Sisters"; **Vladimir Gribunin**, as Stupendieff in "The Lady from the Provinces"; 15. **Yevgenia Rayevskaya**, as Mrs. Stockmann in "An Enemy of the People"; 16. **Varvara Bulgakova**, as Natalia in "The Three Sisters"; 17. **Lyoff Bulgakoff**, as Alyoshka in "The Lower Depths"; 18. **Peter Baksheieff**, as Vaska in "The Lower Depths."

Ralph Barton, *Judge*, 12/29/23:12. Theater caricatures were a staple of 1920s illustrated magazines, including *Life* and *Vanity Fair*.

Issues of *Judge* published during Ross's tenure (April 5 to August 2, 1924) hint at ideas he realized more successfully in the *New Yorker*. He inherited a formula requiring a full-page political cartoon facing a list of the magazine's editors and a page of editorial comments headlined "Judge." With the issue of May 31, 1924, the list of editors disappeared, the heading changed to "Judge on the Bench," and several quarter-page editorial cartoons interspersed among the paragraphs replaced the full-page drawing, in the manner of "The Talk of the Town."

The straight and narrow path in New York

John Liello, *Judge*, 10/27/23:3.

Editors' names did not reappear until August 9, but the previous layout was reinstated by July 26, when writers' names moved back from the end of their pieces (*New Yorker* style) to the beginning, and the "Moving Pictures" department went to George Mitchell from Newman Levy, who had taken over on May 11 (and became a *New Yorker* regular). The coincidence between these changes and Ross's departure suggests that Ross voted with his feet against disagreement over his editorial preferences.

In addition to providing a roster of dissatisfied artists and writers, *Judge* also identified those who could provide the local slant he sought for the *New Yorker.* Contrary to Corey Ford's claim that *Judge* required Ross to reject items with a local theme (113), *Judge* abounded in material with New York topics and backgrounds—traffic, theater, parks—if only because so many artists, writers, and editors lived there. Cartoons and verbal sketches lampooned traffic problems, high-rise living, and other frustrations of New York life. The editorial page regularly called attention to events reported in the New York newspapers. Cartoons with universal themes might have the New York skyline in the background, as in Frank Hanley's vision of a public monument to traffic accidents (7/5/24:13), or they might make fun of urban customs, as in John Liello's ironic commentary on jaywalking, "The straight and narrow path in New York" (10/27/23:3). Regardless of internal editorial politics, the abundance of New York talent and art in *Judge*—including soon-to-be *New Yorker* artists Johan Bull, John Held, Gilbert Wilkinson, Perry Barlow, Donald McKee, Milt Gross, Frank Hanley, W. P. Trent, Eugene McNerney, and Nancy Fay—furnished evidence that a New York humor magazine would not fail for lack of local material.

Judge gave Ross ideas to borrow and reject. He clearly liked Barton's theater caricatures. But he chose not to imitate *Judge*'s political advocacy, despite apparent congruence between the *New Yorker*'s attitudes and the progressive positions in Clive Weed's editorial cartoons—against the Ku Klux Klan and lynching in "Their Christmas Tree" (12/16/22:12) or supporting fair labor practices in "Two Weeks with Pay" (7/14/23:18). Ross had no reason to mimic *Judge*'s College Wits section, nor the digest of world humor, which filled several pages at low cost (perhaps only reciprocal reprinting), but its appeal to universality directly opposed the parochialism that Ross sought. The *New Yorker* did follow *Judge*'s lead in offering a column on motor cars (the sort of consumer advice addressed to computer users today) but rejected a stock market department. (*Judge* absorbed both columns after the merger with *Leslie's*.) Most significantly, Ross rejected *Judge*'s adoption of a weekly theme, such as advertising or athletics, for the cover and main features.

Judge's editorial policies exposed opportunities for a local weekly, even without requiring Ross to reject New York local color humor. The *New Yorker*'s local focus eliminated the need for an external theme to unify its graphic and textual humor. Other departments also had more to offer a New York audience. Reviews of movies, books, musical events, and the theater could easily target a well-defined audience of (self-styled) sophisticates, and the list could easily expand to include the nightlife and shopping that only a local audience would want. But whereas *Judge* envisioned an audience of domesticated middle Americans—its house ads showed beleaguered parents (mostly fathers) seeking comic relief from work and family responsibilities—the *New Yorker* imagined readers with the money, interests, and discretionary time to enjoy the sophisticated entertainments it would review. In this context, Ross's main problem was how to define the target audience in order to make this local weekly viable.

Part of the answer lay in *College Humor*. A relative newcomer among national humor magazines, *College Humor* began in December 1921 as a quarterly spin-off of an anthology, *Best College Humor: The First Collection from the American College*

Dummy Szold's imitation of woodcuts by John Held, Jr. *Carnegie Puppet*, rpt. *College Humor*, 3/25:6. See illustration on page 169.

Humorous Magazines (1920). But where the anthology served an undifferentiated national audience for verbal and graphic humor reprinted from campus humor magazines, the magazine specifically targeted college students themselves, especially the contributors in its pages. To draw these readers, *College Humor* featured introductory essays in which successful writers and cartoonists (always identified by alma mater and class) shared their paths to success. By 1922, college humor publications had become good business. Three in New York City—at Columbia, New York University, and City College—and two more across the river in New Jersey met the minimum circulation of five thousand for acceptance by the Audit Bureau of Circulation (12/22:6,9). Each ninety-six-page issue of *College Humor* made clear what sophisticated, educated young Americans found funny, as

Mr. M'Callum conclusively proves to the Cynics Society the veracity of his slogan,
"You Just Know She Wears Them"

An anonymous cartoonist for *Lord Jeff*, the Amherst College humor magazine, imitated Rea Irvin's style of composition, subject, and caption in a cartoon signed with "Apologies to R. I." a year before the *New Yorker* debuted. In a particularly clever insight, the parody inverts Irvin's typical separation of dignified elites from vulgarly occupied workers (e.g., see p. 39). Rpt. *College Humor*, 6/24:104.

campus cartoonists imitated the work of John Held and Rea Irvin, two of the earliest art contributors to the *New Yorker*. *College Humor's* boasts of its sophistication ("We start with the premise that our readers are educated") likewise found their way into Ross's announcement that the *New Yorker* "will assume a reasonable degree of enlightenment on the part of its readers."[9]

College Humor's growth demonstrated the power of the peer society as a target market. The magazine collaborated with collegiate publications by exchanging reprint rights for advertising, giving college artists and writers a national audience and offering advertisers access, in its own pages *and* those of campus magazines, to a collegiate market. The arrangement allowed *College Humor,* published in Chicago, to expand from ninety-six-page quarterly issues in 1921 to one-hundred-page monthly issues in 1925. On the eve of the *New Yorker*'s debut, such expansion identified the peer society as a viable target market; a house ad valued the market of students and their parents at a quarter of a billion dollars each school year (12/24:87).

In following *College Humor*'s demographic lead, Ross capitalized on contemporary trends in marketing and publishing. The marketing trends began in 1893, according to Richard Ohmann, when Frank Munsey discovered that with sufficient subscribers he could discount the price of *Munsey's* by selling *them* to advertisers (31). Techniques appropriate to mass-circulation magazines for mass audiences did not at first seem applicable to more narrowly defined publics, however. *Judge* relied on subscription sales. Mencken's *American Mercury* (founded 1924) and George Jean Nathan's *Smart Set* (founded 1914) sought many of the same readers as the *New Yorker* at the national level but addressed them primarily as intellectuals and aesthetes, not as consumers. *McClure's, Collier's,* and other muckraking magazines of the prewar period that relied on small ads and large circulations (as *Judge* did) withered away in the 1920s, when movies and radio became competitors for the leisure of middle-class audiences. Large-circulation magazines could not sustain upper-class readers in the postwar period, because the professionalization of advertising that began then privileged the mass audiences identified by mass marketing. These techniques, first detailed in Walter Lippmann's *Public Opinion* (1922) and Edward Bernays and Doris Fleischman's *Crystallizing Public Opinion* (1923), built upon publishing support structures established in the previous decade. The Audit Bureau of Circulation began verifying circulation figures and the advertising rates based upon them in 1914; the Magazine Publishers of America began in 1919 to serve as a liaison between advertisers and publishers (MPA and Kanner). The very trends working against quality monthlies, however, inadvertently fostered target markets.

The *New Yorker*'s focus on local content enabled Ross to adapt newspapers' blend of circulation and advertising appeal to the upscale magazine. In defining the *New Yorker* by its readers' buying power, he understood the magazine's dual needs to sell editorial content to readers and sell readers to advertisers. The *New Yorker* archives show that advertising agencies ranked among early recipients of the *New Yorker* Prospectus, and the head of the J. B. Milgram Advertising Agency near Wall Street replied with a supportive note reporting that he had been thinking along the same lines for six months.[10] Milgram's response demonstrates not only that Ross had timed the *New Yorker* well but also that an advertising professional saw the potential in its editorial hook. In fact, at the beginning Ross understood his market's consumer interests better than their sense of humor.

A truism by 1928, target marketing was novel in 1924, when advertisers sought mass audiences of middle-class consumers. "Tell it to Sweeney," the tabloid *New York Daily News* advised potential advertisers in 1925, "The Stuyvesants Will Understand" (qtd. in Marchand 61). Newspapers thus left the Stuyvesants to the *New Yorker*. By the spring of 1928, just after the *New Yorker*'s third birthday, evidence of that abandonment inspired its own ad campaign. Four-page statistical spreads analyzing the demographics and saturation of New York newspapers, researched by the Bureau of Business Research of New York University, invited the *New Yorker*'s readers—admen and their clients in particular—to reach their peers outside New York by recognizing the affluent audiences for the *Pittsburgh Press, Chicago Tribune,* and other out-of-town publications (e.g., 3/3/28:49–52, 4/7/28:55–58). In 1924, however, Ross and Fleischmann faced the challenge of finding and securing the *New Yorker*'s niche among local advertisers and readers.

The idea of a magazine of New York life capitalized on other contemporary trends in American culture. Urbanization gave New York the caché of leadership, a position enhanced by the increasing importance of industries centered in New York City: the stock market, advertising, entertainment, and mass media. To be sure, film studios had recently relocated to Hollywood, taking some of Broadway's talent with them, but New York remained America's center for book and magazine publication, music printing and recording, theater, and (following the formation of NBC in 1926) radio as well. Through its dominance of media and money, the twin kings of twentieth-century popular culture, New York displaced Boston as America's cultural capital, and daily reinforced its claim.

The peer society saw New York as America's most cosmopolitan city; the *New Yorker*'s formula promoted mutual reinforcement of the city and its peer culture. A 1925 article in the *New Republic* interpreted the (lack of) clothing worn by "Flapper Jane" as evidence that New York was the symbolic and literal center of America's changing culture, in which youth dominated and "feminism" freed women of unwanted children and domestic servitude. "Wall Street . . . is the one spot in which the New Nakedness seems most appropriate," Bliven noted, because "the priestesses in the temple of Mammon . . . should be thus Dionysiac in apparelling themselves for their daily tasks" (65–66). But if Mammon lived on Wall Street, Dionysus had a flat in Greenwich Village. Headquarters of New York's peer society in the twenties, Greenwich Village also housed a local, largely ethnic, working-class population, and thus epitomized Manhattan's cultural shifts during the postwar years, according to Caroline Ware's detailed sociological analysis in the 1930s (43). Floyd Dell revived the romantic mood of the prewar Village when he published *Love in Greenwich Village* in 1926: he defined "love in Greenwich Village" to mean living with a broken heart "in this eager, hard ambitious young world of dreams and struggle" (44). Ross tapped into cultural phenomena larger than American comic art and writing in making New York's peer society his audience.

In 1924 the weekly *Life* surpassed its competitors in addressing humor to this group. A distinguished magazine for fifty years, *Life* is remembered today mainly because Henry Booth Luce purchased its name for his new picture magazine in 1936. *Life* began in 1876 when Harvard *Lampoon* cofounder E. S. Martin collaborated with John Ames Mitchell to establish an American equivalent of *Punch*, the premier British humor magazine; *Life* ran weekly from January 4, 1883, to 1931, then limped along monthly before dying in 1936 (Sloane 83, 142; Mott 224). More attractive in design and contents than either *Judge* or *College Humor, Life* owed its visual character to artist Charles Dana Gibson, whose art debuted in the magazine in 1887, before he was twenty-one, and who (with financial support from friends) outbid F. N. Doubleday and bought the magazine for $1 million in 1920, when its weekly circulation peaked at 500,000 (Sloane 150). Edited in 1924 by Ross's Algonquinite friend Robert E. Sherwood, who had moved there with Dorothy Parker and Robert Benchley from *Vanity Fair* in 1920, *Life* featured artists and writers whose visual style or comic sensibility was too sophisticated for *Judge*: Rea Irvin, Alice Harvey, Don Herold, Gluyas Williams, and Al Frueh among the artists; Donald Ogden Stewart, Baird Leonard, Arthur Guiterman, Parker, and Benchley among the writers. Members of the peer society themselves, these humorists continued publishing in *Life* even after becoming *New Yorker* contributors.

Whether or not Ross noticed that *Life* became more focused on New York City during 1923 and 1924, the trend confirms the timing of his plan for a humorous local magazine. Ellison Hoover's two-page spread, "An Impression of New York By One Who Has Never Been There" takes an insider's view of the outsider's confusion: the Singer Building and Hotel Ritz are on Coney Island, magically connected to Battery Park via the Brooklyn Bridge; Riverside Drive runs to the Bowery via Long Beach; Grant's tomb is next door to the Metropolitan Museum (at Fifth Avenue and Hester Street!); and a devil being chased out of the city by a mounted knight in armor and a fire department car claims, "N.Y. is a grand place, alright, but I wouldn't care to live here" (11/20/24:16–17). The joke is lost on the uninitiated. More typically, cartoons on universal subjects used New York settings, as in Al Frueh's narrative cartoon, "A Nature Study" about human nature on the sidewalks of New York (*Life* 11/20/24:5) or the futuristic unsigned drawing of "The Air Serpent," a snakelike dirigible weaving its way among towers of the Woolworth Building and other landmarks (*Life* 12/24:49). *Life* pioneered cartoons basing visual humor on a comic idea and the drawing's composition rather than on body humor or the caption, and the *New Yorker* took over where *Life* left off.

The *Life* artist most important to the *New Yorker* was Rea Irvin (1881–1972), its founding art director. Irvin contributed not only his own work and his sophisticated eye but also his taste for ironically related images and text. Indeed, what is often called the *"New Yorker* cartoon" deserves to be called "the Irvin cartoon." His 1923 "Skeptics' Society" series for *Life* previewed the *New Yorker* style: a single panel whose caption and image interact, literally in this case, to comic effect. The facial expressions on the skeptics as "They Investigate the Theory That Too Many Cooks Spoil the Broth" enable Irvin to contrast mentation with action: the slender, dignified, discerning diners (dressed in black) clash with the chaos of rotund chefs (white spaces enclosed by outlines) fighting among each other. Irvin's style and sense of humor evidently appealed to the peer society, because the campus cartoonists appearing in *College Humor* frequently imitated him, even though he belonged to their parents' generation.

Life began to look increasingly like the *New Yorker* as the twenties progressed because the two magazines shared so many art contributors. The similarity did not work in *Life's* favor. In fact, the *New Yorker* displaced *Life* as America's wittiest humor magazine even when its circulation trailed *Life's* by 30,000.[11] *Life* conceded its troubles with the May 10, 1928, debut of "the new *Life*"—boasting a new page design and an item titled "The Talk of the Town" by former *New Yorker* staff member Tip Bliss. Two weeks later came a more serious signal, as the Burlesque Number of May 31, 1928, parodied the *New Yorker* along with the *Saturday Evening Post, American Mercury, College Humor,* and the *Nation. Life's* successful truth-in-jest presidential campaign for Will Rogers, which ran from May

THE SKEPTICS' SOCIETY
They investigate the theory that too many cooks spoil the broth.

Rea Irvin and R[obert?] S[herwood?], *Life*, 10/25/23:7.

through November of 1928, proved that its content-based formula could still satisfy readers. *Life* retained a respectable circulation of 70,000 when it folded in 1936, yet its advertising revenues crashed with the stock market—making it sufficiently worthless that Luce bought only *Life*'s name, not its subscribers (Mott 231–32; Elson and Norton-Taylor 291). The *New Yorker*, in contrast, expanded to a second, national weekly edition on October 5, 1929, just a few weeks before the Great Crash.

In replacing *Life* as America's premier humor magazine in the late twenties, the *New Yorker* gave proof to the shift from a manufacturing to an information economy. The new magazine based on consumer demographics outperformed an established predecessor based on editorial content. By the summer of 1930, *New Yorker* insiders considered *Life* a pathetic elderly relative, "a poor thing" subjected to one "operation" after another.[12]

The New Yorker Debuts

Ross explicitly defined the *New Yorker* against the current field. His Prospectus asserted that the *New Yorker* "will not be what is commonly called radical or highbrow," and "not edited for the old lady in Dubuque." Not a newspaper, the *New Yorker* was nonetheless local, timely, and published weekly, and it promoted columnists' mannered viewpoints on current events. Not a newsweekly, like the recently founded *Time* (1923), the *New Yorker* nonetheless maintained a journalistic orientation and weekly scope. Not a tabloid, the *New Yorker* nonetheless used current events more for entertainment than for education and offered gossip and "josh." Unlike conventional "quality" magazines, so-named for their educated and affluent audience, *New Yorker* aimed at singles and childless couples rather than families; the school ads at the beginning of *Vanity Fair* and *American Mercury* had no counterparts in the *New Yorker*. Unlike its competitors among the humor magazines—*Judge, Life, College Humor*—the *New Yorker* sought intellectual and social heights where the air was so thin as to inspire yawns among the uninitiated.

In 1924, the closest competitor for affluent, educated urbanites was *Vanity Fair,* and Ross positioned the *New Yorker* against it, too. In that sense, Tina Brown's 1992 appointment as the *New Yorker*'s fourth editor marked a return to the magazine's beginnings as a sassier, more youthful, weekly *Vanity Fair,* a national monthly with a definite New York slant to its coverage of the arts. Condé Nast's *Vanity Fair* began in 1913 and was edited until 1936 by Frank "Crownie" Crowninshield (Sloane 299–306); during the 1920s it offered extremely sophisticated fare to a well-heeled national audience. (The original American *Vanity Fair*, a domestic version of *Punch*, had run from 1859 to 1863 under the editorship of Charles G. Leland and Charles Farrar Browne, a humorist better known as Artemus Ward.) Crowninshield had studied art at the University of Rome and promoted the Armory Show of modernism and avant-garde art in 1913 (Douglas 20), and he built *Vanity Fair* after the war into a magazine known for its wit, especially as provided by Parker, Benchley, and Sherwood.

Vanity Fair did not entirely lose its sense of humor when the trio left in 1920.

On the recommendation of Edmund Wilson, Donald Ogden Stewart briefly came on staff in 1921 (Stewart 96–97), and Alexander Woollcott, Heywood Broun, Marc Connelly, and Nancy Hoyt wrote witty reviews and occasional pieces. But a high tone predominated before the *New Yorker* came on the scene. Pedantic essays and serious reviews prevailed—Bertrand Russell on behaviorism (VF 10/23:47,96), for example, and T. S. Eliot on English literature in a series of three essays (VF 7/23:51,98; 11/23:44,118; 2/24:29). John Held's woodcuts of folklore topics, seventy of which would appear in the early *New Yorker*, received a heavy-handed analysis as "Interesting Modern Experiments in an Old Method." Readers were advised to note the contrast between Held's popular, lower-class subjects and his careful use of the wood block medium because "It is this underlying seriousness"—that is, the modernist concern for form and method—"which primarily makes these woodcuts worth while" (VF 11/23:76).

A shift toward more comic contents began in 1924, as *Vanity Fair* essays took on some frivolous topics and humorous artwork became more abundant. The January issue featured Heywood Broun's "Higher Aesthetic of the Necktie," accompanied by Miguél Covarrubias's first work for the magazine, a caricature of the writer (1/24:37); amusing artwork by Fish, Benito, and Joseph B. Platt appeared as well. These changes in topic and mood suggest that Ross's idea for an upscale humor magazine was not only well-targeted to the New York scene but also well-timed to its cultural values, as print media sought affluent audiences. Together the ads and editorial content indicated that *Vanity Fair*'s readers could afford the best automobiles, plumbing fixtures, and jewelry. But their interest in the New York social scene was often touristic and voyeuristic, not necessarily participatory.

Ross targeted the most lively local members of *Vanity Fair*'s upscale audience—those with what the Prospectus called the "prevalent query, 'What shall we do with this evening?'" Unlike the old lady in Dubuque, *New Yorker* readers would enjoy nightclubs, galleries, the theater, books, and other signs of the high life, their leisure unhindered by children. (Indeed, Peter Arno's cover of November 16, 1929, showed the bewilderment of both infant and nanny at an elegantly dressed mother's cuddling her child.) Scott Elledge identifies the "old lady" as a character familiar to readers of Burt Leston Taylor's *Chicago Tribune* column, "A Line o' Type or Two" (101), but the implication of the Prospectus did not depend on readers' recognizing the allusion to B. L. T. Rather, the remark expressed a preference for the younger generation and unconcern for the small-town mass audiences that he considered irrelevant to this enterprise—

Irrelevant photographs and ridiculous captions were a favorite staff joke, recurring repeatedly between 1925 and 1930. House ad, 2/21/25:21.

especially readers of the *Saturday Evening Post* and *Ladies' Home Journal,* which (along with *Munsey's*) had revolutionized American magazine publishing by providing national markets for mass-produced goods. Nonetheless, Ross borrowed the *Saturday Evening Post*'s key editorial practice: prompt review of submissions and payment on acceptance rather than on publication, a policy by which contributors give the magazine de facto right of first refusal. (By contrast, according to Corey Ford, *Judge* paid "after publication, and then only when they threatened a lawsuit" [112]).

In part because the editors were more certain of what the *New Yorker* was not than what it was, the magazine did not catch on right away—not even with its editors, who spent much of the first year trying to find a workable formula. During the early months, parts of the editorial puzzle appeared in various places in the magazine under changing titles. Contents of the first issue, dated February 21, 1925, were less compelling than Rea Irvin's cover. The magazine had a number of brief jokes as filler, including the famous "Optimist" joke, a riddle told backwards ("A man who can make it in par." "What's an optimist, Pop?"). Historians typically explain the inverted sequence of the riddle as an attack on two-liners, but *Judge* ran a series of lame optimist jokes during Ross's tenure,[13] and he critiqued them here.

The first issue's stories and cartoons succeeded better than the departments. Except for Ross's witty tale of his run-in with Jumbo Jr., "Of All Things" was a dull string of anecdotes. "Talk" began with an interesting story of International Millennium Week, but layout mangled the punch line. Sawdust's "Story of Manhattankind" had mildly amusing political allusions; the illustration by Herb Roth was wittier. Funnier than the unsigned "Say It With Scandal," a futuristic burlesque of a 1928 newsroom, was a house ad, "Our $25,000.00 Prize Name Contest" (23). Its photograph of a Native American family outside their tepee clashed hilariously with the caption "John Peter Toohey . . . snapped before his home at Manhattan Transfer," while its text parodied magazine contests and contest rhetoric, including their mathematics (eleven $100-prizes totaling $13) and the next week's teaser ("Our Big Anniversary Number"). Of course, the second issue would follow in seven days, but an anniversary issue was a distant hope. In fact, after twelve issues publisher Raoul Fleischmann officially killed the magazine, but (according to Ralph Ingersoll's 1934 report for *Fortune*) he drank so many toasts to "dollars gallantly lost" that he forgot to order a shutdown (82).

Like many good *New Yorker* stories, this one contains some stretchers. Ingersoll reported a somewhat different story in his 1961 memoir *Point of Departure*, conceding that the events had already achieved mythic status when he joined the magazine five weeks afterwards (187–89); Thurber's biographer tracked down the dates (Kinney 112). Their information shows that Fleischmann and Ross met with advisors Hawley Truax and John Hanrahan, and declared the magazine dead at a meeting on Friday, May 8, 1925. They hinted at their ambivalence about the meeting by holding it at 11:00 a.m. at the Princeton Club (then on the corner of East Thirty-ninth Street and Park Avenue)—staying discreetly away from the Algonquin (on West Forty-fourth between Fifth and Sixth Av-

OPTIMIST—*Well, they haven't got me YET!*

One of many optimist jokes purchased during Ross's tenure at *Judge*, this drawing ran the week after he left. Tousey, *Judge*, 8/9/24:3.

enues) and the magazine's offices at 25 West Forty-fifth Street. They could therefore allow themselves second thoughts when they met the next day at F. P. A.'s wedding, and they reversed themselves entirely on Monday, May 11. They determined to ride out the summer while directing financial resources and staff toward a major editorial, advertising, and circulation push in the fall. Acquisitions would continue as Ross built a staff and refined the editorial formula, but the best material would be held until fall and published in conjunction with well-planned advertising and circulation campaigns.

Statistics assembled for the *New Yorker's* second anniversary celebration confirm that circulation did fall below 10,000 copies early in April, and did not return to that level until October. (These numbers put ad revenues at risk because the circulation guarantee was 12,000 copies weekly.) Circulation hit bottom in September, with a rise of 3,000 from mid-September to mid-October. But more remarkable is the growth in subscription copies beginning about October 15: subscription sales grew by 5,000 copies by November 15 and reached 15,000 copies by January 1, 1926, by which time newsstand sales reached 20,000. In-

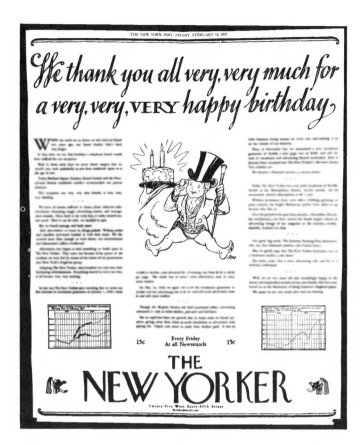

Advertisement in the *New York Post*, 2/18/27, n.p. NYPL. (Poster, The New Yorker
Birthday, Harold Ross—1927, NYer Box 3.)

deed, subscriptions continued rising throughout 1926, so that by the end of volume 2 in February of 1927, subscriptions accounted for half of the *New Yorker*'s
56,000 weekly copies. On its second birthday, a full-page ad in the *New York Post*
boasted paid circulation of 54,748: 44,405 in the New York metropolitan area,
10,343 beyond. Of these, single-copy (newsstand) sales accounted for 26,738
and paid subscriptions, 28,010 ("We Thank You All").

    Ad pages followed a similar pattern. After dropping from eight in the early
months to two during the summer (one for Fleischmann's Yeast), ad pages hovered at eight pages per issue until Christmas trade brought the per-issue numbers up to fifteen (including partial pages) at the end of 1925. In 1926, by

contrast, even the summer slump (now a seasonal pattern) never sent ad pages below twenty-two per issue, and Christmas brought the advertising peak to sixty pages. Advertising rates increased from their 1925 rate of $150 per page to $250 on January 1, 1926, then again to $400 on May 1 (2:11), when the circulation guarantee rose to 35,000 weekly copies. Another increase occurred six months later, on November 1, bringing ad pages up to $500 each and guaranteed circulation to 50,000 weekly copies. Amid all these happy statistics, two details drew the most pride of accomplishment: a positive cash flow in January of 1927, and a number-four ranking among all American magazines for advertising lineage in the previous three months ("We Thank You All").

The reason most often cited for the magazine's turnaround is the publication of Ellin Mackay's "Why We Go to Cabarets—A Post Debutante Explains," which appeared in the issue of 1:42 (11/28/25:7–8) with an illustration by Alice Harvey. Dale Kramer appropriately discounted its importance, but few others have followed his lead. Jane Grant recalled pulling the piece from the bottom of the slush pile (where Ross apparently kept it) and insisting, "even if she has written it with her foot you can't turn it down" because "the promotional value of a story by the glamorous debutante was not to be overlooked"; as she tells the story Ross gave in only after Ingersoll and Woollcott joined her in pressing him (J. Grant 229). Ellin Mackay, daughter of Postal Telegraph president Clarence H. Mackay (Kramer, *Ross* 92), had been formally introduced to New York's elite at the Ritz-Carlton four years earlier, and hence spoke from unassailable authority in declaring that socially particular women could not find their male peers in the stag lines of traditional society parties because they were infiltrated by uncouth young men from the outer boroughs. Although cabarets admit all classes, she concluded, they allow the upper classes to keep to themselves. Grant claimed that Mackay's piece gave the *New Yorker* its first sellout issue (although a letter to contributors claimed that "the first issue virtually sold out in New York City in the first thirty-six hours"[14]) and led Hollywood to offer the magazine $50,000 for movie rights to the article (229–31).

Other principals remember the story differently. According to Kramer, Ingersoll saw the piece as validation of Ross's idea and timing for "a slightly iconoclastic 'class' magazine," though he found it "terrible," and Mackay objected to having it edited (*Ross* 92–93). In 1934 Ingersoll claimed that Mackay's piece "seal[ed] the bargain" of growing ad and circulation revenues that began with a $60,000 publicity campaign in September and, before that, Corey Ford's burlesque series on publishing, "The Making of a Magazine" (82). In fact, after shrinking from thirty-two to twenty-four pages during the summer, the magazine jumped to forty pages on September 12, when three full-page ads sat inside the front covers and another three in the back. Full-page ads in the earliest issues had promoted French perfume, tires from U.S. Royal, Knabe pianos, automobiles, and books; in the fall, these expanded to include hotels, restaurants, supper clubs, and other local establishments. New ads appearing after Mackay's piece suggest that her article inspired New York's retail enterprises to sign on. Bonwitt Teller took the inside cover for December 5, followed quickly by B. Altman (1/2/26), Saks Fifth Avenue, and Helena Rubenstein (both 1/30/26). Some of this growth might have occurred as retailers sought the carriage trade's holiday business, but the drop-off after Christmas, in contrast to the late-summer lull, showed that new advertisers planned to stay.

Local Politics

More than indicating that the *New Yorker* had achieved credibility as a way to reach affluent consumers, these ads show that media buyers and the *New Yorker*'s advertising staff agreed on defining the *New Yorker* as a magazine for women. Full-page ads for cars, tires, and other items addressed men directly, but ads targeting women outnumbered them.

These details emphasize that, contrary to assertions by Thurber and others, "Why We Go to Cabarets" (11/28/25:7–8) did not directly rescue the magazine, but it *did* define the *New Yorker*'s audience for readers, advertisers, and editors alike. The *we* of Mackay's title united readers, editors, and contributors, and clearly distinguished them not only from the old lady in Dubuque but also from the middle-aged folks at *Vanity Fair*. Two years earlier, *Vanity Fair* artist Henry Raleigh had posed "A Problem for Dr. Freud: Why Do People Go to Cabarets?" (11/1923:66–67), a truly rhetorical question because he found the venues too distasteful to explain. Mackay's response, by contrast, defended her own taste as she helped define the *New Yorker*'s. Her piece sneers at everyone outside her smart set—the unattractive, the boisterous, the colorless, the West Sider, the Brooklynite—reserving her greatest contempt for the stag line, with its faith in "male superiority." Then she defends the slumming practice of attending cabarets by reversing the terms of snobbery, claiming that the peasants have so polluted elite parties that only in the peasants' surroundings can the elite stick to themselves. "Yes, we go to cabarets," she concludes, "but we resent the criticism of our good taste in so doing. We go because, like our Elders, we are fastidious. We go because we prefer rubbing elbows in a cabaret to dancing at an exclusive party with all sorts and kinds of people" (11/28/25:8). And there they spend their own money, she notes, not (as in a hotel or home affair) their parents'. Although Mackay used this point to emphasize her generation's independence from parental control, the *New Yorker*'s advertisers and business staff could not have missed the reminder that modern young people—including young women—had substantial discretionary funds.

Ads for Villa Venice at 10 East Sixtieth Street (near Fifth Avenue) explicitly picked up Mackay's theme two weeks later, in the same issue containing her follow-up, "The Declining Function: A Post-Debutante Rejoices" (12/12/25:13–16). The ad offered the restaurant as a place where "one may have one's own party in spite of the fact that other patrons may be of a different social strata [*sic*]," adding that social rules nonetheless remain intact: "The dinner jacket is a requisite, of course" (12/12/27:47). The Business Office probably sold some of the new advertising in this issue—including a perfume ad written entirely in French on the inside front cover and an announcement of "The Cigar of the Bon Vivant" near the back—to run specifically in conjunction with Mackay's second article, but her pieces enabled Editorial to help Business do its job.

Refinement of the editorial program went hand in hand with promotional efforts. A form letter to contributors on August 1 gave strong direction, asserting, "Our aim is to put more life, vigor and ideas into the book, to make it sound like *this week's* New Yorker."[15] The letter also identified concrete ways to achieve the goal. Recommended subjects included seasonal items such as "coming back from abroad and cheating the customs, discarding straw hats, thinking of football, . . . going to first night." Artists were advised to draw "clubs, Fifth Avenue and its shops, the drawing-room, the dining room, the museums, the theatre and so on." Perhaps most important, however, the letter proclaimed a specific point of view as well as a general attitude (though not, of course, a political stance of the sort promoted by *Judge* and *Life*):

The New Yorker, being inclined to opinion, must, it has been suggested, have specific things about which it is opinionated. . . . later this may be done on a comprehensive scale. In the meantime, we suggest that something ought to be done about certain types of social bore—all hundred-percenters and go-getters (includes Rotarians, Kiwanians and conventioneers) all lecturers, society doctors, society painters, all musicians when off the platform, out-of-towners (including buyers, who are very numerous at the moment) all advocates of intolerance, the noveau, etc.[16]

As this list implies an editorial staff who know what they want for their readers, so Ellin Mackay's piece implies a staff who know who those readers are.

Many, apparently, were women. Indeed, the *New Yorker* particularly targeted women readers during this period, though some efforts didn't bear fruit for years. Since Ross imagined readers as consumers—of both editorial and advertising content—much of the early targeting occurred in a traditional women's arena: shopping. After the Mackay piece, fashion advertising from Saks Fifth Avenue, Bonwit Teller, B. Altman, and Russeks featured day and evening wear, hosiery and lingerie, gloves, millinery, shoes, and handbags. Other ads played to women's role as household manager with displays of children's clothing and home appliances. Still other ads, however, addressed the New Woman. The last page of the important September 12, 1925, issue, for instance, carried a notice of the Exposition of Women's Arts and Industries, held at the Hotel Commodore, September 21–26.

By August of 1926, Ross considered the *New Yorker*'s female readership strong enough to suggest that the Advertising Department use it to help clients develop new markets. He advised advertising manager Raymond B. Bowen that London tobacco companies had begun advertising "cigarettes for women" and pointed out that "the Camel Company or some of the other big companies that [are] obviously timid about addressing an ad to women could do it in The New Yorker."[17] Fashionable women smokers had already appeared on covers by Rea Irvin and Ilonka Karasz (3/7/25, 11/7/25), and most recently on Stanley W. Reynolds's cover a week earlier (8/7/26). Later that fall the *New Yorker* targeted women for such male-identified products as automobiles and cameras, and ran Bamberger's ad for women's smoking accessories (10/16/26:4).

Not that regular editorial departments ignored women. The most obvious and conventional approach viewed women as consumers: the shopping department. Although this feature, "On and Off the Avenue," now appears only at Christmastime, it originated as a weekly shopping directory, "Where to Shop" in the first issue. Once this department evolved into its standard form, "On and Off the Avenue" opened with a page devoted to "Feminine Fashions." Two graphic elements marked the department's importance: a department illustration in the corner near the headline and a cartoon with shopping as a setting or theme. Some were drawn by women—especially Barbara Shermund, Helen Hokinson, and Alice Harvey, who all had backgrounds in commercial art—but Harold Denison and other male artists who did fashion work also appeared in this spot. The shopping column clearly addressed women even in the absence of such gendered remarks as Lois Long's "Spee-Dee Guide" to Macy's: "What you cannot carry out in your own hands should go in your husband's" (12/7/29:94).

In a parallel vein, "Motors" and some of the sporting columns (especially

"Polo" and "The Race Track") specifically addressed men. Other departments, although targeting both genders, were conducted by women. These included several very long-running regular departments: Lois Long's "Tables for Two" and "On and Off the Avenue," Janet Flanner's "Paris Letter," Allison Danzig's "Court Games." Dorothy Parker, Nancy Hoyt, and Baird Leonard all reviewed books. Most important, however, was Ross's editorial second, Katharine Sergeant Angell, who headed up fiction and verse acquisitions and helped choose cartoons and covers at the weekly art meeting. Indeed, as late as 1961 Raoul Fleischmann praised her for shaping the *New Yorker*'s standards of taste; he called her "a sensitive, cultured New Englander, imbued with the fine conscience characteristic of that famed rock-ribbed area" and claimed that her "strong feelings involving honesty, decency and believability in the advertising we should accept" defined the magazine's advertising policy (qtd. in Davis 60).

The decision to constitute women as a market and sell them to advertisers began in mid-nineteenth-century American publishing, as shown in Jackson Lears's *Fables of Abundance* and Richard Ohmann's *Selling Culture*. The *New Yorker* exploited rather than conceived it, as have most American mass media, nearly all of which rely on advertising. Nonetheless, the *New Yorker*'s record in hiring and promoting women and their work should make very clear that charges of the *New Yorker*'s misogyny—however much they might apply to individual pieces of writing or art, or to the collected works of certain contributors—entirely mischaracterize the magazine as a whole and the policies of its editor in chief. In fact, several times over the course of the first five years, the magazine explicitly disavowed misogynous contents, though it sometimes erred first.

The most notable example in the early years occurred in the summer of 1927, when Baird Leonard's "Rebuttal" (7/9/27:20) took issue with Ben Hecht's "The Female Bridge Menace" (6/25/27:19–20). Hecht's piece opened with fighting words: "There is nothing which so simply and automatically illustrates the hollowness of the feminine-equality pretense as auction bridge" (19). And it continued in that hostile vein. Its semihysterical tone ("They *will* not play their aces. They will not play their high cards. . . . They will not sacrifice their queens and kings to make one's jack good" [20]) hints that Hecht may have sought irony, but the humor fails after the first page because its chief focus is not the speaker's comic rage but his belief that "the female megalomania of the last ten years" has moved women out of their proper sphere: "making lampshades and Battenberg, writing poetry and attending lectures on Women's Rights" (19). Leonard's "Rebuttal" appeared two weeks later and in roughly the same position but had some disadvantages of defense. Despite an amusing closing quip—"Cut Alice. Cut Edith. Harry, will you take your nose out of that financial section and come over here and *cut?*")—Leonard's best shot was an early double entendre: "Mr. Hecht says that his argument can be summed up in a nutshell. Far be it from me to make any unkind acquiescence on that point" (20). "Rebuttal" could have run as a letter to the editor under the debunking "Our Captious Readers" headline, which began in 1925, but in treating it as featured copy the editors gave Leonard the last word. They did lighten the tone of the page with a W. P. Trent cartoon of a predatory young woman describing a friend's new bootlegger as "simply marvelous—tall, small moustache, and just out of Harvard" (7/9/27:20), but the cartoon's critique of predatory women put the *New Yorker* squarely on the political fence.

The editors became more cautious after this exchange. Gendered attacks stayed out of journalistic or fact pieces but continued in imaginative prose and verse. The distinction between comic and misogynous ridicule certainly affected acquisitions in 1928. About a year after the Hecht-Leonard exchange, Djuna Barnes's text and illustrations for "The Woman Who Goes Abroad to Forget" (12/8/28:23–29) prompted Angell to solicit a series along the same lines. "She is just the kind of person that The New Yorker wants to satirize and I think there must be a lot of others like her,"[18] Angell wrote, but she declined Barnes's "The Crasher" and "The Lost," two other illustrated manuscripts, because they denigrated their protagonists: "their dizziness, if you know what I mean, seems to put them out of bo[u]nds for us."[19] Angell also rejected the "feminine animadversion" of Katharine Brush's "I Do Not Like Department Stores."[20] Cartoons, comic prose, and verse volleyed gender attacks in both directions.

On issues of race and class the *New Yorker* was much less liberal, and somewhat less explicit. None of the writers of the Harlem Renaissance found their way into the *New Yorker*'s pages, and few of the uptown entertainments detailed in Ann Douglas's *Terrible Honesty: Mongrel Manhattan in the 1920s* were reviewed. The editors did know *Porgy* sufficiently well (it opened at the Guild Theater in 1927) to ask Perry Barlow, who hadn't seen the show, to redo a cartoon whose line verged on plagiarism.[21] E. B. White praised Ransom Rideout's *Goin' Home* as "a great idea for a stirring negro story," though he found it "too pat; in places too pat-and-mike" and concluded, "We wish a negro actor played the lead" (9/1/28:41). Nonetheless, Ross declined the opportunity for caricatures of a 1929 "Negro show" as not "worth covering," even though the offer came from a regular contributor, Miguél Covarrubias, whose 1927 *Negro Drawings* of Harlem nightclubs made him the foremost expert on the subject. If only to maintain a cordial relationship with Covarrubias, Ross held out the possibility that an improved show would merit coverage. He valued Covarrubias's contributions and understood his commitment to this ethnic material; the two men were friendly enough for Ross to handle the correspondence himself—his practice only for selected contributors in this period—and for Ross to close the letter "With love."[22]

In the typically American way, the *New Yorker* defined racial "others" mainly as black. Only a few of the five thousand art ideas published in the first five years involve Asians—one of them a cover by Peter Arno in which an Asian houseman uncertainly approaches with a feather duster an abstract sculpture of a voluptuous female nude (12/8/28). With this exception, the servant class of *New Yorker* covers is almost entirely European, and wholly identified (even to their nose-in-the-air snobbishness) with their employers. Equally homogeneous are the crowds in Central Park (8/8/27), Grand Central Station (9/10/27), Macy's (12/17/27), the steps of the Metropolitan Museum (8/4/28), and the subway at Fifty-ninth Street (11/30/29). Even the crowds at Coney Island are unremittingly white. In this context, the magazine's racism institutionalized its target marketing: the *New Yorker* sought the patronage of the carriage trade, not the avant garde, and though it reviewed Carl Van Vechten's *Nigger Heaven* (9/4/26:61–62), the magazine explicitly rejected uptown slumming. Ben Hecht's comic essay "The Caliph Complex" (12/4/26:30–31), like Dorothy Parker's "Arrangement in Black and White" (10/8/27:22–23) and drawings by Reginald Marsh and others, made fun of faddish rather than political liberalism.

Black and brown faces were not entirely absent from the magazine. Though most representations featured conventional types, the *New Yorker* never stooped to the kind of racist joke that appeared on a 1928 cover for *Life*: two black crows perched on a radio, signifying the advent of *Amos 'n Andy* (*Life* 9/28/28). The banjo-playing minstrel in top hat on Vladimir Bobritsky's cubist cover of February 6, 1926, is a stereotypical figure, of course, and (hence) nearly faceless. Still, rays of light and inspiration exude from him to help constitute the dancer, whose white skin and red cheeks make her clownish, as if she's in whiteface makeup and he's the natural. The African dancer with tambourine who performs in the center of the Coney Island cover for July 3, 1926, is framed, rendered exotic, and diminished by a series of three well-defined female figures: a bathing beauty in Gibson-girl pose on the left, the fat lady promoted on a huge banner just behind the dancer, and a shapely white knee and thigh framing the scene from the foreground. In addition to these conventional representations of race, many other cartoons (discussed in chapters on comic art) satirized racism.

The *New Yorker*'s audience took liberal positions on related issues. Readers protested anti-Semitism in editorial matter, although they apparently tolerated it in ads for apartments and resorts. The "Notes and Comment" of March 9, 1929, drew many complaints from readers who perceived it as "pernicious propaganda" (as Assemblyman Julius S. Berg put it).[23] Written by E. B. White (Hall C594), the item reported that "America's three most prominent young men—Tunney, Lindbergh, John Coolidge—have all three chosen the same kind of girl for their helpmeet, educated, Christian, beautiful, proper, well-to-do, American," and proclaimed exasperation with the sheer conventionality of their choices. "We would see more hope for the country," the column went on, "if at least one of the three young men had fallen in love with some quite impossible goddess—not somebody's daughter, but somebody's mother, or somebody's stenographer, or somebody's second wife, or a Jew," and it ends with a call for diversity: "wouldn't the nation be safer if . . . there was one Magda, or one Goldie, or one Mrs. X?" (3/9/29:11). The ending quite justified the *New Yorker*'s defense that "there was no intent to disparage or belittle any faith or race mentioned therein."[24] When complaints arose, the *New Yorker* claimed that readers had misunderstood, a position supported by archival evidence. Indeed, the editors had sufficient sensitivity to such matters that they changed "race apart" to "class apart" in a 1926 manuscript by Oliver Claxton.[25]

Humor always risks offense, of course, when taking up issues of social prejudice, especially when audiences' backgrounds differ from humorists'. In-groups may tell jokes that out-members may not. Had they belonged to the *New Yorker*'s peer society, African-American readers would surely have joined the Jews and Catholics to protest items they found offensive. In fact, the *New Yorker* gave most of a "We Stand Corrected" column in the issue of October 29, 1927, to a letter from A. Lincoln Perkins, "a respectable colored gentleman" who wrote to correct Gardner Rea's "Dirty Work at the Union League" (9/24/27:30) for depicting employees as white. Perkins defended the club, founded during the Civil War, as a "progressive organization" with a fifty-year history of hiring only "gentlemen of the colored race" (60). More important than Rea's error and Perkins's correction, however, is the blindness to diversity, the assumption that all cartoon figures will be white unless the comic idea demands otherwise. The *New Yorker* focused on the white, upper-income New York of the peer society, not the polyglot, multi-ethnic city of Africans, Greeks, Syrians, Chinese, and other immigrants described in Konrad Bercovici's *Around the World in Manhattan* (1924).

At a time when ethnic, class, and racial prejudices openly merged, the *New*

Yorker avoided ethnic put-downs. New York's large Jewish population meant that Rea Irvin could title a two-page cartoon "The Kibitzers" and expect readers to recognize the Yiddish for "jokers" (2/1/30:14–15), and that Al Frueh could title a drawing "Yom Kippur" to invite laughter at empty New York streets and sidewalks at lunchtime on Judaism's holiest fast day (9/22/28:26). Other *New Yorker* cartoons likewise found humor in social difference but steered clear of advocacy by staying focused on their dominant, target readers.

These readers were defined by socioeconomic status, thereby making class central to the magazine—in both content and advertising—as defined in the 1920s. Class figured so importantly in the definition and shaping of the magazine's humor that it is a key theme of my individual chapters on "Talk," comic art, storytelling, and departments, but in the context of the magazine's gender and racial politics, I should note that race and dialect often served as convenient or shorthand class markers. Leonard Dove's 1929 drawing of a little girl standing frozen in fantasy before an elegantly dressed mannequin in a store window probably could have stood with a white or black child, and it probably could have rendered a Bronx or Brooklyn accent instead of black dialect for the antiromantic remarks of the impatient mother, "don' stand dere gettin' ideas in yo' head" (10/26/29:29). By making the child black, however, Dove not only creates an amusing silhouette of a small child against an Amazonian upper-class mannequin but also establishes a series of other contrasts, some more amusing than others: the multiribboned head of the child against the elegantly coiffed mannequin, curly hair against smooth fur, real vs. fake, big vs. small, white vs. black, rich vs. poor. And the contrasts of rich and white against black and poor get reinforcement from a second pair of figures in the drawing, a dowdy black mother near the right edge and a slim upper-class shopper (demurely ignoring the scene) near the left. In the political context of these additional figures, the mother's dialect and sharp words cut the sentimentality of the scene. And by reducing sentiment, the cartoon not only sustains the comic idea of the drawing but also downplays any political message in it. The *New Yorker* reader can relax in her own fur coat, protected from the child's guilt-provoking wishes by the mother's acceptance of the status quo.

New Yorker cartoons and text support such detailed analysis because the editors chose and edited them rigorously. The archives overflow with acceptances, rejections, and memoranda detailing editorial requirements for cartoons, and every idea—even if drawn by an amateur, or merely described—received consideration. Ross had the final say on every item printed. Rejections didn't require his permission, but acceptances did, and no manuscript went to press without his "R" in the corner—and the expectation that readers would like what he did.

Comic art hit the mark earlier than humorous journalism, fiction, or verse in part because the *New Yorker*'s policy against photography clearly distinguished it from the competition. *Vanity Fair* regularly used photographs of its contributors and occasionally featured art photography, including nearly nude figures by Edward Steichen (VF 11/23:45). Thus the *New Yorker*'s exclusion of photographs did not originate in technical or social concerns. Nor was cost a factor, since the *New Yorker* regularly licensed photographs for use by its caricature and portrait artists. Rather, the key issue seems to have been making the *New Yorker* unique.

Given the local focus and newsy flavor of the early *New Yorker*, replacing photography with comic drawings helped distinguish this new magazine from the tabloid press, a notoriously low-class genre whose hallmark in midtwenties New York was the news photograph. Ross needed to avoid readers' confusing the *New Yorker* with the weekly newspaper digest, a nineteenth-century tradition best known for *Leslie's* and *Harper's,* and surviving today in the weekly *Washington Post.* His contemporaries knew this genre as a country cousin of the big-city paper, a context that would have damned his new magazine. The decision to offer cartoons as well as illustrative art emphasized the absence of photography and etchings and thus reinforced these distinctions.

Quite aside from the etchings in *Leslie's,* New York audiences had a long history with cartoons. As Stephen Becker traces the history, the *New York World*'s Sunday editor Morrill Goddard pioneered newspaper comics in the 1890s. By 1893, New Yorkers had two outlets for color comics: artist George Turner, formerly of the *World*, published America's first color page, "Cosmopolitan Sketches—Annie, the Apple Girl," in the *New York Recorder* on April 2, 1893, six weeks before the *World* published "The Possibilities of the Broadway Cable Car," by Walt McDougall, May 21, 1893. After Richard Felton Outcault invented the modern comic by integrating the caption into his first drawing of the Yellow Kid, published July 7, 1895 (Becker 5–13), New York readers were treated to an increasingly wide array of comic art. By the 1920s New Yorkers had not only Bud Fisher's *Mutt and Jeff* but also upscale strips by *New Yorker* artists, including Rea Irvin's *The Smythes* and Alan Dunn's *Gladys and the Young Moderns.*

Ross drew on this popularity in planning the *New Yorker*, noting in the Prospectus that "the New Yorker expects to be distinguished for its illustrations, which will include caricatures, sketches, cartoons and humorous and satirical drawings in keeping with its purpose." So well did he fulfill this goal that within eight months, he could brag to his old army friend Hugh Wiley in California, "Everybody talks of the New Yorker's art, that is its illustrations, and it has just been described as the best magazine in the world for a person who can not read."[26] Two years later, a writer for the *New Republic* declared that he and his grandmother in Dubuque would continue to buy the magazine "so long as the pictures are good" ("A New York Diary" 97). And as recently as December 12, 1997, television journalist Ted Koppel, host of ABC's *Nightline,* confessed as he opened a program on the magazine's special cartoon issue to be published three days later, "I know 'The New Yorker' has this great reputation for brilliant writing and sophisticated humor, but there's only one reason I ever pick up the magazine. You know what I'm talking about" (ABC News).

The "purpose" of *New Yorker* art, according to the Prospectus, was "a reflection in word and picture of metropolitan life." Pictures established the *New Yorker's* aura of eliteness through the elegant figures populating them. Captions typically undercut the characters' superiority, and *New Yorker* humor critiqued all ages and both genders of the upper class, yet the critique stayed within a frame of class complacency. This was a magazine for people who could laugh at themselves while they enjoyed the expensive cars, furs, jewelry, sportswear, perfume, and cruises advertised in its pages, admired the people and places mentioned in Janet Flanner's "Paris Letter," and decided whether to buy theater tickets, own radios, visit art galleries, or challenge the bootlegger who charged more than the street prices listed in its pages. Or people who aspired to.

Urbi et Orbi

Expectations that contributors and readers shared experiences went beyond metropolitan New York and New England across the Atlantic to Paris. Early advertisers included Parisian couturiers such as Paul Poiret. The *New Yorker* was just a few months old when Ross solicited the biweekly "Paris Letter" from Janet Flanner (who signed herself "Genêt"), yet he continued to reject offers for Chicago and San Francisco letters as late as 1929.[27] From the start, Flanner recalled, Ross wanted her to explain "what the French thought was going on in France" (Flanner xix). What she saw as "a new type of journalistic foreign correspondence"—"precisely accurate, highly personal, colorful, and ocularly descriptive" (xix–xx)—thus helped readers maintain their own French connection.

As early as 1917 young American intellectuals such as Kenneth Burke and Malcolm Cowley saw New York as the American Paris (Burke and Cowley 36). By the midtwenties, most *New Yorker* writers had some experience of France— James Thurber had even met E. B. White's sister Lillian Illian en route to Paris in 1925 (Kinney 36)—and some of them seem to have spent most of their time abroad socializing with one another. In 1922, for example, Donald Ogden Stewart toured the Verdun battlefields with his mother, Alexander Woollcott, and Edna Ferber, then fetched up elsewhere with *Masses'* editor Max Eastman, *World* music critic Deems Taylor, and the (future) *New Yorker's* John Mosher (Stewart 109–11). Among the 437,000 Americans who left the United States in 1928 (Cowley 196), those in Paris could keep up with the *New Yorker* every week.[28]

Because *New Yorker* artists belonged to an international culture centered in Paris, they felt an even greater pull than the writers. Gluyas Williams and Alan Dunn studied formally in Europe, Dunn as the 1924 recipient of the Louis Comfort Tiffany Foundation honorary traveling fellowship in painting.[29] Most New Yorker artists made it their business to go regularly to Paris.[30] Julian De Miskey considered an extended stay there important enough to justify giving up his assignment as "Talk" illustrator in the fall of 1930.[31] In publishing the covers, spot illustrations, and multi-image layouts resulting from these visits year after year, the *New Yorker* acknowledged that its readers' world included Paris and that its contributors and readers belonged to the same peer culture.

In this context, Ross's success with the *New Yorker* illustrates the validity of Ortega y Gasset's observation in "The Dehumanization of Art," published the same year the *New Yorker* began. As Ortega surveyed the changes constituting modern art and life, he concluded, "Obedience to the order of the day is the most hopeful choice open to the individual" (13). Certainly by 1928 everyone involved understood that Ross had assembled the right audience and contributors in the right place at the right time. Less clear, however, was the degree to which the European modernism that Ortega explicated would affect American popular culture generally or manifest itself in the *New Yorker*. Through the French connections of *New Yorker* artists and writers, high culture influenced the comic products they sold to popular media, including movies and magazines.

A large and complex subject in its own right, modernism is typically associated with fine art and literature, not humor. Nonetheless, scholars of American humor have long recognized the origins of Don Marquis's *archy and mehitabel* in poetry by e. e. cummings, and more recently Sanford Pinsker pointed out affinities between T. S. Eliot and Thurber, and between Joyce and S. J. Perelman ("On or About" 191–98). Earl Rovit has called for scholars to contextualize the radical modern ideas of Nietzsche, Freud, Einstein, Kafka, and Picasso with the new information systems represented by the products of American popular culture, including the *New Yorker, Reader's Digest,* and other magazines of the twenties (552). Contrary to the conventional view of art historians that American modernism was a dead movement by 1920, Susan Noyes Platt has demonstrated that the 1920s were precisely the time when modernism moved from the galleries of elite intellectuals into the mainstream press, especially in New York (1–2). Murdock Pemberton's art reviews in the early *New Yorker* participated in that process.

The *New Yorker* shares modernism's origins in urbanization and the commodification of media audiences. Modernism grew out of dramatic changes in public communication and cultural production, as Raymond Williams has observed (25). Photography, motion pictures, audio recording, and early broadcasting—all commodified fine arts for mass production and commercial consumption, and thereby displaced painting, theater, and live musical performance. At the same time, urbanization and war stimulated mass relocations of people, including artists, fragmenting and defamiliarizing their experience. In the 1920s these trends converged emphatically in New York City—Williams calls it "the City of Emigrés and Exiles"—promoting an "intense, singular narrative of unsettlement, homelessness, solitude and impoverished independence: the lonely writer gazing down on the unknowable city from his snappy apartment" (25) This particular narrative typifies the *New Yorker* of the '30s more than the '20s. Nonetheless, the process that Williams describes helps explain why the *New Yorker* was created and constituted by provincials—Ross from Salt Lake City via California, Irvin from San Francisco via Honolulu, Angell from Boston via Cleveland, White from Westchester via Seattle, Thurber from Columbus, Hokinson from Mendota, Illinois—and why their images of city life so convincingly captured its essence.

Although Malcolm Cowley attributed this phenomenon to postwar resistance to small-town small-mindedness (170), modernist elements that Ortega identified in "The Dehumanization of Art" underscore just how accurately Ross timed and targeted the *New Yorker*. The *New Yorker* adopted wholesale three key trends of modernism cited by Ortega: treating art as play, taking an ironic stance, and rejecting transcendent purpose. A perhaps more important trend, which Ortega called "inversion," also links the *New Yorker* with the modernist movement, though the link hinges on Ortega's 1949 expansion of his earlier ideas. His 1925 essay pointed out that modern art inverted the process by which symbols operate as representations: "If, turning our back on alleged reality we take the ideas for what they are—mere subjective patterns—and make them live as such, lean and angular, but pure and transparent; in short, if we deliberately propose to 'realize' our ideas—then we have dehumanized and, as it were, derealized them. For ideas are really unreal" (38).

Developing this concept nearly twenty-five years later, in "On Point of View in the Arts" (1949), Ortega pointed out that painters (like all viewers) choose where to focus their eyes, and their decision determines the relation of foreground to background; when European cubists and expressionists of the 1910s and 1920s zoomed in on the foreground, they fractured close-up forms into their component shapes and blurred objects into backgrounds (109–10). In a similar process of inversion, Ross made the city the subject, not the background, of his magazine. Thus the *New Yorker* featured comic art and writing and the enjoyment of city life as ends in themselves, not vehicles for enlightenment. Complaints about the *New Yorker*'s smugness miss the point, as does criticism of modernism's "aesthetic self-mystification" (to use Karl Kroeber's term [172]).

Modernist tendencies flattered the elite consumer Ross sought. They not only appealed to readers' education and experience, but also reinforced the hierarchies of taste and the class distinctions embedded in them. Thus the *New Yorker* promoted, even protected, sophistication at a time when economic and educational democratization threatened it. If, as Ortega insisted, modern art "acts like a social agent which segregates from the shapeless mass of the many two different castes of men"—the educated elite who appreciate it and the mass population who resent their exclusion (5)—then modernism provided the perfect vehicle for identifying the *New Yorker*'s audience. In an editorial process that packaged the Stuyvesants as a commodity to be sold to advertisers, modernism provided *New Yorker* readers and contributors with a screen to conceal the subversion.

It worked. As Marcus Klein has pointed out, modernism cushioned the sense of dispossession among America's privileged classes but this right-wing response to modern dislocation did not displace left-wing movements, except perhaps in literary history (12, 39). In this context, it is particularly intriguing that artists and writers associated with proletarian and left-wing movements, from Ashcan art to anticapitalist arguments, often published their work in the 1920s *New Yorker*: Reginald Marsh and Gardner Rea, Elmer Rice and Ruth Suckow. Even Art Young, one of the defendants in the *Masses*' espionage trial, published a cartoon during the *New Yorker*'s first year. The *New Yorker*'s commitment to the everyday life of the city, despite its focus on the top, reflected this complex cultural dynamic.

The *New Yorker* absolutely resisted modernism's elitist extremes, however. Considering how Karl Kroeber and Andreas Huyssen have described these elements, Ross seems to have worked deliberately against them. Rather than separate art from daily life, the *New Yorker* integrated them. Graphics and text commingled on nearly every page of the magazine, and layouts became more interdependent as the twenties went on. The rural tradition of local color humor found new zest in the *New Yorker*'s urban topics, especially in mock-oral prose humor. *New Yorker* cartoons remained steadfastly representational, topical, and thus social while geometric abstraction reigned on covers. More important, *New Yorker* practices also rejected what Kroeber calls the modernist "expression of a purely individual consciousness rather than of a Zeitgeist or a collective state of mind" (8–9). The collaborative "Talk of the Town" blended ideas, writing, and editorial insight from many quarters; not until Tina Brown's editorship did "Talk" items receive bylines. In fact, the *New Yorker* acquired a table of contents only in March of 1969, nearly twenty years into William Shawn's tenure. Until then, readers could find individual items only by flipping pages and identify authors only by seeking the names at the end. The policy subordinated individual contributions to the collective effort, as did the reliance on initials, pseudonyms, and, in the case of artists, signatures (some nearly illegible). Archival evidence and memoirs have cleared up many of these mysteries, but readers in the early years received a magazine quite deliberately produced by many unidentified New Yorkers.

By itself this collaborative spirit provides evidence that the *New Yorker* embraced rather than rejected mass culture. Weekly reviews of movies, piano rolls, and (after 1927) radio programming demonstrated an enthusiasm for mass culture. But the *New Yorker* also saw mass culture reflexively, as a springboard for humor. Stories, poems, and cartoons burlesqued shops and shoppers, consumption and wealth—as objects of fun, if not social critique. Advertising contents, styles, and processes also came under regular comic attack. As a result, the *New Yorker* developed a complicated relationship with what Richard Wightman Fox and Jackson Lears have called "The Culture of Consumption": some of its ads presented conventional claims for the product's merit or the user's benefits (Lears's "therapeutic ethos"), while others adopted a comic tone or featured cartoon characters, and still others—notably the *New Yorker*'s own ads for subscriptions—poked fun at typical advertising rhetoric. Advertising also entered editorial content as a feature of contemporary life, and thus a topic for cartoons and verbal humor (see chapters 3 and 6). Nonetheless, Ross and the Business Department relentlessly pursued advertising for their own survival. Thus, in its early years, the *New Yorker* bridged the "Great Divide" (Huyssen's term) between modernism and mass culture, moving toward the postmodern. The process explains, in part, why the *New Yorker* remains spirited and modern at the age of seventy-five. In a postmodern context, the elite join the mass, all constituted as consumers.

The bridge to the postmodern also reflects New York's unusual position during the magazine's first five years. Nineteen-twenties New York had already begun to shift from an industrial culture based on manufacturing to a postindustrial culture based on information. Scientific advertising, which produces categories of consumers, led the way in this effort, but advertising also supported other information businesses headquartered in New York City: publishing, broadcasting, and finance. The growing importance of the New York capital markets in the twenties mirrored the declining significance of midwestern commodities markets, a restructuring most dramatically expressed in the stock market crash at the end of the decade, but *New Yorker* cartoons marked the momentum gathering in the late twenties. The same shifts toward equating information with capital explains the consolidation of newspapers and the demise of magazines during this period. By 1920, the number of cities with monopoly newspapers surpassed those with competing dailies; by 1930, four times as many American cities had monopolies as competition (Sloan, Stovall, and Startt 302). And a host of monthly magazines—*Everybody's, Munsey's, McClure's,* the *Century,* the *Dial*—had died, along with other representations of the nineteenth-century industrial culture that nourished them. More ephemeral information media took their place. Radio displaced newspapers; the United States had 30 licensed commercial stations 1920 but 618 in 1930 (Folkerts, Lacy, and Davenport 209). Weekly magazines, such as *Time* and the *New Yorker,* replaced the monthlies.

Other changes in publishing also created opportunities for the *New Yorker.* As journalism increasingly became a profession of college graduates, elite newspapers aimed for objectivity, creating a vacuum for opinion and interpretation of (local) events. The advent of the "Colyumists" marked the urbanization (and, on the pages of large metropolitan dailies, the industrialization) of the first-person social commentator who stands at the center of what Blair and Hill called America's "native" comic tradition, which includes Huckleberry Finn and other rural observers of the American scene. With newspapers declining in number, and the continuing success of New York's Colyumists—including F. P. A., Don Marquis, Christopher Morley, and Heywood Broun—the *New Yorker* had a sure thing in offering readers more of what they already knew and liked. As radio picked up traditional news functions, newspapers needed to enhance their entertainment offerings, including verbal and graphic humor, to maintain their circulation and advertising base. At the same time, rises in literacy and income levels made newspapers more suited to mass marketing. Niche marketers seeking the carriage trade saw their options for reaching local targets decline.

Other narrowly targeted magazines also thrived in this period. *Town Topics,* the *American Mercury, Vanity Fair,* and other so-called "smart magazines," like the *New Yorker,* simultaneously informed readers and delivered them to advertisers. In these cases, tone and attitude were everything. Consider, for example, the announcement for "a Revolutionary and Not a Reform Magazine; a Magazine with a Sense of Humor and No Respect for the Respectable; Frank, Arrogant; Impertinent; a Magazine whose Final Policy is to Do What it Pleases, and Conciliate Nobody, Not Even Its Readers." This manifesto, by which Floyd Dell launched the *Masses* from Greenwich Village in 1913 (Dell 25–26) could have described the *New Yorker,* except that Ross respected readers as customers.

And Something Blue

Ross's much-rehearsed fear of publishing sexual material makes sense in light of the *Masses'* history. The Espionage Act of June 15, 1917, allowed the postmaster general to prevent use of the U.S. mail for distribution of material containing pacifist or antiwar sentiment or items opposing American or Allied war policies. On the basis of one poem defending anarchist Emma Goldman and four cartoons opposing the war, the *Masses* lost its mailing privileges that August, when its editors were also indicted (Emery and Emery 256). The charges were dismissed in 1919, but the post office retained enormous power over magazines, declaring birth control publications as well as pornography obscene until 1954, when the Supreme Court removed the power of prior restraint in a case involving *Esquire.* Ross did not overestimate the threat to his new magazine. In its first summer "Talk" reported Horace B. Liverright's indictment for publishing *Replenishing Jessica* by Maxwell Bodenheim (7/11/25:1). In 1926, H. L. Mencken was arrested for publishing a story by Herbert Asbury (also a *New Yorker* contributor) in *American Mercury.* Mencken's legal fees, some $10,000, would have destroyed the fledgling *New Yorker.*[32] Unlike editors of political publications, Ross had no reason to test the tolerance of postal authorities or his financial backer. If he wanted to avoid having issues of the *New Yorker* suppressed or his postal permit suspended, he had no choice but to scrutinize every bit of copy and every cartoon for material that a hostile reader might find obscene.

Thurber's claim that Ross "nursed an editorial phobia about what he called the functional" seems true enough. In a 1935 letter to E. B. White, Ross explained at length why the *New Yorker* must resort to genteel euphemisms such as "Satin Tissue" for "toilet paper": "the word toilet paper in print inevitably presents a picture to me that is distasteful and, frequently, sickening. It would, for instance, ruin my meal if I read it while eating. It might easily cause vomiting. The fact that we allow toilet paper to be advertised, under the name 'Satin Tissue' has nothing to do with this matter. I have never been nauseated by a Satin Tissue ad, possibly because I have never read it."[33]

While these remarks reveal vestigial Victorianism, they are also self-parodic, and in any case identify the chasm separating advertising from editorial policy. No archival evidence documents Ross's objections to ads for functional products such as Kotex sanitary napkins (a recently developed product) or graphic claims for the digestive benefits of eating Fleischmann's yeast (an illustration of a woman with an empty large bowel [5/22/29:31])—the latter from the family business of Ross's partner. The publication of these ads after the *New Yorker* had become profitable demonstrates the balance achieved between advertising and editorial priorities.

Nonetheless, a fair amount of what Thurber called "bathroom and bedroom stuff" (*Years* 9) got through in the 1920s despite Ross's fastidiousness—all of it too bald to justify as having gone over Ross's head (as Thurber does; Kramer recognized sex as a comic ingredient [*Ross* 202]). Ross could not have missed the double entendre in Barbara Shermund's cartoon of a woman telling a hotel clerk, "Such a heavenly night I spent in your bed" (6/1/29:13), nor the jokes about nudity in H. O. Hofman's February 27, 1926, cover of cubist nudes evoking scrutiny from gallery-goers in winter coats. In an October 1929 letter to Dorothy Parker, Katharine Angell blamed Ross for revisions required in the name of "taste" (his word) but took credit for getting such items into print: "I have the reputation with our editor for possessing the dirtiest mind on the magazine because I've fought so many times for phrases or drawings that seem to his puritanical mind slightly off color."[34]

That truce along with many others signified the degree to which Ross, Angell, and their colleagues—editors and contributors both—succeeded in defining *New Yorker* humor.

CHAPTER 2

Comic Business

Humor and Criticism at the Office

The one thing that has made The New Yorker *successful is that it is a collaborative effort,*
switching ideas back and forth to find the man best adapted to doing them.
Harold W. Ross to Gluyas Williams, 1934

Among the many contemporary trends that the *New Yorker* bucked in its
early years, the blend of consumer advice and advertising caused the most difficulty. In the 1920s, when *Vanity Fair* and *Vogue* offered shopping services to their
readers, the *New Yorker's* adoption of a policy prohibiting advertising influence
on editorial content required media buyers and sellers to learn new practices.
Historians have had almost as much difficulty as the 1920s staff in understanding the *New Yorker's* approach. On the one hand, following Dale Kramer, they
have overlooked Ross's financial investment in the magazine and declared the
New Yorker "the only example of a publication, dependent for its livelihood on
advertising, being dominated by its editor rather than by its owners" (*Ross* 70).
On the other, as in Mary F. Corey's analysis of "mixed messages" from the 1940s,
when socially austere content clashed with nearly decadent advertising appeals,
historians have overlooked the degree to which Ross designed the *New Yorker's*
journalistic departments to sell readers to advertisers.

"Our regular departments are all written fairly straight, as you know,"
Katharine Sergeant Angell wrote Willard "Spud" Johnson in February of 1929,
allowing herself a little asperity as she chided her former *New Yorker* colleague;

64

"facetious comment isn't what we want."[1] Johnson had fetched up in San Francisco, and now wrote a "page of facetious comment" for *Sunset* magazine, but still sent ideas to the *New Yorker*,[2] this time proposing a regular "Letter from San Francisco." Angell conceded that anecdotes about California might well fit into the "Out of Town Department" or even into "Talk" but rejected the column. "We are certainly not in a position to start a regular San Francisco Letter," she replied, "and even if we were we would not do it in this fairly cheap vein."[3]

Angell's comments show how firmly the *New Yorker*'s leadership in 1929 understood the purpose and style of the regular departments. "Fact" departments held the key to the magazine's identity. They not only provided journalistic ballast for comic art, verse, and fiction but also gave the Advertising Department a specific product to sell. Whether produced by salaried staff members (full- or part-time) or under term contracts with freelancers, departments fell into three main categories: criticism, consumer service, and news. Criticism departments reviewed theater, art, music (live and recorded), restaurants and nightlife, books, cinema, journalism, architecture, and radio. Consumer service departments critiqued goods and services, including fashion, household goods, automobiles, apartments, and travel. News departments covered sporting events (including notable collegiate contests), personality stories, and urban features, including "The Talk of the Town." Collectively these timely reports justified the magazine's weekly appearance to readers and advertisers.

Written "mostly straight," departments validated the *New Yorker*'s journalistic credentials. Reviewers' personal viewpoint enabled the departments to veer toward the witty or ironic comment appreciated by the peer society—an audience that justified upscale advertising wasted on the Sweeneys. As a result, as E. B. White put it in his obituary of Ross, "humor was allowed to infect everything."[4] Thus departments expose what historical fantasies of Algonquinites' antics only suggest: as the flip side of modernist angst, humor expressed and assuaged the anxieties of the Jazz Age.

Tensions between departments' economic purpose and their editorially pure viewpoints squeezed the fledgling F-R Publishing Corporation. Like its peers, F-R encompassed two parallel organizations. Fleischmann supervised two main departments of the business side, Advertising (a sales office, headed by Ray B. Bowen) and Business (including accounting and purchasing, headed by E. R. Spaulding). With one or another lieutenant (a "Jesus," in local parlance—part genius, part savior [J. Grant 216–17]), Ross ran the editorial side, overseeing three operations: fact departments, freelance submissions (including art acquisitions), and production. The managing editor supervised the fact departments, which had full- and part-time staff members, while Angell coordinated acquisition of freelance material from prose writers, poets, and artists after the art meeting evaluated each week's submissions of cartoons, drawings, and covers. These responsibilities strained Ross's already fragile nerves. By all accounts he exuded nervous tension. Poker inspired him to tremendous "arm waving, coin jingling and hair mussing" (J. Grant 21), and the stakes of this game were substantially higher.

Ross's reputation as an administrator has suffered greatly—and unjustly—at the hands of Thurber, Gill, and other comic memoirists. Ross reinvented the humor magazine in a modern mode, and made it succeed. To be sure, his primary motivational tools were the harangue and the lecture, and his high standards and voracious appetite for material infuriated staff and freelancers alike. In the privately published 1926 parody issue in honor of his thirty-fourth birthday, Lois Long ended, with the driest irony, an allegory about a man who set a baker on a monumental task, not once but twice, and then swallowed the finished product on the spot: "Harold W. Ross's outstanding characteristics are his dignity and his tact." Less oblique, Morris Markey described a descent into publishing hell as "A Reporter in Chains."⁵ The compilation of so many hostile jokes into a birthday present, however, suggests faith that Ross could take it as well as dish it out. In fact, E. B. White told Frank Sullivan that Ross's rages had more bark than bite and that the steam he ventilated produced some benefits: "[Ross's] rage, actually, was one of the sustaining things at the magazine because it was usually a sort of cosmic rage directed not at the person he was shouting at but at the enemy. . . . In retrospect I am beginning to think of him as an Atlas who lacked muscle tone but who God damn well decided he was going to hold the world up *anyway*."⁶

To develop the *New Yorker*'s fact departments, Ross needed first to identify suitable editors, writers, and artists, and then guide them toward a yet blurry goal. The process required Ross to negotiate sometimes contradictory editorial and business demands and to adapt each newfound formula to changing talent, economics, and taste. That he did—for twenty-six years. Humor bound these elements into a successful publishing formula. In the early years, the more professionally that fact departments secured the *New Yorker*'s finances, the more playfully art, poetry, and prose could experiment with humor.

Components of Comic Journalism

Departments helped *New Yorker* advertisers, readers, editors, and contributors find each other. They did not need to be funny, but humor infected them because the magazine's payment practices rewarded, and thus selected for, department writers with a comic bent. Staff members able to contribute humorous prose, verse, and art could augment their salaries and cement their editorial posts; freelancers, likewise, could secure regular income through part-time department contracts. But whatever their topic and whoever their authors, departments identified the interests of *New Yorker* readers: books, theater, and piano rolls, but not vaudeville; horse racing, football, and tennis, but not baseball; Fifth and Madison and Park Avenue shops, but not Fourteenth Street stores; New York and Paris and London, but not San Francisco.

Ross sought to provide a new kind of journalism. More visible at the end of the first year than at the start, this journalism aimed to be (as he put it in his Prospectus) "interpretive rather than stenographic." Ross could not have chosen a better time than 1924 to propose such a shift in emphasis; in the midtwenties, radio and film had barely begun to displace print's domination of the news function known as surveillance, leaving print the role of correlation, or relating developments to one another. But his statement of purpose also recognized that other components would have to compensate for the absence of hard news. Thus the Prospectus promised a magazine "so entertaining and informative as to be a necessity for the person who knows his way about or wants to" while keeping "its integrity . . . above suspicion." Balancing news and entertainment, art and text, criticism and humor, the *New Yorker* negotiated the contradictions of modern media that Walter Benjamin identified in "The Work of Art in the Age of Mechanical Reproduction" (1936), though Ross sympathized with the capitalists instead of the masses.

The Prospectus did not translate into precise instructions for contributors. A 1924 draft call for submissions shows the blurriness of the initial vision at a point when Ross hoped "to print immediately after January 1st,"[7] and the six-week delay in putting out the first issue suggests that his invitations did not soon yield what he sought. In fact, early issues of the magazine followed conventional patterns familiar to readers of *Judge* and *Life,* even though Ross abandoned verbal and cartoon political editorials; overlap among the three magazines' contributors cost it a claim to individuality. Page after page of brief anecdotes, verbal sketches, news items, jokes, short verses, and so forth, characterized the *New Yorker* as a humorous miscellany. Only the "Profiles" biographical department and Ross's opening tale of Jumbo Jr. featured extended narrative. The *New Yorker*'s substantial reviews of theater (p. 13), music (20), art (21), movies (28), and books (26) did provide a thread of currency to draw readers through the magazine, but Ross did not indulge in false modesty when he apologized to contributors, "We had not intended to look so much like a humorous magazine and regret that the appearance, together with the contents, tend to give a wrong impression."[8]

The problem came partly from having insufficiently differentiated departments. The local interest departments in particular lacked direction. In the first issue, all three brief-mention departments' columns of paragraphs overlapped, although ostensibly "In Our Midst" focused on personalities, "Jottings About Town" on incidents, and "Of All Things" on epigrammatic observation. The conflict grew after the fourth issue, when "The Talk of the Town" moved permanently to the front of the book (magazine parlance for the full pages of text before the centerfold) to set the tone with a series of "insidey" observations. "Talk" evolved into narrative and commentary, as detailed in chapter 3, but it tended to overlap with the short biographical notes in "The Hour Glass" in providing background on figures in the news. The magazine's wrong impression also came from the out-of-town columns, as if Ross wanted to hedge his bets on the concept of a city magazine. The first three numbers included "Washington Notes," expanded in 1:4 to include "Indianapolis Notes" and "Nassau Notes." He specifically solicited contributions for "notes . . . from anywhere" to draw readers to the partial-page ads at the back of the book and accumulate enough material for a full-size department.[9] These departments diluted the local theme, indicating a lack of strategy for attracting the local audience.

Newer departments added in the early weeks showed more promise. After the third issue, Ross invited suggestions for "a department of bunk, blah, etc."[10]—the comically infelicitous excerpts known today as "newsbreaks," which debuted in that issue (3/7/25). From the start, these carried both the original example and an ironic commentary on its unintended implication, known as the "kick line"; the ironic headline came later. The first examples came from staff and regular contributors, but soon readers began sending them too. The simplicity of the idea obscures the attention they received from editorial talent, an investment entirely disproportionate to their small space on the page. Their role as humorous content apparently entitled them to such treatment, however, from E. B. White (as a part-timer late in 1926) and Tip Bliss (first as a staff member, then as a freelancer from 1926 at least through 1930).[11] Eventually Ross moaned, "They arrive by the hundreds—by the thousands, I guess,"[12] but quantity did not lower his expectations for quality. Unable to meet Ross's comic standards, the celebrated F. P. A. quit within six months. "To spend the best part of a day at it," he complained to his poker buddy, "do ten or a dozen, copy them accurately with the contributor's name and address, and then get paid for one, if I'm lucky. No. I ain't in no prize contest."[13] Despite the high standards, some 2,500 newsbreaks ran in volumes 1–5. As the magazine's first comic innovation bringing tangible feedback of readers' approval, newsbreaks earned their keep.

In fact, Ross saw little difference between newsbreaks and original comic submissions: he paid only for publishable newsbreaks and used the department to test staff members' comic sensibilities. In the summer of 1936, when William Shawn had already risen from "Talk" writer to editor, Ross asked E. B. White, "How well does he do your newsbreaks? He's bright, by all indications."[14] Thus it's not surprising that Ross also expected the makeup department to treat newsbreaks with respect. He complained when makeup staff reused newsbreaks to fill out a page,[15] and Angell asked them to keep newsbreaks away from poetry because "the two don't fit in juxtaposition."[16] Newsbreaks functioned as filler only for purposes of layout; in every other way, they contributed editorial content because they did not simply recycle unconscious humor, in the clippings tradition of *Judge* and *Life*. Instead, ironic kick lines transformed others' editorial errors into demonstrations of the *New Yorker*'s superior discernment and wit.

Subsequent innovations developed this attitude further. A month after newsbreaks came the debut of "The Sky-Line," a column of architectural criticism in the April 11 issue. Author R. W. S. (probably R. W. Sexton)[17] promptly denounced both architecture and criticism. "We declare that this is all wrong," concluded the first paragraph, after describing journalists' typical account of a new building. "The designer of the building deserves much more credit than is usually allotted him" (4/11/25:28). The same issue saw the first nightlife column, "When Nights Are Bold" (temporarily renamed "Around the Clock" the following week) written and illustrated by Charles Baskerville, who signed the column but not the drawings as "Top Hat" (4/11/25:20). Soon after came "Sports," an unsigned discussion of the Gibbons-Tunney fight, walking races, tennis, and collegiate rowing, probably by Peter Vischer (4/18/25:25).[18] Sports

ALMOST BEDTIME

"Economy Is Idealism in Its Most Practical Form."

Calvin Coolidge was a favorite target of humor during the twenties, although the *New Yorker* avoided explicit political advocacy. Miguél Covarrubias, 3/14/25:5.

and architecture coverage originated to compensate for the end of the theater and music seasons, to maintain audiences and hence advertisers during the summer.

These departments spotlighted individual writers and their "insidey" views, the tone informal while criticism remained "fairly straight." Editorial policy in the form of an undated "Note to staff" from a pseudonymous "Mr. Fall, the late secretary of the Interior" urged writers to speak their minds: "All contributors should be entitled to differ with the opinions of the conductors of another department . . . it would probably be best to denounce the original opinion as what

*Evangeline
Adams*

Caricature for "Profiles: Lady of the Stars." Ralph Barton, 10/27/28:28. Potentially libelous gambling tools were removed from the figure's hands.

might be expected from a fathead. A few feuds and honest quarrels won't hurt. It is thought, in fact, that this practice should be encouraged as a step to putting more life and personality into the magazine."[19] Injecting personality meant expressing opinions and prejudices. Thus the *New Yorker* substituted social snobbery for the *Judge* and *Life*'s political advocacy.

The *New Yorker*'s emphasis on individual expressions of taste and value intensified its New York focus and therefore unified the book. Allowing writers to maintain their own voice kept departments unpredictable and amusing—as when John R. Tunis ended a 1926 column on tennis by repeating an exchange, rendered as dialect, between "two young ladies of the Connecticut nobility" who didn't recognize an aging tennis star in the actor on the stage (6/12/26:24). As the bottom line, however, the process of tightening departments clarified the market for readers and advertisers both.

Injecting personality into journalistic departments had risks, however, and Ross approached them by protecting financial flanks, not by curtailing editorial expression. Architecture columns resulted in libel charges against the magazine in 1926 and 1927, the latter against James Thurber.[20] The hazard prompted additional scrutiny by attorneys of items for fact departments,[21] and the risks grew as the magazine acquired assets worth shielding. In addition to sundry cautions about referring to Al Capone in a story about gangsters and unintended slurs against the Yellow Cab company, J. A. Stevenson advised Angell in the fall of 1928 that Ralph Barton's drawing of astrologer Evangeline Adams, commissioned to accompany Alva Johnston's profile "Lady of the Stars" libelously associated Adams with gambling. The attorney recommended two changes in Barton's drawing: eliminating the small rake in her left hand and deleting the gambling terms *passe* and *pair.*[22] Adams's oddly empty left fist and the white spaces on either side of the horoscope wheel in the published drawing (10/27/28:29) show the effects of these changes. Removal of the details blurred the drawing's association of astrology with roulette, and thus protected the magazine.

Injecting personality also translated into inside jokes. In the context of local news, inside jokes meant gossip. But the *New Yorker*'s peer society also had its own jokes. Ross's brash "Not edited for the Old Lady in Dubuque" topped the list, followed closely by jokes about optimists. In 1:9, for example, the sports columnist announced, "Of course, if Gibbons and Tunney weren't contenders for the heavyweight championship it wouldn't make much difference to folks outside of Dubuque and away from the East Side if they fought or not" (4/18/25:25). Optimist remarks not only debunked the boosterism of the day but also extended the fractured "optimist" riddle, which so tickled the staff that it reran in subsequent issues and provided a theme for cartoons. A Gilbert Wilkinson drawing from the *New Yorker*'s first spring, for instance, shows two women golfers discussing a third, who insists on playing by herself because "her husband is an optimist" (5/23/25:20). Their reasons escape the rest of us, but *New Yorker* staff remained loyal to these jokes as expressions of themselves.

Art policy likewise promoted humor through personality. Header illustrations brought visual humor to departments even before the opening sentence, while caricatures emphasized the *New Yorker*'s interpretive stance. Comic drawings thus sustained the *New Yorker*'s humorous view of the metropolitan scene, unifying disparate departments with a common attitude to enhance their common New York themes.

The decision to use drawings instead of photographs represented a rhetorical as well as economic choice. Photography was expensive in the 1920s, to be sure, but it also had editorial implications. Tabloids made it an instrument of sensationalism, while more traditional newspaper publishers limited it to rotogravure supplements whose production costs included glossy paper and half-tone engravings. These layouts maximized the number of photographs and minimized the amount of text, leading editors to privilege photographs of people and events needing little explanation. As early as 1921, Ralph Barton saw the typical rotogravure section as a stale idea ripe for burlesque and drew caricatures in a department subtitled "Camera Shots" (*Judge* 4/5/21:12). Because sports, concerts, theater openings, and similarly routine events did not typically win photo space in the supplements unless they featured celebrities, figures needing identification and explanation were represented in the regular news sections by line drawings. These factors applied to the *New Yorker,* which certainly did not want to be confused with a tabloid weekly, yet needed to keep costs within bounds.

Substituting caricatures for photographs enabled the *New Yorker*'s premier fact departments—"Sports," "Theatre," and "Profiles"—to look askance at leisure, culture, and fame. This tone remained important even after "Profiles" illustrations incorporated portraits as well as caricatures. In fact, the policy of avoiding photographs in favor of drawings remained in force until Tina Brown added photography in 1992, and her choice of Richard Avedon's highly mannered photographs continued the spirit of the caricatures. They maintained the *New Yorker*'s comic attitude by subjecting fact to humorous interpretation.

Theater caricatures constituted a distinct genre of popular art during this period. Important *New Yorker* artists contributed to American caricature, which comics historian Stephen Becker has called "the most significant artistic development" of 1920s popular art; Becker notes that Al Frueh of the *New York World* helped launch the movement in 1922 with his collection *Stage Folk,* and that Ralph Barton and Miguél Covarrubias soon followed with their own books (149). Reginald Marsh drew cartoon reviews of burlesque and vaudeville productions (Cohen 203) as a staff artist for the *New York Daily News* from 1922 to 1925. Newspapers led the movement, but magazines also featured caricature reviews. In 1923, Barton's theater caricatures for *Judge* might fill a full spread ("The View from K-12, E-7, and a Left Lower Box" 1/24/23:8–9) or run opposite George Jean Nathan's review column (12/29/23:12). Barton's work achieved such renown by January 1924 that *Vanity Fair* used it to introduce Miguél Covarrubias, recently arrived from Mexico: "The Pleasant Art of Caricature" included not only a series of Covarrubias's caricatures but also Barton's caricature of *him* (38).

By featuring the art of Frueh, Barton, and Covarrubias, the *New Yorker* borrowed *Vanity Fair*'s social sophistication and editorial credibility for its own

FENNIE BRICE IN ERIZONA

To save good, kind, Miss Leah's money Miss Brice, in "Fanny", rolls down her stockings, ties a Cleopatra girdle about her hips, and turns her sex appeal on the wicked foreman of a ranch. A scene which restores the Fannie Brice they love to her audiences just as they've grown fearful that she's gone Republican on them.

Miguél Covarrubias, 10/30/26:30.

more playful purpose. The art committee seems to have considered the three caricaturists indispensable but interchangeable: nearly every issue contained at least one page (not necessarily theatrical) by one of the three. Frueh contributed idea drawings rather than caricatures in volumes 1–2, probably because these drawings remained under contract elsewhere, but he missed only six issues in the first six months, contributing some forty items to volume 1, including several multipage cartoon narratives. His regular theater caricatures, engravings

"MAN'S ESTATE"

Although it has to do with nothing more cosmic than that quaint old love-or-a career problem, the Guild's comedy at the Biltmore is made worth-while by several fine performances. From the right: Earle Larimore, as the young man with the fancy ideas; Margalo Gillmore, as the lovely lady who causes all the trouble, and Dudley Digges, representing the humdrum as a midwestern hardware merchant.

Al Frueh, 5/4/29:29.

more subtly and modestly witty than his colleagues' work, began near the end of volume 2 (1/29/27:34), as Barton and Covarrubias gradually contributed less. Rotating caricatures among several artists gave variety to individual numbers of the magazine while maintaining a consistent graphic tone over time.

Theater caricatures by Covarrubias and Barton shared some stylistic elements, figures having oversized, spherical heads and compositions having frozen, somewhat cubist fragmentation of motion. Barton drew caricatures for the second and sixth issues of the magazine but then disappeared until the summer, when his news caricatures began, usually with his own copy. Running almost weekly from July 4, 1925, to April 3, 1926, his appearances in the magazine alternated with those of Covarrubias, who contributed weekly from 1:2 through the end of March and regularly until June 13, 1925, then left to draw monthly caricatures for *Vanity Fair,* returning February 6, 1926, to begin weekly theater caricatures.[23]

Joined by lesser-known artists, these signature caricaturists established the *New Yorker*'s high sense of humor and gave comic character to the texts they accompanied. The biographical "Profiles" department exemplified this pattern in the extreme. Described in an early contributors' letter as "pen portraits," profiles had their inspiration in graphic art and always included a mannered, if not comic, drawing of the subject. In a comic inversion of writing and drawing as sister arts, the drawing named the subject, while the article title—always elliptical, sometimes cryptic—did not. The writer might claim heroic accomplishments for the subject, but the artist's satiric image made its humanizing point first.

The *New Yorker* attracted first-rate artists despite its comparatively low rates because photojournalism was restructuring their work, and because art editor Rea Irvin gave it attractive layouts. As the magazine began to thrive, moreover, Ross developed an attractive drawing account system, already in place by the end of 1926. The *New Yorker*'s system adapted the book publisher's advance against royalties: it designated rates for specific contributions without promising to buy them but provided for a weekly wage as an advance against earnings. For instance, whereas *Life* paid Robert Benchley $300 for his 1928 drama column and paid Ralph Barton $400 in 1929,[24] Barton's 1928 *New Yorker* contract offered a weekly draw of $350 while specifying minimum art rates of $250 per page ($400 for double-page drawings, $75 for theater caricatures) and $0.12 per word for prose (about $30 per manuscript page).[25] Designed for prized freelancers, the system attracted Dorothy Parker as a book reviewer in 1927. But it also served to push staffers out, as Philip Wylie learned in the winter of 1926–27, when Ross gave his "Talk" job to newcomer E. B. White and put Wylie on a "soon-terminated drawing account" (J. Grant 254). Departments thus kept the door to the editorial offices in regular motion, offering opportunity to newcomers while pressuring staff to produce or leave. The door revolved rapidly in May of 1925, when publisher Raoul Fleischmann commuted the *New Yorker*'s death sentence and agreed to bankroll the magazine through the summer while the editorial, circulation, and advertising operations regrouped for a simultaneous push in September.

Funny Business

The magazine's near-death in early May 1925 led to a general revamping of departments. First came consolidation. Brief-mention columns disappeared to emphasize a multipage "Talk" section as the signature department and Howard Brubaker's half-page "Of All Things" as the collection of short quips. Consolidation also brought the several review sections together in 1:16 (6/6/25) as a single "Critique" department initialed by Herman J. Mankiewicz as the drama critic, Frederick J. Smith for movies, and Murdock Pemberton for art. "Books" spun off as an independent department on September 12, just in time for both the *New Yorker*'s advertising push and publishers' announcements of their fall lists, but "Critique" remained a consolidated department through 1:50 (1/30/26) probably because theaters and galleries seldom bought more than a few inches of space, and other advertising remained insufficient in the early days to sustain separate review departments.

Other changes sharpened existing formulas. The issue following the reprieve (5/23/25) moved publication from Tuesday to Friday, the day before the cover date, giving the information more timeliness while allowing the staff a few more days to find it. The out-of-town column had already disappeared. "Sports" got more attention, beginning with John R. Tunis's "Hard Boiled Golf" (6/13/25:18–19), as the department expanded to cover sufficiently elegant physical activities, including polo, tennis, horse racing, and football.[26] "Hard Boiled Golf" also featured the first of Johan Bull's sports caricatures, which satirized the people and feats chronicled in the text. The text might praise skill or mourn errors, but the illustrations showed athletes in awkward positions or embarrassing moments and thus brought a comic sensibility into sports.

Revisions to the nightlife department followed the lead of "Sports" in targeting the peer society more explicitly. Lois Long as "Lipstick" took over "When Nights Are Bold" from Charles Baskerville with the issue of August 1 (not May 9 as Corey Ford recalled [118]). The title changed to "Tables for Two" six weeks later, on September 12, the start of the fall circulation and promotion campaign that would determine the magazine's fate. Ross, Fleischmann, and consultant John Hanrahan had agreed in May to accept the verdict of the marketplace on the idea of a local magazine aimed at affluent consumers and, in the absence of encouragement come fall, to declare the *New Yorker* dead. With these stakes in mind, "Talk" formulas also received fine-tuning in late summer, the main changes involving the August 15 introduction of "Notes and Comment" and related illustrations on page one.

New developments required, and reflected, the talents of new contributors. Joseph Moncure March replaced Tip Bliss as managing editor in May (Kramer, *Ross* 75). March sponsored Fillmore Hyde as a staff writer (Kramer, *Ross* 76), and he in turn recruited his neighbor Katharine Sergeant Angell later that summer. Ralph Ingersoll had come on board June 13, 1925. During the summer, Lois Long moonlighted as the *New Yorker's* nightlife columnist while on staff at *Vanity Fair*; Morris Markey moved from the *New York World* to handle "Talk" rewrite and a department of journalism criticism, called "Current Press" on August 15 and "In the News" after September 5. Long made the move herself after Ross offered her a second column and bettered her salary (Kramer, *Ross* 83–84); directly targeting affluent female readers, she launched the "Fifth Avenue" department (10/3/25:31), renamed "On and Off the Avenue" on November 21. Although credit for Long's hiring has gone to March and others, Long herself attributed it to Herman Mankiewicz (Kinney 378, 1133), the *New York Times* assistant theater critic, which may explain his fury when Ross fired him as the *New Yorker's* theater reviewer in January 1926.

Kramer saw the newcomers as evidence that Ross had abandoned expectations of help from his Algonquin associates, but many celebrity friends did come through, even in the earliest days. As the pseudonymous Search-light, Robert Benchley contributed half a dozen "Profiles" and other nonfiction for volume 1. Ralph Barton certainly did his part for *New Yorker* art. Other Algonquinites also participated. Murdock Pemberton originated "Art" (and continued it for thirty years) and edited "Goings On About Town" until June 1926; Herman Mankiewicz first came on as drama critic over the summer. Among the lesser-known Algonquinites, Art Samuels (formerly of *Harper's Bazaar*) joined the Business Department to help consultant John Hanrahan write the fall 1925 promotional materials (O'Connor 102–3) and eventually joined Ross's staff in Editorial as managing editor in 1928.

Among the Algonquin auxiliaries, Corey Ford was a stalwart contributor, both in "The Making of a Magazine" and in his urban art series, a group of burlesques that hold up remarkably well after seventy-five years not only as ridicule of city life but also as satire of 1920s art, especially dadaism. Ford had published regularly in the *New Yorker* since 1:1, but the mock-journalism of "Blotters: An Absorbing Medium" (5/9/25:22) and "Laundry Art: Study in Wash" (5/16/25:22) provided the first successful expression of *New Yorker* prose humor: a mock-essay treating an urban subject held dear by educated readers.

"The Making of a Magazine" extended this ironic spirit and, more important, pointed freelancers in the desired direction. The new series originated when Ross asked Ford in the summer of 1925 to "fill the goddam inside cover"— embarrassingly empty of advertising—with a promotional series for the magazine, and Irvin suggested lampooning house organ brochures (Ford 119). Recently hired as staff artist, Johan Bull drew the illustrations, representing "Our Mr. Tilley" with a figure in evening dress modeled on Rea Irvin's dandy from the inaugural cover and "Talk" header. While Ford and Bull worked, full-page cartoons by W. Heath Robinson and Will Owens ran in the inside spot on July 11 and 18, followed by two weeks of house ads. The twenty-one installments of "Making of a Magazine" began August 8 and continued through January 2, 1926. In contrast to earlier house ads that had run inside the book (for example, the one-column "HYLAN FUND SOARS TO HEIGHTS WHILE TRACTION PRESS RAGES" [5/30/25:23]), "Making of a Magazine" stood out from other copy. Each chapter appeared with Irvin's figure in the corner of a frame descending from one arm and ending in a curlicue near the other. After the fall promotion campaign, advertising pushed all but two episodes to the back of the book; the bulging fifty-six-page issue of December 12 (1:42) ran without one.

Ford's series burlesqued a genre of public relations, a relatively new profession, but it had a precedent in the parodic testimonials that opened each issue of *Vanity Fair* under the title "In Vanity Fair." These melodramatic parables detailed the successes achieved by reading the magazine. As an appeal to readers, "Making of a Magazine" went further than "In Vanity Fair," however, by mentioning the five-dollar cost of a year's subscription at the end of each installment. The mock-advertisement thus became a real ad as well. In mid-September, Hugh Wiley, one of Ross's army buddies writing for the *Saturday Evening Post,* proclaimed the important September 12 issue a huge improvement over earlier numbers and cited "Making of a Magazine" as "the best stuff in it."[27]

The introduction to "Making of a Magazine" set the comic pattern for the series—and the magazine's early tone—as playfully hyperbolic. Subtitled "Some Statistics, the Funny Little Things," the introduction did have plenty of statistics, but they had little to do with the *New Yorker.* Unlike Mark Twain's "The Danger of Lying in Bed," which cites death rates in various locations, including trains and beds, to reach its comic conclusion that beds are lethal, Ford's introduction to the "vast circulation of the New Yorker" considers the 8,657,000 fingers and toes on "the great body politic" in order to ask the irrelevant question, "What is this heart that so faithfully beats for us each week, pumping us our weekly subscription?" The answer, we learn, lies in still other statistics, includ-

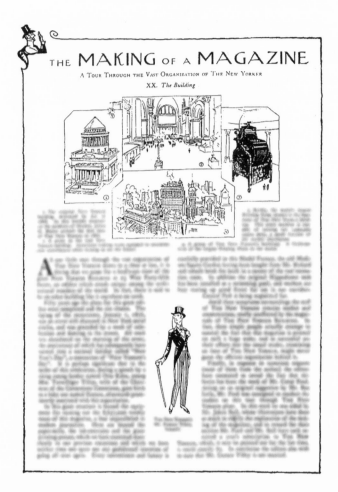

Illustrator Johan Bull matched Corey Ford's banter about the *New Yorker*'s "sumptuous surroundings" with joking images of Grant's Tomb (left), purportedly "the original New Yorker building, destroyed by fire in 1868," and Grand Central Station (upper center), identified as the place where contributors wait to see the editor. 1/2/26:[24].

ing an elaborate computation of twenty thousand (unspecified somethings) from the Willimantic (Connecticut) Iron Pipes and Gadgets Company. Still, the introduction aims mainly to inspire readers to join the upcoming metaphorical "tour through the vast organization of *The New Yorker*," slated to include parts of Tennessee (scene of the recent Scopes Monkey Trial) and requiring participants to bring "a complete change of clothing, two blankets, . . . and (ah yes)—The New Yorker" (8/8/25).

This last item, which also stands as the last line and last phrase of the text, specifically parodies the parodic "In Vanity Fair." Just a few months earlier Nancy Hoyt's "Confessions of a Man-Eating Débutante," for example, ended with this injunction: "Lady, get your man: get him and marry him. But *why* use the old, out-of-date Neolithic methods? Why not follow my example and subscribe to VANITY FAIR!" (VF 3/25:25). Whereas *Vanity Fair* served its parody straight, the *New Yorker* enhanced its foolishness with Johan Bull's illustrations. The clash between Bull's simplistic style and Ford's complex descriptions makes the series playful. Bull's drawing for the "Introduction," for example, contains just three components, each clearly separate from the other. Yet the drawing identifies each by letter (as if illustrating a complex system), and (gilding this lily) the letters are used out of sequence: "A" designates the leaning tower at Pisa, "C," a character named Eustace Tilley, dressed in top hat and cutaway but not yet identical to the dandy on the first cover, and "B," a linear squiggle made by rubbing a pencil along the side of the point while moving the hand vertically down the page—the squiggle identified by the caption as "The New Yorker."

The numbered chapters following the introduction made no bones of their function as house ads, as the speaker admitted with broad winks. For example, chapter 1, "Securing Paper for the *New Yorker,*" plays with the marketing idea of magic ingredients. The guide points out the miracle by which fifty-two issues emerge from a "single scrap" of special material: "an oblong sheet of green paper issued by the United States Government, and bearing the words: 'Five Dollars.'" And the chapter ends with the joking promise that anyone sending in such a scrap will receive a free subscription (8/15/25). By the end of chapter 4, the slow-motion saga had progressed only to the point where rags become paper (but only after such distinguished New Yorkers as Otto Kahn averted the paper famine by supplying the shirts off their backs); claims to superior proofreading included the details that "so perfect a magaxine [*sic*] is well worth the price of a year's subscription, or $500 [*sic*]" (11/14/25).

Ford's narrator constituted one of the funniest elements of the series because his bright-eyed naïveté contrasted so strongly with his detailed pseudoinformation and aggressive salesmanship. Deadpan narration enhances the story's stretchers in the typical manner of tall talk, but the narrator disappears behind the comic presence of the multitalented protagonist. "Our Mr. Eustace Tilley" provides the series' signature goofiness. With a different job and title in every chapter, Tilley becomes a superhuman jack-of-all-trades: field superintendent (chapter 1), Director-in-Chief of Rag Cleaning (chapter 4), General Superintendent of Inking (chapter 6), Field Superintendent in Charge of Porcupines (chap-

Johan Bull, 11/23/29:70.

ter 7), Syntax Engineer (chapter 9), Director-General of *Italicization* (chapter 14), and so on down until his final role, Superintendent of Recreation (chapter 20). In contrast to the vast expertise and intense activity that the text accords Tilley, the illustrations tell a story in which other people labor as Tilley supervises through his monocle.

The series' visual humor contributed irony as well as representation, as a sketch of Grand Central Station ran as the *New Yorker*'s "sumptuous waiting room" (1/2/26:48). Or consider the illustration for chapter 8, "Digging Type for the Printing." The text's joke hinges on how Tilley had successfully mined all letters of the alphabet except *W* on three thousand acres purchased from J. P. Morgan in Chile but was stymied by the absence of *W* until Joseph Pulitzer "discovered that what was being exploited as an M vein was really a rich strain of an inverted W," requiring only that machinery and operators work upside down to extract it. The illustration offers a different joke: young Pulitzer with his head caught between his knees, tottering close to the edge of a mine shaft in a position enabling him to see that a box of *M*'s (the wholesale size of the type case) could also serve as a box of *W*'s. While this physical humor occupies the center of the drawing, however, Tilley stands in the doorway off to the side, observing the scene through his monocle with "polite, though conservative, surprise" (10/3/25:26). His entirely incongruous presence sums up the comic vision of the series: contrasting the rough mining scene with his eastern elegance, the madcap activity of the text with its visual tableau, the series' blatant commercialism with its euphemistic declaration that Tilley sends a year's subscription to correspondents sending five dollars "just to show his appreciation and good will."

A detail in the final installment—"Mr. Eustace Tilley is not married"—concludes the series by appealing to the *New Yorker*'s target audience: Ford's youthful peers, women especially. The remark shows how differently Ross approached this audience than Frank Crowninshield, who inaugurated *Vanity Fair* in 1914 with what Nina Miller called a "self-congratulatory . . . [and] patronizing" admiration for women's contributions to contemporary culture (784). Instead of trumpeting his policy toward women, Ross hired women and men to write departments, some of which (e.g., fashion or polo) assumed a single-gender audience while others (theater) targeted both. More important, Ross sought to attract rather than preach to his target. "The Making of a Magazine" winked at single women and men while feigning other concerns.

New Departments, New Readers

The August 1925 changes not only honed existing parts of the formula but also introduced new departments with an eye on the September 12 promotion and female readership. During this period staff could tinker with departmental formulas without much notice; Ingersoll reports that circulation that month dropped to 2,819, though archival statistics claim nearly 5,000 (Ingersoll 201).[28] Reviews of art, music, books, theater, and architecture had familiarity to recommend—perhaps even require—them, but to avoid appearing redundant with newspapers the *New Yorker* also needed unique departments.

Janet Flanner's "Paris Letter" filled this need, capitalizing on the peer society's experiences abroad. Whereas news from American hinterlands blurred the distinction between New York and Dubuque, a Paris department put the *New Yorker* in an elite class. The Paris Letter declared the sophistication of its audience and announced its own affinity to *Vanity Fair,* which shared a Paris office with its sister Condé Nast publication *Vogue,* a fashion magazine requiring a French connection. *Vanity Fair* described its Paris office, located near the Opera and Café de la Paix, as a private club, "Charmingly decorated rooms . . . every convenience for writing, telephoning, resting between appointments, or meeting one's friends" (7/1923:20)—a description especially geared to women readers. Instead of an actual office for Americans, the *New Yorker's* Paris department provided insight into things French.

Jane Grant took credit for suggesting her wartime friend as its author (J. Grant 223; Rood 156), but Ross knew what he wanted. "The only specific guidance I had received," Flanner recalled in *Paris Was Yesterday,* "was his statement that he wanted to know what the French thought was going on in France, not what I thought was going on. This was a new type of journalistic foreign correspondence, which I had to integrate and develop, since there was no antecedent for it" (xix). Like much *New Yorker* lore, the remark makes much more sense within its historical context. By her own account Flanner belonged to the Left Bank expatriate group congregating at Sylvia Beach's Shakespeare and Company bookstore; *Maison des Amis des Livres,* the French bookstore across the street, attracted their francophone counterparts (Flanner viii–xix).[29] By advising Flanner to report on the French, Ross asked her to downplay celebrity expatriates and American tourists, two communities that his target readers already knew, and present a French viewpoint instead.

The important issue of September 12, 1925, carried Janet Flanner's first "Paris Letter" (30), though it has gone unrecorded. Following Jane Grant's listing, without verifying the facts, the *Dictionary of Literary Biography,* Kramer, and other sources cite October 10 as the date of Flanner's first letter, all claiming that the opening reference to "the last two weeks" (26) exposes Ross's sloppy editing (J. Grant 223; Rood 151, 156–57; Kramer 126). In fact, October 10 marked the third installment of Genet's department (the circumflex in *Genêt* came later).

Genêt's biweekly letters kept the cognoscenti in the know. From her initial advice that "All right-minded persons should dine their first evening in Paris at Ciro's or at the Château Madrid" (9/12/25:30), she advised readers on local trends, with an accent on women's fashion. Flanner provided advance news of the new gray shade of women's stockings (10/10/25:27) and described books not for sale in the United States because of censorship, including early chapters of

Finnegan's Wake and Gertrude Beasley's *My First Thirty Years* (11/7/25:26). In February she reported on the weather, nudie revues (at the Folies Bergere, Moulin Rouge, and elsewhere), theater, laws on serving game in restaurants, new art shows, and works in progress by Gertrude and Leo Stein (2/6/26:38–39). As her column passed the one-year mark, Flanner shared an insider's confidences with her audience, whom she envisioned in her own image, just as she distinguished them from more vulgar types: "'Around the opera sector, business booms in honor of Brooklynites and Britishers. But in the more French quarters the side streets are dotted with closed shops. Your favorite tradespeople are taking their solemn summer holiday. . . . your old coiffeur, poorer, has locked his door and retired with his white whiskers to the back of his shop. You let your hair grow'" (9/25/26:66).

Genêt's "Paris Letter" enabled readers to experience the Paris scene at one remove. Her success spawned C.B.T.'s "London Notes," begun the week after the first anniversary (2/27/26:45); within a year this department graduated to the "London Letter" (1/29/27:75), written by Beverly Nichols in the fall of 1927.[30] A year later, Angell advised Flanner of plans to add a Berlin letter as well,[31] though it did not materialize by the fifth anniversary.

Among efforts to foster an intimate relationship between the *New Yorker* and its readers, "Why I Like New York" had special importance. This incidental column promoted the magazine's plans for "a more definite metropolitan tone" (as announced to contributors on August 1),[32] by remaking an old tradition of audience participation. The contest by which the *New Yorker* invited readers to praise the city differed dramatically from typical magazine contests. When *Judge* offered $50 plus publication for the best second-line of a he-she joke, the contest appealed to readers' competitive instincts. The *New Yorker* offered such contests only in jest. Whereas *Judge*'s contests month after month reinforced social hierarchies by producing a cash prize, one winner, and several losers, the *New Yorker* promised only entreé into a select group of wits. Contributions to "Why I Like New York" earned the token sum of ten dollars each, the magazine's standard payment for ideas and small items, because "Why I Like New York" flattered rather than ranked participants.

It also enabled staff to scout for writers among its readers and to stimulate readership by writers. Over the column's run of two and a half years (8/15/25 to 5/28/27), two or three entries appeared every few weeks—including early appearances by freelance verse writers Margaret Fishback and Irma Brandeis (9/11/26:84; 10/10/25:31), as well as E. B. White (8/22/25:10), who as a contributor the first spring probably received the call for contributions. The department also inspired contributions from staff members Katharine Angell and Elsie Dick (12/19/25:37; 8/7/26:49) and spawned the tradition of reader participation in Otto Soglow's manhole cartoons (1928–30) and Arno's couch series (1928, 1930). These audience-participation events, like newsbreaks, engaged readers as participants in the process of defining *New Yorker* humor instead of feeding the twenties' craze for contests as a consumer activity.

Not that Ross opposed consumerism. On the contrary, new fall departments included Lois Long's "Fifth Avenue" column, which began in 1:33 (10/3/25). The department took a very different tack from the "Where to Shop" listing of the previous spring and summer, and from the shopping column of *Vanity Fair,* where Long had worked previously. The *New Yorker's* original shopping column provided a classified listing of advertisers, inviting readers to patronize them, while *Vanity Fair's* "Metropolitan Shopping" department singled out individual items, described their virtues and prices, and sold them directly to readers as a personal service, presumably paid by the stores involved. The *New Yorker* offered fashion judgments and predictions, taking a viewpoint snobby about style but stingy about money—and kept editorial hands out of the till. Long's first column, relying on the conceit of her friend Jerry, "boarding school roommate, perennial flapper, and graceful idler" (evidently the department's target reader), noted that the new Paul Poiret silver lamé dress at Bonwit Teller's "would be a perfect SNAP to copy" and that "one of the most attractive models of the Winter . . . will have just about one more month of smartness" because soon it will move from the Fifth Avenue salons to Forty-second Street and sell for $19.75.

Although early installments of "Fifth Avenue" ran at the very back of the book with the "Where to Shop" ads, Long's narrative department moved forward as the fall campaign swelled the book while the ads remained in place. The split acknowledged the difference between advertising and editorial copy, granting Long's department progressively more importance; eventually it led the last third of each issue. In keeping with this stature, beginning November 14 the department acquired a new look and title. "On and Off the Avenue" boasted a full-page opening having three columns of text, a header illustration, and a cartoon. The cartoon usually made shopping its theme, as in Barbara Shermund's linocut of a fashion show with a discerning couple in the foreground (11/14/25:28).

Over the next several months, Long found her stride. She advised women how anyone with "faultless taste" could save money by buying cheap clothing, stripping it of tacky ornaments, adjusting the fit, and adding stylish accessories (11/14/25:28). She recommended holiday hostess gifts from H. Hicks (675 Fifth Avenue) and hip flasks made from baby bottles purchased at Woolworth's (12/19/25:32–33). Her discussion of social and stylistic innovations on display at the annual Auto Show (1/23/26) anticipated the inauguration of the "Motors" department, which debuted June 12, 1926, as a subdivision of "On and Off the Avenue,"[33] and became an independent department on September 18. The split may have aimed to direct "Motors" specifically to men, in contrast to Bowler's "As to Men," an "Avenue" subdivision directed ambiguously at men or the women who shopped for them.

Even after seventy-five years Long's prose retains an appealing directness in both her annoyance over sartorial difficulties and her determination to solve them. Women whose bobbed hair exposes an untidy hairline need a Zip treatment by Mme. Berthé; those who want men's pajamas "in swell colors" and sizes to fit women should go to Saks-Fifth Avenue (1/30/26:34–35). More to the point, Long's column and its function as a proving ground for new consumer-service ideas illustrate Ross's overlapping commercial and editorial purpose. He sought to constitute *New Yorker* readers as a market, not to sell them goods directly.

House ads served the dual purpose of entertaining readers and doing business. Written by editorial staff, they filled space not taken by paid advertising and set the comic tone of the magazine. The first ads established the *New Yorker's* fondness for parodies of other magazines and for a visual humor of incongruity, using illustrations irrelevant to the caption or surrounding text. "Our $25,000.00 Prize Name Contest" in the first issue already resolved elements of the comic formula, but the hyperbolic silliness of these early ads gave way in 1927 to a more subtle, though no less funny, humor.

Where Corey Ford's burlesque "Making of a Magazine" waxed hyperbolic, E. B. White's Sterling Finny series parodied advertising rhetoric with quiet irony. The ten-part series from 3:8 to 3:20 (7/2/27) began with a dramatic half-page photo of Sterling Finny swooning in the arms of his wife, Flora, over the headline, "Darling, he bought everybody a soda but me!" There follows a familiar tale of woe: his employer had snubbed him by inviting everyone else for an ice cream soda, and even the newspaper vendor sneered, he moans, because "I am not au courant"—that is, he explains to Flora, "not tidy." But not to worry, the ad assures us: "Do you know it is just as easy to be *au courant* as it is to be a Baptist?" (4/9/27:61). "She married me for my muscular system," Finny wails near the end

They giggled when he stirred
the soup with his finger

As E. B. White's text parodied advertising rhetoric in the Sterling Finny ad series, so the illustrations ridiculed ideas about photography and visual representation. Mannequins borrowed from a local department store portrayed Finny and his wife Flora. This photograph from the fifth installment extends that joke—a variation on the incongruous photos and illustrations in earlier house ads—by contrasting the pair with a real human and making that human a waiter, the mannequins' social inferior. 5/28/27:47.

of the series; next to the photo of Sterling's artificial body comes a report that the paragon of steel muscles had "collapsed" into tears because "acquaintances at the bathing beach plunge into the water"—no matter how cold—to avoid his ignorant company. Each week *New Yorker* readers saw Sterling or Flora confront a new calamity that a weekly dose of the *New Yorker* could remedy. Reading the *New Yorker*'s weekly departments would solve the problem, the ad promised, and soon people would rush *out* of the water, exclaiming, "Here comes the man whose body is like a god's and who is well informed, too" (6/25/27:45).

The series' visual and commercial elements reinforced its basic joke. Each installment's reply coupon (coded to identify the source) invited the subscriber to participate in the joke by signing a confession, such as "My chest measures 48 inches, but otherwise I am terrible" (6/25/27:45). Even funnier, the series reinvented the photographic joke of the first house ads by featuring photographs of two store mannequins posed in tableau. These photos debunked photographic realism as well as commercial art while the text parodied advertising rhetoric. "Making of a Magazine" had evoked a similar ironic contrast between text and image when the tableaus of Eustace Tilley supervising the scene contrasted with his activities in the text, but the Sterling Finny series made the contrast its central joke. The series underscores the close relationship between advertising copy and editorial copy in the early *New Yorker,* not because of trespassing between publishing units but because both sought approval from the same reader.

The Sterling Finny series appeared amidst battles between Ross and advertising chief Ray B. Bowen, and its ridicule of advertising surely fed the flames. But Ross gained the upper hand in part because he and Angell had recently persuaded White to accept a full-time staff position. Thurber arrived soon after, strengthening Ross's hand further. With Thurber and White on board early in 1927 and other departments running well, Ross had no need to bluff in the showdown with the Advertising Department.

Skirmishes between Editorial and Advertising

Consumer journalism was always separate from advertising inside the pages of the magazine, but separating them within the *New Yorker's* organization took much longer. The issue concerned journalistic vision at least as much as the "utter contempt for businessmen" reported by James M. Cain, a 1931 "Jesus" interviewed by Kinney (333) and Kunkel (194). The contempt has received so much attention, however, that it has obscured the collaboration between the *New Yorker's* editorial and publishing sides in making the magazine a success. To be sure, Ross expected editorial independence from advertisers and their resident lobbyists in the Advertising Department, but he also collaborated with the Business Department. Knowing that magazines run on ad revenues pegged to paid circulation rates, Ross sought readers' loyalty first and assumed advertisers' faith would follow.

For instance, during the magazine's most difficult period in the summer of 1925, Ross sent business manager Eugene R. Spaulding a series of subscription and promotion ideas. Each resulted in an action step or explanation, evidence of mutual respect among professionals. Formerly business manager at *Town and Country,* Spaulding joined the *New Yorker* in late April or early May as part of Hanrahan and Fleischmann's rescue effort (Ingersoll 75); he did not dismiss Ross's ideas as amateurish but rather gave them a respectful try. Ross did not advance them scattershot either. He followed up systematically after suggesting on June 15 that the *New Yorker* seek syndication revenues by emulating O. O.

McIntyre's New York letter; notes on the carbon copy of his proposal record bi-weekly follow-ups, the last reporting, "100 weekly mailed for during past 2 months. Still being done."[34]

Ross also sought advice from knowledgeable friends and acquaintances about every means of boosting circulation. He advised Spaulding on July 8 of a trick recommended by newspaper columnist Ben Hecht, to give closing theatrical productions free ads in exchange for tickets, then trade the tickets to newsstand dealers for "good will and better display."[35] Ross did not reveal whether he knew that Hecht's own weekly *Chicago Literary Times* lasted barely sixteen months, from March 1, 1923 to June 1, 1924 (Kramer, *Chicago* 335), but notes show that Spaulding tried the idea, despite the legwork required. Other collaborations also demonstrate cooperative, even cordial, relations between the Editorial and Business Departments amid the financial tensions of the *New Yorker*'s first summer.

Not that desperation didn't surface. Ross's involvement in the business office's activities reflects not only skepticism over Spaulding's abilities and Hanrahan's leadership, as Kramer has claimed (*Ross* 69), but also worry about the *New Yorker*'s survival. By March of 1925, Ross had already sunk all his $25,000 savings into the magazine and lost another $29,000 when he tried to raise capital at a Thanatopsis poker game (J. Grant 71). Ross had his own investments of money, time, reputation, and imagination to protect, and these cast his suggestions as cooperation with the Business Department as they jointly sought success for the novel magazine he envisioned.

Ross saw himself as a professional on a quest for perfection. His efforts to establish efficient procedures struck his staff as variously comical, annoying, and frustrating. An unsigned contribution to the 1926 parody issue burlesqued his penchant for systems in a spin-off of the current reader-participation column, "If I Were King":

> Ten cardex files I'd buy for him,
> And let him try his every whim;
> A system here, a system there,
> A system hanging in the air:
> He'd try them all, and then he'd clean
> Them out and run the magazine.[36]

Despite such joshing, Ross persisted in the Taylorite spirit of the day. After ten years he still bemoaned that "Talk" lacked the journalistic timeliness and efficiency of *Time* and *Newsweek*.[37] But in January, 1926, when advertising contracts guaranteed an average for the year of 26 ad pages per issue, Ross had the foresight to seek copyright protection for Rea Irvin's New Yorker type font as well as various department titles.[38] And he persisted when Fleischmann let six months go by without acting on the idea: "It will mean thousands of dollars some day."[39] On paper, at least, congenial relations between Publishing and Editorial continued despite advertisers' occasional disappointments about treatment in editorial copy.

Some of the congeniality stems from the professional etiquette of the day, especially staff members' practice of referring to each other politely as "Mr. Ross," "Mr. Fleischmann," and "Mrs. Angell." In line with this practice, Ross typically approached Fleischmann respectfully, even deferentially, and calmly received what he regarded as just criticism or appropriate business concerns. For its part, the publishing side forwarded concerns ranging from potential causes of libel and embarrassment to the impact on newsstand sales when cover designs interfered with the magazine's name.[40] Far from being touchy about criticisms or suggestions from the publishing side, Ross declared a willingness to take on all comers, "and if we discover therefrom that we are doing something wrong I will undertake to correct it."[41]

Nor was this braggadocio. When Fleischmann asked how to handle a bona fide criticism about art department commentary, Ross replied, "We should print it, I guess."[42] As late as April, 1930, Ross insisted that the publishing office had an obligation to forward "sensible suggestions and complaints" to help him improve the book.[43] The same sense of professionalism that propelled him to seek criticism and reinvent systems, however, made him intolerant of colleagues' unprofessional conduct or poor systems.

Cooperation between Editorial and Business has received little attention from historians, whereas their conflicts have become legendary. Conflicts make better stories than smooth operations, of course, and leave more paper for historians, but Kramer overstated the case in casting Ross's power as inappropriate for his role as editor rather than publisher (*Ross* 70). Ross had unusual authority, to be sure, but as a stockholder he *was* an owner, and his holdings increased with each annual salary bonus.[44] Corey Ford's exaggerations planted more misunderstandings. Ford claimed that Ross's colleagues at *Judge* had so ridiculed the idea of a local magazine supported by local advertising that he segregated the *New Yorker*'s business and editorial offices "in separate buildings two blocks apart" (113). Quite the contrary: in April of 1926, the entire business operation, Advertising included, shared a single floor with Editorial in the building that Fleischmann's family owned. More to the point, as willingly as Ross addressed criticism he considered reasonable, so deeply did he resent trespasses onto editorial turf or any failure of responsibility.

The most important conflict began on April 17, 1926, when Ross alerted Fleischmann to what he considered inappropriate fraternization between salesmen and the book and movie reviewers, a problem exacerbated by the proximity of editorial and advertising offices. Though he may have felt differently, Ross did not originally formulate the problem as a matter of turf. Rather, he sought Fleischmann's partnership in protecting the editorial integrity of service departments for the ultimate success of the *New Yorker.* Arguing that writers burdened with the magazine's financial concerns "lose their spontaneity and verve," Ross cited new accounts, including Rolls Royce, as evidence that editorial had found the right tone, and asked that advertising staff stay away from writers. "In this kind of publication the flavor is practically the whole thing,"[45] Ross explained, and he warned that the magazine would fail with readers and advertisers unless staff writers remained "independent, uninfluenced, honest and—more important than all—slightly aloof" from the magazine's business concerns.[46] Ross saw editorial and advertising success as flip sides of the same coin, with Editorial face up.

The publisher agreed, and obliged with a memo restating Ross's case as his own. Specifically he advised Bowen "to instruct your Department that there be no unnecessary contact with the Editorial group," and asked him to handle communication with Ross's office,[47] but Bowen's staff broke ranks within two weeks, and war began. On May 1 Ross abandoned formality and presumed on his peer relationship with "Raoul" to protest a series of violations. A salesman had sent a request directly to Lois Long's assistant, who resigned in protest; the ad man claimed that Bowen had never passed on Fleischmann's policy about communication channels. (Ross evidently made a fetish of channels: a 1931 letter from Frank Sullivan teased him by requesting that he "ask Fleischmann to ask Brindley to ask you to ask Jim Cain to ask Ralph to ask John to send me some envelopes and stationery."[48]) Adding insult to injury, a staff member from Business had twice interfered with Editorial business: he sent the office boy home on Saturday afternoon, a busy day finalizing copy for the printer, then interrupted Mrs. Angell's dictation on Monday with an urgent request for her secretary's presence. Ross raged, "The fact is that Bowen has NEVER PAID ANY ATTENTION TO THE 1,000,000 THINGS I HAVE SAID ON THIS SUBJECT and that your decision to notify the staff that they were not to deal with editorial personnel has never been conveyed to the advertising salesmen."[49] Ross's anger did not arise simply from the salesmen's trespassing nor, as Corey Ford had it, from total antipathy to business (113). The incident made the Editorial Department subordinate to Advertising.

Fleischmann was contrite.[50] The documentation on this incident shows not only that Ross had good reason to mistrust some of Fleischmann's staff, but also that Fleischmann took Ross's complaints seriously and shared (at least on this topic) the editor's sense of how the organization should and should not function. In 1926, Publishing and Editorial united to guarantee financial success by insulating service departments from pecuniary interests because, as Ross put it, "All we have is our virtue."[51] Ross's vision of the magazine prevailed as the publisher's policy.

The straw that broke the camel's back hit a year later, in the middle of 1927, when the magazine reached a turning point. Weekly numbers regularly exceeded 100 pages beginning in March of 1927, and editorial pressures intensified as Ross juggled administrative tasks with editorial innovations, including new directions in cartoons and prose humor as well as changes in the books, press, and sports departments. Advertising had celebrated the *New Yorker*'s second birthday a few weeks before, bragging that the magazine had succeeded through editorial excellence alone: "Without premiums, short term offers, clubbing, guessing or prize contests, the bright Manhattan public have taken us up because they like us," ran the announcement in the *New York Post* ("We Thank You All"). As if trading compliments, the second anniversary "Notes and Comment" pointed out the connection between the magazine's newfound success as an advertising vehicle and readers' validation of its contents: "our circulation is at least twice what we thought it ever would be" (2/19/27:17). Advertising faced the burden of funding an expanding editorial operation, and Editorial had to find quality copy for these additional pages.

A few weeks later, Advertising once again interfered with "On and Off the Avenue." Bowen absorbed most of Ross's fury, though some attached to Fleischmann for not keeping his staff in line. The conflict began March 7, 1927, when Lois Long complained to Ross that "the Advertising Department seems to be getting a little fresh again":

> No less than five messages from the Advertising Department came to me today through one way or another practically demanding that I go to see Russek's [*sic*] Spring Opening this afternoon. All the important shops are having Spring Openings now and Russeks is not in the class to which I am used to giving publicity.

That however is not the annoying thing. It is: that Russeks does
not communicate with me at all, but tries to bully me through the
Advertising Department.[52]

Long proposed a solution, that Ross ask the Advertising Department to have
stores submit their publicity requests directly to her or her assistant, and Ross
followed up immediately, asking Long's assistant for clarification before passing
on Long's complaint. Typically Ross observed organizational formalities, trans-
mitting the request through Fleischmann, rather than directly to Bowen. And
rather than pass on Long's incendiary claim about Advertising's "collusion" with
clients, Ross concentrated on the need to solve a persistent problem—though he
dumped the problem in his partner's lap. "Everything is useless," he claimed,
"unless the publishing office shows some force in insisting upon the observance
of its instructions."[53]

The Editorial Department fueled the feud by failing to take scrupulous care
with advertisers' products in editorial copy. A week before the 1927 blowup over
Long's column, a comment about a chambermaid's brand of perfume in the
"New Apartments Column" (3/12/27) dismayed the perfume importer's ad
manager to the tune of thirteen full ad pages and eighteen single columns.[54]
Faced with Fleischmann's charge to be fair, Ross consulted with the writer, and
explained her intention to compliment the hotel on the elegant and expensive
taste of its staff.[55] When another occasion arose within the month, Fleischmann
too lost patience, insisted that editorial integrity could not excuse "wallops"
lacking "the saving grace of wit," and pointed out that such items injured the
morale and operation of the Advertising Department.[56] Though Ross loyally defended the humor of the piece (and thus the honor of his staff), he accepted responsibility for the item and for finding "rules" to prevent a recurrence.[57]

More egregious trespassing from Advertising followed within three weeks.
On March 31, 1927, the department head Ray Bowen notified Ross that an advertiser's representative wanted to take Lois Long to dinner the next night and
asked Ross to forward the invitation to her.[58] Incensed that Bowen would make
a date for her, Long complained to Ingersoll about advertisers' attempts to influence her via internal channels, but asked Ingersoll not to fuel the feud by reporting the incident.[59] Ross had no such reservations. Within a week he charged
at Fleischmann, insisting that the problem between Advertising and Editorial
"is right at the top" and warning—almost threatening—that their tenuous success was threatened. A practice of influencing Editorial through Advertising

"cannot but destroy respect for the magazine among advertisers and everybody else," he insisted, urging him to communicate this point to Bowen "in some way, possibly by the use of nitro-glycerine."[60]

Hard feelings between Advertising and Editorial increased after this incident, which came at a critical time. However, Ross relished his fierceness, perhaps as a first line of defense against interference, and acknowledged as much in 1943, when he told E. B. White, "I am the God damndest mass of tact known to the human race."[61] Though the exchanges indicate that Ross deserved as much blame as Bowen for feeding (or, at least, not putting out) the fires between them, they also demonstrate that Ross had more institutional power than Bowen or Fleischmann as the one person indispensable to success. And Ross periodically flaunted it. Fleischmann tried to mediate the conflict by expressing each side's viewpoint to the other, but if the problem lay in the novel conception of Long's department, and *New Yorker* service departments generally, then no operational procedures could resolve it, especially when the organization was still defining and shaping itself. Perhaps in recognition of this factor, Fleischmann sought to improve internal communication through venues other than personal mediation. On May 2, 1927, noting the growth of the organization, he announced the establishment of a Wednesday newsletter "to secure better meshing of our organization machinery" by informing staff members of developments in other departments.[62] The timing of this action characterizes Ross and Bowen's conflict as part of the organization's shift from survival to growth.

On the other hand, some animosity involved individual personalities. Ross disliked Bowen, but so did others, and he probably deserved some of it. Many years later, the typically mild E. B. White allowed himself some harsh words about Bowen's inability to distinguish editorial treasure from trash: he donated the magazine's 1925–1934 manuscript archives to a World War II paper drive.[63] (According to White, on learning of this patriotic generosity Ross "blew all seven gaskets, and there was a goddamming that could be heard as far as a Hundred and Tenth Street. He goddammed for three days without letup."[64]) The animosity served more than its participants' egos, however. Barring influence of the Advertising Department on Editorial enabled editorial content to draw advertising revenue. Maintaining the organizational wall between the departments kept both the journalism and advertising on edge—where humor as well as anger lives.

Equally important, much as Fleischmann's failure to get Bowen in line implies resistance to Ross's editorial imperialism, so his actions toward Ross point to his faith in the *New Yorker* as Ross imagined it. Indeed, Kunkel reports that Fleischmann declined a three-million-dollar offer to buy the *New Yorker* late in 1927, despite Ross's own willingness to sell, because he foresaw greater success if Ross would sign a new contract as editor (Kunkel 157). However entangled with a gambler's hope to recoup his losses in the next hand, Fleischmann's decision testified to faith in Ross's editorial vision.

The originally equal partners of the F-R Publishing Corporation redefined their contributions as the magazine began to make money in 1927 and when Editorial and Business jockeyed for power. Ross and Fleischmann each owned 10 percent of the stock in 1924, but Fleischmann's monthly subsidies brought his share to 50 percent by 1927, when he began giving loans instead of taking more stock. His investment climbed to $700,000, including $100,000 from his wife, before profits began in 1928 (Kunkel 210–11)—dwarfing Ross's ante nearly fifteen times over. The imbalance rewarded Ross much less than Fleischmann for his investments of time and money, and their relationship bore the strain. Ross's grudge at his dwindling share of the rewards increased when he sold his stock in 1934 to meet personal financial demands. Fleischmann's resentments found a sympathetic ear in James Thurber in 1958; after Thurber's series on Ross appeared in the 1957 *Atlantic Monthly* (which became *The Years With Ross*), Fleischmann complained to Thurber that Ross saw businesspeople as "beneath contempt" (qtd. in Kunkel 215). In the 1920s, however, the partners understood that Fleischmann could no more edit the *New Yorker* than Ross could fund it, and they worked accordingly.

Keeping Departments Vital

Ross listened receptively when Bowen had information he could use, as when the advertising head criticized the books department late in August of 1926.[65] The books department, like theatrical and music reviews, helped define the *New Yorker* as a magazine for the cognoscenti. The *New Yorker*'s most notable reviewer, Dorothy Parker, came on board halfway through volume 3, and her contribution lay precisely in providing what Harry Dounce ("Touchstone") did not. The department aimed at an unconventional, individualized approach to reviewing, and Dounce took care to advise publishers of the *New Yorker*'s plans to "choose a few books that I think combine high quality with likelihood of interesting a good many intelligent people"; he emphasized that the *New Yorker* would provide a personal evaluation, not an objective or authoritative one.[66]

Dounce reviewed on this basis, both in the stand-alone column and the consolidated "Critique" section through November 20, 1926.

Deservedly in Parker's shadow, Dounce's weekly columns lacked brilliance rather than taste or humor. His second effort announced, "This column is not a geyser. We don't gush if we can help it" (2/28/25:26); six months later he made good on the promise by explaining that "Theodore Dreiser is big, significant, etc., . . . [because] Stuart P. Sherman finds him morally objectionable" (8/15/25:15). Changes in the department followed Ray Bowen's report to Ross late in August 1926 that "the opinion among all publishers is one of sorrow, rather than anger, because the New Yorker falls down so miserable in its book reviews."[67] Bowen also forwarded a summary of publishers' "impartial reactions" to the *New Yorker*'s reviews: they cheerfully paid the *New Yorker*'s high ad rates because it suited certain books perfectly but faulted the department because recommendations came too late to "discover" new books, old books stayed too long on the "Tell Me A Book to Read" list, and recommendations "more closely correspond with books recommended by the critic in Dubuque than those boomed by the more sophisticated critics of Manhattan."[68] The editorial leadership had its own concerns about the department, dating at least to June 24, when Angell considered John Chapin Mosher for book reviews.[69] Although Ross rejected Baldwin's suggestion to expand the department as "unwise" because it would change "the nature of the magazine,"[70] he continued seeking a new reviewer who could provide readers' services that advertisers would support.

Humor arrived in the department along with "Alceste"—Ernest Boyd, *Vanity Fair*'s 1925 book reviewer[71]—on November 27, 1926, and the department acquired a new look for the occasion: expansion from three columns to four (Ross's previous reservations notwithstanding) and an attractive new header by André de Schaub of a neoclassical pair of fashionably dressed readers in stylish contemporary chairs. In addition to wit, Boyd brought more intellectuality than Dounce to the column. He occasionally opened with an theoretical perspective. "Now that the moral wave is engulfing New York and the police have discovered that tights are indecent," he began on February 26, 1927, introducing Supreme Court Justice John Ford's *Criminal Obscenity: A Plea for Its Suppression,* "[Ford's] views and his aims . . . have more significance than the usual outpourings of the spinster mind . . . because they represent the mental condition of the militant moralists who threaten the amenities of civilized life in New York" (78). Boyd counted on readers' awareness of Broadway news and thus used the book as a springboard to remind readers about the lucky death of the Clean Books Bill (a proposal to censor literary and theatrical works on the basis of individual words) and the ability of play juries to represent the sensibilities of "the average New Yorker above the age of twelve" (79). Not all Boyd's columns took such high ground. But many columns had a wry humor, as when he introduced the eight-hundred-page *American Caravan* edited by Van Wyck Brooks, Lewis Mumford, Alfred Kreymborg, and Paul Rosenfeld as a self-proclaimed effort to provide an audience for writing unjustly excluded from magazines, and concluded: "if there is a single contribution which has not been rejected for good reasons, the editors have failed to find it" (9/24/27:97).

Boyd might have continued for more than ten months had Ross not contracted for regular contributions from Dorothy Parker, who wrote under the title "Recent Books" for four weeks, until "Reading and Writing" became her signature headline in 3:37 (10/29/27). Parker's department lasted only thirty-six weekly installments during this portion of the magazine's history—barely nine months' worth—but fifteen years later Ross still felt he owed her a "mountain of indebtedness" for it. "Her Constant Reader," he told E. B. White in 1938, "did more than anything to put the magazine on its feet, or its ear, or wherever it is today."[72] Contracted in half-year increments from October 28, 1927,[73] four weeks into the project, the department ran with only three lapses between 3:33 and 4:9 (4/21/28); *Vanity Fair* regular Nancy Hoyt wrote a supplementary "More Books" column beneath Parker's.

Parker merits recognition as one of the most important contributors *not* to write for the *New Yorker.* Ross wrote her in November that "the book stuff is going sensationally well,"[74] but the arrangement began to falter by April, as her first contract expired. That agreement, which allowed her occasional pieces for *McCall's* and *College Humor* as well as short fiction beyond the *New Yorker's* 3,500 word limit,[75] climaxed months of letters and telegrams praising submissions and begging for more: "Now, Dorothy please write more stuff" (2/7/27), "Is there any chance of getting any more verses . . . ?" (2/17/27), "Dottie, please do a lot of things for us" (5/31/27), "Dorothy please do some others" (7/8/27), and "I am not hounding you, but please remember that less than three days ago you said you would do more pieces right away" (7/20/27).[76] Ross had negotiated the contract himself, promising her $2.00 per line of poetry and $0.12 per word for prose, payable in a weekly drawing account of $100, with additional fees paid at the end of the contract. In addition to this regular income, however, Ross promised her publication "in a medium that is (and this is unquestionably true) the best vehicle for it."[77]

Parker began audaciously, dropping the editorial "we" for "I" and dispensing with preliminaries about literature and taste. Through her use of the first person, Nancy Walker points out, Parker created a comic persona that brought humor of character to the reviewing process: she could feign shock at literary failure to ridicule books she disliked and express reverence for writing she loved ("Re- markably" 7). The approach already marked her first review for the *New Yorker,* which attacks both the marketing and the execution of Cosmo Hamilton's *Caste,* a tale of American anti-Semitism and class prejudice. She dismisses claims of "a superb love story" and "biting social satire" in less than a sentence: "In either of which cases, I am the entire Hanneford family, including the nice white horsie" (10/1/27:86); without a single negative word she savages the plot ("So the book ends with *Max Lorbenstein,* gentleman if J-w, Going Away" [87]) and the writ- ing ("Mrs. Hamilton's inimitable, please God, style" [88]). The next week she condemned Dr. Will Durant as "the worst reporter that the Snyder-Gray trial ever had (and that's no faint praise)" and advised that he not take vacations if they inspire him to write such books as his autobiographical novel *Transitions* (10/8/27:96). Though she panned most books—most famously on October 20, 1928, when she announced that "Tonstant Weader Fwowed up" while reading *The House at Pooh Corner* (98)—she did find some to applaud. She declared André Gide's *The Counterfeiters* as "too tremendous a thing for praises," claiming that to call it a "magnificent novel" was like describing the Grand Canyon as "quite a slice" (10/22/27:101). And the "spare and beautiful stories" of Ring Lardner's *Round Up* nearly (but not quite) left her speechless: "What more are you going to say of a great thing than that it is great?" (4/27/29:106). "Reading and Writ- ing" did not so much review books as display the Constant Reader's tastes as a reader and skill as a writer, offering the *New Yorker* audience a model of culti- vated passion for letters.

As her commitment waned, the staff struggled to compensate. "SWELL JAM I'M IN STOP," Wolcott Gibbs declared on March 26, 1928, in a telegram to Parker at Hotel New Weston at Madison Avenue and Forty-ninth Street, just a few blocks from the New Yorker, "COMMITTING SUICIDE IF NO COPY FROM YOU TODAY."[78] She came through with "A Very Dull Article, Indeed," for the issue of March 31 (4:6), and managed to keep going through 4:9 (4/21/28), but then the interruptions grew longer and more frequent. Morris Markey as "Asper" con- tributed a trial "More Books" section in 4:8 (4/14/28), and Angell gave him the department on April 16 "except for Constant Reader's column."[79] The exception soon proved the rule. Most of 1928–29 went to press without it; she finished up with 5:4 (3/16/29) and 5:10 (5/27/29).[80] In Parker's absence, a "B. L." (Baird Leonard?) wrote most of the columns in the summer and fall of 1928, and R. L. L. took over in the winter, but E. B. White also had a turn (6/9/28), as did Wolcott Gibbs (12/1/28).

"Reading and Writing" ran sporadically until 1933 (Updike 111), but Parker's departmental contribution to the fledgling magazine was concentrated in the small period between the fall of 1927 and the spring of 1928. Angell rued the loss for coming "even faster . . . than we expected,"[81] and Ross insisted that he'd be willing for Parker to "take a book now and then, and write a piece on it . . . no matter who was reviewing books."[82] Considering how Parker's failure to write has added to *New Yorker* lore—including her famous "Someone was using the pencil"—Ross's gratitude for her actual contributions seems generous.

To a certain degree, Ross's begging and appreciation reflected a modesty and persistence essential to great editors: if they granted themselves the same arrogance as writers, nothing would get done. In dealing with outside contributors, however, the modesty trope reigned, and Ross perfected the stance by 1928. "YOU MAKE ME BETTER BOY," he cabled Ralph Barton on February 4, 1928, enthusiastically agreeing to a list of ideas sent from Paris, "PLEASE DON'T MAKE ME CYNIC BY NOT DOING THESE," following up with a letter offering to pay at least two hundred dollars per prose piece, "illustrations additional." A key feature of Ross's letter, however, is his description of himself to a friend close enough to receive cables signed "LOVE ROSS." "Me, I am the same fretful, bewildered youth," he told Barton, bringing him up to date on his plans; he concludes with an effacing disclaimer: "That is, I will if I am enough of an organizer to do it."[83] Arrogant in the pursuit of his goals, Ross evinced modesty in equal measure when dealing with the artists and writers whose creativity he sought.

Local Color Departments

When increased ad pages in 1927 created a need for editorial ballast, the *New Yorker* expanded its serious coverage of the local scene. The opinionated tone of Robert Benchley's press reviews and Morris Markey's "Reporter at Large" enabled these departments to do double duty as local color humor. As coverage of entertainment targeted the peer society as actors and consumers, so local color departments also flattered *New Yorker* readers as insiders in the know.

Benchley, who had supported the early *New Yorker* by writing "Profiles" and other pieces as "Search-Light," signed a contract in the summer of 1927 to write

for the *New Yorker* as Guy Fawkes, because *Vanity Fair* owned his nonfiction signature.[84] Benchley's "Press in Review" began with "An Eight-Point Roman Holiday" in July 23, 1927, and appeared every three to five weeks through
December 3,[85] after which it became "The Wayward Press," also signed as Guy
Fawkes during this period. With a few exceptions (among them, the 5:20 installment written by E. B. White as S. Finny, the mannequin protagonist of his
1927 house ads [7/6/29:26–31]), Benchley continued producing this department even after he began weekly theater reviews under his own name in September 1929—a plan enabling the *New Yorker* to feature Benchley in nearly
every issue, and sometimes twice, beginning in the spring of 1929.

Benchley's press reviews advanced the *New Yorker*'s aim of distinguishing itself from a newspaper by deflating newspapers' self importance and thus arming
New Yorker readers with sophisticated critiques. Benchley brought a jaundiced
eye to press coverage of large and small events. He inaugurated his department
by tweaking New York newspapers for their sentimental handling of Lindbergh's flight to France ("a bottle of warm, remarkable news, needing care only
in the adjustment of the rubber feeder to keep the chin dry"), and went on to ex-
tol accounts of Commander Byrd's upcoming polar expedition: "We have seldom read of anything more exciting than the momentous movements of Acosta's
elbow within a radius of two inches" (7/23/27:28,30). The next installment devoted nearly three columns to ridiculing the *New York Evening Post* for reporting
with "almost the lyrical quality of an Elsie Dinsmore story" that Calvin
Coolidge had declined to seek reelection (8/13/27:28). After "The Press in Review" became "The Wayward Press" on December 24, 1927, Benchley retained
his ironic wryness, but the title's implication of incorrigible failings apparently
inspired him to accentuate the negative. He abhorred dullness, both for its own
sake and for inviting journalists to compensate (12/24/27:23). In a week full of
newsworthy events, he resorted to observing, "There is almost nothing to complain about this week. . . . This makes it tough for us" (1/14/28:26).

Press reviews allowed the *New Yorker* to acknowledge the importance of news
media after declaring newspaper work and writers' troubles taboo subjects for
fiction. Press reviews helped the *New Yorker* set itself apart from other weekly
media, giving opinions on controversial events without having to describe them.
In particular, "The Wayward Press" advanced a goal Ross set forth in the
Prospectus for local commentary not advocating a political party or position.
Even without a specific affiliation, the column could reach an appropriate audience because appreciating Benchley's opinions required sharing both his knowl-

edge and his viewpoint—promoting the homogenous readership of his peers that Ross and advertisers sought.

Like Constant Reader, Guy Fawkes played with sarcasm. After pointing out the accuracy of his predictions for "acres of space and platoons of special writers" at the 1928 Democratic Convention, he switched to deadpan: "We can hardly wait until 1932 for another brace of conventions, and the excitement of opening our newspaper directly to the shipping news" (7/21/28:28). Less justifiable was his sneer that "the metropolitan press went cultural with a bang" in giving newspaper readers simplified accounts of Einstein's *"Zur Einheitlichen Feldtheorie"* (3/2/29:34). But his exasperation when discussing Lindbergh's conflicts with the press over his wedding arrangements balanced critique and wit. "Wholly aside from the point of what the hell right the Public has to insist on knowing anything that a perfectly law-abiding citizen doesn't want to tell," he asked, "are not the editors a little sanguine in their estimate of the eagerness with which the Public devours the morsels which are set before it in the Press?" (6/8/29:28). His left-handed compliments—he called the *New York Times* a "compendium of printable news" (1/26/29:30)—relied on wit to keep pomposity at bay.

The art accompanying "The Wayward Press" enhanced its comic edge. Julian De Miskey's department header of three smiling, nearly identical photographers running eagerly toward an assignment characterizes journalists as ambulance chasers and pack creatures. Nor could Benchley deflate reporters more swiftly than Otto Soglow's cartoon of a reporter asking a woman in a bathtub, "what was your most embarrassing moment?" (11/10/28:40). Cartoons made fun of readers as well. Benchley's essay on the difficulty of "Educating the Public" on Einsteinian field theory becomes all the more ironic in conjunction with I. Klein's drawing of two men comparing the legs and posture of the woman seated opposite them with those on the front page of a tabloid whose headline screams, "CUTE KILLER MISSING" (3/2/29:34). As the image juts into two columns of text, John Reehill's drawing of a middle-aged man reading his paper for the *Katzenjammer Kids* undercuts Benchley's philosophical ruminations on the public versus the press (6/8/29:28).

Benchley's press column succeeded where earlier incarnations had failed. Ross had tried "Behind the News" in the first weeks, "In the News" and "The Current Press" during the September 1925 campaign, and "Review of the News" in November. Between attempts to guess what Ross wanted in a press column, Morris Markey wrote "Talk" items and a few casuals until "A Reporter at Large" debuted on December 26, 1925 (13–14). These efforts show how much Ross wanted a department of press criticism and how much he valued Markey. But although Markey's column began, like Benchley's, by combining critique of journalism with witty commentary on news items themselves, Markey's reportage eventually veered off into a genre combining local color humor and depth journalism, "A Reporter at Large."

Early "Reporter at Large" columns bore vestiges of "Behind the News," offering commentary on recent news items. Beginning, however, with "Sunday Morning," his March 6, 1926, account of services at the Church of the Ascension in Greenwich Village, Markey began to experiment with topics of local, if not conventionally journalistic, interest. In fact, this column mentioned newspapers primarily as a foil for his own, very different experiences and observations of superb music, unoffensive sermonizing, and pleasant (if not fully appreciated) surroundings. The next week, Markey moved his investigation into downtown life further south to Wall Street for a look at the investment pools that accelerated the recent stock market fall (one of many early warnings of the Great Crash yet to come). Sympathetic to the misery that professionals took in stride but amateurs found bewildering, he noted "the helpless, inexperienced boom-traders" who could not cover their margin accounts, and described "red-eyed and desolate" faces: "clerks, owners of insignificant shops, ancient maiden ladies—their dreams broken, their precious bankbooks worthless, their brave plans for tomorrow's opulence all gone awry" (3/13/26:26). After a brief step backward for a revival of "The Current Press" (3/20/26:22), Markey continued this approach to the department, reporting on local people, places, and experiences with the eye of a witness.

The reporter was an outsider looking in, however, and naïveté propelled many of his accounts. "Day at the Races" (9/18/26:36–38) characterized him as so new to racing that he didn't know how to read a racing form, but the novelty of the experience justified his appreciation of the specialized talk, characters, atmosphere, and rituals of racing. These continued even as his narrative ended: "the throng rushed toward the cigar-smoking gentlemen, who spoke in monosyllables, and handled rolls of money with entire carelessness, and stuffed little slips of paper into their bulging pockets" (38). By the second anniversary issue, Markey had perfected this stance, and his "Men of Affairs" recorded his descent into New York's underworld (2/19/27:36–40). There, guided by a modern-day insider named "Joe" he observed a high-stakes gambling operation, complete with checkpoints (the first manned by "a grim- faced Irishman with the manners and carriage of a traffic policeman" [36]), fascinating characters (including "a flat-chested fellow, all but bald, with a nervously twitching mouth and horn-rimmed spectacles" [36]), and the specialized talk of the games as they progressed ("Point is six, and the gentleman threw seven, to lose ten thousand" [38]). Markey's variation on the Tenderfoot posture that Mark Twain used so well in his early writing did not, however, make the narrator the subject of the writing. Because he observed rather than participated, Markey's reporter retained his innocence from one experience to the next while maintaining a credibility that comes from not being the object of jokes.

Markey's perspective balanced irony, awe, sentimentality, and wit in faithful portraits of city life. As a result, "A Reporter at Large" offered the affectionate detail of rural local color humor, with its emphasis on unusual characters and specialized practices, but adapted the mode to the urban environment, where his experience as a narrator could provide amusement when the incidents he described did not.

An innovation late in the first year, "A Reporter at Large" ran almost weekly for its first eighteen months, from 1:45 to 3:10, when other signatures displaced Markey's. April and May issues featured columns by other local journalists, including Ben Hecht (3:11), Elmer Davis (3:12), Forbes Watson (3:13), and Karl Schriftgeiser (3:16). Offended, Markey wrote Ross of his dissatisfactions with the editorial operations, and the two jockeyed over Markey's ability to meet Ross's demands for quality and timeliness.[86] Considering that the magazine went to press on Sunday and that writers got paid on acceptance, it is hard to know how realistic Ross's demands were, but his reminder that Markey controlled his own future exposes faults in the *New Yorker*'s drawing account system. While Ross emphasized the system's generosity, advising Markey, "upon your return you can start writing and turn in as many pieces as you want and get paid for them,"[87] the writer still had to satisfy Ross's standards before getting the check.

Markey managed with only a few lapses to conform to the new policy from September 17, 1927, to June 9, 1928, when midway through volume 4 "A Reporter at Large" changed from a solo department to a heading, like "Profiles," that covered contributions by many writers. The new policy opened the door to E. B. White, who contributed the never-reprinted "My Little Cabin Monoplane" to the issue of October 6, 1928 (36–42). The change reflected an idea that Ross broached in his June 1927 letter to Markey but waited a year to institute: increasing the variety of journalistic topics and viewpoints without increasing the space devoted to serious nonfiction.

Nonfiction departments filled 12 pages in the front of the book and 33 in the back of the 84-page third anniversary issue (2/25/28). Freelance writing and art also expanded during this period. By May 12, 1928, three years after the magazine's near-death, the book ran 106 pages. Full-page departments in the front included 3 pages for "Goings On," 5 for "Talk," 4 for a profile (by Alexander Woollcott), and the first page of "A Reporter at Large," the transitional department before the ad-filled back, where new departments such as "Out of Town" (recreational suggestions) and "The Oarsmen" (on college crew) kept the focus youthful even as the original members of the peer society grew older. The shopping department took their aging into account with subdepartments divided between fashion and domestic purchases. The expansion of original departments and their multiplication into more specialized columns indicate that journalistic departments became more, not less, important as the *New Yorker* began paying its own way.

When the August slump shrank the book to a mere 64 pages, in fact, department coverage remained strong. Freelance writing diminished, however, apparently held back for New Yorkers' return from summer vacations. The August 4, 1928 issue, for example, had art by regulars Al Frueh, Barbara Shermund, Peter Arno, Perry Barlow, Helen Hokinson, Otto Soglow, and Johan Bull along with casuals by Frank Sullivan, E. B. White, Katie Spaeth, and Reed Johnston; a ballad by Clarence Knapp; and verse by Baird Leonard, Genova Charlot, Elspeth, Oliver Jenkins, Olive Ward, and Ruth Brown. But these contents totaled only 17 of the 64 pages, and full-page ads just 7 more. The rest of the book—some 40 pages—belonged to departments, including separate discussions of "Paddocks" and "The Race Track." Equally important, departments covering goods and services increased along with those devoted to arts and experiences, a sign that the expanding media culture of the 1920s, to which the *New Yorker* contributed, was transforming experiences into commodities.

In this context, it is not surprising that the commercial and editorial merged in the *New Yorker*. Advertising adapted to the editorial context by following similar graphic or literary style, often by hiring the same people who published in the magazine as freelancers. In fact, the first Gluyas Williams drawings in the *New Yorker* were his full-page ads for McCreery's department store. E. B. White's Sterling Finny series, like "The Making of the Magazine," enlisted the magazine's top comic talent for its own commercial purposes. And vice versa, as Julian De Miskey and Corey Ford produced promotional materials for the advertising department. By 1928 and 1929, Peter Arno and De Miskey often had bigger drawings in ads than in the editorial pages. Other ads imitated the *New Yorker* verbal and visual styles, though not its type font. This blending underscores why Ross and Bowen were doomed to disagree: although magazines need both editorial and advertising copy, editorial contents sell readers to advertisers, while advertising steals attention from editorial content.

Indeed, by the beginning of volume 5, *New Yorker* departments had achieved sufficient success that Alexander Woollcott agreed to write a weekly page, "Shouts and Murmurs." Tina Brown revived the department's title, which came from his 1922 collection of theater reviews, for the comic essay facing the magazine's inside back cover, but the original "Shouts" ran a full three-column page in the middle of the book, just before "Sports," with a header loosely modeled on the masks of tragedy and comedy. The department, which represented Woollcott's first major commitment to the magazine, debuted just before the fourth anniversary (2/16/29:40), and rather like Woollcott himself, made style its substance. He speculated on the identity of the pseudonymous Lynx, who wrote "a mordant monograph" for each "brilliant and telling" caricature of a British notable collected in *Lions and Lambs*: "I am sure that Lynx is none other than the great Miss West. And I don't mean maybe. And I don't mean Mae" (3/16/29:34). Like Dorothy Parker, Woollcott gave his department a conversational tone while maintaining a highly literate wit.

As the magazine neared its fifth birthday, it realized Ross's goal of a successful local magazine for the peer society. By the summer of 1929, the organization had grown so large that twenty-one professionals were eligible for police-issued press passes.[88] Even during the late-summer lull, the book ranged from 60 to 72 pages, and the weeks before Christmas—the 1929 crash notwithstanding—brought a peak of 168 pages (12/7/29). Departments covered the whole range of upscale entertainments. Sports changed with the seasons with "Yachts and Yachtsmen" (signed by Binnacle) and "The Tennis Courts" (by Allison Danzig) in the summer, "Football" (R.F.K.) and "Horse Shows and Hunts" (by "Touch and Go") in the autumn. Robert Simon's music department had long since expanded to include regular reports on phonograph records. Reviews covered "New Apartments" (by "Penthouse") as well as film (John Chapin Mosher) and radio (A. S.). Ross ignored Gibbs's recommendation to replace Howard Brubaker's "Of All Things" with a Washington letter[89]—but Gibbs's assessment of all the *New Yorker's* departments exemplified the editorial commitment to serve readers.

Today some *New Yorker* departments remain as Ross envisioned them, indispensable for the sophisticated person-about-town. New Yorkers lined up for dis-counted theater tickets at TKTS booths in Manhattan make their choices with help from "Goings On About Town." The position, layout, illustration, and tone of "Goings On" absorbed substantial editorial energy and imagination early in the *New Yorker's* history, as did other departments. Not until 1:49 did the apparently simple department secure its present position between the opening ads and "Talk" and acquire caricatures of featured figures and a decorative frieze (1/23/26:4). Six months later the department continued to cause such concern that Ingersoll announced a "divorce" by which Murdock Pemberton, the art critic presently writing the column, would now assist the recently arrived Jesus, Oliver Claxton, in assembling it.[90] The tinkering continued. "Goings On" had enough importance by 1927 that Ross invited Fleischmann's approval before suggesting a new layout idea,[91] but new illustration policies for the department a decade later aimed at the same goal: "to have the New Yorker more accurately and more promptly reflect the events, life, and characteristics of the day."[92] Those same goals spur today's New Yorkers, resident and transient, to buy the magazine.

The *New Yorker's* early departments show Ross at his most innovative and his most exasperating. Nonetheless, service and news departments stood at the heart of the *New Yorker's* mission—"to be so entertaining and informative as to be a necessity for the person who knows his way about or wants to." In setting that goal as early as his 1924 Prospectus, Ross intuited that even journalistically serious departments created opportunities for humor that advertisers would pay for. Press reviews and the "Reporter at Large" department always appeared above a cartoon; so did "On and Off the Avenue." Opinionated reviews of art, music, vacations, and other activities of the elite created an audience who could appreciate ironic humor in graphic and verbal modes, cartoons that teased the eye and mind, prose that pushed boundaries of fact, verse in specialized stanzas, comic characters from the present scene. Departments led the way in fulfilling the promise of the Prospectus to provide "a reflection in word and picture of metropolitan life." The *New Yorker* unified its diverse contents with humor, and departments funded it.

CHAPTER 3

"The Talk of the Town"

The Merger of Verbal and Visual

If you can't be funny, be interesting.
Harold W. Ross

Ross envisioned something like "The Talk of the Town" as the *New Yorker's* signature department from the time he wrote the Prospectus, although it took many months to reach its familiar form. If the legend of Ellin Mackay's "Why We Go to Cabarets" discounts the many editorial experiments contributing to the *New Yorker's* successful formula, it particularly ignores "Talk," which changed more than most. As originally conceived, the department would define the magazine's niche in matter and manner: local color interest and urbane humor. "Talk" thus sought a conversational tone of clubby superiority appropriate for the magazine's target market. The Prospectus identified three key elements: advice on popular entertainment, lighthearted news items, and gossip.

Through The New Yorker's Mr. Van Bibber III, readers will be kept apprised of what is going on in the public and semi-public smart gathering places—the clubs, hotels, cafés, supper clubs, cabarets and other resorts. . . .

There will be a page of editorial paragraphs, commenting on the week's events in a manner not too serious.

There will be a personal mention column—a jotting down in the small-town newspaper style of the comings, goings, and doings in the village of New York. This will contain some josh and some news value.[1]

Initially dispersed among several departments, these goals finally merged in

108

"Talk." From the start they aimed to fulfill the promised "reflection in word and picture of metropolitan life." What kinds of words, what kind of pictures, and what aspects of urban life remained far from clear—as did its "josh and news value." After much tinkering, however, "Talk" opened the magazine with the *New Yorker*'s distinctive voice and vision.

Simply settling on a format took the better part of volume 1. "Talk" went through six distinct incarnations in the first six months and another two before its first birthday; refinements continued through volume 5. Most changes represented successive trials of the formula, each aiming nearer the goal of merging news, commentary, and humor. This idea, quite radical in 1924, when journalism had just professionalized itself as an objective lens, had no model. *Time* magazine advanced the trend toward hard, unembellished news by publishing weekly news summaries with its March 3, 1923, debut. The *New Yorker*'s more intimate, conversational approach to news seemed retrograde by contrast. So did its decision to use caricatures and other handmade art at a time when serious newspapers and quality monthlies joined illustrated tabloids in documentary and portrait photography. *New Yorker* staff needed not only to define "Talk"'s purpose, but also to help readers appreciate it.

While the *New Yorker* broke new ground in targeting consumer audiences, it revived an old idea in the humorous news section. As early as the 1850s, before either Dan De Quille or Mark Twain arrived on the scene, the *Virginia City Territorial Enterprise* had a local jottings column offering comic witticisms on minor events. An item from December 17, 1859, for example, took the perfectly ordinary fact that a donkey will eat anything and combined it with the then-controversial argument over Darwin's newly published *Origin of Species,* to create the kind of witticism that marked the *New Yorker* seven decades later: "Passing up Carson Street the other evening, we saw a donkey pick up a newspaper and deliberately swallow same, editorial, correspondence, items and all, without bolting a single statement. The circumstances clearly demonstrated to our mind the identity of the two and four legged specimens of the species donkey."

The newspaper wits known as "The Colyumists" borrowed this tradition as they urbanized local humor late in the nineteenth century. Chicago launched the movement with Eugene Field and George Ade in the 1890s, followed by Burt Leston Taylor (*B. L. T.*) in the early 1900s (Blair and Hill 383–85), but the next cohort of column writers, including Finley Peter Dunne, moved to New York dailies after beginning their careers in Chicago and elsewhere. Franklin P. Adams, Christopher Morley, Don Marquis, and Heywood Broun all belong to this group of urban humorists, and all published in the early *New Yorker*. In 1923 Carl Van Doren saw their topical wit as evidence that modern readers wanted humor "more edged, more sophisticated, more varied, and more continuous" than their predecessors (315). Ross may not have read Van Doren's argument for this new trend in newspaper humor, but it certainly justified his concept for "Talk."

Local antecedents to "Talk" drew particularly on the gossip column, reinvented by Walter Winchell in 1925 for Bernarr Macfadden's *New York Evening Graphic*. Winchell's column began in 1924 in the same mode of theater and vaudeville lore as F. P. A.'s "Conning Tower," but in 1925 Winchell produced a single stream of gossip items that established a new genre of newspaper writing, because he violated existing standards of what was newsworthy or publishable (McKelway 27–28). Not surprisingly, Winchell became a source for "Talk," funneling details to the department on people or events that he chose not to develop. The coincidence between Winchell's reorientation of news and Ross's plans for personal mentions with "insidey" viewpoints underscores how accurately Ross felt the journalistic pulse of his day.

In aligning the *New Yorker* with local newspaper genres, Ross distinguished "Talk" from the editorial departments of *Judge* and *Life*, with their political affiliations and national scope. Not surprisingly, early "Talk" staff had newspaper backgrounds. The first "Talk" writer was part-timer James Kevin McGuinness, a sports columnist for the *New York Evening Post,* which also supplied "Talk" writers Russel Crouse, Nunnally Johnson, and James Thurber.[2] Nonetheless, the *New Yorker*'s interpretive mode—in word and picture both— worked against the newspaper model to distinguish "Talk" from the daily Colyumists, who would always scoop a weekly.

Ross's first call for contributions, issued when departments still lacked titles and he still hoped to publish by mid-January, called for two kinds of items now familiar as "Talk" pieces. What he called "topical stories" would "review, summarize and interpret" the news, especially local events. For these he sought "an enlightened viewpoint and . . . a behind-the-scenes atmosphere." Items in the second category, described as "Comment," would constitute a distinct department—a rationale that Tina Brown seized upon in the fall of 1992, when she removed "Comment" to a separate spot in the front of the book. Ross downplayed the didactic and political potential of "Comment," however.[3] In lieu of political humor, "Talk" emphasized humor of situation and character, as shown in local incidents.

Who Speaks in "Talk"?

Experiments in the early weeks sought to establish the department's personality. Both verbal and graphic content mattered. Evidently Ross knew the visual imagery he wanted: every issue since number 1 has opened with Irvin's bemonocled dandy with quill pen and paper (denoting the cosmopolitan reader and writer), an owl (wisdom and nightlife), and the urban skyline at night (urban vitality). The header itself antedates the inaugural cover, which Irvin created at the last minute, but finding the right text to go under the header involved trial and error.

In fact, "The Talk of the Town" did not open the first issue. Rather, the first issue began with the dandy presiding over "Of All Things" (1–2), a two-page miscellany of one-liners, jokes, and anecdotes leading up to the comic essay on the editor's tribulations with Jumbo Jr., the switchboard. Three pages of "The Talk of the Town" signed by "Van Bibber III" followed, and the personal mentions column "In Our Midst" filled pages 18 and 19 in the middle of the 32-page book. The first week's "Talk" lacked subheads and local humor, but it had some similarities with the final product. It began with a story about a recent celebration of "International Millennium Week" and tied it to an irreverent anecdote about a New York farmer who in 1844 fell asleep in a hay stack while waiting for the end promised by the Millerites; he awoke when some boys set the hay on fire ("In hell!" the farmer cried. "Just as I expected" [2/21/25:3]). Following this bit of old news were several shorter and more personal items—about the new rage in "cross-word puzzling," possible calling cards for unemployed actors, rules for a new parlor game, and editorial turnover at *Collier's* magazine. Local events did not yet constitute the "Talk" formula.

Instead, it relied on the fictional persona of Van Bibber III. Early readers would have recognized the character as a joke, a personification of Van Bibber cigarettes, whose ads targeted "the devil-may-care, swagger young man about town all dressed up for the opening night" (*Judge* 11/17/23:11). As an insider's view of the urban scene, Van Bibber's accounts featured casual conversation— that is, talk. His first-person singular and intimate manner set "The Talk of the Town" apart from the other departments, especially "Of All Things," with its editorial "we" and third-person anecdotes. "When speaking of cross-word puzzling I intended to tell you about the gradual identification of the Simon & Schuster firm," he said by way of introducing a statistic about their unexpected success (2/21/25:3). So important was the first-person account to "The Talk of the Town" that another narrator stepped in to report firsthand about New York City Zoo director William Beebe's scientific expedition to the Sargasso Sea. Van Bibber's transition to the new speaker will sound familiar to longtime *New Yorker* readers. In a variation of the late "Talk" trademark, "A friend writes," which died during Brown's editorship, Van Bibber announces, "I've a friend who is a member of the group of scientists which sailed off" (2/21/25:4). The framed report enables several local jokes—about how New Yorkers are so easily bored that they need to stay in the city, and how New Yorkers are so easily bored that they need to *leave* the city—but its significance lies less in content than in rhetoric. From the first, "Talk" featured the wit of one friend writing to another.

Overlap among early departments hindered the development of "Talk." "Of All Things" was as miscellaneous as the title promised (including a remark about the magazine's having hired "the men who took the antitoxin to Nome" to shovel out New York's side streets [1]), but so were "In Our Midst" and "The Talk of the Town." "In Our Midst" assembled gossip and quips, mostly about newspaper and theater people, in paragraphs of five to seven lines. "Talk" items ran longer, but only Van Bibber unified them. By contrast, the artwork for "Talk" and "Of All Things" inspired hope. In addition to the department header of an owl in evening dress greeting a rooster as dawn breaks in the city, "Talk" artwork consisted of a silhouette of a dancer on the first page and a caricature-report "At the Beaux Arts Ball" across the inside spread. Frueh's "Co-operation" appeared on the second page of "Of All Things," opposite the start of "Talk." Already Irvin and Ross had established a policy that important text have equally important art: if not a heading, then a humorous drawing. And already "Talk" featured a two-page drawing of local activity—in this case, a society ball.

Moving "Talk" to the front in the second issue (2/28/25) strengthened the link between Van Bibber's arch rhetoric and the dandy in Irvin's header, underlining the magazine's interest in the elite. The second issue not only rearranged the three personality departments but also added a new two-page department of press commentary, "Behind the News." The new section fulfilled Ross's promise to contributors to "be a little more serious and purposeful," yet its contents were livelier than those in "Talk." Reginald Marsh's two-page caricature reinforced Van Bibber's brief account of Mary Hay and Clifton Webb at Ciro's supper club. Van Bibber, on the other hand, presented himself as a snob and a wannabe. As he fawned over Fifth Avenue's liveliness and sneered about "men popping up from the South for a few days with offensively tanned faces" (2/28/25:1), Van Bibber left "Talk" without humor or interest.

More tinkering with department sequence in the third number (3/7/25) emphasized commentary and inside information, not conversation. Now "Behind the News" came first, expanded from two to three pages and lightened by two unsigned pen-and-ink drawings (probably by Eldon Kelley) of fashionable young ladies buffeted into coquettish postures by March winds. The first item explained the decision by *World* columnist (and Algonquin Round Tabler) Heywood Broun to resign: editors had scolded him for a column on how the *World*'s censorship stories might stimulate attendance at dirty plays. Covarrubias's caricature of Broun faced the story, but at a distance indicating layout problems. The second item, by contrast, described how two women pressured their estranged husbands for legal separations by planting unfavorable stories about them in the *New York American,* thereby generating coverage in other newspapers, including the *Times*. "Of All Things" (4–5) followed with a series of anecdotes and one-liners, signed "The New Yorker," while Van Bibber's "Talk of the Town" hid on pages 13 and 14.

Its static drawings of "Moss and Fontana at the Mirador" lacked value as art or reportage, while its flat remarks on taxi drivers, Fifth Avenue shoppers, and newspaper vendors distracted from its sole amusing item: a very tall story by Donald Ogden Stewart about a journey by covered wagon from 125th Street to Hollywood. Aside from this tale, the third attempt at "Talk" deserved to be cut altogether. It began uninspiredly with an extravagant remark about Fifth Avenue ("Fifth Avenue is consistent only in being the most feminine thoroughfare in the world"), sneered at "the amoebae in . . . audiences who don't know when to laugh," condescended to praise an uptown theater company for selling Esquimaux Pies at intermission, and ended with a weak complaint about how "the business of peddling . . . newspapers around town is rapidly becoming a nuisance of no little concern." On his third try, Van Bibber had become a caricature of the *New Yorker*'s target reader.

Despite Van Bibber's failure, displacing "Talk" seems to have helped Ross clarify his goals. The letter reviewing the second and third issues for contributors said, "We want anecdotal material etc. for the Talk of the Town department which, we think, is more or less set to style in the fourth issue."[4] In fact, the issue of March 14 returned "Talk" to page 1, where it mixed witty anecdotes with the kind of "insidey" items previously in "Behind the News." Now a quip to a theatrical producer ("What . . . do you want to buy a new shirt for? You'll only lose it next week" [2]) alternated with the details of how public relations expert Ivy Lee outsmarted newspaper reporters and reflections on George Jean Nathan's decision to step down as coeditor of *American Mercury* ("One sheds a tear" [2]). Front-page art now included a drawing as well as Irvin's header, but Van Bibber himself was (mercifully) gone. In his place, the anonymous, bemused, somewhat distant voice of "Talk" represented the magazine as an organizational entity, an embodiment of stylish New York, not an eccentric individual.

After its separation from Van Bibber, "Talk" remained anonymous through the editorial tenures of Ross, Shawn, and Gottlieb. Among the writers who enjoyed its collaborative, institutional nature, Lillian Ross (no relation to Harold) declared it "a rare writing experience . . . precisely because it means being part of a group effort, dependent upon many colleagues—an effort that speaks for the magazine" (3). Tina Brown's decision that "Notes and Comment" should stand alone lasted only until October 1998, when David Remnick restored it to "Talk." But E. B. White would have applauded Brown's allowing writers to sign individual items, a change that he could not persuade Ross to make. "Your page is stronger anonymous, as an expression on an institution, rather than of an individual," Ross insisted in 1935, denying White's request, "I feel this very strongly. I feel that the strength of The New Yorker is largely that strength."[5] Perhaps to deflect a charge that anonymity deprived White of recognition as author of the magazine's "keynote page," Ross also defended anonymity as an editorial practice.

The policy began in necessity. The names of Ross's early staff members had little currency, though McGuinness and Bliss had published in *Life* and *Judge*. Their signatures would have given the impression of a magazine produced by amateurs and nobodies—a counterproductive move for appealing to the smart set. For their part, the advisory board members whose names graced the Prospectus and masthead (and who supplied inside information from newspapers, Broadway, and other magazines) had more lucrative opportunities elsewhere or contractual limitations on their bylines. By 1935 these reasons no longer applied, but other considerations replaced them. The collaborative nature of "Talk" loomed largest. Unlike Lois Long's columns, which gained authority by eschewing outside influence, "Talk" needed informants, especially anonymous informants. As a variation on the gossip column, "Talk" replaced scoop with interpretation but depended almost as much on collaboration between staff and outsiders. Attribution kills sources of gossip.

Scrupulous about paying contributors, Ross sought to reward ideas, not just writing, to attract suitable material to "Talk." Early columns drew heavily on information from the Algonquin and Thanatopsis groups—too few sources, in fact, to credit them without exposing the shoestring operation. Aleck Woollcott or Marc Connelly, for example, might pass on an anecdote to Ross, who would write it up before forwarding it to be rewritten by a "Talk" writer—if not

McGuinness, then Bliss (at the beginning), Markey or Hyde (from the summer of 1925), White (from late September 1926), Crouse (by February 1927), Thurber (from August 1927), or Gibbs (later in 1927)[6]. The manuscript that moved back from the "Talk" writer to Angell or Ingersoll for copyediting and preliminary approval would have its provenance noted as "Talk-F. P. A. (through Ross)-Thurber"; if the item received Ross's approving *R,* payments went to all contributors. Ideas were paid at five and ten dollars each in the 1920s, whether from Broadway celebrities or Brooklyn readers. The procedure gave "Talk" a covert presence throughout the city but made public acknowledgment of contributors impractical. The practicality of anonymity pressed hard, however, against writers' needs for credit.

Visual Counterparts

Along with resolving matters of "Talk"'s position and persona, the fourth issue changed its local color art. Two-page spreads within the "Talk" pages now featured local events and familiar places from the Easter Parade outside St. Patrick's to dance halls in Coney Island. Over the years, artists who seldom contributed cartoons—Reginald Marsh, Constantin Aladjalov, Federico Lebrun, and Victor Bobritsky—frequently drew these "Talk" spreads. Graphic counterparts to "Talk"'s verbal humor, local color art lay at the heart of the *New Yorker's* mission, bringing a humorist's eye to the New York scene.

Reginald Marsh's "Greenwich Village: Playground of the Bronx" occupied the slot in 1:4 with a busy collage-like ink drawing that points out such landmarks as Washington Square Arch, elevated tracks, and the Brevoort Hotel, and identifies salient neighborhood types: "drummers, finale hoppers, hicks, fake highbrows, suckers, old ladies from Dubuque, bank runners, jazz boys . . . native drunks" (3/14/25:2–3). Marsh ridiculed this bastion of bohemianism with a careful composition portraying its subjects as full of energy and absent of dignity. He filled the space with figures in motion, buildings overlapping and cut away, vehicles facing in all directions, and labels borrowed from the tradition of newspaper comics. Marsh's casual style contrasts dramatically with spread for the first issue, Eldon Kelley's "At the Beaux Arts Ball," with its stylized close-ups of the elegantly costumed party-goers. Kelley probably also drew "Moss and Fontana at the Mirador," the spread for 1:3, but over the next few months, Reginald Marsh's crayon drawings, so teeming with activity that the figures seemed alive, displaced Kelley's stilted tableaus of upper-class subjects.

Marsh is more often associated with the social realist painters of New York's

A Safe and Sane Fourth

_____

Reginald Marsh, 7/4/25:2–3.

Ashcan school (he studied with Kenneth Hayes Miller and *Masses* editor John Sloan) than with the *New Yorker*, though his 1930s breadline drawings are deservedly famous. But Marsh contributed frequently to the early *New Yorker*, with some 140 drawings appearing in more than half the 261 issues in volumes 1–5, and he signed twelve of the seventeen local color features running through 1:20 (7/4/25). Elements that art historians have praised in his paintings also apply to this early *New Yorker* work. A theme from Marsh's paintings that Lloyd Goodrich described as "the public's pursuit of pleasure in its many forms" (Sasowsky 10) suited "Talk" extremely well. Marsh's "Talk" spreads also have the same "documentary specificity[,] . . . the dated headlines and the price signs[,] . . . the agitation of his forms" that Marilyn Cohen found notable in his paintings as expressions of "the excitement, alienation, and restlessness of the new commercial environment" (11). Though Cohen associates these elements with mass marketing of the thirties, they already existed in the twenties and contributed to the *New Yorker*'s founding, though Ross sought more elite commerce.

In place of the cool elegance and mannered individualism of Eustace Tilley

and of Eldon Kelley's figures, Marsh presented crowds at play. He showed urban masses enjoying the circus (4/18/25:2–3), cavorting in Central Park (4/25/25:2–3), attending an imaginary parade (5/16/25:2–3), and swarming on Coney Island sands (7/4/25:2–3). More important, his groups include lower-class as well as "smart" people. Indeed, in 1933 he declared, "Well bred people are not fun to paint" (Cohen frontispiece). When he did portray "Elegant America," as in "Elegant America Does Its Duty By the Other Great Scotch Invention" (5/9/25:2–3), his panoramas shrink socially grand individuals to small members of a group, and most of these he ridicules. "Greenwich Village," which reduces even so grand a figure as Otto Kahn to half an inch, labels the figures inside the Provincetown Theatre simply "Gene" (O'Neill), "Kenneth" (Burke), and "Hav'd Graduates." "The Dutch Treat Show" lampoons it as "'The D.T.'s of 1925'" (4/11/25:2–3), and "A Safe and Sane Fourth" ironically imagines summer at the beach as a chaotic swarm of bodies writhing on the sand (7/4/25:2–3). Heightening the irony from the standpoint of "Talk" as a whole is the contrast between Tilley's New York on the front page, and Marsh's on the next. Text and graphics presumed substantial "insidey" knowledge shared by contributors and readers: we all know Kenneth, and the celebrations at Coney Island, don't we?

Marsh's early "Talk" drawings share with his later paintings a key feature that

Cohen identified: his crowds consist of undifferentiated individuals who barely interact with their environment, much less with each other. "What interested Marsh was not the individuals in a crowd," she concluded, "but the crowd it-self—the urban masses brought together randomly on subways, at the beaches and sideshows":

> Marsh detailed the world his figures inhabited but left the inhabitants anonymous. . . .
> even his individual figures function as types—the city slicker, the fashion plate. . . .
> Like crowds, they personify the city in the abstract.
>   The typecasting of Marsh's characters was in part the result of the new popular cul-
> ture propagated by movies and radio, media that created a uniformity of style and taste.
> (Cohen 12)

Together with Cohen's claim that Marsh's work was stimulated by the anonymity and hegemony of mass media, the context helps explain why the *New Yorker* abandoned Marsh's two-page "Talk" panorama in the summer of 1925.[7] If Marsh's view of urban life expressed an affinity for the new mass media in American popular culture, then his style suited the *New Yorker*'s newly added film car-icatures better than reports on human society. Marsh may have had reasons of his own, of course. He went to Paris at some point in 1925 after quitting the *New York Daily News,* where he specialized in vaudeville caricatures (Sasowsky 9). Since all drawings, even those assigned by the editors, required final approval from the art committee, Marsh may not have wanted to undertake the spreads on speculation when film caricatures for the *New Yorker* would still provide reg-ular income and take him to sites suitable for his own artwork. Marsh's panora-mas gave "Talk" a sense of "the city in the abstract" and thus fulfilled the promise of the Prospectus to reflect urban life with "sophisticated" yet not "highbrow" humor; but shifting Marsh from local color spreads to caricature film reviews saved money for the fall promotion while keeping "Talk" open to more individualized graphics.

Talk Tactics

After the department and its persona settled into position, "Talk" writers and editors sought an appropriate rhetoric. In the spring and summer of 1925, "Talk" items ran to three main topics—names, money, and fashion—and invited readers to join the editors in bemused superiority. A few items in each issue made jokes from news—for instance, the paragraph about "the old subscriber" to the Philharmonic who wondered if the new subway beneath Carnegie Hall would allow the orchestra to dispense with double-bass players (5/16/25:4). For the most part, however, "Talk" featured abbreviated narratives beginning with an amused attitude and ending with a punch line.

Name pieces led the field, calling attention to New York as a small town. These pieces put their subjects' names in the first sentence (usually as the opening words), implying that they needed no introduction or identification. A lead story in April began, "Mrs. William Randolph, as all the world, figuring on the guest list alone, should know, recently gave a party at the Hotel Ritz" (4/4/25:1). "George Luks did a characteristic thing when he dashed off a brilliant sketch of himself to illustrate the word study in last week's NEW YORKER," an inside item led off in mid-May (5/16/25:4). The technique blatantly borrowed subjects' fame to announce the local, gossipy orientation of "Talk." As a result, name stories tacitly invited readers to join a select circle of intimates. At first the Art Department emphasized these rhetorical functions with illustrated or enlarged capital letters for lead-off names, but self-conscious treatment gave way to more casual reference as "Talk" writers became more certain of their purpose. "So Mr. Donald Perry Marquis has triumphed at last," opened a report of how the humorist, best remembered today for *The Old Soak* (1921) and *archy and mehitabel* (1927), sought release from the contract for his daily *Herald-Tribune* column, "The Lantern" (8/29/25:3). By giving a comic twist to names already in circulation, celebrity stories helped differentiate between newspapers, which reported events, and the *New Yorker*, which found amusement in them.

Potentially libelous jokes, by contrast, conspicuously refused to name names, thus coyly generating rather than reporting gossip, and encouraging readers to speculate on subjects' identity. An early example is the story of "a certain angular dowager, whose name appears frequently in the society columns": the woman offered a restauranteur her business and the attendant publicity in exchange for a fifty percent discount, but the manager discovered through the grapevine that for all her public status, her neighbors knew her "for stealing the milk bottles off the dumb waiter" (4/11/25:6). Facts about well-known people required no such restraint, however. Under the heading "Piracy" ran the news that Arthur Brisbane had recently purchased "what was once a pirate island" both to jab at newspaper publisher William Randolph Hearst and to prove that some childhood dreams come true: "Consider the case of the boy who dreamt he would become another Captain Kidd and grew up to be a Hearst editor!" (7/18/25:2). Similarly, instead of simply identifying the model for Garet Garrett's *Saturday Evening Post* story about a Jewish man who got rich by ignoring his stock investments on Yom Kippur, "Rewards" recounts how Bernard Baruch expressed incredulity at the tale, only to reveal at the end, "I told Garrett that story myself. It's about me" (6/27/25:1).

As these bits of gossip show, name and money stories overlapped somewhat, reflecting the trend by which New York's economic vanguard pushed hereditary society aside in the 1920s at the same time that mass media like the *New Yorker* transformed the gentry into high-class consumer markets. The tension between social and economic values found its way into money pieces' focus on sharp business practices. As they joked about innovative or dubious business tactics, money pieces featured a kind of Yankee 'cuteness long celebrated in New England folklore, now tempered to admire originality while disdaining the vulgarity always associated with frank discussions of money. Thus an early story about a supper-club's foray into radio began irreverently, "Broadcast your bread upon the air and it shall return buttered," before noting that the evening's considerable profits did not so much validate the publicity concept as expose rivalry among competing establishments: representatives from other clubs dined elaborately at their employers' expense while spying on the event (4/11/25:5).

In addition to reinforcing New York's capitalist culture, money pieces expressed the *New Yorker*'s contradictory ambitions in these early years, when it sought to associate with elite New York while still allied with middle-class peer society. Nineteenth-century New England humor had straddled similar contradictions, and it solved them in much the same way as the *New Yorker*'s early "Talk" stories. Brother Jonathan's combination of common sense and uncommon shrewdness, Cameron Nickels has observed, valorized him as "an exemplary representation of the American ways of doing and seeing"—particularly in contrast to the English, who considered themselves superior—while also recognizing that the same rusticity by which Jonathan triumphed over his social superiors defined him as inherently uncouth by contrast (9). "Talk" items often invoked this paradox of admiration and mockery. For example, a series of anecdotes in "Prohibition Threatens—Again" concluded, after explaining how Scotch distillers began supplying American importers unaged whiskey as soon as they understood the economics of Prohibition, that "the Scots deserve their title of 'the Yankees of Europe'" (4/25/25:3). A report on William Jennings Bryan's fortune (the so-called "Great Commoner" sold Florida acreage to a church for half a million dollars) noted that the silver-tongued orator agreed to preach eight sermons in the church they built on the land and thus attract additional worshipers to fill the collection plate. "For this service," the *New Yorker* noted in conclusion, "there would be no charge" (5/23/25:1). "Talk" stories thus revived old-fashioned Yankee 'cuteness.

Fashion pieces, which commented on news and trends, took a similarly conservative attitude toward innovation. "Talk" writers particularly enjoyed catching social leaders as they violated proclaimed values. "The Craze for Royalty," for example, played with Americans' ambivalence about class. "No social set feels satisfied with its activities these democratic days" began the lead story for May 16, 1925, the issue following Fleischmann's reprieve, "unless it is entertaining, or has entertained, or is planning to entertain royalty" (1). Noting that 1926 would mark the tricentennial of "that famous real estate deal . . . when Manhattan Island was purchased from the Indians," the item pointed out that Queen Wilhelmina of the Netherlands would make an ideal guest to mark the event. Carefully chosen words identify how appropriate her appearance would be: "Her home life is admirable. Her tastes are simple. She drinks tea without needing the extra stimulus of jazz orchestras. She is the sort of majesty Queen Victoria would have approved; and so, if she will voyage here, the descendants of the New Netherlands settlers are willing to yield a point to modern custom and receive her into their homes as an equal" (5/16/25:1). Other items on fashion asserted the *New Yorker*'s superior taste. "Source" ponderously approved the "noble work that Steiglitz and John Quinn and other press agents of modern art have done" to popularize the work of Matisse, Hartley, Demuth, and Brancusi before reporting its logical consequence: "To-day sees the dress houses and even the Fifth Avenue department stores displaying 'Cubist fashions'—scarves patterned like composite photographs of all the abstruse countenances in Euclid's book of open curves . . . sports blouses done in bands of gradated color and roundish forms which proclaim their nepotal relation to Cézanne" (7/4/25:4). When identifying new styles in clothing or entertainment, "Talk" spoke for "We Sophisticates"— as the ironic lead item about "really snappy hoofing" in Dayton, Tennessee, put it (1).

The peer society populated "Talk" items in July and August as the editorial staff prepared for the fall circulation and advertising push. Fashion pieces, for example, began drawing humor from the frisson between old and new. In the issue of July 25, "Old-fashioned Fashion" sniggered over the incongruity of young women using antique cameos to decorate the stocking roll below their modern bare knees; "Neighborly" observed how "the better clientele" have ignored the temptations offered to them by the "energetic, artistically-impelled movement to take the theatre off Broadway . . . to Greenwich Village, to upper Madison Avenue" and have settled in comfortably among themselves at two midtown movie houses, the Plaza and the Lexington (7/25/25:3–4). At the same time, "Talk" began endorsing the viewpoint of the young modern, and inviting readers to share it. "Purple," for instance, reports the opinion of "the best-dressed girl we know" that fashionable colors serve better in the country, where "one forgets that the streets are glutted with it," than in town, because new fashions move from Fifth Avenue salons to Fourteenth Street mass merchandisers in a week—making life doubly unpleasant for those stuck in the city. "Only pity us," she concludes, "who have to cross Fifth Avenue a dozen times a week-day" (7/11/25:4). The report on "Southampton's latest protest against scanty bathing costumes, 'worn usually by strangers'" gently ribbed high society for scorning parvenus, declaring the younger generation's power in the process. A series of drawings by Helen Hokinson reinforced the youthful viewpoint: her briefly clad young women smoking, playing bridge, and cavorting at the beach put the peer society quite literally in the midst of "Talk" (7/11/25:3, 8/1/25:12–13, 8/22/25:2). In these early months of outreach to the peer society, "Talk" stuck to the singular *I* or the reportorial *they*—the legacy of Van Bibber III—rather than the editorial *we*. Despite the group signature of "The New Yorkers" at the end, "Talk" did not yet unite readers with the writers and artists of the peer society.

The new emphasis coincided with staffing changes over the summer. "Talk" writing passed from James Kevin McGuinness to Morris Markey and Fillmore Hyde, who gave "Talk" the voice of the peer society. Oversight of the department went to the new staff expert on the elite, managing editor Ralph McAllister Ingersoll, whose great-uncle Ward McAllister invented the concept of New York's Four Hundred. Ingersoll verifies the famous story that Ross hired him to make up for spilling ink on his Palm Beach suit (*Point* 164–65), but Jane Grant trumpeted the appointment as a deliberate effort to give the magazine an insider's view of society (228). Regardless, Ingersoll's hiring on June 13, 1925, brought "Talk" a competent journalist with society know-how.

Innovations in the Fall of 1925, or, The Guns of August

Pressure on "Talk" for the fall circulation and ad campaign brought format changes to the issue of August 15 (1:26). This point exactly halfway through volume 1, when according to Ingersoll circulation dipped to 2,819 (*Point* 201), allowed trial of new ideas at a time when no one would notice mistakes. To lead

off the department, the new formula put an illustrated group of short items under the general title "Notes and Comment" in place of a substantial story and
unrelated art. Explanations of the formula's origins vary. Kramer credits Joseph
Moncure March, who replaced Tip Bliss in the spring, with proposing that
"Talk" open with several short paragraphs, an idea refined to current events (*Ross*
79); March's successor as managing editor, Ralph Ingersoll, claimed credit himself (*Point* 164–65). These accounts suggest that Ross led the change and let others think they created it. Archival evidence documents a category called
"Comment" in his prepublication call for contributions, which sought "brief,
snappy, humorous or satirical observations and comment on current events, local and otherwise"—exactly the formula adopted in August.[8] No one disputes,
however, that Fillmore Hyde wrote these starters (Kramer, *Ross* 79), which debuted with Johan Bull's illustrations four weeks before the fall promotion campaign.

The first "Notes and Comment" presented eight topics in a series of one to
three paragraphs each, ending with a punch line. In contrast with the lengthy
opening items of previous weeks, the new paragraphs move swiftly from lead to
punch line. Whereas earlier issues had detailed activity such as the annual "In-
vasion" of buyers who displaced the Van Bibbers from Fifth Avenue restaurants
(8/8/25:1), and ended with a bit of repartee ("it were well to remember in our
wrath that they are buyers, after all, primarily because we are sellers"), "Notes
and Comment" concludes a story about horse carriages with understatement and
irony, noting their utility as a "fresh air treatment" for the "flushed and uncer-
tain"—that is, drunk (8/15/25:1). The next week, remarks on the greater hardi-
ness of the oriental ginkgo tree over its native cousin end cynically: "we are
inclined to smile dubiously, and to wager a small amount that if the Gingko tree
survives New York, it will be due to sentimental assistance on the part of people,
rather than to the hardihood of the tree itself" (8/22/25:1). In concert with the
fall campaign, "Talk" emphasized pithiness above all in the key issue of September 12: its eight items ran just one paragraph each, the longest of them nine
lines. The editorial *we* displaced Van Bibber's vestigial *I*, uniting contributors
and readers as a single group of New Yorkers and giving institutional weight to
the magazine's signature department.

The fall "Notes and Comment" focused on society rather than politics. In the
process, the liberal politics trumpeting modern science over the biblical pseudo-
science that marked the substantial text and graphic coverage of the Scopes trial
during the summer gave way in the fall to conservative attitudes toward race,

gender, and class. "Here it is only September, and the name on every lip is not Dayton but Charleston," Hyde quipped, while Johan Bull's illustration showed a pair of black youth with blackface features, one dancing while the other claps, to the amusement of two white businessmen (9/12/25:1). The advent of the Atlantic City Beauty Pageant, a forerunner of the Miss America Contest, inspired this misogynist item: "The winner of last year's beauty contest, Miss Ruth Malcomson, tells how she won it in a recent issue of *Liberty;* and from these writings we leap hastily to the conclusion that the very very beautiful are also very simple" (9/19/25:1). The same week that Ellin Mackay's "Why We Go to Cabarets" declared the *New Yorker's* alliance with the highest echelons of the smart set, "Notes and Comment" sneered at vulgar gawkers invading the Vanderbilt House. "Curiosity knows no caste," Hyde insists, but he implies that the lower classes have no right to indulge them: "The Vanderbilt House, beautiful as foam, wasteful, wealthy, incredibly carved, is being tramped through this week by a cross section of the nation to the tune of radios and entertainers. . . . The scene by the stairway was a little like Paris tramping through the Tuilleries in '92. Farewell forever, most exquisite of exteriors" (11/28/25:1). Not surprisingly, in this context, the next week's "Comment" praised women who continued to ride sidesaddle ("It looks so much better") and declared debutantes' acceptance of stags' drinking as proof that "the female always objects to the way the male treats her, and loves it" (12/5/25:1). The conservative politics of "Talk"—produced by staff writers and overseen by Ingersoll—stood far apart from the liberal attitudes on race and gender expressed everywhere else in the magazine.

The *New Yorker's* freelance art, prose, and verse consistently ridiculed the very misogyny, racism, and snobbery that marched boldly across the early "Notes and Comment." Ross oversaw every item that went into the magazine, but the different purposes of fact and fiction departments and their separate acquisition processes may have promoted different politics. "Fact" items targeted the Stuyvesants, while fiction, verse, and art aimed to entertain the peer society. The gap emphasizes, most important, the inaccuracy of defining *New Yorker* humor by one genre—whether "Talk" or prose fiction—rather than examining them all.

Drawings by Peter Arno and Helen Hokinson reinforced the conservatism of "Comment" as their renderings of the smart set in smart settings gave "Talk" a visually consistent tone and theme. Attractive young subjects especially emphasized the importance of the peer society. Further visual stabilization came later

Johan Bull, 8/15/25:1.

in the summer, when shuffled priorities and staff responsibilities gave "Talk" a staff artist, Johan Bull (1893–1945). A Norwegian who had arrived in the United States just a few years earlier, Bull had begun at the *New Yorker* as caricaturist for the sports department, but his illustrations for "The Making of a Magazine" had proved his ability to mimic Irvin's style and, thus, to represent the magazine.

The August debut permitted four weeks of trial and error, but Bull's first efforts worked surprisingly well. The three drawings have some funny details, such as the gas mask worn by the horse-carriage driver who asks, "FRESH AIR TREATMENT SIR?" Furthermore, while each illustration sums up the nub of one item, the images and cut lines remain ambiguous enough to direct the reader to the text. In this context, even the first "Notes and Comment" accomplished a major goal for "Talk": uniting word and picture in lighthearted coverage of city life.

Models of comic economy, Bull's illustrations relied on two basic jokes. First, the drawings' small size reduced their subjects to absurdity, if not insignificance. They minimized, and consequently ridiculed, even such serious comment as the protest over the Health Department's plan to promote "I Have Been Vaccinated" buttons (8/15/25). In addition, the drawings' simplicity, a function of their size, contrasted with the elegant precision of the text, creating an amusing incongruity between the rudimentary image and the arch narrative. Bull's drawing of library lions transformed into wolves, for example, gave humor to "Talk"'s eloquent complaint: "If the policy of drawing our Public Library's purse strings tighter endures, either the strings will break, or the library will be deftly strangled. Even now, on stormy nights, passing revelers have sworn that they saw those smug lions before the portals rise, change their shapes into wolves, and leap up the broad expanse of stone stairs to sniff and whine at the very doors" (8/29/25:1). Bull's approach intensified Marsh's strategy of comic reduction by composing simple rather than chaotic scenes. The combination of comic reduction and verbal-visual contrast suited "Talk" well enough that it remained the pattern throughout the early years.

With social conservatism safely contained in "Notes and Comment," and comic skepticism registered in its illustrations, the rest of "Talk" moved away from the formula of name, money, and fashion stories to a more liberal array of topics drawing on experiences and places familiar to New Yorkers in the peer society. "Nicotine" celebrated tobacco for stimulating writers' "great dynamic urge toward composition" and proposed that New York Public Library provide "a room . . . for writers, with redoubled restrictions in the matter of silence, but with full smoking rights for all" (9/19/25:2). Reverse snobbery animates the complaint in "Wheat Cakes" that "It simply isn't possible to be democratic any more": our writer finds the upscale decor and prices at the new Childs restaurant on Fifth Avenue "a most ungrateful denial of Childs' origin"—not to mention a cramp in the style of those who enjoy "winding up an hilarious evening at breakfast among the flannel-shirted proletariat" (9/19/25:4). As the art and music seasons opened, "Talk" stories drew conclusions about exhibits, concerts, and other local events. Admiration for the George Bellows exhibit at the Metropolitan evinced the magazine's bias toward readers in their twenties: "Bellows was young . . . and the young like him best—action, experiment, refusal to accept authority" (11/28/25:2). The new Madison Square Garden, with 17,000 seats and the latest technology for ventilation and ice making, evoked punning praise for the structure as "(the gods forgive us) . . . a veritable Foresight Saga"

(12/5/25:3). Wit distinguished "Talk" reporting from the poles of objectivity and gossip in New York newspapers, while its youthful viewpoint spoke to and for the peer society. "Tell me all the gossip that isn't in the *New Yorker* or the *World*—" F. Scott Fitzgerald begged Maxwell Perkins in a letter from Paris in December 1925, "isn't there any regular dirt?" (Fitzgerald 132).

Pleasure in uniquely New York events and experiences extended naturally to contrasts with the attitudes of visitors from Dubuque and elsewhere. "We visited friends from placid California and found them in bed in the Waldorf," "Comment" reported, noting that the friends had declared New York "a mad house," and thus retreated. The *New Yorker*'s response proved the superiority of the local species: "We commiserated and rushed uptown feeling comfortably insane. We had exactly fifty minutes to get to Ninety-third Street[,] change our clothes, and get to Washington Square for dinner" (12/12/25:1).

By the fall of 1925 "Talk"'s sophistication meant conspiring openly with readers to flout Prohibition as the new "Liquor Market" section enhanced "Talk"'s iconoclastic, trendy stance. It began with a single joke July 18, when the "Market Note" that closed "Talk" had nothing to do with Wall Street and everything to do with "quickly convertible gin." The joke lay in the financial conceit: after noting various market conditions, including a prohibition blockade and warm weather, the department reported prices for case lots of scotch, gin, wine, and beer before concluding, "Indication for increasing prosperity, slight cutting in price, coupled with increase in volume" (7/18/25:5). Two weeks later, an untitled section identified by an enlarged capital *T* reported on "The Liquor Market," noting "Further improvement in Summer gin," along with comment that "recent increases in Prohibition Enforcement costs are forerunners of Mr. Coolidge's supreme effort to dry the country" (8/1/25:4). By the issue of November 7, the joke asserted the importance of bootlegging to the *New Yorker*'s New York as "The Liquor Market" became a regular "Talk" section replacing "In Our Midst," the paragraph and personal mentions department.

"Talk" had absorbed "In Our Midst" in 1:13 (5/16/25) as part of the general consolidation of departments in May, and the section gossiped about celebrity comings and goings for most of the summer. Among other changes to "Talk" in mid-August, however, "In Our Midst" added information about liquor. The August 15 column noted only flappers' expectations that fashionable dress shops serve "a cocktail for every dress bought" (4). Two weeks later, the last paragraph of the column began specifying prices—noting the bargain of $88 for imperial quarts of fine Canadian Club from a "falling off in restaurant consumption due to continued use of teapots and cups in distribution" (8/29/25:5). The frisson of blatantly trading in contraband (if only verbally) got a boost from the Peter Arno cartoon below it, which showed three people shushing an irate cabbie. After a few weeks without liquor information, the column closed more boldly in the promotional issue of September 12 with a recipe for a sloe gin fizz (7), and the next week revived the stock market conceit: "Prices unchanged despite heavy sales due to rainy Labor Day. Continuing hot weather helping light wine market, especially in retail restaurant trade" (9/19/25:5). That column marked the end of "In Our Midst"; beginning September 26, 1925, "Talk" closed most weeks with a paragraph on bootleg prices or a related news item, anecdote, or recipe.

Refinements in January 1926

Tinkering with "Talk" resumed as the magazine approached its first birthday in the flush of success following the fall campaign. The weeks before Christmas saw full-page ads for the French designer Paul Poiret, Mayfair House, the Little Shop at Macy's, Pathex home movie systems, Bonwitt Teller, and other premium brands. In contrast to the lean issues of 1925, 1926 began (according to boasts in the first anniversary issue) with contracts in force for 1,350 ad pages, "an average of twenty-six pages per issue for the entire year"; when that statement went to press, circulation also had risen—to approximately forty thousand, "almost all of it in the city and suburbs" (2/20/26:15). Refinements to "Talk"'s comic formula now aimed first to withstand scrutiny by new advertisers and subscribers and then to stimulate further growth.

Revisions concentrated on the look of "Talk" and included alterations in Irvin's department header, despite the claim in his *New Yorker* obituary that his original "Talk" heading was never changed ("R. I."). (In fact, the heading graced "Of All Things," not "Talk," in the first issue.) Changes reflected "Talk"'s shift from snobbery to trendiness. The early iteration of the heading enclosed the skyline and owl in a window frame; Eustace Tilley wrote from either a penthouse or a garret, but he observed the city from a superior position. The new variant on this scene, debuting three weeks before the first anniversary issue, balanced the emphasis between the dandy and the city. As redrawn, the scene switched from night to day, the frame disappeared, and the block of low-rise buildings gave way to an abstracted skyline of three high-rises. In addition, a swirl and zigzag curve replaced the straight lines of the windowsill, putting the buildings on a

Small changes to Irvin's "Talk" headings near the end of the *New Yorker*'s first year mark the huge improvements in the department between 2/21/25:1 and 1/30/26:7.

slight rise and letting New York borrow the caché of a city on a hill; Eustace Tilley and the owl grew larger and their outlines more refined as the owl moved from the windowsill to offset the dandy on the right side of the header; and the light in the drawing, which originally came from inside buildings, now emanated from the city itself, as buildings gave off rays like the sun (1/30/26:7). This scene still announces "Talk," though its width has shrunk from three columns to barely two. Small in themselves, these changes nevertheless symbolized the huge refinement in "Talk" over the *New Yorker*'s first year.

The resumption of local color spreads inside "Talk" after a six-month hiatus made an even stronger statement of fiscal and editorial health. These layouts reappeared nearly a month before the header change, in the first issue of 1926. Rather than feature a single artist or represent the text, like the "Comment" illustrations, layouts provided news and commentary from varying points of view. Three layouts by staff artist Julian De Miskey inaugurated the revived feature. His first layout, a highly geometric rendering of couples dancing at a costume ball, offered a much more comic view of the scene than Eldon Kelley's spread a year earlier: as the drawing jumped the fold, dancers' angular poses gave the illusion of motion, while their stylized costumes and bodies signified their high

A "Talk" layout of Central Park. Constantin Aladjalov, 4/9/27:18–19.

social status (1/2/26:4–5). De Miskey's second layout, "The Automobile Show at Grand Central Palace," offered even more visual humor: it contrasted the furry, round shapes of the customers in their winter coats with the long, slender bodies of the salesmen in morning dress and cars so light that they look like toys (1/9/26:4–5). His third layout featured a hockey game, with naïve, sticklike figures contorted variously on the ice (1/16/26:6–7). Like their verbal counterparts, these layouts covered subjects across class lines, while the point of view remained dependably playful and ironic.

Other artists followed De Miskey to the inside "Talk" spread, and their layouts broke up the drawing into multiple images projecting into the text. Alice Harvey's seven sketches of "The Junior League's Red and Gold Ball" invited chuckles on its events: a dramatic performance (drawn so indistinctly as to imply its irrelevance), a Charleston contest (represented in extremis by the winners, an exuberant woman and exhausted man), a waltz contest (portrayed as a comic contrast between the elegant Miss Gertrude Lawrence judging it and an absurdly costumed couple who failed to win). Her sketches' casual style emphasizes their origin in live action while gently challenging the dignity of high society; less gently, the pictures of a woman selling programs and of "Stuyvesant, the demon balloon smasher," expose the event's commerce and vulgarity (1/23/26:8–9). Over the next few weeks and months, this more elaborate docu-

mentary humor prevailed, though few layouts filled half the spread, as Harvey's did. The five images in Helen Hokinson's "Portraits From the Poetry Society— By One Who Should Not Have Been There" contrasted the intellectual and romantic aspirations of the society's women with political infighting among the men. Two men stand at the center of the spread and dominate the discussion with the length and directness of their criticism, but they are outflanked, literally and figuratively, by the portraits of delicate and mousy matrons who outnumber them eight to two (1/30/26:10–11). When De Miskey drew "The Beaux Arts Ball" for the following issue, his geometric abstraction of the ball's costumes and its seventeenth-century pretensions emphatically ridiculed high society. Artists brought a modern sensibility—social and artistic—to "Talk" reports on the New York scene.

"Notes and Comment" toned down its misogyny and cynicism in this period, addressing criticism to matters of style and taste, and firmly speaking in the editorial "we." A bemused note in the issue of January 2, 1926, that the Daughters of the American Revolution had recently dedicated a plaque commemorating the "lost thoroughfare called Petticoat Lane," led to a low-key concession of urban pleasures. "While not one of those fortunate creatures . . . who can find joy and beauty in everything, we nevertheless agree with the man who does not mind the shortest day in the year if it means that the Woolworth Building is illuminated that much longer" (3). The snobby opening holds out a critic's difficult life for admiration before deigning to endorse someone else's praise, but praise comes through anyway. The more moderate tone prevailed over the next weeks. In remarking that The Woman Pays Club, an organization encouraging "girls to pay their own way when taken to lunch by gentlemen," has no position on other kinds of men, "Comment" concludes, "Probably the Club takes it for granted that in the latter case the woman pays anyway and so deserves to get her lunch free" (1/9/26:3). Similarly "Notes and Comment" in this period celebrated the incongruity leading the public library to catalog books on bridge and mah-jong under "Fine Arts" (1/23/26:7) and the propensity of boxholders to spend the intermission in their seats but retire to their vestibules to play bridge during the performance (1/30/26:7).

At the end of the first year, the humor of "Notes and Comment" separated New York insiders—who could nod knowingly when "Talk" decried the front window of the Flatiron Building as "the dullest in all New York"—from outsiders (who couldn't get the joke about how "according to the researches of social scientists, the geographical society center of New York has moved northward two blocks in one year. . . . it must have gone on a Madison Avenue car" 2/6/26:10). The insular focus on Manhattan went so far as to explain the building of a new subway station under the Public Library as a means "to assist our more eccentric citizens to get to Corona and Astoria when the madness seizes them" (4/3/26:9)—not (apparently) to give residents of Queens access to Fifth Avenue and Forty-second Street.

Prohibition jokes now opened "Talk" as well as closed it, an increase that corresponded to a broadening of "Talk" topics generally. Name stories continued, but money items diminished (testimony to the *New Yorker's* increasing self-assurance), and local places and events generated more and more amusing anecdotes. "Epicurean," for example, bemoaned how "There may be another Delmonico's one day but . . . it will be Delmonico's with the apostrophe, and not Delmonicos, without . . . [as] when the four members of the same family held interest in, what was then the city's most distinguished restaurant," and a story underlined the point: Lobster á la Wenberg, a Delmonicos trademark, bore the name of its inventor, but a rift between Ben Wenberg and Charles Delmonico inspired the latter to rename the dish the Lobster á la Newberg, an anagram of the original (3/6/26:8). Other stories took up the Elm Street widening project, which unexpectedly gave the city its most dense row of gasoline stations ("Justice," 4/3/26:11), the zoo (4/10/26:8), and Washington Square (4/24/26:10). Many of these stories had the "insidey" quality that Ross had told contributors he sought in the personal mentions department, into a compendium headed "This Week" following "Notes and Comment." Here, however, inside knowledge meant not gossip but details separating the real New Yorkers from the wannabes. "Keys to the City," for instance, described how the organizers of a national meeting at a large hotel provided free tickets, in order "to make the delegates feel at home," to the aquarium, Stock Exchange, the Metropolitan Museum, and other such sites, which New Yorkers of 1926 would recognize as free already.

Hangouts *outside* Manhattan likewise exploited regional inside knowledge. When "Black and Parisian" reported on the unfriendly competition that summer between Josephine Baker and Florence Mills, the place names dropped in the story—the Folies Bergères, the Ambassadeurs outdoor restaurant, the Théâtre Femina, the Bienvenue Française in the Faubourg Saint-Honoré—flattered the sophistication of readers who knew or dreamed of them (7/17/26:10–11). Seasonal reports also came from Florida in the winter, summarizing hotel rates, available entertainment, and ways to distinguish the Four Hundred from the "*nouveaux*" ("Florida This Year" 1/1/27:10). By June of 1928, the peregrinations of New Yorkers became such staples of "Talk" that the *New Yorker* could reject news from London with an airy "we are already pretty well stocked with trans-Atlantic material."[9]

Graphic layouts reinforced and extended this variation on local humor. "Talk" spreads in 1926 began featuring scenes of New Yorkers' playgrounds— including Coney Island (Aladjalov 7/10/26:12),[10] Central Park (De Miskey 8/14/26:10–11), Southampton (Harvey 8/28/26:10–11), and Belmont Park racetrack (Arno 6/28/27:12–13). Most stood as "Talk" items in their own right, not as illustrations of the text, but prime topics ran in both media. On the same page that "Talk" reported on the number of Americans going abroad with the end of the opera season, for example, Alice Harvey particularized the exodus with a scene from Café de Paris, a Manhattanite favorite located a few thousand miles east of the Hamptons ("Cycle"; "Café de Paris" 4/24/26:12–13). Layouts of city sites scrupulously ignored uptown Manhattan, however, especially Harlem, as they privileged the activities of the peer society. The Stock Exchange ([Hokinson] 10/16/26:18–29), the Easter Parade on Fifth Avenue (Hokinson 4/10/26:10–11), the opera (Hokinson 11/13/26:18–19), and similar "smart" venues prevailed.

Nonetheless, "Talk" layouts varied along with the sensibilities and artists presenting their work to the editors. In addition to the hauteur recorded by Aladjalov in "Sunday Morning at St. Bartholomews [*sic*]" (3/2/29:16–17), layouts also featured public sites where New Yorkers assembled democratically en masse, such as Central Park (Aladjalov 4/9/27:18–19) and the subway (Marsh

The dining car—wine is thicker than Evian

They shall not pass

It's the people you meet

Garrett Price reported European experiences of the peer society in "Boat Train."
6/1/29:24–25.

11/2/29:34). Indeed, "Talk"'s graphic humor of place grew even more important as the twenties went on. By the time Garrett Price drew his layouts on France for volume 5, including scenes of the boat train (6/1/29:24–25) and Paris (7/27/29:16–17), the *New Yorker* valued such "covering art" at one hundred dollars a spread.[11] Outdoor scenes especially furthered the humor of place defining "Talk," and their public mood offset the insularity of the single-panel cartoons, with their domestic settings.

Layouts' realism contrasted with the primitive, modernist style of Julian De Miskey's illustrations for "Notes and Comment" when he succeeded Johan Bull with the issue of May 29, 1926. As De Miskey substituted stick figures and other rudimentary shapes for the more detailed, rounded figures of Bull's caricatures, "Talk" replaced the earlier humor of character and situation with a humor of style. Bull's drawings usually summarized a story and graphically represented

"Il est dangereux
de se pencher en dehors"

Elwood Swift, of Ohio Wesleyan,
and baggage

its punch line, as in the scene of Eustace Tilley walking down the street as a woman's slender leg follows her into a limousine. The drawing remains cryptic despite its caption, "A DAY'S WORK," but the text shows how caption, item, and drawing come together to celebrate the serendipity of "Talk" reporting and, by extension, life in New York among the celebrated: "We unexpectedly came face to face with Miss Raquel Meller debouching from a store. . . . within five seconds she dived into an enclosed car and hastily departed. It was a great moment, and a very gratifying [sic] to one whose business it is to write down his experiences. . . . in five seconds we had done a day's work" (4/24/26:9). De Miskey's drawings, by contrast, seldom overlapped with "Comment" text in this way. Instead of reporting an event, they expressed an attitude toward it.

Indeed, De Miskey's work emphasized generalities, rejecting the specifics on which caricatures such as Bull's depend. To illustrate a "Comment" about Jack Dempsey's refusal to fight Harry Wills, for example, De Miskey drew a symmetrical pair of boxer icons, equally unspecified, the white cringing as the black

THE TALK OF THE TOWN

Julian De Miskey, 6/5/26:15.

advances. The cryptic drawing nonetheless ridicules the racism that "Notes and Comment" attacks more directly when noting that "the greatest colored champion we have ever had" would have to be "Dempsey, not Wills—the color being yellow" (7/3/26:7). The extreme naïveté of De Miskey's illustrations not only provides a lighthearted mood that keeps "Talk" amusingly arch instead of pedantic or snotty but also directs attention back toward the text. Indeed, the only way to know who is represented in the little drawing of a mature man in tuxedo holding out a jeweled necklace to a little princess jumping up and down is to read through "Talk" until reaching the item about how "the ten-year-old daughter of Billie Burke and Flo Ziegfeld has been robbed of ten thousand dollars' worth of jewelry" (7/3/26:7). The tiny size and emphatic abstraction of De Miskey's drawings defined "Talk"'s sense of humor as the formula evolved in the middle of volume 2. No archival evidence identifies another reason that De

Miskey took over this assignment from Bull, who remained on the *New Yorker* staff, specializing in sports illustrations. Although Bull occasionally contributed "Talk" layouts such as "The Spring Meeting of the United Hunts, 1926" (5/1/26:12–13), "Comment" drawings belonged exclusively to De Miskey until he left the staff late in 1930 to work in Paris and Otto Soglow succeeded him.[12] In this context, De Miskey's assignment to "Talk" suggests that Ross, Ingersoll, and Irvin preferred his ambiguous modernism to the more conventional caricatures Bull drew.

By representing absurdity visually, De Miskey's illustrations injected "Talk" with the silly spirit animating New Yorker fictional prose humor in the summer of 1926. Silly drawings particularly enlivened text that lacked its own humor, and they became more important as "Comment" grew increasingly acerbic. A drawing of straphangers dangling like droopy marionettes gave a comic context to the complaint that the crowds packed into the Long Island Railroad recently made it "difficult to indorse" a new express to Southampton (7/10/26:7).

The July subway strike brought special demands, and "Comment" broke the policy against political editorials by siding with labor. More evidence of liberal politics came as the column satirized the responses of others, especially the *New York Times,* the bus company, New York Central Railroad, and others it deemed equally ineffectual: "We heard of several people who revived the old war-time custom of having brown instead of white bread and of inviting a Hoover child to the table in order to help out in the great emergency" (7/17/26:7). For its part, "Comment" granted management's concern over "the wanton breaking of contracts" but concluded that "the plaintive protests of the motormen and switchmen . . . appeared justified." With a thumbnail sketch of a tiny motorman dwarfed by a rotund plasterer, De Miskey conveyed the gist of the *New Yorker's* argument that "If there is any good reason why a plasterer should get fifteen dollars for a day's work and a motorman six dollars we don't know it, the responsibility of the motorman being incalculably greater." Staff rated the drawing important enough to run it twice, as mirror images, on the front page.

De Miskey's visual humor here, as on topics of less economic and social import, came from a vaudevillian contrast between large and small. Throughout the twenties, De Miskey's tiny drawings for "Comment" emphasized the small scale of insignificant topics while putting major ones in comic proportion.

The acerbic tone of "Notes and Comment" in the summer of 1926 shows how much "Talk" needed De Miskey's sense of humor to offset "Comment"'s rising hostility. Nearly every issue brought a new complaint. "There is always one horror of summer which we fail to anticipate," began the "Comment" for July 17: the Coolidges' vacation activities. An item about colors on the Rotary Club's official hatband similarly evoked a hyperbolic "We are horror-struck" (7/31/26:8). Solutions evinced as much indignation as offenses. To resolve the conflict between traffic and pedestrians, "Comment" proposed a "compromise" in which the police would "wait a few seconds before starting traffic at an intersection when the light changes." This procedure would let people finish crossing—but only those already halfway across the street. "If they are caught less than halfway," the *New Yorker*'s Solomon continues, "let them die" (7/24/26:7–8). Although Hyde became known for his "caustic" tone in "Comment" (Kramer, *Ross* 188), this harshness shows how "Talk"'s sense of humor suffered over the summer when illness took Ross from the office, and Ralph Ingersoll, who earned a "crack-up" for his efforts, ran the magazine in his place.[13] The tone softened a bit after Ross returned in August, when lead items took up the "sore subject" of new procedures for paying bus fares (9/4/26:7) and noted the "disturbing" reluctance of otherwise "adventurous" Americans to rise on the front platforms of subway trains (9/11/26:17).

Other changes over the summer refined the formula, which now linked every "Talk" item to New York. An old joke about lawyers' corrupt billing practices reappears "with Long Island as the mise-en-scene" (7/10/26:8), and a report about Santa Fe claims attention as "one of New York's most popular summer resorts" (7/10/26:9). A report on "Fashion" from "Our New Mexico correspondent" begins by describing various men's styles "stolen from the Indians" by eastern tourists, including the concept of wearing several shirts in layers; the tale ends (in the manner of western stories by Mark Twain) with a joke on the tenderfoot, the urbanite as comic victim:

> The plan has other advantages, our correspondent points out. . . .
> "Why don't you wear that lavender shirt on top, Trinidad?" he asked. "It's a beautiful one."
> "Yes," said the Indian wistfully. "I liked that one, too, but it got dirty." (7/24/26:10)

Thus the story about Taos became, like stories about George M. Cohan, Spring Lake, and Fifth Avenue, a tale about New Yorkers and New York.

Character sketches and other narratives now entered "Talk" via hooks to contemporary events. Some occasioned thoughtful, even profound, observations. A story about the advertising genius Milton Feasley illustrates how humor ran in two directions. After introducing Feasley as the creator of Listerine's halitosis campaign, "whereupon, it is said, was born the principle of advertising through fear," one narrative recounts Feasley's refusal to prove the truth of a perfume testimonial unless his accusers do likewise for an ad proclaiming "Milk from contented cows" (9/4/26:11). A second story develops the item's modest title, "Obit," pointing out that news of Rudolph Valentino's death squeezed notice of Feasley's into a mere seven lines. The piece emphasizes the irony of the "simultaneous decease in New York, also through peritonitis, of . . . another young man in his thirties, whose audience had been perhaps twice the size of the screen star's." "Talk" thus not only nods perfunctorily at a well-known event while zeroing in on a more novel one but also holds up paradoxes of publicity for *New Yorker* readers to consider and invites their appreciation of the "cynicism" by which Feasley performed his halitosis ads at parties (9/4/26:11). This shift from a news orientation to a narrative mode reversed "Talk"'s priorities of the first year, and it gathered strength after E. B. White joined the staff.

Enter E. B. White and James Thurber

As in the inaugural issue's tale of Jumbo Jr., the second anniversary issue "Comment" despaired, in the manner of the daunted Little Man, of the tribulations of running a magazine. "Sordid material problems have continued to be practically insurmountable," ran this trope, reviving the frustration of the *New Yorker*'s first number: "Partitions, desks, telephone—where they all go; office boys whistling; words misspelled and commas out of place; an office of such unusual acoustical properties that even 'Lipstick's' charming girlish shoutings are made to sound like a mob scene in 'Lulu Belle.' A new reception room papered in silver tea papers doesn't get all these things out of the way" (2/19/27:17). The continuity between this celebratory item and earlier bits obscures the major change occurring in "Talk" when this issue went to press: E. B. White had arrived. His contributions to this number consist of a brief paragraph in "Comment" speculating on the promised improvements to the now abandoned "Vanderbilt château" at Fifty-eighth and Fifth (17), an account of the auction scene in "Hammer" (19–20), and a frame tale *cum* personal narrative on "Why Albert Ferncroft Is a Bitter Man" (28). Neither White nor the *New Yorker* considered these items important enough to reprint, but they demonstrated his already substantial contribution to the magazine's reportage and comic fiction.

Even from the vantage point of seventy-five years, among the most momentous developments in "Talk" occurred when E. B. White began writing it. "I can't remember a piece by anyone but E. B. White that Ross ever really thought just right," Ralph Ingersoll recalled in his memoir (*Point* 203). By 1944, Ross so trusted White's instincts that he encouraged him to editorialize in "Comment" on behalf of the United Nations or any other cause, insisting that White could not harm the magazine however he deviated from *New Yorker* policy. "You made the Comment page what it is, God knows," Ross declared, "and I have for long regarded it as yours to the extent that you want to use it. That is not only the right way to look at the matter, but very sound business, I am convinced."[14] The admiration ran in both directions. As early as 1929, White credited the magazine for helping him develop "a special kind of writing which has always amused me," and he was frankly grateful. "Not till the New Yorker came along," he told his brother Stanley, "did I ever find any means of expressing those impertinences and irrelevancies."[15]

Exactly when White arrived remains fuzzy. According to Scott Elledge, with whom White cooperated on an authorized biography, Angell recommended that Ross hire White in the spring of 1926 because "Always" (5/8/26:31) and "Lower Level" (5/22/26:20) so neatly fit the magazine's needs, but White resisted until fall, evidenced by details in his "Life Cycle of a Literary Genius," the story of an author who learns about a staff position during lunch with a Great Editor and "dies of nervous indigestion" immediately thereafter (Elledge 109, 114; 10/16/26:31). Other sources offer different accounts, however. Family friend and *Letters* editor Dorothy Lobrano, who also collaborated with White, reports that White dodged several offers before he and Ross agreed to a part-time job at thirty dollars a week in January of 1927 (Kunkel 146; White 72).

The specific date matters less, of course, than the process by which the writer and the magazine adopted each other. White had contributed to the magazine since 1:9, which contained "A Step Forward," followed a month later by "Defense of the Bronx River" (5/9/25:14). He took a part-time job with the advertising firm of J. H. Newmark in October 1925 (Elledge 105) but clearly enjoyed freelancing. In an undated letter to his Cornell classmate Howard Baker Cushman, White announced his success at piecing together a living from the *New Yorker*, the Cunard Line, and other sources; he implies a reluctance to give up his professional independence in remarking that the *New Yorker* "has been quite receptive, rejecting little, buying much, and even asking me to lunch once in a while."[16] Freelancing offered a bachelor of twenty-seven glamour and excitement too. In July 1926 he seized a last-minute opportunity to make travel films while sailing to Europe with college students on the Cunard line, and began considering a career at the magazine only after his August 7 return, when he discovered six checks totaling $178 from the *New Yorker* waiting for him (Elledge 112–13; White 27). Casuals based on his trip appeared in the *New Yorker* within a week of his return; his work had run five weeks straight (2:28–2:33) when he debuted in "Talk" (Hall 231–32). A total of two more "Talk" paragraphs and ten casuals between October and December of 1926 argues against his having joined the staff that fall, however. In any event, even after he signed on with Ross, White kept the Newmark job until satisfied that the *New Yorker* would support him (Elledge 105; White 72). This decision point probably came in February 1927, when White began taking over "Notes and Comment" from Hyde, the week before Thurber came on the scene as managing editor.

White's first "Talk" piece reveled in the drama at Woolworth's when a customer tendered a ten-dollar bill for a ten-cent purchase. Extolling the experience as "more fun than eating a ham sandwich in a polo box at Meadow Brook," the item appeared as a single paragraph of "Notes and Comment" for October 2, 1926. The piece indicates that White brought to "Talk" real, if brief, experience as a "colyumist." He had conducted the daily humorous "Personal Column" in the *Seattle Times* from early March to June 20, 1923, after six months as a reporter there.[17] Fired from the *Times,* White returned that fall to New York and began submitting to F. P. A.'s "Conning Tower" in the *New York World,* where twelve of his pieces appeared before he sold anything to Ross (Hall C226–C239). In homage to colyumists F. P. A. and B. L. T., White usually signed himself *E.B.W.,* although early in his association with the *New Yorker* he experimented with other representations of himself as an author. Thurber, recalling these in a 1938 piece for the *Saturday Review of Literature,* razzed him for having signed himself "Elwyn (as God is my judge) Brooks White" (8), but White did so only once, in his second contribution to "Why I Like New York" (10/10/25:31), and he appeared just twice as "E. B. White"—in his first "Why I Like New York" (8/22/25:10) and again nearly two years later in "Lower Level" (5/22/26:20)—before retreating to a discrete *E. B. W.* or (more frequently) the anonymity of "Talk." As a venue for writing colyums, stories, and verse, the *New Yorker* suited White as well as he suited it.

Katherine Hall's bibliography shows that White wrote a paragraph or two of "Comment" each week and five titled items in the first eight weeks of 1927, a period of apprenticeship leading up to his first solo "Comment" in 3:2 (2/26/27). Not that he needed much practice. In the New Year's Day issue, a cranky report on the loudspeaker-bedecked Christmas tree in Times Square as representative of "the Holiday Spirit of 1926–27" led to White's much funnier paragraph proposing "government ownership of all speakeasies" as a solution to the problems of Prohibition: "The citizenry would be assured liquor of a uniformly high quality, and the enormous cost of dry enforcement could be met by the profits from the sale of drinks" (1/1/27:7). The mock naïveté of White's piece stands out clearly against the rest of the section, which sneers at the cultural aspirations of boxer Gene Tunney ("it would be a shame if the profession got so cultured that there was nobody in it who fought because he was so tough he loved it") and bemoans the annual departure of domestic employees ("wily persons . . . [who] stay in a place until they have received a Christmas present and then . . . leave"). In contrast to the cynical paragraph remarking that the new municipal curfew has "nobly" provided the "public . . . a new law to break," White elevates girl watching to a high aesthetic, sociological, and euphemistic plane as he describes "one of New York's most distinguished tribute-payers" (7). Although Kramer saw the difference between Fillmore Hyde's "Comment" and White's as a contrast between the "caustic" and the "easygoing" (*Ross* 188), their humor differs in rhetoric as well as tone. Whereas Hyde assumed a superior pose and invited readers to join him in comic condescension, White saw incongruities between matter and manner and elevated them for readers' admiration and amusement.

These differences showed less in the inside pages of "Talk," where essays ran longer and attitudes varied more. White's "Harbinger," an auspicious choice for the New Year's Day issue, told how sanitation workers met the challenge caused by the mysterious appearance of a lawn mower on the city sidewalks one cold morning: after voting to salvage the machine and ceremoniously installing it on a new truck ("one of the squad making the supreme sacrifice and donating his jacket so it wouldn't scratch the paint"), the crew "drove off, vernal-hearted, down the wintry street" (1/1/27:8). This celebration of urban serendipity stands out among the other items. "Rehearsal" offers a stern account of work at Carnegie Hall. One character sketch describes how Lee Schubert saved the three-thousand-dollar cost of retuning the organ in his theater by requiring the orchestra to match *its* pitches ("Two More" 9). Another uses George Gershwin's work-in-progress, "An American in Paris," as a springboard for discussing his work and spending ethics, his classical music training, his family connections, and his collection of orchestral scores ("Celebrity" 9–10). Unlike these gossipy character sketches, White's writing emphasized the color in local humor.

White specialized in "Talk" stories that elicited surprising implications from slim subjects. "Royal" reported that a cruise aboard a former royal British yacht allowed passengers to book the king's suite (complete with bathtub) before turning to dilate on Americans' shipboard behavior: apparently the democratic impulses by which "American tourists get so chummy with the stewards as to unfit them for return to the trans-Atlantic service" also explain why some women would rather remain aboard ship than tour the ports (2/12/27:19). An on-the-scenes report of Manhattan's twice-weekly horse auctions (at Twenty-third Street between Lexington and Third) begins by noting the excitement and danger of the trade ("Lured by a man ringing a dinner bell, we disappeared into the gloom. . . . We almost got trampled to death"). His account of the "amazing speed" with which the auctioneer dispenses with "a flying team, immense in the half-light, [as it] bears down at a full gallop" and the other two hundred animals for sale each week leads to observations that the trade sustains trucking companies as well as horse-meat packers ("Horse Mart," 6/18/27:10–11). A few items ended without a witty nub, however. Reviewing the new reptile hall at the Museum of Natural History in "Snakes," White starts by appealing to our interest in "The slimy, poisonous things of the earth" and notes along the way "Rule Number 1" for treating a snake bite—"Make sure that you are bitten by a poisonous snake"—before ending with an ambiguous appreciation: "The Gila monster, emerging in the glow of an Arizona sunset, will disturb and vitalize our dreams for many nights to come" (7/2/27:10–11). Close-ups in prose, such "Talk" items emphasized the personal viewpoint in city life, connecting public experience and mental life.

White joined the "Talk" staff at an opportune time, because Ross and Fleischmann contracted on January 21 and 27, 1927, for the Bell Syndicate to recycle the department as a newspaper feature about a week after each issue appeared.[18] An early example of the *New Yorker*'s present practice of maximizing revenue via audio books, anthologies, and the internet Cartoon Bank, among other venues, the Bell deal began February 1 with "Talk" but immediately expanded to include theater reviews and other features, and thus served several purposes. Over the next twelve months the Bell contract not only produced revenue—half the syndication income—but also allowed the magazine to test the value of first-run material and reprints for an out-of-town audience. Fleischmann agreed in June to a second six-month run, but in October he decided "to take a whirl at our own syndicate," and instructed Ross to limit Bell to "Talk" material only and to terminate the arrangement effective January 1, 1928.[19] Ross complied, but reluctantly, because their own syndicate gave greater play to art than to "Talk" and because he feared alienating the newspapers who would soon be his customers.[20]

For that reason Fleischmann agreed to let Charles Brackett's theater reviews continue, but by mid-November withdrew them again, and Ross wrote his Bell contact, John H. Wheeler, withdrawing Brackett's letter at Fleischmann's behest and declining with an embarrassed disclaimer the invitation to extend the agreement.[21] Although the end of the Bell contract on January 31, 1928, paved the way for the magazine's own syndicate, it also anticipated a development making syndication moot: the *New Yorker*'s split into two editions—city and out-of-town—beginning with the issue of October 5, 1929.

Thurber also arrived at the *New Yorker* shortly after the start of the Bell venture. Thurber joined the staff by a more direct route a few weeks behind White, around March 1, after selling Angell two poems and a casual: "Villanelle of Horatio Street, Manhattan" (2/26/27:74), "Street Song" (2/26/27:79), and "An American Romance" (3/5/27:63–64). But he came aboard as managing editor, not as a writer. "Writers are a dime a dozen, Thurber," Ross countered his new employee's request for a writing post, as Thurber recalled the scene thirty years later in *The Years with Ross;* "What I want is an editor" (3). Within five months, however, Ross conceded his mistake and renamed Thurber a staff writer for "Talk," giving him his famous office with E. B. White and raising his salary (Kinney 353). Thurber, on the other hand, nursed a grudge for thirty years that his original administrative salary of $5,200 allowed Ross to avoid paying for his first eight casuals.[22]

White's "Talk" item about tourists' fraternizing with ship stewards had already run by the time Thurber arrived—more evidence that Thurber exaggerated Ross's fear of bedroom humor, among other misrepresentations. Even if Ross had missed the risqué implications of "Royal," he could not have overlooked those in the adjoining column, which put sex in the punch line literally and figuratively. "She's a fine actress," begins the speaker in a joke linked to the recent closing of E. H. Sothern's *Ghosts,* "but she ought to have a better show. They ought to get whoever wrote 'Sex' to write one for her" (2/12/27:19). Indeed, sex remained a subject for cartoons and an undercurrent of "Talk" throughout the twenties, and in 1929 White published a "Comment" opposing Mary Ware Dennett's conviction on obscenity charges because the "offense, if any, was not criminal but editorial. . . . she overwrites" (5/4/29:13). If Ross offended Thurber over the suitability of topics, more likely he quashed Thurber's ideas for the department. Or he may have required too many revisions; Ross demanded so many from White in 1927 that the writer put a jibing note on his Christmas present: "At first I resented the idea of having to give anything to my employer.

I don't owe you anything! Everything I have had at your hands I have worked for, often twice" (White 78).

By the time Thurber joined him in "Talk" rewrite in the fall of 1927 after five months as an editor, White had already hit his stride. He had written at least part—and usually all—of every "Comment" since the first of the year, and usually contributed a "Talk" item as well. White's wit set a genial standard for the other pieces as well, often by devoting elegant vocabulary to mundane experience. Other writers and the editors also contributed to the development of a "Talk" style, though their activity remains difficult to trace. Edited manuscripts in the *New Yorker* archives from 1927 show a consistent effort to avoid editorializing and tighten sentences, making them more like newspaper than magazine writing. Ross reviewed most of the manuscripts, putting his "R" on "Comment" items to go to De Miskey "For illus" and occasionally tinkering with a line or two. He changed a line in White's "Comment" on American Forest Week, for example, turning "have fewer special writers" into "have smaller newspapers." But he sought Angell's approval of the change, calling her attention to it and adding, "I don't know whether it's wise. R[.]"[23]

More important, another variety of humor emerged in 1927: lyrical appreciations of the city alternated with ironic ones. In the issue of September 3, for instance, "Change" hung a punch line about a hostler turned chiropractor on an otherwise unremarkable anecdote about "a westerner, arrived in the city last week, [who] sought to look up a friend, an ardent equestrian," by querying the Manhattan livery stables that might keep his horses (9–10). The next item changed the mood entirely: "Fiesta" described the "sizzling little Italian boys" with the other sights and sounds of the Lower East Side's Feast of San Giovanni, where "Squalor became subdued in the majesty of music." Enthralled by a beautiful young girl, the author (not White) gave way to rapture: "In the East Side is the sort of beauty that exhausts you" (10). In the fall of 1927 "Talk" presented anonymous writers' personas, not just their topics, as amusing.

Thurber resumed editorial responsibilities for "Talk" early in 1928 and recorded the department's official and implicit policies in his correspondence. By this point "Talk" staff included reporters as well as rewriters, and relied on information from a cadre of local journalists as well as Algonquinites and friends. Sources in 1928 included Finley Peter Dunne of the *New York World* (a.k.a. the Irish-dialect humorist "Mr. Dooley"), who supplied the information on fliers headlined "Heroes of the Week" (5/12/28:17–18), and Groucho Marx, who provided inside information on Hollywood.[24] In addition, staff encouraged freelance artists and writers to submit ideas. Katharine Angell marked two items for "Talk" in a note from Frank Sullivan explaining (a) his having abandoned a nearly completed casual on laundries because it duplicated one just published by White, (b) a new story idea on which he solicited her opinion, (c) an idea "that might be either a 'Talk' or a picture," and (d) an anecdote relayed by someone from the *Tribune*.[25] The *New Yorker* bought information and ideas, not writing, for "Talk," and sought ideas everywhere. The 1920s established the *New Yorker*'s hunger for facts that inspired amazing submissions—such as Lewis Mumford's 1949 suggestion to mention "Global Weather Changes" diverting the Gulf Stream and thawing Northern Canada[26]—that sustained "Talk" for many years to come.

Sex was not among them, but by 1928 the *New Yorker* had assembled a long list of taboo topics for "Talk." The taboos set limits much more refined than the first summer's list of declared "prejudices" against "hundred-percenters and go-getters (includes Rotarians, Kiwanians and conventioneers) all lecturers, society doctors, . . . all advocates of intolerance, the nouveau, etc."[27] The 1928 department brushed off name items on local media and theater people. Thurber counseled Abel Green of *Variety* that daily newspapers covered them adequately and that the *New Yorker* sought "the significant, interesting and amusing figures . . . [outside] the little Broadway circle."[28] Historical New York pieces sustained an important strand of local color humor, but a large supply in the bank led Thurber to reject new ones.[29] Ditto what he called "Villagy and wet" stories— anecdotes set in Greenwich Village and those featuring alcoholic excess.[30] Assigning Thurber to work the "Talk" slush pile had the advantage of allowing him to choose material amenable to rewrite by himself or his colleagues as well as inviting his insight into who might turn into a regular contributor. This process led him to advise S. J. Perelman that he could earn twenty-five dollars, the equivalent of a five-hundred-word casual at a nickel a word, for supplying information for a substantial "Talk" piece.[31] (Perelman joined the staff of *Judge* in 1924 after dropping out of Brown University, but his first *New Yorker* work did not appear until 1931 [Perelman xi; Toombs 85]—despite his reputation as an early *New Yorker* humorist.) In general, by 1928 "Talk" aimed at newsy, local ideas "too slight for a casual"[32]— an independent comic sketch—but worth the time White and Thurber put into styling them. For that reason, Arthur Samuels, who took over the managing editorship in 1928 and handled some of Angell's work that summer, instructed Ingersoll to ensure that Thurber and

White receive news clippings and "Talk" ideas throughout the week, even on Saturday or Sunday mornings, in order to maintain the department's focus on news.[33]

The issue of June 2, 1928, shows the distance "Talk" had come in the three years since Fleischmann's reprieve. White's "Comment" runs smoothly through a series of local topics, each of them drawing amusement from local people, places, or events. He begins with a name item—Thornton Wilder decided not to go abroad with Gene Tunney because the playwright couldn't compete with the boxer's knowledge of *A Winter's Tale*—and continues with reflections on how the Navy ships anchored forlornly in the Hudson would make splendid housing, spacious and airy, for Manhattanites. Then a paragraph tweaks Grover Whalen for calling a banquet "remarkable" and notes that a display of tadpoles meant to illustrate the need for a telephone on every desk affected him quite contrariwise: "the tadpoles had sensibly *given up* rising to the surface, wise little frogs! We departed, vowing never to answer the phone again" (17). The section closes with racist nostalgia for the demise of Chinese laundries, which had given children pigtails to pull and fantasies to elaborate; the new French laundries simply do not compare, since their managers don't even speak French (17–18). Headlined items in the body, running through Johan Bull's layout of horse racing at Belmont Park, run the gamut of narratives with punch lines. Jokes include a tale of the trickster who got tricked ("Life in a Big City" 18), a governess who turned out to be the girlfriend of a famous flier ("An Aviator" 18), and a survivor of the Pennland ship collision who took the experience graciously in stride: "When I got aboard I was supremely happy, and it was a pleasure to wake up a short time later and find myself being so gently and efficiently rescued" ("Fog" 19). A lengthier item considered the impact of Eugene O'Neill's eight-hour drama *Strange Interlude* on local restaurants and on a taciturn theatergoer, who, as if in a contest, reduced the plot to eight words: "Well, if it ain't one thing it's another" ("That Play" 18–19). White took readers on a tour of Bedloe's Island, where Lady Liberty and her minions reside (19–20).

This sense of commonality between "Talk" and its audience led David Sloane to compare "Talk," in his guide to American humor magazines, to "a small-town newspaper reporting on current events in a folksy way that implies that the writer and reader know each other, share the same beliefs, and are on familiar terms" (186). In the 1920s "Talk" flattered readers as no small-town paper can. Its educated vocabulary pegged class membership high, as did its use of inside information—gratifying the cognoscenti by referring to knowledge in circulation, informing the novice with gentle reminders and subtle details, and delighting the witty with humor between the lines.

The job was not easy, and Angell tried recruiting Frank Sullivan for it in the fall of 1928, when Thurber retreated from "Talk" editorial work.[34] But he declined the opportunity even as he wrote more fiction for the magazine, though he supplemented his income with ideas and anecdotes for "Talk." Now the department ended with a quip summing up the attitude of the New Yorkers who signed it. One installment recommended a list of "ten words nobody can spell," which, accompanied by "a little astuteness in laying wagers . . . should take anyone through a long winter" ("Bee," 10/20/28:17). Another told of a yet-to-be-discovered practical joke perpetrated on two "impeccable spinsters" in Palm Beach who swam unaware while a wag used their camera to shoot "a reel of gentlemen lolling carelessly about in the altogether" ("Men Without Women," 3/2/29:17). These stories, like the simple department signature, "The New Yorkers," reinforced the spirit of "Talk" as the *New Yorker*'s collective voice: a pluralistic, modernist (if white and elite) view of New York City as the sum of many individual voices, distinctive though anonymous.

New Trends in "Talk" Layouts

Graphic layouts inside the department changed as "Talk" stories grew longer and their verbal humor more subtle. Instead of the single panoramic scene, layouts beginning October 9, 1926, splashed two to six drawings (occasionally captioned) of various sizes about the inside pages. The earliest examples, such as Peter Arno's "Fashions in First Nighters: A Broadway Revue, the Theatre Guild, the Super-Movie" (10/9/26:18–19), demonstrate the shift from a caricature report of New Yorkers at work and play to non-narrative, nonlinear glimpses of activity from many angles. Arno's uncaptioned drawings contrast three classes of audience: sharp-nosed Broadway types and their youthful audiences, the more subdued intellectual audiences for a Bernard Shaw play, and elegant movie stars who need a police escort. Each drawing shows theatergoers entering from the right and heading left as they climb the stairs toward their seats—but this composition sets them marching backwards across the page, against the flow of text. That comic layout decision led to another: the drawing cuts across all three columns on the second page, bifurcating the page. In this case, only one figure's head juts into the column, but by the fall of 1927 layouts began regularly to take on a such comic relations to the "Talk" text, jumping around the page and wrapping text into odd shapes about them. Consequently, "Talk" layouts created humor not only from the contents and composition of individual drawings, as when the two drawings in Alice Harvey's "The Flower Show" put the audience instead of the flowers on display (3/26/27:18–19), but also from relations among the drawings and their interaction with columns of text.

Clarence William Anderson's "The Club Locker Room: Mens Sana in Corpore Sano" scattered men in amusingly varied states of dress and undress, activity and repose, across two pages in five images. The sequence evokes humor from incongruity and contrast: first a trim naked man in glasses (quite unself-consciously signing for drinks delivered by a uniformed busboy), then a fat man playing racquetball (seen unattractively from behind), next another rear view of a round man on the scale, and finally two clinchers: nude and nearly naked men in the locker room in conversation with a man in evening dress; a man stretched out on a sofa, apparently asleep with a drink on his belly (3/19/27:19). The arrangement of the drawings adds to the amusement, as four drawings march from left to right down and across the spread and the fifth bounces upward. Although Anderson published only one more layout among his thirty-one drawings in the early *New Yorker*, he shared his approach to visual humor with other alumni of the Art Institute of Chicago—Helen Hokinson, Alice Harvey, Garrett Price, and Perry Barlow, all frequent contributors of covering art who combined an illustrator's hand with a satirist's eye.

Federico Lebrun's layouts relied on a bold line more akin to Arno's than to Hokinson's, and an equally bold approach to people and page makeup. The beach scenes in his first layout contrast the people who hide from the sun and from other people with those who flaunt either their bodies or their clothes. The drawings, set symmetrically on the two pages, interject themselves amusingly into the text—a knee here, a cape there, a sunhat somewhere else (8/27/27:12–13). Lebrun's preference for active subjects such as "October Football" (10/22/27:14–15) and ice skating in Central Park (2/11/28:10–11), added a sense of movement as image pushed into the text. The ice-skating drawings gave the editors some difficulty because the mild winter of 1928 allowed only a few days for skating in the park (as Angell reported to Lebrun, who had gone to Paris to paint).[35] "Talk"'s aim of mirroring the local reality put special pressures on artists doing covering layouts because art required more lead time than copy. Covering art had to anticipate the facts, whereas "Talk" writing could reflect them.

As graphic components of a news department, "Talk" drawings had to meet

Layouts offered a comic slant on the news, interpreting events with a humorist's ironic eye. Federico Lebrun, 1/14/28:12–13.

high standards of realism for such details as location, season, and fashion. Artists needed to dress their figures and settings appropriately, and the New Yorker assisted artists doing covering layouts by arranging permits and press passes for them to sketch in museums, the Stock Exchange, sports stadiums, and other sites. High aesthetic standards explain why Lebrun distinguished these layouts from what he called "real commercial stuff" and insisted, "the New Yorker's covering work is the only one I can stand besides painting."[36] It also explains why, having found an artist who could combine high aesthetic and comic values with the requisite reportorial realism, Angell invested large amounts of time in the late twenties locating photographs of Coney Island, Forest Hill, and golfers on courses to help Lebrun represent them accurately while living in Paris.

Layouts focused more on public activities than domestic relations, the purview of cartoons, but Alice Harvey often incorporated domestic elements into her covering art. Her oversize drawings of children and parents in the park,

The *New Yorker* treated text and images as interrelated graphic elements by 1928, creating humor as drawings encroached on text and pushed columns aside. Alice Harvey, 4/14/28:16–17.

for example, ran in two issues: four drawings on April 14, 1928 (16–17), five more on November 24, 1928 (30–31). The two layouts boldly seize space from the text and play with columns as graphic elements of humor. Her April layout of an unlikely entourage—a fashionably dressed mother walking a dog and pushing a scooter while her child straggles behind—violates the separation between image and text as the scooter pushes its wheel into the nearby column. To emphasize the joke, two other drawings likewise shape the copy on the facing page, where another scooter bangs into the text as a girl chases a bird atop the center column. The November layout focuses more on the activities in each drawing, including a father awkwardly following a toddler on a leash. The short column over the father's head and the longer one over the child's emphasize the comic contrast between the figures' sizes, just as the wobbly columns surrounding a young roller skater's elbows express the youth's instability. Along with other drawings about children in the late twenties, these drawings hint that some members of the peer society had lately become parents themselves, though

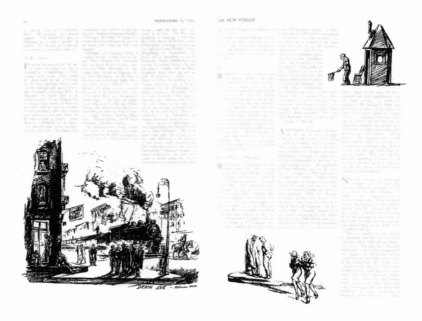

Reginald Marsh, 11/5/27:10–11.

the *New Yorker* had yet to advertise schools, as *Vanity Fair* regularly did. Harvey's layouts extended to such nondomestic sites as the Stock Exchange ("Bull Market" 4/28/28:26–27), cabarets ("The St. Regis Roof" 7/7/28:10–11), and Venice (8/11/28:18–19), but they concentrated on displaying the vitality of life in the city from the viewpoint of the privileged.

Reginald Marsh resumed "Talk" layouts with the "Six-Day Bike Race" (3/12/27:20–21), but his covering art often took on lower subjects, including those below ground, as in "The Interborough Subway 3 A.M.," three large drawings of activity in the cars and stations of the Seventh Avenue Local (10/5/29:20–21). As early as 1927, however, the New Yorker supported his interest in lower-class subjects. "Eighth Avenue Subway" featured the massive public works project, with men like ants engaged in various forms of physical labor (6/11/27:10–11). "Death Ave" portrayed Hell's Kitchen with grotesque imagery: the locomotive belches smoke as it bears down on a horse in the way while men lounge dejectedly about the margins or congregate in aimless groups in the foreground. Two women look stricken as they run across the street away from smiling men who have evidently harassed them; a trainman with a stop flag, who might in a less-chaotic world exert some control, stands by his hut two columns and larger psychic distance from the activity he aims to direct (11/5/27:10–11). Whereas Helen Hokinson's "Library Fauna" (6/9/28:12–13) found amusement in readers' concentration and frustrations (her largest drawing shows a group of readers staring at the book indicator "Waiting to be told that whatever they want is not to be found"), Marsh's "N. Y. Public Library" shows diverse men and women intent on their individual tasks (9/21/29:20–21). Not surprisingly, Marsh's version of the Florida "Talk" layout—a quasi-annual feature—depicts train, track, smoke, and a desolate landscape, reducing rich tourists to a very small size and satirizing their talk—"Hot, ain't it?" "Yeah, but that's what we're down here for"—as empty (2/15/30:14–15).

Marsh's layouts provided contrast in setting and tone to the upscale norm of Aladjalov's tableaus arresting activity at "The Southampton Beach Club" (8/10/29:12–13) and "Columbia University" (10/19/29:26–27). In contrast to explorations of local color by Harvey, Hokinson, and Lebrun, however, and unlike Aladjalov's jokey caricatures, Marsh's renderings of the local scene shaded over into social satire and critique. Thus their dark tones and busy crayon lines.

Layouts' comic reports on *New Yorkers*' activities confirm W. J. T. Mitchell's assertion that verbal and graphic representation differ "by a history of practical differences in the use of different sorts of symbolic marks, not by a metaphysical divide" (69). *New Yorker* editors and staff considered many ideas "available" (to use their editorial euphemism) for rendering in either art or word. In 1930 E. B. White queried "Mrs. White" (as he called her professionally) about an idea that he received for "Talk" asking, "Better as picture?"[37] More important, after 1928 "Talk" transcended the metaphysical divide between image and text. Editors conceptualized "Talk" as a single space composed of text and images. Graphics asserted their equality through the devices of the bleed, by which borderless drawings come close to the text, and the wraparound, by which images impose upon and steal textual space.

Tweaking the Formula

As the twenties ended, "Talk" stayed bold through controversial topics. White's "Birth-Control Hearing" not only acknowledged that "Sex is scary"—thus summing up the attitudes of spectators and prosecutors in Margaret Sanger's trial for illegally dispensing a contraceptive device—but also identified the limits of free speech: "There are things you can tell in the State of New York, there are things you can't. Mum's the word." Yet he concentrated on ironies rather than outrage, noting that the trial brought "the germ of life" to court but could not affect it; hence "Life went on" (5/4/29:14–15). On the other hand, White's cocky description of the Great Crash as "a fat land quivering in paunchy fright" would surely have given way to a more somber metaphor had anyone understood that, unlike the summer thunderstorm, it would not blow over by morning (N&C 11/2/29:17). "Talk" left substantive discussions of Wall Street's problems to "Behind the News," commenting only when discerning some little amusement in them—as when "Ticker News" noted how "the Great Days in Wall Street spread their effects in ever-widening circles" and trolley conductors and motormen check the latest market reports when passengers bring newspapers aboard (11/9/29:20). White's "Comment" just before Christmas noted the stoicism of the "*nouveau* poor," criticized them for adopting the elevated posture of "the shabby genteel"—an undeserved set of airs—and then zapped a comic reversal: "Nobody is going to high-hat us just because he happens not to have a cent" (12/21/29:17). This joke underlines two facts about "Talk" at the end of volume 5. First, the *New Yorker's* financial success insulated its staff from the Crash. In addition, social humor often runs to the edge of good taste.

The limits of good taste in the twenties are restrictive by today's practices. The sudden spate of Wall Street jokes, a dark strand of humor, led White to shake his head over the "melancholy prospect" that new the humorists of tomorrow would cut their teeth on it (12/28/29:9), though that very issue featured lots of money and stock market humor. Gossip caused discomfort to some celebrities named in "Talk." Five years after her cabaret piece brought notoriety to the magazine, former debutante Ellin Mackay Berlin, now married to composer Irving Berlin, sent a handwritten letter to Ross confessing, "It makes me very uncomfortable to know that my casual gossip can so easily find its way into print."[38] Ross declined her request for the names of his informants.[39] More important, he did not apologize to her, nor did he retract an item from May 25, 1929, disclosing that Milton Cross used a speechwriter. After investigating the complaint, Ross offered to run Cross's complaint letter but defended the story as a "plausible and, moreover, harmless" tale from a reliable source. He extended a token "regret" for the embarrassment but insisted with pride, "We rarely make mistakes."[40] "Talk" humor began in facts and opinion but ended in stylistic precision.

As White himself put it in his notes on the history of the *New Yorker*, "to Ross, if you can't write, your opinions are of no consequence."[41] Ross acknowledged White's leadership both at the time and later. "Benchley says you are the only writer that will make him laugh out loud when alone," Ross reported after an April 1929 party for Dorothy Parker. "He said that you were not only the best humorous writer of the day, but the greatest man of the day. I had never thought of this before, but I think it is so."[42] White summed up his own and the department's accomplishments with appropriate comic modesty in "Talk" itself. Observing that the magazine had acquired sufficient caché to inspire a sandwich (an open-faced spread of Roquefort and cream cheese toasted under the broiler and topped with bacon and paprika—its developers hoped the combination would "appeal, as your publication, to the sophisticated"), White ponders "just how far we've really come with this magazine": "Five long years of hard plugging," he muses, "and when finally a sandwich is created in our image; it hasn't so much as a bit of roast beef inside it. Just a bunch of cheese" (11/9/29:17).

This bit of self-deprecation points out how any magazine, but especially a humor magazine, must repeatedly reinvent itself to remain fresh to its readers. The braggart invites deflation. In nineteenth-century American humor, that job went to the yarn spinner's audience, the implied listener or frame narrator who voiced suspicions about "stretchers." Once deposed from his pedestal, the braggart loses his comic authority. Probably for this reason, Mark Twain abandoned the four poses of superiority he used early in his career—the Gentleman, the Sentimentalist, the Instructor, the Moralist—for poses of inferiority such as the Sufferer, the Simpleton, and the Tenderfoot (Gerber). These postures allow the self-deprecating humorist to confer superiority on the reader—a more durable comic strategy for Twain. It also suited the *New Yorker*. In adopting a modest inferiority to its readers every time it took account of itself, "Talk" reasserted a rhetoric that flattered the peer society. Through its editorial process and rhetoric, however, most of "Talk" promoted a view of readers and writers and artists in a joint endeavor. Ross joined himself equally with them in a process that White eulogized in his draft, though not in print, as a seriocomic endeavor: "Ross set up a great target and raised a tremendous hue and cry in an attempt to hit it in the middle. He dreamed of a magazine that would be good, and funny, and fair."[43] In the process, the snobbish voice of Van Bibber III, who inaugurated "Talk," gave way to the inside humor of peers, jointly creating and enjoying a comic view of New York.

CHAPTER 4

Comic Art

More Than Meets the Eye

Cultural historians who offer explanations for this sudden flowering of the New Yorker *cartoon seem to share an owlish tone, and cite the same roster of names and sources in their accounting. . . . I can't disagree, but I have a different conclusion: I think it was a miracle.*

Roger Angell

It is a truth universally acknowledged that the *New Yorker* pioneered the modern gag cartoon, but exactly what the achievement entailed has been much less clear. The *New Yorker* did promote witty one-line captions to replace traditional two-line illustrated jokes, but it did not invent the one-liner, contrary to claims by *New Yorker* historians such as Dale Kramer (129) and Janet Flanner (12) or cartoon historians such as Stephen Becker (149). The first modern one-liners antedate the *New Yorker* by at least three years, and in any case, the number of lines in the caption quite misses the point: some of the most beloved *New Yorker* cartoons have had two lines, such as Carl Rose's famous spinach cartoon (12/8/28:27), while a whole genre of narrative cartoons lacked captions altogether. M. Thomas Inge correctly points out that the *New Yorker* innovated by making the image, not words, the comic focus, but he errs in following Kramer's conclusion that the results stemmed from Ross's fetish over knowing "Where am I in this picture?" and "Who's talking?" (111). The nearly six-thousand comic graphics published in volumes 1–5 make clear the *New Yorker*'s distinct innovations: it created a new kind of captioned cartoon by uniting image and text in a comic relation of irony or literalism, and it redirected visual humor from the theme to the lines and shapes composing the picture. In the process, the *New Yorker* shifted the role of comic art from representation—an accompaniment to a verbal joke—to expression, in keeping with the modernist manifesto of art for art's sake, even for play.

The *New Yorker* fostered this achievement because its several varieties of comic art attracted fine artists as well as illustrators during a time when commercial markets shrank from the combined pressures of photography and media mergers in the 1920s. At least six other genres joined the cartoon in expressing the *New Yorker*'s visual sense of humor: (1) illustrations of text, especially the naïve illustrations of "The Talk of the Town," (2) caricatures in various "fact" departments, including "Profiles," theatrical reviews, and sports, (3) covers, (4) local color spreads known as "covering art" or "layouts," (5) small, "spot" illustrations, and—the most innovative type—(6) drawings made comic by their layout on the page. Cartoons have dominated discussion because *New Yorker Album* series and artists' own anthologies have kept them in the public eye, while other genres remained buried in the pages of the magazine. Anthologies emphasize timeless and easily reproduced graphic forms over the four-color covers, text-related graphics, and time-linked jokes that show the *New Yorker* at its liveliest. But anthologies' efficiencies (reducing three thousand gag cartoons to a hundred-plus) have skewed understanding of the weekly magazine.[1] Taken together, the many genres of visual humor in the *New Yorker* show that when humor "infected everything," as E. B. White put it, humor penetrated even the white space on the page.

Ross promised such variety and intensity of visual humor in his Prospectus, and made good on it by naming Rea Irvin (1881–1972), then at *Life,* art director. In contrast to the famous profile of Eustace Tilley, Irvin kept his own quite low. No one has recorded exactly when he arrived in New York to try his hand at acting after working as a staff artist for the *Honolulu Advertiser* and other newspapers (Horn 317), and sources differ on what Ross paid him for the part-time job of choosing cartoons and other art—either seventy-five dollars per week plus stock (Kramer, *Ross* 69) or eighty dollars total, half in stock (Lorenz, *Art* 15). But everyone agrees that Rea Irvin understood better than anyone exactly what the *New Yorker* aimed to achieve.

Irvin gave the *New Yorker* its graphic signatures. Not its most prolific artist (Peter Arno, Barbara Shermund, Julian De Miskey, Helen Hokinson, and Alan Dunn, in that order, all published more cartoons, covers, and illustrations than

Irvin in the first five years[2]), Irvin designed the *New Yorker*'s typeface, drew its chief department headers, determined its page design, and chaired the art meeting—all as a part-timer who came to the office once a week. Irvin's personal style also dominated the book. For the first volume alone, Irvin drew 10 of 52 covers, along with 14 cartoons (6 as full pages), and a host of department headings. His creativity during the *New Yorker*'s first five years enabled him to supervise its art acquisitions, produce commercial drawings, continue publishing in *Life,* try his hand at a color comic for the Sunday *New York Herald Tribune* (Blackbeard and Williams 79, 82), and still contribute 45 covers (17 percent), 91 cartoons (16 of them multi-image graphic narratives), and illustrations for 22 stories and fact pieces in the *New Yorker*. Irvin also picked up the ball from artists who dropped it. When E. B. White submitted an idea for a twelve-scene narrative cartoon with the hope that Gluyas Williams would execute it, Angell sent Williams the outline with the committee's suggested improvements,[3] but when the two-page "No Fork, or Catching The Waiter's Eye" finally appeared seven months later (7/13/29:14–15), Irvin had drawn it.

Creating the dandy who personified the *New Yorker* on its first cover stands among Irvin's most significant work for the magazine. Named "Eustace Tilley" by Corey Ford, Irvin's dandy graced every anniversary issue from 1925 to 1998; without comment, editor Remnick replaced him with a cover celebrating New York City landmarks for the seventy-fourth anniversary issue in 1999 (2/22 & 3/1/99). Irvin originally planned the inaugural cover to depict a theater curtain rising over New York's city lights—a suitable metaphor for the magazine's performance of urban drama—but at the last minute Ross asked for a design that "would make the subscribers feel that we've been in business for years and know our way around" (Kramer, *Ross* 64; Lorenz, *Art* 14). Irvin's cover may have reflected the influence of the *Chap-Book*, a humorous miscellany whose first cover featured a similar figure; the *San Francisco Examiner* reviewed the magazine when it appeared in 1894, when Irvin was a teenager there (Blair and Hill 380–81). More intriguing, the *Chap-Book* popularized the artwork of Toulouse-Lautrec and other Europeans blending commercial and fine art into the poster (Lupton and Miller 181), the genre that became the *New Yorker* cover. Whatever his origin, however, Irvin's dandy descended from the same top-hatted comic "disreputables" as Simon Suggs, the roughneck who metamorphosed into the more respectable Uncle Sam during World War I (Blair and Hill). The process urbanized a traditional folk antihero and pushed him up the social ladder, making the representative *New Yorker* an object of humor and a figure of dignity.

As a personification of the magazine, the dandy helped establish the *New Yorker* as the companion of fashionable New Yorkers. Not coincidentally, the August 8, 1925, issue that identified Irvin's dandy as Corey Ford's Eustace Tilley in "The Making of a Magazine" also carried on the back cover a house ad, drawn by H. O. Hofman, of a stylish young woman reading the inaugural *New Yorker* while a couple in the background plays golf. The angular, geometric style of Hofman's drawing and the woman's chair characterize *New Yorker* readers as up-to-date and identify Irvin's dandy as the quintessential image of the magazine, an ironic symbol of contemporary sophistication.

The Inside Story

Cartoons and covers were chosen at the art meeting. One artist called it "the Tuesday inquisition,"[4] and it apparently made Ross as nervous as his contributors: Spud Johnson joked that a typical meeting consisted of Ross rearranging desks and exhorting staff to "'be playful in makeup,'" before he finally "Vetoes two covers that were commissioned, [and] Okehs one cartoon for 'Comment.'"[5] The rejection rate meant that only prolific contributors kept checks rolling in, and as late as 1969, when Alan Dunn had already published more than three thousand cartoons in the magazine, he still worked around the clock on Mondays to assemble an ample portfolio.[6] Submissions went without screening to the committee, whose sense of humor joined the artists' in shaping the magazine's. Originally consisting of Irvin, Ross, and Philip Wylie, the group expanded in the fall of 1925 to include Katharine Angell. No one seems to have replaced Wylie after he left the magazine in March of 1927 (Lorenz, *Art* 16; Keefer 35), but archival evidence shows that Scudder Middleton stepped in for Angell during a leave of absence in the spring and summer of 1929. From the artist's standpoint, portfolio submission acknowledged that most ideas would fail, while bringing acceptance, rejection, and payment together in the same envelope. From the art meeting's standpoint, portfolio submission meant reviewing hundreds of drawings each Tuesday. By 1934, with the depression and mergers restricting outlets for cartoons, the magazine received submissions of six hundred to a thousand drawings every week, and one week had three thousand (Ingersoll, "*New Yorker*" 90).

The art meeting dispensed three verdicts: accept (with payment and perhaps a request for minor revision of the caption), reject (with explanation to discourage resubmission of the same or similar items), revise (with specific recommendations or objections). In addition to fully rendered works, the art meeting also evaluated art ideas in various states for assignment to artists. Assignments resulted when appealing ideas came from amateur artists or "idea men" (often professional gag writers); the $10 payment for the idea came off the artist's fee. Artists need not accept assignments, however, even if submitted with them in mind.

Most submissions were rejected. During the 1920s most issues contained a dozen cartoons, two or three caricatures, a few small decorations, and six or eight text-related illustrations. The vague dismissals of 1925 became by 1929 frank reports of the art meeting's acquisition policies. "We heartlessly turn down ideas which are good, but which we consider outside our field," Ross wrote Bruce Bairnsfather, returning two of three submissions by his British colleague from *Stars and Stripes*. The field—which Ross defined as "topical journalistic value" and "what goes on in town"[7]—explains the magazine's most infamous rejection: James Thurber's drawing of a seal, submitted by E. B. White with the caption "Hm. Explorers!" As usually told, the story accuses Irvin of failing to appreciate Thurber's artistic sensibility: the item, rejected because the seal's whiskers went the wrong way, came back with White's insistence, "This is the way a Thurber seal's whiskers go" (Kramer, *Ross* 203). More likely the problem was that seals are not a New York species. Except at the start, the art meeting stuck with the topical and metropolitan during the first five years; Thurber's first *New Yorker* cartoon appeared just after the end of this period, in 6:1 (2/22/30), as the magazine entered a less restrictive phase.

Ross included a check for Bairnsfather's third drawing with the two rejected ones; thus one envelope sealed the deal, softened disappointment, and transformed criticism of rejected ideas into advice for future success. This strategy also gave the editor the upper hand in determining price, an important matter because the *New Yorker* paid less than its competitors. Payment on acceptance discouraged negotiation over price and challenged artists to let quantity and speed replace the quality of each payment. But money did not drive acquisitions: no bargain price would tempt the committee to purchase inappropriate material, such as four covers commissioned by but unacceptable to *Vanity Fair*.[8] On the other hand, they passed up items very definitely the *New Yorker* type that duplicated art on hand.[9]

These cornerstones of the *New Yorker*'s art policy, prompt attention by the art meeting and payment on acceptance, persuaded artists to give the *New Yorker* their best work, and rewarded those who hit the mark. The policy attracted not only commercial artists such as Helen Hokinson but also aspiring fine artists such as Alan Dunn, who abandoned his career as a painter, despite a fellowship from the Tiffany Foundation, because "one a week in [the *New Yorker*] means a living wage and publicity to break in on other magazines."[10]

Early Visual Jokes

New Yorker staff and artists' first success in sharing a comic vision came in covers. Foremost was the visual sophistication implied by their nonverbal humor. When Wylie told artists, "Covers for the *New Yorker* are posters,"[11] he linked them to an important contemporary art form. *New Yorker* covers relied on an amusing topic or rendering, not an implied story. This focus differentiated the *New Yorker* from *Life* (which titled its covers), *Judge* (which used slapstick cartoons to announce the week's theme), and *Vanity Fair* (which tended toward the intellectual and the painterly).

Al Frueh's cover for the second issue introduced what became a staple contrast, borrowed from vaudeville, between large and small shapes. His two rotund policemen overflow their tiny vehicle (a cross between a velocipede and a golf cart), a visual joke repeated in the large golfer and little caddie of A. E. Wilson's cover for 1:13 (5/16/25), and Julian De Miskey's cover for the debutante season of a tall, skinny daughter and her short, fat mother (12/19/25). Geometric or thematic doubling often intensified the basic incongruity. Frueh has *two* big policemen aboard a tiny vehicle. De Miskey's mother and daughter both have bare shoulders and pale skin, dangling earrings, puffy muffs, dresses decorated with zigzags, and demure looks on their faces. H. O. Hofman depicts a gallery with two cubist nude paintings, small and large, each with a pair of perky red nipples holding the attention of his three spectators (2/27/26). In 1927 these jokes also ran inside the magazine in small spot illustrations breaking up large blocks of text, but on the cover visual jokes about contrasting pairs provided a rhetorical continuity that, along with New York settings and characters, explain why, as Gerald Weales observed, the *New Yorker* can "wear so many and such diverse faces and still manage always to look like itself" (510).

The comic contrast also encompassed incongruous doubles. Julian De Miskey's first cover pairs human lovebirds on a park bench with avian counterparts in the tree above (6/6/25); two years later he depicted a hairdresser giving a woman and her poodle, both in curlers, the same treatment (9/17/27). Bertrand Zadig's cover on the Scopes trial, similarly, symbolizes the descent of man with a wallpaper pattern of angels rising and apes climbing down the evolutionary ladder, its repeats and inversions expanding the association from a single man and ape to all humanity and animals (7/11/25). H. O. Hofman's zoo scene the next week shows humans and apes viewing each other through bars ambiguously placed to make the two groups equivalent (7/18/25). Religious and mythical subjects receive similar treatment: Pan playing his pipes for a bird and bunny (3/14/25), an angel wearing halo *cum* Easter bonnet (4/11/25).

More important to the theme of New York are covers that pair the personal and the public. Love scenes take place in public: with the skyline in the background (3/21/25), in the park (5/23/25), at a dance (6/6/25), at a soda shop (8/8/25), amid other cars with lovers (12/5/25). Individual figures appear against a backdrop of crowds (5/15/26), a sea of headlights (6/13/25), or confetti (3/7/25). Situating individuals within the city made humor from the isolation and alienation that Ortega identified in "The Dehumanization of Art" as the modernist vision.

Local scenes such as Ilonka Karasz's views of Columbus Circle (5/30/25) and Central Park (2/26/27) point out the limitations of the categories of *New Yorker* art suggested by Gerald Weales and Lee Lorenz. Weales separates cover artists into those who tell jokes and those who create settings (503), while Lorenz classifies them into illustrators such as Garrett Price and Carl Rose, satirists such as Gluyas Williams and Al Frueh, stylists such as Peter Arno and Helen Hokinson, and clowns such as John Held and Otto Soglow (Lorenz, *Art* 53). But both emphasize the artists rather than their work, in contrast to the categories developed by historians of American humor: humor of character, the earliest nineteenth-century narrative tradition in English; humor of place, or local color humor, which developed in the late nineteenth century to celebrate rural, regional customs at risk from rapid industrialization and national development; and humor of situation, a tradition from the late nineteenth century that became increasingly important in the twentieth. *New Yorker* covers merged these three categories into one, identifying distinctive characters as local types engaged in amusing local activities.

A variant of American literary realism focused on authentic regional settings, characters, and customs, local color humor has two distinct nineteenth-century traditions. Southern local color stories looked back at a simpler time, their nostalgia and folk fantasies tempered by scrupulous attention to dialect and other details, as in Joel Chandler Harris's Uncle Remus stories. In New England, however, as Josephine Donovan has shown, local color writing became a women's tradition promoting female-associated values of rural communitarian life over male-identified values of urban capitalism (7). These strands came together in *New Yorker* covers, which characterized the city as a small town governed like any rural area by season and custom, and which veered between individuals and crowds.

The results gave a comic viewpoint to realistic and fantasy scenes. Frueh's cops might have come from Boston or Chicago, but the skyline in Carl Fornaro's cover of March 21, 1925, could only signify Manhattan—viewed from its best vantage point, across the river in Brooklyn, an irony much enjoyed by residents of the outer boroughs. From the start, springtime and summer scenes allowed annual events—the Easter parade, Saratoga races, Christmas, even the opening of the opera season and the annual auto show—to bring predictable rhythms to the year. The best of these scenes combined geographical realism and seasonal details, as in the first of Ilonka Karasz's many covers grounded in local color humor, pairing a red tulip on a windowsill with red rooftops (4/4/25). This scene links tulip-colored buildings with a conventional sign of spring, and typifies her vision of the city as a gay, exciting place where the natural and built worlds co-exist—in the waters off Coney Island (7/4/25), the grass of Battery Park (8/14/26), the train running through Riverside Park (9/24/27), even in Times Square, where crowds fill the street (3/10/28). Present from the earliest issues of the magazine, covers' local color humor explains the proud claim, despite bleak advertising and circulation figures in August of 1925, "to date, we feel that our covers have been consistently good."[12]

Other art had a rockier start. Local color "Talk" spreads stopped for six months beginning in mid-July 1925 despite such funny, appropriate scenes as the writhing bodies of Reginald Marsh's "Safe and Sane Fourth" (7/4/25:2–3) and the narrow shape reiterating the topic of Peggy Bacon's "Sunday on the Coney Island Boardwalk" (7/18/25:2–3). In the spring of 1925, cartoon representations of the elite seemed particularly flat compared to the lively, middle-class population of Frueh's cartoons, such as the antics featured in the burlesque newspaper-collage, "Gay Undergraduate Days at the New Police Academy" (5/16/25:5). Elegant characters seemed more dead, and less funny, than the men in Hans Stengel's hilarious "One of Our Clubs on the Avenue Arranges Its Spring Window Display": ancient club members being artfully positioned—with hooks to keep them upright—by a window dresser (4/11/25:6). By contrast, the illustrated jokes by *Judge* cartoonists Gardner Rea, Donald McKee, and Gilbert Wilkinson, like Eldon Kelley's elegantly dressed figures, offered little

Co-operation

Al Frueh, 2/21/25:2.

amusement. The first advisory letter to art contributors, sent out when Ross still expected a mid-January debut, solicited "cartoons with a snap, local or national, and . . . humorous drawings, [especially] those with a smart, or rather a metropolitan, setting,"[13] but in the spring of 1925 cartoons had much the same failing as "The Talk of the Town": they lacked a tone as sophisticated as the journalistic topics the *New Yorker* covered and the audience it sought.

As cover art transferred local color humor from verbal to graphic humor, so *New Yorker* cartoons eventually moved comic irony from the caption into the visual text. But only three cartoons succeeded in the first month. The decidedly urban characters and New York scenes of Al Frueh's "Cooperation" and Wallace Morgan's "The Bread Line," both in the first issue, and Donald McKee's "We-el, that's not so bad," in the fourth, invited readers to enjoy local ironies. Accompanying the editor's tale of woe with Jumbo Jr., "Co-operation" depicts a train carrying a frumpy, nearsighted businessman who, trying to see out the window, uses his handkerchief to wipe it and thus unwittingly fulfills the injunction in the sign posted nearby: "HELP US KEEP THE 'L' AND SUBWAY CLEAN" (2/21/25:2). The ink drawing's firm outlines and white spaces reinforce its theme of tidiness as they emphasize the action of the figure, whose lunch bucket and submissiveness twit his middle-class status. Class jokes of a different sort structure Morgan's two-page centerfold, "The Bread Line," which compares the clients of charity bread lines with the stylishly dressed young women waiting for their escorts in the hallway outside a hotel dining room (2/21/25:16–17). The title puts these wealthy young women in the same state of economic dependence as dispossessed men, despite the social distance between them, and Morgan's ink-washed crayon-sketch in the style of fashion advertisements hints that only money differentiates them. For its part, McKee's cartoon contrasts class extremes more explicitly as a well-dressed older couple decides to "take a chance" on a cabbie whose prison record replaces the rate card posted at the door (3/14/25:17). The local dimension of these cartoons not only announced the magazine's subject and viewpoint to audience and advertisers but also reinforced the hometown feeling essential to local color humor. All three capitalized on inside jokes—the grime of industrial America, the economic challenges for women in the peer society, and the complicated, non-uniform rates of New York taxis. The interdependence of text and image as a vehicle for irony became the *New Yorker*'s trademark, but the success of just three among several dozen drawings emphasizes that the art committee took some time to recognize what they wanted and then help artists achieve it.

From Decoration to Illustration

Uncertainty about *New Yorker* cartoon humor ended in the summer of 1925, about the same time that the art meeting dropped Marsh's local color spreads. "The art in THE NEW YORKER has been leaning toward the decorative rather than the illustrative," began an undated contributors' advisory letter, probably from early June of 1925, as the editorial staff refined its formula for the intensive fall advertising and circulation push. "Henceforth we want to tend definitely toward making our art *illustrative of ideas*."[14] Despite the contradiction of "tend definitely toward," the editors moved swiftly to guide artists to understand idea drawings, insisting at the end of June, "We want character stuff, with a situation."[15] By August 1, editors took artists' awareness of the new direction for granted as they spelled out the desire for "plausible situations with smart backgrounds" and declared, "We do not want preposterous, custard pie situations. The test ought to be, could this have happened."[16] Smart subjects and values entered the magazine most vividly when Peter Arno and Helen Hokinson began contributing early in the summer of 1925, but Al Frueh, John Held, and Gardner Rea led the way in making comic ideas central to their art.

Judging by numbers of drawings published, the new preference for idea drawings made Al Frueh's work particularly important in the summer of 1925. He published some thirty idea drawings in the magazine by the end of the first summer, most of them using multiple images. Some were captioned narrative cartoons, such as the three frames of "The Liberal Modernists Open Their Own Speakeasy" (5/2/25:5); some, pantomime (uncaptioned) narratives, such as the thirty-four frames of a wild goose chase concluding with the confession, "My son, there isn't any Santa Claus" (6/13/25:11–13); and some, non-narrative layouts or collages, such as "When 'You Can't Win' Crime Ads Become Prevalent," which extends *ad absurdum* the ironic idea that one person's loss is another's gain (5/23/25:5). Frueh studied in Paris with Henri Matisse, whose influence shows in Frueh's naïve lines and open shapes, emphasizing broad comic conception over subtle details.

This style adapted easily to the single-panel idea drawing, and Frueh led the way in local color cartoon series. A drawing from late April, "One That Mayor Hylan Hasn't Thought of Yet" capitalized on an inside joke among New Yorkers, though outsiders could also appreciate it: as they carry the occupants of a burning building down the ladder, firemen wear signs advertising, "This lucky lady [or man] is being rescued by MAYOR HYLAN's firemen" (4/25/25:5). The idea grew into a series, "Mayor Hylan's People's Concerts," a few weeks later, shortly after the editors announced the shift toward idea drawings. The series ran in the ten summer issues from June 27 to September 5 crediting the mayor for various urban sounds: birds chirping (6/27/25:1), sanitation workers throwing trash cans (7/4/25:10), peddlers announcing their arrival (7/11/25:13, 8/1/25:7), drunks carousing on street corners (8/22/25:4), even a father picking up his screaming infant during the night (9/5/25:2). Though specifically local, the silly situations do not veer off into political satire. The Mayor Hylan series takes more pleasure in celebrating city life and the artist's imagination than in chastising the mayor.

Or in flattering the rich. The absence of "smart" backgrounds and characters in these drawings identifies middle- and lower-class New Yorkers as the quintessential urbanites. Frueh's characters frequent the subway, not cabarets, and live in small apartments, not townhouses; even his comment on evolution, "700,000 Years of Progress" (7/25/25:5), compares an ape with a less-than-dashing straphanger. Any ideology his drawings advance ignores the activities of the peer society in favor of the pleasures and frustrations of rather frumpy, mostly middle-aged characters—an antithesis of stylishness that Brendan Gill saw in Frueh himself, who despite his Greenwich Village address, was "village-like, not Village-like" (197).

The early ideas contributed by John Held Jr. also ignored smart people and places. Best known for his flat, abstract flapper drawings for *Judge* (imitated by Benito and Fish for *Vanity Fair*), Held gave the *New Yorker* a series of distinctly different items: woodcuts of old folk songs in an old graphic style. The technique garnered enough interest for a show at the Brown-Robertson Gallery in October 1923, and *Vanity Fair* instructed reader in its modernist virtues as technique (76). Irvin and Ross liked them enough to run seventy-seven of these prints during the *New Yorker*'s first five years; they became his signature style for the magazine, much as his round-headed Betty Coed and Joe College became his signatures for *Judge*. Just five woodcuts appeared in the four months before the *New Yorker* announced its commitment to idea drawings: all ran within a period of seven weeks, beginning with "The Rumrunner's Sister-in-Law" (4/11/25:5) and ending with "The Shot-Gun Wedding" (5/30/25:5).[17] Beginning in late August, however, as the magazine readied its formula for the fall push, eleven more woodcuts appeared in as many weeks, and after a break in mid-November, six more by the end of volume 1 in February—a pattern indicating that Held and the art meeting increasingly saw eye to eye.

Held's woodcuts contributed to *New Yorker* humor more than the "freshness" that his biographer Shelley Armitage has observed (171). Her claim that they offered a view of contemporary America as an ironic reflection of the Gilded Age—"destroy[ing] the validity of the past by taking its rosily viewed situations and values to ironic task" (171)—sums up implications of the folk materials and situations he chose, but magazine readers would probably not piece together such a coherent theme from items published individually week by week, as opposed to prints in book collections such as *The Wages of Sin and Other Victorian Joys and Sorrows* (1931), on which Armitage based her analysis. More important, some of the magazine images differ from those republished in book form: The *New Yorker*'s version of "Johnny and Frankie Were Lovers," for example, lacks the book version's explicit sexuality—and the nipple winking dead-center on Frankie's breast (11/14/25:5; Held 19). The books, moreover, print

John Held, Jr. 5/30/25:5.

each image alone, framed by the white space of the page as well as by the black frame of the wood block, whereas the magazine set Held's images against a margin and marked at least one edge (usually two) by text. In this reading environment, featuring one image at a time, Held's idea drawings gave the *New Yorker* a humor of anachronism, built on tension between content and context.

Indeed, all of Held's *New Yorker* woodcuts play with the ironic relation between the modern urban life represented by (and elsewhere *in*) the magazine—down to its modernistic sans serif typeface—and the self-conscious archaism of the prints themselves. Individual plates offered their own humor. Given the intensity of the love between "Johnny and Frankie," their frozen positions in the print has the kind of irony that Wallace Stevens identified in Keats's "Grecian Urn": these lovers will never get their kiss, despite their passion, comically symbolized by the woodstove burning between them (its kettle seems ready to whistle). Held's reworked lyric for the second line of the caption, "OHO MY GOD . .

HOW THEY LOVED!," has a salacious leer to it, all the more amusing in light of the unrequitable passion in the print. Held puts the rigid lines of the woodcut to comic use in most of these prints. Arresting their motion makes the characters look foolish. The technique works especially well in "Love Comes to the Paper-hanger," where a workman sits perched on a ladder, wallpaper in one hand and paste brush in another, ready to be knocked onto the floor as soon as his sweetheart opens the door (9/5/25:5). This kind of literalism is quite different from the irony of Held's earlier "Shot-Gun Wedding," which greets an illegitimate birth with death images: the minister looks like the Grim Reaper, the bride stands Madonna-like with her child, and the bridegroom and her brother (he looks too young to be her father) look like West Point regulars (5/30/25:5). Held's reversal of the song lyrics "Frankie and Johnnie were lovers" into his "Johnny and Frankie" parallels other comic reversals in the print and points up the intellectual nature of idea humor.

The comic anachronism of Held's block prints intensified through the first fall and winter. By the end of volume 1, Held began calling even more attention to anachronism by referring to contemporary incidents and inscribing the date—usually with one numeral backwards—on his plate. "Back Scratching at the Algonquin" featured eight unidentifiable men scratching each other's backs while seated at a round table—an unmistakable reference to the Round Tablers—with the annotation, "FROM AN OLD ENGRAVING BY JOHN HELD JR MADE IN 1–26," a ridiculous claim for a print published five weeks into the year (2/6/26:16). Three weeks later he repeated the joke in "Whisker Inspection at the Century Club," which made fun of his own New York club, still notable today for its literary membership, by portraying the members as centenarians and adding below the title, "INDEED A QUAINT OLD ENGRAVING BY JOHN HELD JR 1926" (2/27/26:18).

These ironic references to time reinforce the modern qualities of Held's woodcuts. His rigid lines not only abstract form but also freeze motion even as they imply it. Combined with this graphic irony, the captions' textual ironies connect Held's art with the modern topics of the *New Yorker*'s text. But not all readers liked these works, even several years into their run. A 1929 reader complained, "Everybody I know thinks the *New Yorker* has the best cartoons and humorous illustrations ever published . . . Why spoil your record with John Held's stuff?" The answer, that "they are distinctly a part of the present day art which goes to make up our magazine,"[18] explains the editorial commitment to fine comic art, rather than newspaper cartooning.

"My Man, There's a Fly in the Room"

One of the earliest idea drawings, by Gardner Rea, in a new style notable for its white space. 6/27/25:11.

Frueh's and Held's early idea drawings could hardly differ more in style or subject, yet their work shared a key element of the *New Yorker* idea drawing: an ironic relationship between image and text. Irvin evidently admired this comic vein, considering his role in choosing and promoting it, but his own *New Yorker* art seldom employed it. Irvin contributed only three cartoons before the fall campaign—"Brother, thy tail hangs down behind" (6/6/25:1), "The Rise and Fall of Man" (6/6/25:3), and "As It Might Have Been In the Beginning" (6/27/25:5)—all related to the Scopes trial, none particularly ironic. Even as his

Indignant Side-Show Proprietor: Yeah, lot you care 'bout the gettin' on in life! Ten kids and not a decent freak in the lot!

MADAME BARBINE /

In an earlier issue, Rea used the busier style of his illustrated jokes for *Judge*. 4/25/25:22.

New Yorker art expanded to include idea drawings and narrative cartoons, Irvin's humor avoided irony in favor of comic literalism. Both his *New Yorker* drawing of "Tomato Surprise" (10/10/25:11) and an earlier drawing for *Life*, "The Skeptics' Society: They Investigate the Theory that Too Many Cooks Spoil the Broth" (10/25/23:7; see p.39), show his preference for the straightforward rather than ironic comic idea.

The *New Yorker*'s shift from decoration to illustration required the art committee to identify artists who could imagine and execute comic ideas. This difficult process lasted well into the magazine's second year and continued through volume 3, but Lee Lorenz exaggerates in claiming that the *New Yorker* lacked real cartoons until the end of 1927 (*Art* 37). In fact, other artists joined Held and Frueh in launching idea drawings during the spring and summer of 1925. Gardner Rea led the outer circle of freelancers in making the transition from illustrated jokes; his style changed from the detailed compositions of his *Judge* drawings and earliest *New Yorker* work to a more visually open and amusing style of curvy outlined shapes and comically used white space. Rea's first drawing in this new style, "My Man, There's a Fly in the Room," ridiculed the demands of the rich through a series of visual contrasts: between the vast spaces of the room and the size of the single occupant, his overstuffed chair dwarfed by the high ceilings and fat columns, between the size of the room and the fly (invisible) that

Ralph Barton's burlesque illustrated newspaper supplement in the early *New Yorker* acquired local faces. *Judge*, 2/23/24:12.

bothers him, between the huge capacity of the room and its minimal contents, between the speaker's complaint and his spectator's posture (6/27/25:11). Although Rea's illustrated jokes continued to appear for some weeks, following "My Man" he made comic use of space a central idea of his cartoons, and turned his attention from the lower-class figures of his earlier drawings toward club members and other "smart" characters.

Another set of visual jokes emerged from the *New Yorker*'s policy of illustrating fact departments with caricatures instead of photographs or portraits. Perhaps because the policy automatically brought humor to illustration, an early strand of *New Yorker* humor twitted this policy and satirized its journalistic background. The earliest examples, brought over by Ralph Barton from *Judge*, burlesqued newspaper photography by substituting caricatures for photos—first in "The Graphic Section," which ran for four weeks in August of 1925 (1:24–1:27); then in "The Inquiring Reporter," which ran for the next five weeks, until the end of September (9/26/25); and finally "Heroes of the Week," which ran almost weekly until March 20, 1926.[19] The joke had enough appeal that Barton sold a similar page (perhaps *New Yorker* rejects) to *Life* in November ("News in Pictures," 11/26/25:15), but the art meeting seems to have particularly enjoyed this kind of the comic reversal, substituting one graphic image for another.

Variations on the theme created visual jokes from wrong, inappropriate, or irrelevant illustrations. Staff made such jokes a staple of house advertising, as in the mock-contest announcement, "see Wilkes-Barre . . . for Nothing," featuring a photograph identified as "The River Common" but actually the Roman Coliseum (4/11/25:21). Incongruity between image and text grew even more emphatic after Julian De Miskey took over "Talk" illustrations, beginning with the issue of May 29, 1926. The joke spilled over into illustrated fiction too. James Thurber had yet to arrive when the Wilkes-Barre ad ran, but four years later his "Two Ships Bring Americans of Note and English Author" illustrated his vignettes of six individuals with just two photos printed three times each (6/8/29:18)—head shots of mannequins from White's Sterling Finny 1927 house ad series. The occasional uncomic historical illustration, such as the etchings by Thomas Nast accompanying an installment of Russel Crouse's "That Was New York" (10/27/28:40–44), also sustained this rather cerebral strain of graphic incongruity. As improved technologies made photography cheaper and more familiar, the *New Yorker*'s drawings appeared more comically eccentric. Thus they reinforced Held's humor of anachronism.

The arrival of Peter Arno and Helen Hokinson in early summer accelerated the shift from decoration to illustration. Rea and Barton visualized comic ideas, but Arno and Hokinson populated them with the peer society, whose absence from *Life, Judge,* and *Vanity Fair* brought a fresh look to the *New Yorker*. Arno and Hokinson's enduring reputation as the quintessential *New Yorker* cartoonists reflects not only the number of drawings they contributed but also their leadership in characterizing the peer society in them.

Arno debuted first, with a small, wide drawing of an elegantly dressed couple crossing the street in the issue of June 20, 1925 (6); two weeks later, in the July 4 issue, Helen E. Hokinson's first matron graced the opening page of "Talk." Either Arno or Hokinson, and frequently both, appeared in most issues from mid-

Peter Arno, debut drawing, 6/20/25:6.

June through August. Both had an eye for the local scene already the focus of Frueh's series, a welcome relief from the overdose of drawings about evolution and the Scopes trial. More important, both artists preferred the drawing to speak for itself. Neither Arno nor Hokinson had a talent for inventing captions (both eventually used partners for ideas and text), but each contributed distinct visual ideas that shaped the *New Yorker*'s sense of humor.

An uncaptioned drawing contrasting the elegant couple in evening dress with the crude pair of youths loitering under a street light, Arno's first contribution featured the stylish figures that soon became his—and the *New Yorker*'s— trademark. The composition makes the class contrast funny by inverting the pairs' social importance: the happy, cultured couple walks in the background, apparently moving toward the loiterers in the foreground. The art committee began buying his work in profusion. Four more of Arno's cartoons appeared by the end of August, all populated by smart people, all displaying "situations," and all placed in the front of the book; two appeared on page 1 with "Talk." By September 5 the magazine was publishing two Arno cartoons a week, a pattern that continued through 1929, when appearances dropped to one a week. But his prime traits as a cartoonist showed even in the fall of 1925: he had a hard time coming up with ideas, an easy time executing them. Most of his cartoons featured the same top-hatted elegant man ranging about town, sometimes with women, sometimes with other men, as sociable as he is attractive and successful. Some repetition reinforced Arno's themes, but others just repeated them. His cartoon of August 29 depicted a situation repeated three years later as the cover for September 15, 1928: when a collision between a taxi and a chauffeured sedan inspires the cabbie to outrage, the chauffeur and the other adults signal the cab-

One of the neighbors drops in at the Neighborhood Playhouse.

Like other *New Yorker* cartoonists, Peter Arno satirized racism, here also combined with class prejudice. 6/5/26:19.

bie, with fingers on their lips, not to shout obscenities in front of the child sitting with them. With their abundance of top hats and fashionable dresses, their confident presence at entertainments, and their flamboyant violations of the Volstead Act, Arno's figures brought high society to life.

Nonetheless, a close look at these cartoons shows that the jokes come at the elites' own expense. The frisson of his humor comes from its ambiguity: for all their beauty and elegance, Arno's characters demonstrate in word and act that they are selfish, dissipated, and undeservedly smug. The most obvious examples came in volume 2. "One of the neighbors drops in at the Neighborhood Playhouse," which jokes about the theater's location on the Lower East Side, exposes the racist snobbery of its well-dressed patrons, so homogeneous that all wear the

"It will rise fifty-five stories into Manhattan skies—a scintillant spire gleaming aureate in the sun's rays—a crowning monument to my career."
"Who's doing the plumbing?"

Peter Arno's portrayal of elites celebrated their attractiveness *and* ridiculed their pride. 8/7/26:8.

same face, as together they sneer, aghast, as a man in Chasidic dress enters the theater (6/5/26:19). Similarly, the developer who waxes eloquent about his new building—"It will rise fifty-five stories into Manhattan skies—a scintillant spire . . . a crowning monument to my career"—is ripe for deflation; his companion's business suit and square build mark his lower status as efficiently as the developer's morning suit and nipped waist signify his wealth, but the plain-talker has the last word: "Who's doing the plumbing?" (8/7/26:8).

Arno began his mild critique of attractive, elite characters near the end of volume 1, about six months into his association with the magazine. A December 1925 drawing of two men and a woman in evening dress asking a sewer worker on the night shift to check his manhole for "a perfectly—ah—ravishing lipstick" (12/19/25:20) intensifies the class reversal of Arno's first cartoon. This drawing sets the upper-class figure parallel to the high-rise buildings in the background and allows him to tower over the half-submerged body of the sewer worker, but the joke is on the rich guys. They need the sewer man to satisfy their curiosity and this woman's need, and why should he care about a lipstick? (For that matter, why do they?) As Arno's characters express their dissipation, by mistaking two policemen for a taxi (9/19/25:3) or borrowing money to send an actress home in a cab (2/6/26:24), they invite readers to admire their attractiveness yet smirk at their smugness.

Not that Arno's cartoons sneer only at the deserving elite. Drawings from volume 1 in particular scorn the nonrich and nonbeautiful—targets that the *New Yorker* gave up as success brought self-confidence. "Pick the professional in the audience" (1/23/26:27) gives grotesquely deformed arms to its featured character, a vigorously applauding actress, suggesting not only that her behavior but also her very person does not belong in refined company. A similar snobbery animates a drawing in which a box office worker asks an obese couple, "How 'bout a coupla boxes?" (11/7/25:10). Arno's typical characters—beautiful, beautifully dressed couples, usually young (all but one of Arno's twenty-nine drawings for volume 1 featured characters in evening dress)—suggests that he saw humor in any deviation from this standard.[20] That aesthetic snobbery helped create the Whoops! sisters, with captions written by Philip Wylie after the first drawing in the series, "Tripe? Oh, I'm mad about tripe!" (4/17/26:30). The series encompassed fifty-one cartoons and a cover across three years (until 1/26/29:26), but forty-five appeared within fifteen months, by which time a writer for the *New Republic* pronounced the series tired, although he originally judged the sisters "preposterous and delightful figures, in incredible situations, wholly refreshing" ("A New York Diary" 96). The art meeting may have agreed: the six installments after the review stretched across thirteen months. Wylie recalled Arno's original plan as emphasizing the women's disconnection from their environment—he drew them headed to fall into one of New York's many open sidewalk elevators (Lorenz, *Art* 17)—but the first drawing framed the women quite tightly, eliminating the sidewalk hazard and thereby focusing on character, not situation. The drawing shows two eccentrically dressed women conversing intently while walking under a street lamp, and the caption creates humor by identifying the vulgar topic that they find so engaging: tripe. The characters hardly needed a situation to be funny, however, as the largely irrelevant dialogue eventually proved. The two old ladies dressed with Victorian propriety but demonstrated a total lack of breeding (not to mention sobriety) as they trotted with glee through one raucous situation after another, deviants from social rules.

In the classic manner of clowns, the Whoops! sisters maintained an inner sense of dignity while frolicking from roller rink and construction site to department store and restaurant. "Who has babies these days—what with everybody gettin' so refined an' all?" asks the first sister, insulted by a store clerk's mention of the babies' department, as they race down an up escalator (10/23/26:31). "Lordy, ain't that a pretty how-d'yuh-do!" she huffs, irate that an impolite man would call himself a "civil engineer" (8/14/26:24). "Literary, my eye!" she sniffs, as they're evicted from a Parnassus club lecture and reading (6/12/26:17), presumably because they remarked on its sexual content—as in another drawing two weeks later (6/26/26:14). As these captions show, the series' humor drew on the conflict between the women's undisciplined behavior and their claims to delicate sensibilities. The popularity of the series, in Janet Flanner's memory, "sold the magazine on the newsstands" (13), but the characters appeared on the cover just once, June 18, 1927, in a slapstick scene along the Coney Island ropes, which helped waders keep their footing: one sister is swinging on a rope; the other, tiptoeing (bloomers and all) into the water, cannot grab it for her hands full with muff and collar. While the series' visual humor relies on character and situation, its captions reflect—indeed, parody—traditional two- and four-line textual jokes. The Whoops! sisters helped *New Yorker* emphasize visual humor by making captions comically irrelevant.

The Whoops! sisters stand as exceptions among Arno's women characters, most of whom function as foils for men, not protagonists in their own right. Nonetheless, Lee Lorenz's claim that Arno's cartoons have "kept *The New Yorker's* testosterone level well above the national average" (*Art* 30), perhaps accurate over the long history of Arno's contributions to the magazine, misrepresents his influence in the 1920s. During the twenties Arno's humor scarcely dominated the magazine, nor did it represent *New Yorker* humor generally. The top-hatted drunk was Arno's comic signature, to be sure, and thus resonated with the figure of Eustace Tilley and other representatives of the smart set appearing in the magazine. And Arno did characterize his beautiful people from a predatory, masculine point of view. Nonetheless, in the pages of the early magazine, though not

Helen Hokinson, debut drawing, 7/4/25:3.

in histories of it, the male viewpoint did not go unchallenged nor did women's views remain unarticulated.

Women artists had a substantial presence in the early *New Yorker*. The *New Yorker* career of Helen Hokinson followed a trajectory parallel to Arno's, but despite her reputation as the sole woman in the men's art club, she was not alone there. Barbara Shermund (who drew almost much as Arno for volumes 1–5) and Alice Harvey contributed a large body of *New Yorker* art during the early years. More to the point, the art committee had no design to exclude women or bias against their ideas. A mailing list compiled too early to include Hokinson or Ilonka Karasz as potential art contributors included a dozen other women, including the then-known Edna Ditzler, Wanda Gag, Neysa McMein, and Ethel Plummer.[21] These women did not equalize the armies in the war between the sexes—the cadre of artists remains largely male to this day—but they drew different types of women and invented different kinds of amusing situations for them. Hokinson's women, in particular, were more engaged in living, working, and exploring than in courting, and she presented their bodies as more amusing than seductive.

Hokinson's earliest comic ideas concerned women's daily activities and vulnerabilities. (She also illustrated some prose text in her first months' association with the magazine, evidence that the art committee, which made those assignments, wanted her in the book.)[22] Her first drawing, of a woman standing on a pier and waving her handkerchief at a departing ship, expressed the poignancy

Helen Hokinson's visual humor included presenting figures from odd angles, such as the rear, and imagining regressive series, such as our looking at the figures looking at the mummy. 9/19/25:21.

of the woman left behind—and amusingly seen from behind. The odd vantage point from behind, above, and so forth, became an enduring technique of the *New Yorker*'s visual humor, used with particular effectiveness by Julian De Miskey, but Hokinson initiated it. Her other early drawings, also uncaptioned, similarly survey varieties of New York women and record their daily lives in the kind of varied smart settings that the editors specifically sought. Her women play bridge at Manhattan Beach (7/11/25:3) and study paintings at the Metropolitan Museum (7/25/25:16).

After this first summer, Hokinson homed in on three types of ideas: shopping situations, local color "layouts," and lifestyle narratives. All three types fulfilled the requirements for smart settings, realistic incidents, and "character stuff" while finding amusement in individuals' responses to familiar activities. Exemplifying her gentle approach, an early uncaptioned drawing shows a handsome young man and woman at a museum, where they study the annotation to an open mummy case on exhibit but ignore the artifact itself (9/19/25:21). The drawing acknowledges their personal attractiveness and intellectual sincerity yet ridicules their misplaced attention—a charge applying equally to the cartoonist, who has put *them* on display and shown them from behind. Hokinson's drawing thus matches comic idea with comic execution, exactly the relation of matter to manner that the art meeting sought. Not surprisingly, in this context, they purchased 115 items from Hokinson even before her first cover appeared July 16, 1927, midway through volume 3.

Hokinson's shopping scenes featured a diverse range of female types, although they characterized women's lives most conventionally. The foolish matrons who became her signature figures coexist alongside younger, explicitly modern representatives of the peer society. In the fall of 1925 she played with the comic potential of the domineering, impatient matron, a variant of the familiar shrew of world folklore. In "Henry—I wish you'd buy yourself a muffler," a four-image narrative cartoon, the wife does the buying (11/21/25:4–5); in "Young man, just what is the difference between alligator and lizard?" she overwhelms the shoe salesman physically as well as verbally (11/28/25:2). But a collage of early Christmas shoppers, "The Vanguard," adds a number of other types: the indulgent mother, the eccentric aunt, the frustrated saleswoman (11/28/25:13). Perhaps because of parallels with her own life as a young working woman, Hokinson presented the tribulations of women workers with particular empathy: however comic their situations, the characters themselves always merit respect—if only for their forbearance—though they are physically attractive too.

Hokinson's young women reached out directly and indirectly to their counterparts in the *New Yorker*'s audience. The first drawing of the multi-image "The Auction: One of Our More Popular Winter Sports" implies that Judgment Day has arrived for two young women standing opposite two middle-aged men while the auctioneer sits at a desk high above; the caption identifies the young women as readers. "That terrible moment when the auctioneer says, 'Sold! to the lady on my right, for fifty-five dollars and fifty cents!' You and Margie had just dropped in for a few minutes and hadn't intended to buy anything at all" (2/6/26:14). By contrast, the last image on the page, a framed portrait of a dowager camped out to claim the "reversible cushioned living room suite," makes fun of the older generation, reversing respect for elders. Judging by its frequency, the art committee and Hokinson had a special fondness for this joke, which she first drew in "This is 'N'Aimex Que Moi,' madame—'Don't love nobody but me,'" in which a young woman (in this case a clerk, badly educated and hence lower class) instructs a mature, more worldly woman in the art of seduction (11/7/25:5). "The Auction" similarly undercuts the matron's presumed dignity while contrasting her weariness and wealth with the younger women's impulsiveness and impecuniousness.

Hokinson's strongest sympathies go to young independent women, whom she characterizes as naïfs and sufferers—the opposite of nineteenth-century comic braggarts. Not surprisingly, she extends extra empathy to artists, such as the woman earnestly opening her portfolio to a gallery attendant who dismisses her with an undeservedly haughty "No we don't buy no drawings" (12/19/25:3). His puffed up chest asserts his economic and physical power over the slender young woman, yet his words declare the opposite; his insistence that "We make our own drawings" adds insult to injury—how can someone who speaks in double negatives make good art?—and thus deflates him. Hokinson's feminism shows most clearly, however, in a little-known genre, narrative cartoons. A feminist counterpart to the Little Man theme of modern life's travails, her illustrated tales of single urban women's trials and triumphs began in August 1925 with "'Why Don't You Come Out for the Week End?'" (8/29/25:12–13). The gauntlet begins with the crush at Grand Central Station "and the democracy of day couches," continues through the boredom of "heavy bridge (no-smoking)" with the host's aunt and uncle in the afternoon and "poor lights and worse books" in one's room late at night, all the way through to her return train ride. As the text offers the young woman's priorities and values for peer readers' approval, so each successive picture reveals her more daunted by the experience. Standing on the train for the ride home, she barely shows her face for the gifts, flowers, and belongings she has carried aboard. Although she brags about her sufferings rather than her achievements, the tale ends in anticlimax like nineteenth-century comic yarns. As the speaker repeats the question from the start, "Yes, why don't I?," she transforms an invitation into a rejection that is also a declaration of independence.

Thus began Hokinson's series of sixteen narrative cartoons depicting young women bloodied and bowed but finally successful in their urban quests. A few took up seasonal topics, such as "The Boulevards of Paris—Even the French Can't Cross Them" (9/4/26:14–15), but most stuck with local travails: "So You're Going to 59th Street!" (10/8/27:28–29), "So You're Going to Let Your Hair Grow!" (1/14/28:16–17), "So You're Going To Buy A Mop!" (10/5/29:24–25). An exception to the feminist theme occurred just once, when the male protagonist of "So You're Going to Hire a Secretary!" displayed unreasonable expectations to match his interviewees' unreasonable demands (4/13/29:22–23). For the most part, however, from their titles' challenges to their heroines' Pyrrhic victories, Hokinson's cartoon narratives celebrated the independence and fortitude of New Women in their urban adventures. These characters spoke directly to the *New Yorker*'s female readership, unlike Hokinson's more famous matrons, whose displays of childish pleasure and extreme fastidiousness spoke to male readers particularly and the peer society as a whole.

New Emphasis in Covers

Late in August of 1925, two months after the art committee asked artists for cartoons illustrating comic ideas, they sought covers that "tend strongly toward the elegant." Editors pronounced previous covers "consistently good" but rued their "scattered" tone, specifically rejecting sailor suits and "character studies of the lower classes."[23] This criticism amounted to a change in policy even though only four of the twenty-seven covers published to date featured lower-class characters, because three were by Irvin and other artists ranking high among the early contributors, and not one involved a sailor suit. Probably as a result, no more covers appeared from Al Frueh, who continued drawing middle- and lower-class figures inside the book, or from Carl Fornaro, whose lovers admiring the Manhattan skyline from a Brooklyn rooftop remained his sole contribution (3/21/25). A few holdovers of lower-class subjects remained, notably S. W. Reynolds's sailor courting a flapper (5/29/26) and Vladimir Bobritsky's white-shirted and black-skirted workers seeking refuge from the heat by sleeping in Central Park (7/31/26), suggesting art held over from the previous summer, but the smart set predominated.

Bobritsky's disappearance from the cover, although he continued drawing illustrations inside the book, hints at the cost of this new policy. Bobritsky's modernist designs evoked motion and, therefore, the speed and intensity of urban life; his debut cover paired cubist renderings of a flamenco-style dancer and a minstrel singer *cum* banjo player. Playing with the class and racial meanings of minstrelsy that Eric Lott details in *Love and Theft* (1993), Bobritsky's cover put a person of color on the front of the magazine for the first time two weeks before the end of volume 1 (2/6/26). A black musician the same size as the white dancer stands in the foreground, his stylishly rakish top hat and profile making the two partners equal—as performers, geometric shapes, and social-sexual opposites. A few months later, Bobritsky brought a similarly contemporary theme and technique to his cover on baseball (5/8/26), a sport so lacking the caché of the horse races, polo, and tennis matches covered by *New Yorker* reporters that Ross refused it space inside the magazine.[24] Bobritsky gave his batter a pugilistic stance and an angry look quite unlike the expressions of the elegant figures appearing just before and after it, but his July 31 cover of neatly dressed men and women sleeping in a park was decidely proletarian. Here are workers whose prominently placed alarm clock signifies not only a scene from 1:25 A.M. but also their need to wake up for work in the morning (7/31/26). After this cover, despite its fine rendering of local customs, Bobritsky's work graced the front just once more in these early years: a year later, an Independence Day scene of Coney Island roller-coaster riders (7/2/27), and thus a suitable time for democratic sentiments about the lower classes.

Bobritsky did not return to the cover until late in 1930, when (signing himself "Bobri") he depicted upper-class figures as connoisseurs of modern art (11/29/30), patrons of the pony rides outside the Central Park Zoo (5/22/37), and bicycle riders in the country (5/28/38). By contrast T. C. Haupt, a cover artist new to volume 3, used geometric style to evoke humor from upper-class experience. The figures in his fashion show cover (10/15/27) have shapes like cutouts, as do the architectural and human forms in his Grand Central cover (9/10/27), Christmas shopping scene (12/17/27), and Florida beach scene (2/18/28). Representing ordinary events and activities in high aesthetic style put a cerebral humor on the *New Yorker*'s face.

Julian De Miskey, by contrast, promptly turned away from the classless activities of his first covers in the summer of 1925—snuggling on a park bench (5/23/25), dancing (6/6/25), swimming (6/27/25), sipping sodas (8/8/25)—and depicted smart characters and situations instead. Elegant subjects did not demand admiration, however, and covers often gave smartness a jaundiced eye. De Miskey's opera cover of October 31, 1925, elevates the audience above the performer in height but not in value. Visual parallels and asymmetries link the smart patrons in their box seats halfway up the right edge with the singer on stage in the lower left: the rounded box matches the rounded stage, the red ring around the box matches the singer's belt, the round-faced singer matches round-faced listeners; even their cheeks have matching ovals of pink against their pasty white oval faces. But a chasm separates them. A deep blue space isolates stage from box, performer from audience, passionate involvement from aloof observation; the center of the drawing—its ostensible subject—is empty. Cartoon-like figures make this an amusing twist on conventional reverence for opera and society, and De Miskey consistently put his stylized characters to such anti-conventional use. The flapper-dowager pair on his cover for December 19, 1925, announces that the more fashions change, the less difference they make. De Miskey's care to balance and imbalance the pairs in his covers kept his skewed look at smart subjects gaily humorous rather than sharply satiric.

De Miskey's pairs violate expectations of symmetry to ridicule such elegant subjects as doorman service (10/9/26), society hunts (10/22/27), and the cabaret (1/14/28). The strong, geometric design of his covers, borrowed from modernist experiments, declared them playful aesthetic objects, not social critiques. By rejecting satire for domestic comedy, De Miskey's covers met the art committee's request for situations about "wife and husband, mother and child, servant and mistress, hostess and guests, borrower and lender, lovers, newlyweds, beginners in any sports, revelers."[25] These topics, circulated to artists late in August of 1925, not only unified artists' diverse styles around a core set of themes but also located *New Yorker* humor in unequal relationships of power and ability, a topic dear to the iconoclasts of the peer society.

This satire, which peaked in 1927–28, emphasizes eccentric individuals and interpersonal relations over society in the aggregate. Gardner Rea's three covers from volume 3 exemplify the comic strand. Smart figures share the page with servants, implying that each defines the other, but the servants mimic and thus ridicule their superiors, and claim more importance—ironically—by filling more of the page. Rea's first cover set the pattern, contrasting a snobby, snappily-uniformed butler with a flabby, mischievous truck driver: the butler exaggerates his employers' fastidiousness as he protects a goldfish bowl from a burly barbarian in blue who sticks his tongue out in mockery as the butler struggles with his burden (10/1/27). The appearance of this cover after Rea had published forty-four cartoons inside the book suggests that he had some difficulty satisfying the art committee, but variations on this theme followed shortly: a smart matron parades with her nose in the air while the doorman behind her bears a tiny, but evidently precious, package aloft (12/10/27), and a haughty butler nearly fills the whole space as he carries a bootlegger's calling card on a tray (2/4/28). Comically reversing the importance of server and served, all three covers skewer the snobs whose noses point toward the sky (a feature also of Rea Irvin's servants), yet each figure has enough eccentricity to limit the critique to the individual. The butler, so much smaller than either the moving van driver or the plant atop the truck, contorts himself, nearly twisting his head around his neck, in asserting his superiority over the driver, becoming all the more ridiculous in the process. The doorman cover multiplies comic clashes: between his hauteur and his preposterous act of service, between his pretensions and his official role (his uniform matches the awning of his building, implying his function as a fixture) among the members of this procession, led by a dog (amusingly left out of the picture) and capped by himself. Like the looming presence of the valet bearing the bootlegger's bill, these incongruities—together with the similar jokes in covers by

Rea Irvin, Helen Hokinson, and Peter Arno—sum up the *New Yorker*'s vision of smartness: it comes from the servant class. Equally funny: servants, as representatives of the elite, metaphorically join their club.

Covers by Irvin and Hokinson, also from volume 3, illustrate how the *New Yorker* focused comic attention on the smart set without satirizing wealth, capitalism, or smartness. For instance, the carriage driver on Irvin's November 26, 1927, cover has a haughty profile that matches the hood ornaments of two vehicles in the background. These parallels not only undercut his hauteur by characterizing him as an ornament like those on the car but also (because the driver holds a whip that bisects the drawing and separates him from the cars) ridicule his role as a vestige of horse carriage days. This period also saw Helen Hokinson's first covers, watercolors of matrons requiring assistance from their valets to perform such minor acts as clipping roses (7/16/27) and picnicking (8/20/27); the six other scenes in volumes 4–5 include a fishing expedition causing her to avert her eyes from the violence to the worm as her valet baits her hook (6/30/28). The series ended in volume 6, but throughout its run the matron's self-indulgence and incompetence coexisted with her joy for living, albeit a certain kind of life. These and other scenes from what Gerald Weales termed "the land of pamper" (508) make fun of upper-class comforts as gifts from social inferiors, but generally sustained the burgeoning consumer culture promoted by the *New Yorker*, which celebrated what money could buy.

The art committee's discomfort with displaying lower-class sympathies on the cover of the *New Yorker* kept its focus on innovations in idea and design, which gave an edge to work by Ilonka Karasz and other scene makers. Beginning in 1928, Adolph Kronengold contributed five covers, for the most part joining Karasz in using bright colors and abstracted shapes and taking a well-defined physical point of view on the local scene. His first cover, a bird's-eye view of city skyscrapers, elevated trains, and traffic, appeared September 22, 1928, a few weeks after an atypical scene by Karasz of children frolicking in the fountain at the Fifth Avenue library (8/18/28) and a few weeks before an almost signature Karasz design of urban folks parading along country roads to admire the autumn leaves (10/6/28). I. G. Haupt's colorful designs sustained that panoramic tradition in volume 5, when Karasz's contributions temporarily declined. But a few of Haupt's covers during this period also brought a broadly comic sensibility to the front of the magazine, notably his Thanksgiving tableau of a butcher presenting a turkey for approval (11/23/29) and his mildly risqué scene of a window dresser frantically working to cover a naked mannequin as a crowd watches

(1/28/28). Together these covers avoided issues of class while nonetheless looking beyond the world of elites.

Crowd scenes by Sue Williams and others celebrated the communal dimension of urban life. Williams's gay scenes of the circus (4/14/28), New York harbor (6/2/28), the opera (11/17/28), and other crowded places invite a pleasure in community quite distinct from the humor of Irvin's eccentric individuals. Moreover, whereas Ilonka Karasz's local color covers typically make the landscape their subject, Williams's designs blend people, environment, and event into a single whole. The result is typically dehumanizing, though visually amusing. Her 1929 Palm Beach auto show cover makes people's heads look like coconuts fallen from the palm trees and cars like so many flowers between pillars that could pass for trees (1/5/29); fans at a hockey game disappear into their seats (2/2/29), while the people in her Paris landmarks cover add color but no specific action or meaning to the scene (6/15/29). Toward the end of volume 5, however, Williams's aquarium cover put humans, animals, and architecture into balance (1/11/30). Williams's covers attribute humor not to their subjects, as in Irvin's covers, but to the artist and her audience, who can appreciate their jokes.

Julian De Miskey's "Memories" series in volume 4 restored lower-class characters and situations to the cover, this time in the context of local color humor. Like nineteenth-century local color dialect writing, the twelve "Memories" covers placed lower-class subjects such as tattooing (4/28/28) and barn dancing (9/8/28) safely in the past. In this series, which ran from April 18, 1928, to June 8, 1929, class snobbery gave way to historical condescension as De Miskey replaced the stiff, formal contemporary figures of his modernist covers with characters who curve sinuously, display a sprightly energy, and engage in informal activities. The first covers depict a port city where sailors acquire a new tattoo for each new love (4/28/28), dignified equestrians ride through Central Park (5/12/28), and fish gleefully evade capture (7/7/28). "Memories" evokes a time when New York was not only a small town but a country town of uncrowded beaches (8/4/28), sleigh-borne Christmas shoppers (12/15/28), and other simple pleasures of the seasons. Participants in the Easter parade (3/30/29) had their noses in the air, to be sure, but a photographer looked down on *them* from his perch in a tree. The series emphasized fond feelings, including nostalgia (a typical mood of local color humor), not social satire. But lower-class characters do not displace the elite, who remain present by implication in Leonard Dove's construction worker, backed by a skyscraper he'll never inhabit (7/20/29), and Gardner

Rea's overheated street sweeper, advised by an ad in the trash, "The Swiss Alps Beckon You" (8/3/29).

The Series Solution

Coherence in covers emerged partly because the art committee bought multiple contributions from individual artists in addition to soliciting specific subjects and themes from artists on the mailing list. Cartoon series accelerated this process. Series combined familiar graphic styles with recurrent themes, matching artists' ideas with the art committee's agenda. The earliest series began as artists first visualized comic ideas in the summer of 1925, when Frueh's early Mayor Hylan drawings expanded into his "People's Concerts" series. By depicting smart subjects, early series reinforced the magazine's emerging identity by sustaining successful comic formulas over many weeks.

A bold blend of verbal and visual humor, Hans Stengel's "Our Sermons on Sin" drove a wedge between illustrated jokes and idea drawings from September 19, 1925, to March 20, 1926. The series featured a six-frame comic strip over doggerel commentary on recent news; each installment's ballad rhymes inflate its story while primitive illustrations deflate it. The idea originated in July in an untitled single-panel satire of the Scopes trial: Stengel drew a group of apes admiring a modern businessman rising above a volcano, and his rhymes mocked the equation of evolution with progress:

> Onward and up from clam to brute
> all things were meant to evolute,
>
> . . . .
>
> And, lo, a vision caught their eye,
> the lovely Arrow Collar Guy

(7/18/25:5)

Although scholars since Walter Blair have identified advertising as a particular theme of *New Yorker* humor, references to the Arrow Collar Guy did not reappear in the next variation on this comic-strip-and-rhyme format two weeks later, when Stengel continued his visual and verbal slams at the peer culture. The second effort, also untitled, lampooned women's fondness for artists, pointing out that the artist "feeds / The soul with beauty" and she reciprocates with "toast and tea" (8/1/25:14). Similarly amateurish rhymes and primitive drawings became the ironic hallmarks of the eleven installments of Stengel's "Our Sermons on Sin."

The series transformed the original joke into a burlesque of tabloid journalism. Each sermon's text came from an unspecified newspaper headline, as impressionistic as an imagist poem: "Wife Stabs Husband to Death, Blames Bright Lights" (9/19/25:8), "Radical Falls Into Coils of Law" (10/17/25:8), "Charleston Causes Collapse of Another Building" (1/9/26:10), "Prodigal Son Returns Only to Find Tomb of Mother" (3/20/26:16). The verse narrative then details the story in six rhymed quatrains before ending with a moral. The conclusion of "Gambling, Menace to Nation, Says Divine" [sic] followed its pictures—of one "Red" Milton Silverleaf praying to the king of dice (on a throne), playing cards all night, and amassing piles of poker chips while his wife wails "hopeless broken and dispairing" [sic] and Fortuna eludes his grasp—until the last frame shows him reduced to begging with a tin cup in the rain, and concludes:

> Now he's poor and godforsaken,
> lost his wife, his home, his soul.
> Silverleaf, his spirit shaken
> begs the passers's cheerless dole [sic].

(12/19/25:8)

Mannered punctuation and spelling call attention to inept writing: bad journalism, bad poetry, bad moralizing. The same comic amateurishness appears in the drawings, whose figures and settings lack detail and perspective, though the compositions fill the frames effectively. Such mock-naïveté ridicules not only the stories and pictures of tabloid journalism but also the public who enjoy them. And considering that the art committee ran the series irregularly for half a year, from 1:31 to 2:5, the editors' evident approval of mock-naïveté amounts to a declaration of the New Yorker's superiority to low-class printed matter. Like John Held's woodcuts, Stengel's series comically contrasted the primitive and the sophisticated, a joke extended later in volume 2 to De Miskey's illustrations for "Talk."

From these beginnings, cartoon series eventually brought the magazine an important balance between familiarity and novelty. Later series lasted longer than earlier ones as artists and editors learned to milk them. Frueh's two urban solutions series from the winter of 1926, "Solving the Traffic Problem" and "Solving the Parking Problem" quit after just three appearances, whereas their counterparts by Otto Soglow ran much longer. "On Beautifying the City" lasted nine installments in the summer and fall of 1927, "On Enlivening the City," nineteen between March and August of 1928.[26]

So You're Going to Sublet

Your Apartment!

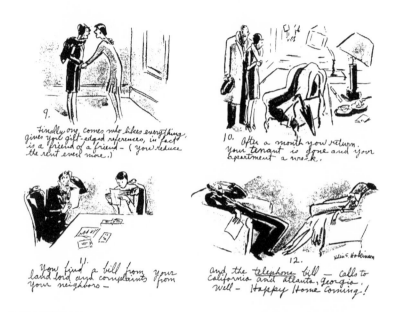

Helen Hokinson's narrative cartoons, an important genre of *New Yorker* comic art, featured women's viewpoints on the demands of urban life. Women cartoonists gave women's issues an important place in the *New Yorker* of the 1920s, though scholars have not recorded it. 2/11/28:20–22.

Series cartoons' recurrent themes enabled social critique as solo drawings did not. Irvin's "Social Errors" series provided smart figures and settings while developing the theme that elite society has specialized codes of knowledge and behavior. Ridiculing the problems of both rich and poor, Irvin's four cartoons illustrated such faux pas as asking a Dunhill's clerk for a package of Camel cigarettes (10/17/25:10), telling a clean story at a party (10/24/25:13), snubbing the bootlegger (11/7/25:14), or failing to discard all the pieces of a now-obsolete mah-jong game (12/19/25:13).[27] Kramer traced Irvin's idea to *Punch*'s "Our Social Outcasts" series (*Ross* 126), but the similar drawing by R. B. Fuller for *Judge,* "Man Who Used the Wrong Spoon" (11/28/25:8), which followed Irvin's, shows the *New Yorker*'s leadership in the themes and techniques of idea drawings.

Early in 1927, as the magazine's focus on smart subjects peaked, Irvin's "Surprises of the Social Season" extended the class consciousness of the "Social Errors" series into a comic critique that did not so much offset the visual appeal of the elites portrayed by Arno and others as declare class differences funny. The

SOCIAL ERRORS

The Woman Who Cut Her Husband's Bootlegger

Rea Irvin's "Social Errors" series in the *New Yorker* (11/7/25:14) was followed by R. B. Fuller's "Wrong Spoon" in *Judge* (11/28/25:8), showing that even in its early months *New Yorker* visual humor raced ahead of the competition.

main joke of the series, which began as a single drawing, the two-page "Surprise of the Social Season: Oil Is Struck Under the Mills Hotel" (1/1/27:12–13), tweaks the bottom of the social ladder. "The Third Avenue Elevated Puts on a Club Car," for instance, envisions an ethnically diverse group ostentatiously lounging on the "El" (1/22/27:14), and "Max Rosenblatt, 412 Bowery, stages a spring fashion show" pits ready-to-wear against couture with ethnic, even racist,

THE MAN WHO USED THE WRONG SPOON

overtones (4/2/27:24). Although later installments subjected the upper classes to ridicule, as in "The Salvation Army Makes Some Converts at the Ritz" (2/19/27:24), Reginald Marsh's "Upper Crust" series from the same period stung more sharply.

Running from March 5, 1927, to November 5, 1927, Marsh's seven drawings declared the elite decadent: busy lithographic crayon compositions detail self-indulgence while smug captions expose social ignorance. The series began with a bold half-page of three figures in evening dress who fill a space already crowded with signs of wealth: a Victrola, grand piano with turned legs, lamp with curved silk shade, Sheraton side chair, and model of a sailing ship. The caption indicates a conversation in progress among the three figures, but the drawing shows them interacting more with the objects than each other: a fat middle-aged man sits on the piano bench, smoking a cigar and leaning against the piano; a tall, balding man stands far to the left; a fashionably dressed woman also leans against the piano, balancing the scene on the right. Neither the caption nor the drawing clarifies the speaker, who warns, "Don't go to *that* part of France—it's been ruined by the tourists" (20), but the ambiguity indicts the three as equally unaware of their own complicity as tourists and snobs. Marsh compounds the speaker's denial of being a tourist with the ambiguity of who speaks the line, suggesting all are the same.

More damning satire arose from the serious topics introduced near the series' end, but for the most part publishing Marsh's social critique did not amount to the editors' biting the hand that fed them. Appearing at the height of twenties' prosperity, these drawings surely stung their targets, such as the husband and wife of "What! Have more children?" (in a drawing whose background shows a nanny chasing a single child across a vast estate replete with servants and mansion [7/16/27:14]) or the matron who insists that girls "should have enough will power not to become unfortunate" (8/20/27:17). However, the targets of these jokes were probably not *New Yorker* readers but rather the readers' older siblings, parents, or (considering the Victorian settings) grandparents. A logical extension of the peer culture, tensions between the generations displaced class tensions as a comic theme during the late twenties, as the magazine settled comfortably into its economic success.

Ironic ideas

Ironic series sustained the editorial preference for idea drawings from 1925 to 1927, as artists learned to produce such cartoons. An important sign of success, however, came in Otto Soglow's debut drawing from mid-November, "Here Y'are, Read the Lord's Prayer on the Head of a Pin" (11/14/25:15), which appeared at the same time that Alice Harvey, Barbara Shermund, Isidore Klein, and other artists began responding to the call for idea drawings. The size of Soglow's drawing, two-thirds of two columns, implies how important the editors saw it. Artists submitted drawings in whatever size they preferred; the art

"Here Y'are, Read the Lord's Prayer on the Head of a Pin."

This early idea drawing, Otto Soglow's first for the *New Yorker*, plays with many incongruities. In addition to the basic visual contrast between huge buildings and tiny figures (and the invisible pin purportedly containing miniscule text), the composition treats the background scene as more important than the subject and uses a rough line for a drawing whose declared subject requires highly refined script. The caption adds another incongruity by suggesting that despite the size difference separating metropolis and small town, they share the same wonders—and scams. 11/14/25:15.

meeting decided how to use each item, and, consequently, how much to pay for it. Enlargement or reduction followed in the printing process. Soglow's drawing shows a dense cityscape of skyscrapers with a tiny plaza in a crevice, where crowds leave a small space for the vendor to display his ware through a telescope. The composition creates comic contrasts between the huge buildings and tiny figures, between the roughly suggested buildings and the comparatively detailed people, between the promise of the engraved pin, and the image we're given—which makes us viewers dupes of a parallel scam. This incongruity between the image and the caption, between visual and verbal elements, eventually became the hallmark of *New Yorker* cartoon humor when the majority of contributors understood how to achieve it.

Early drawings by Barbara Shermund used the same comic techniques as Soglow's but presented Arno's elegant world from a woman's standpoint. Although Shermund's characters appeared in smart settings, their commentary reversed conventional associations of elegant appearance. Shermund's foremost message was that women did not need men, a theme developed in both covers and cartoons. Her two covers from volume 1 feature a lone woman—one blissfully enjoying a summer night atop a double-decker bus (6/13/25), the other portraying a female Bacchus, her hair interwoven with leaves and her earrings bunches of ripe grapes (10/3/25). Each woman fills her space: both are sensuous, self-assured, and complete. Considering what these and Shermund's other virtually unknown images add to our understanding of *New Yorker* humor, her invisibility in *New Yorker* history tells a lot about the politics of reputation that obscured her contribution to the magazine.

Barbara Shermund signed more than 300 items in volumes 1–5, not quite as many as Peter Arno (with a total in the 400 range) or Johan Bull (about 350), but more than Helen Hokinson (275), Julian De Miskey (275), Alan Dunn (175), Al Frueh (175), or a dozen other artists. While these sums do not measure historical merit, they do indicate relative worth to the art committee, which chose, paid for, and determined the use of each drawing (depending, of course, on what they received). Nonetheless, Dale Kramer gave Shermund only a brief mention as an artist who drew flappers (Ross 135), and Lorenz merely listed her among artists in the first *New Yorker Album* (where she's erroneously indexed as "Sherman") (*Art* 35). Shermund was not pictured in the group portrait of artists in the 1997 cartoon issue (12/15/97:103–5) or cited in its pages.

Gender alone does not explain such undeserved obscurity. Another of the *New Yorker's* most prolific artists, Julian De Miskey, received brief posthumous recognition for the quantity of his contributions—from Lee Lorenz in *The Art of "The New Yorker"* (19, 21) and the recent cartoon issue (12/15/97:124) and from John Updike in his introduction to *The Complete Book of Covers from "The New Yorker"* (*New Yorker* Magazine)—but he does not appear in any of the *New Yorker* memoirs or histories that have formed the basis of historical memory. De Miskey believed that Brendan Gill deliberately omitted him from "the family album," effectively snubbing fifty years of work—some one hundred covers, thousands of cartoons and illustrations, and dozens of promotional booklets, including one in the permanent collection of the Metropolitan Museum of Art.[28] Even before that, he complained to E. B. White, "I'm a forgotten man," grateful that White had mentioned him in a 1971 column at a time when the magazine's staff cared so little that they misspelled his name, their legendary passion for accuracy notwithstanding.[29] (The problem continues; the 1997 cartoon issue designated him *Julian De Misky* [124].)

Like De Miskey, Shermund produced work of many kinds. In fact, on a 1926 spreadsheet on which the art committee charted who contributed what type of art, only De Miskey appeared in all categories (which differentiated covers and "covering art" layouts, cartoons, and idea drawings),[30] yet he remains unknown today. These details underscore how reputations of *New Yorker* artists have depended more on external factors, such as comic biographical details and reprints in cartoon collections, than on their contributions to the magazine's pages. Shermund's reputation has suffered similarly, though probably for different reasons than De Miskey's.

The variety of Shermund's work diffused its impact throughout the magazine. The magazine's byline policy and the range of media in which she worked—including block print, ink and wash, and lithographic crayon—diffused it further. Different items had very different styles, and often different signatures as well: *Shermund, Sher Mund, B. S.* In this she followed an established editorial pattern. Artists and writers signed their name just once per issue in the early years, identifying additional work by initials or publishing it pseudonymously. The policy, which insinuated a larger cadre of contributors than Ross had amassed, was relaxed later in the decade. Elements within Shermund's drawings also contributed to her invisibility. Although her subjects compared to Arno's, her lithographic work lacked the boldness of Arno's ink-lines; her drawings of women lacked the visual wit of Hokinson's compositions. Perhaps for these reasons, the art committee designated them as half-pages or less, but their small size, whatever it meant to the committee, downplayed her radical themes. Shermund called a plague on conventional women *and* men. By addressing women's behavior and the battle between the sexes from the point of view of a New Woman skeptical of fashion, courtship rituals, and marriage, Shermund's art offered an amusingly bold viewpoint quite valuable to a publication needing to reexcite readers each week.

Still, the sexual (and homosexual) politics of these cartoons probably prevented their inclusion in the book collections that confer lasting fame. Shermund never published a volume of her own drawings, unlike Arno, Hokinson, Gluyas Williams, and Dunn (who collected his unpublished cartoons as *Rejections*). With a few exceptions, her cartoons exist only in back issues of the *New Yorker* and other magazines. But the very limitations of her work in the more universal context of book publication testify to its appropriateness to the mission of the weekly magazine, and underscore how much the art committee valued it to buy and publish it so often.

Shermund's drawings, which often appeared twice per issue in volumes 2 and 3, met the idea drawing's primary test: "Could this have happened?" Her cartoon of two maids talking through nearby windows illustrates an old, familiar joke as they remark on the city's springtime air while shaking out dust (4/3/26:25), but most of her early drawings, run in small sizes as department headings, visualize the social contrasts at the heart of idea humor: a salesgirl helping a matron try a hat (1/23/26:36), an elegant woman working her way through a sea of shoes while the clerk struggles to help (1/23/26:36), a couple in love on the movie screen and a second in the audience (2/13/26:36). A few of these early drawings fall flat, like the bus scene with a mother urging a child to say "Bye, bye Hudson River" (2/27/26:14), but most of Shermund's characters displayed an amusing spontaneity and expressed pride in upscale New York.

Beginning in the winter of 1925–26, however, Shermund's drawings brought a new topical humor to the *New Yorker* on sexual politics. Her characters ran the gamut of contemporary types, but her sympathies clearly went to the New Women in the cast. A few were smart only in dress—such as the one who looks at a still life and exclaims, "It's egg plant! I simply loathe it, don't you?" (3/27/26:26), or the one who mumbles "sort of—sort of a—well, you know" when her escort asks whether she enjoyed the show (5/22/26:18). Shop girls who call dignified matrons "dearie" (e.g., 9/4/26:26) ridicule both ends of the spectrum at once. To these familiar female types, Shermund added androgynous women. She portrayed them neutrally rather than critically but poked fun at would-be sophisticates. The eggplant drawing and another set in an art gallery, "Well—you have to look at it through your eyelashes, silly" (6/19/26:26), together make clear that ignorance about art has less to do with gender or style than with intelligence or education.

More interesting, Shermund made androgyny itself a theme. "What is that, a boy or a girl?" depicts two men talking about a figure with short hair, jodhpurs and tie, smoking a cigarette in a long holder while walking through the park (7/31/26:14). The humor exploits the visual ambiguities of gender by taking its caption from another context, a look into a baby carriage. The character could hardly have violated more taboos of women's behavior all at once (the early 1960s still judged smoking in the street "unladylike"), but the dialogue declares appearance and manners irrelevant. Apparently gay himself, one man insists that the smoker is a woman; he can tell "By the sex appeal," implying clearly that anyone who can't recognize it is sexually deficient himself. Shermund apparently held that the gender debate was not itself gendered, because her drawing of a highly geometric (hence, modern) middle-aged couple does not distinguish which one says, "A very brainy girl, that," and which replies, "But she's not a bad sort, really" (6/5/26:29). The ironic relation among image, caption, and speaker in these early Shermund cartoons became the *New Yorker's* comic signature.

Cartoons featuring women speakers advanced Shermund's more radical ideas. "I do say I'll never marry," a woman earnestly assures her friend on the next stool at the soda fountain, but she adds wistfully, "I've always wanted to be a widow" (5/29/26:10). In addition to its illogic, the caption identifies women's ideal state as combining adult privilege with independence from men. The large size of this drawing, more than a quarter-page, emphasizes the attractiveness and self-possession of these well-off young women who imagine happy lives without men. In fact, they constitute a happy couple facing each other, excluding the male at the next stool. (On the other hand, they're eating sandwiches and drinking sodas at a counter, not cocktails at a cabaret, a setting that suggests their youth and naïveté.) These pairings silently clash with the heterosexual theme of the captions, presenting an incongruity especially pleasing to 1920s readers, including privileged bohemians and feminists committed to lesbianism or companionate marriage. A summer 1928 letter from Ross to Gardner Rea indicates Ross's specific desire during this period to please homosexual readers,[31] and Shermund's humor may have fit the bill. A quarter-page drawing the next month euphemistically made homosexuality its topic, and the editors signaled the cartoon's importance by letting it encroach on nearby text. As two attractive women huddle in confidential conversation on a matched pair of chairs and their floppy hats imitate the palm tree behind them, their similarity implies that they are two of a kind, frilly and feminine in their daytime dresses. The implication that the pair are lesbians comes from their conversation, and their insistence that "he's [not] abnormal—he's just versatile" transforms homosexuality from a defect to a virtue (7/21/28:12), a good joke for gays and straights. Shermund's drawings about love and marriage consistently, but quietly, affirmed homosex-

•   •

"What is that, a boy or a girl?"
"A girl."
"How can you tell?"
"By the sex appeal."

Barbara Shermund's drawings made friendly jokes about gender identity and sexual
preference. 7/31/26:14.

ual love by replacing male-female couples with pairs of conventionally beautiful
women.

Less radical than Shermund, Alice Harvey also began contributing idea drawings about women in the fall of 1925, probably inspired by her friend Helen
Hokinson's success. Harvey published only three cartoons before the end of the
first year, although she illustrated the important Mackay cabaret piece. Reflecting her experience in fashion advertising, Harvey's drawings (most in crayon but
a few in pen and ink) have sketchy, apparently casual lines giving the composition energy by suggesting bodies in motion. The art committee apparently liked
this style well enough to assign her illustrations despite the ambiguous effect of
her technique in her first idea drawing, in which a woman asks, "Do my nails
shine from there?" (10/24/25:7). The remark addresses an indeterminate figure
of head, torso, arms, legs—if the joke hinges on this rudimentary shape, the hu-

mor doesn't come through today. For the most part, however, Harvey visualized figures as individuals, creating a humor of character. And in the spring and summer of 1926, when her work appeared almost every week (eleven cartoons in sixteen weeks), she ridiculed men and women alike.

Harvey's drawings put men and women together, and doubt over who speaks in the captions keeps the sexes equal. For example, in her drawing of three young women flirtatiously greeting an older man at the entrance to the Plaza's Palm Court, the caption "Well! This is a surprise!" (4/17/26:25) could apply to either the man or one of the women—and it doesn't matter. Harvey and the art committee found the joke worth repeating in a drawing of two couples playing bridge (a recent vogue), whose humor depends on *all* four characters' disengagement from the game, any one of whom might be asking, "Who dealt?" (5/8/26:17). Harvey added visual ironies to those between drawing and caption. Her cartoon of an imperious but shapely young matron directing a furniture mover carrying a huge cabinet builds a visual joke from the contrast between their postures: hers staunchly vertical, his nearly horizontal. His complaint plays on this visual bit. By griping, "I'm so tired, if you was to ask me to dance now, I wouldn't go" (6/19/26:21), the mover asserts his power to decline even though their roles put her in charge; moreover, by contrasting them to a conventional male-female pair, Harvey reverses the typical roles of asker and asked. As this example shows, Harvey's early vision of *New Yorker* humor refused to privilege one gender or social class, though she typically drew attractive, affluent figures. Indeed, she made equal fun of country folks and their summer invaders when an old country man and woman meet on the road and he remarks (in the local dialect) on how many people are waiting for the train to New York, and she replies, "Must be something going on down there" (7/10/26:17). Their diffidence about the New York experience—perhaps the *New Yorker*'s most sacred topic—provides at least as much humor as the old folks' naïveté.

Despite these successes in the summer of 1926, the art well ran dry in the issue of July 24. The issue recycled Hokinson's and Arno's first cartoons from the previous summer along with S. W. Reynolds's drawing of a woman blowing smoke rings (12/5/25:4). New art included an unremarkable page drawing, more suited to *Life,* by Rea Irvin, "Does Your Home Reflect Your Personality? Living room of a family devoted to horses" (12). But along with this stagnation came a few signs of impending change. A preview of "waggishness" in layout, a new genre of *New Yorker* visual humor that grew increasingly important in 1927, came in an H. O. Hofman drawing on the inside pages of "Talk": the drawing, divided in two by the fold, showed a woman archer aiming her bow on page 8 and a target with arrows on page 9 (see p. 228). Not particularly amusing if conventionally printed, this drawing acquired comic elements of time and space from its whimsical treatment. Pantomime narratives (uncaptioned cartoon sequences) would more fully exploit time and space as comic graphic elements later that fall.

Even more promising, drawings by Hokinson, Arno, and Isidore Klein in the July 24 issue invoked ironic relations between image and text, the key discovery of the idea drawing. Hokinson's drawing of "a race to see who gets to the baby first" ridicules the tiny size of the organizer and participants (13). At the opposite end of the spectrum, Arno also makes size a visual theme in his drawing; his thin florist serves a fat customer who rejects a bunch of peonies by asking, "Haven't you any larger flowers?" (19), though in the absence of irony this effort hardly differs from an illustrated joke. Greater success came in I. Klein's half-page drawing, which creates irony not only from the incongruity between the caption and its visual context but also from the reversal of class relations in image and text. One would not expect comments on a restaurant's "beastly service" and "real exotic atmosphere" to come from two plaid-shirted workmen rather than from the primary patrons, every one of them a businessman in a suit. But this example demonstrates, along with other successful cartoons from the first eighteen months, that the *New Yorker* invented not the one-line caption but rather the comic relation of verbal text to visual context. With these drawings, and a new concern for "space and pliability of make-up," the art committee earnestly sought "first class idea drawings."[32]

CHAPTER 5

Two into One, and Then There Were None

The New Yorker *is a movement*

Harold W. Ross to Raoul H. Fleischmann

With the promise of rewards for idea drawings, the late summer of 1926 saw a second period of editorial experimentation with art. "More space and pliability of make-up" meant giving artists more money (for the larger size) and more attention (in relation to adjacent text)—two major incentives. They worked. The proportion of idea drawings increased beginning July 31, as a wider group of artists brought varied sensibilities and styles to the common problem of visualizing comic ideas. In addition, the art committee began more aggressively shaping *New Yorker* humor with its own decisions over subject, size, and makeup. As a result, the illustrated two-line joke not only gave way to drawings integrating image and caption, often ironically, but also to narrative cartoons telling comic stories without words. Featured drawings and the figures within them grew larger as the decade progressed. By the end of volume 5, cartoons reshaped columns as images jutted into text, while copy constrained narrative cartoons as individual frames stepped down the page. Word and picture united as graphic elements for humor.

First-Class Idea Drawings

Several cartoons in the issue of July 31, 1926, visualized comic ideas by relating image and caption. In "The Very Great Artist," a full page by George

Shanks, the scene exposes the caption as a lie (7/31/26:12). The drawing shows an artist directing two visitors to "a little thing I just dashed off"—a huge panorama with figures larger than the artist and his visitors, the canvas partly blocked from view by scaffolding three stories high. Shanks, whom *Judge* readers from the early 1920s knew well but whose reputation today rests on his cartoon of an acrobat who fails to catch his partner, saying, "Oop—sorry" (7/16/27:16), gave this simple idea very careful design. The detailed scaffolding and picture-within-the-picture on the left contrast with nearly empty space on the right; a dog lounges before a small blank canvas on an easel, an ironic metaphor for the artist's greatness. Small people, dog, and door in the foreground emphasize the vastness of the canvas in the rear. Other idea drawings in the same issue, including Shermund's "What is that, a boy or a girl?" (14), confirm that the magazine had turned the corner. Text moved from the caption line into the frame in two other cartoons, Frueh's "The Power of the Printed Word," a narrative cartoon ridiculing tabloid journalism's semipornographic tendencies (19), and I. Klein's wizened old men *cum* film critics, who leer at a movie poster of Mexican bad guys threatening a nearly nude "Flora Flooie" in *Oh the Brute* and remark on what "tough babies those guys must be!" (26). The ridicule of mass media in these cartoons links them also to the magazine's prose humor, which made the topic a staple.

The pace of idea drawings picked up further the next week, August 7, when cartoons by I. Klein and Alan Dunn made clear that the number of lines did not define *New Yorker* cartoons. A noted animator who worked on *Mutt and Jeff* and other silent cartoons for the Hearst International Film Service in the years following World War I and for Walt Disney Studios in Hollywood in the late 1930s, Klein has received little attention as an early contributor to the *New Yorker*, perhaps because *The New Yorker Album, 1925–1950* reprinted only one of his cartoons, "The Chess Player and the French Pastry" (2/1/30:34). However, Klein began selling work to Irvin and Ross soon after cartoonist Milt Gross told him of the new magazine "where my New York drawings would fit" (Klein 53–56); more than half the issues between 1:9 and 5:52 carry his 148 cartoons from this period. Klein often used lengthy, two-line captions, but even his very early contributions worked from visual ideas, which captions sharpened. Visual humor thus set his ideas quite apart from the mainly verbal illustrated jokes of *Judge* and *Life*.

Visual details of Klein's cartoons typically depict a cockeyed world that renders incongruous dialogue hilarious. He used the technique as early as his second drawing for the magazine, of a chaotic, filthy office in which one of two beefy cleaning women demonstrates moral refinement in her report that she declined the night watchman's proposition: "I ain't gonna break up no happy home!" (4/25/25:20). The larger of his two items in the issue of August 7, 1926, sharpened those dynamics. The drawing shows two men in top hats actively engaged in their business. Mayhem abounds. As they clip newspapers with oversized scissors, dictate into a recording machine, and read a huge volume through binoculars, the men add to the mess: a telephone (off the hook), a cash register, piles of books, a typewriter, globe, and stacks of advertisements (promising "EASY PATH TO CULTURE," "BECOME POPULAR OVER NIGHT," and other kinds of success). The comic calm amid this chaos comes from the clean ink lines and shapes as well as from two details in the background—bars on their window, and the armed keeper marching past it—and the caption, which presents a model of civilized conversation, albeit of the commercial type. "Tell me, my dear Perkins, how you, with nothing more than a college education . . . have filled your mind with such a treasure house of fascinating information," says one. "Tut-tut! It is nothing," replies the other, who finally lets us see that the cartoon burlesques self-help advertising, "I saw the advertisement [and] knew it was my chance. . . ." (8/7/26:20). Here the men in top hats are crazy, and (they think?) they are running an advertising business. The parodic caption adds irony to the comic idea, joining satire to burlesque. The humor owes something to Klein's characters (every bit as loony as the Whoops! sisters, who ran in the same issue) and their dress (Arno and Irvin had already made top hats a trademark), as well as to the topic (advertising received a lot of ridicule). But its sophistication lies in Klein's integration of verbal, visual, and conceptual incongruities, and in readers' ability to appreciate them.

The length of Klein's captions underscores how historians have misunderstood the *New Yorker*'s innovations. *New Yorker*-style cartoons displaced the old formula of the illustrated joke not by reducing the length of the caption but by uniting it with the drawing. Because illustrated jokes typically identified speakers, often as "He" and "She," Kramer (among others) claimed that the *New Yorker*'s one-line cartoon grew out of Ross's particular prejudice against lengthy captions as distractions from the graphic image (129). This explanation overlooks the chief fact of the illustrated joke: the irrelevance of its art to the humor. Frustration with the old style evidently ran high in *New Yorker* circles. Eight months before the *New Yorker*'s debut, Benchley's introduction to a cartoon collection by *Life* artist Ellison Hoover scorned illustrated jokes as evidence that

"Tell me, my dear Perkins, how you, with nothing more than a college education and no time to read, have filled your mind with such a treasure house of fascinating information. You answer all questions, you hold us hypnotized with your knowledge, your witticism, your aphorisms. All men admire and envy you."
    "Tut-tut! It is nothing. I was blind, I was dumb, I was a bore—and then came that day. I saw the advertisement: Personality in Three Easy Lessons. I knew it was my chance. I feverishly clipped the coupon and—popularity, great Heaven, popularity! I was a made man."

I. Klein, 8/7/26:20.

"nothing at all went on in the mind of the artist" (Hoover n.p.). *New Yorker* cartoons, on the other hand, required mental effort from artists to visualize comic ideas and from readers to interpret them. Some ideas required long captions. The caption in Klein's crazy admen cartoon added 50 percent to the space required to run it, Leonard Dove's cartoon of two women gossiping took three lines (6/22/29:15), and Carl Rose's famous spinach cartoon, often singled out as the quintessential example of *New Yorker* graphic humor, also has a two-line caption. Only after the mother identifies the vegetable as broccoli does little girl let go with "I say it's spinach, and I say the hell with it" (12/8/28:27).

Klein's crazy admen would not be half so funny if they were not making advertisements, suggesting the possibility that real advertisements—especially those on radio, recently commercialized in 1926—were made by people in asylums. (New York's importance as a media and advertising center made this hu-

"It's broccoli, dear."
"I say it's spinach, and I say the hell with it."

Often cited as the quintessential *New Yorker* cartoon, this drawing demonstrates that the key to the *New Yorker*'s comic art lay in the relation (typically ironic) of art to text, not the reduction of two-line captions to one. Carl Rose [caption by E. B. White], 12/8/28:27.

mor local—maybe even personal—for the magazine's readers.) Nor would the spinach cartoon be funny if it depicted two boys from tenements snatching food off outdoor tables at a restaurant rather than a cultured mother and her daughter. The humor here arises primarily from the contrast between the extreme vulgarity of the line (written by E. B. White) and the extreme gentility of the image. The well-dressed mother speaks gently as she leans solicitously over the tablecloth, so we are astonished that this little girl—so small that her Orphan-Annie head doesn't even clear the chair back, so prim in her puffed sleeves and with her elbows off the table—swears like a sailor. That incongruity delighted *New Yorker* staff members as well as readers. Audax Minor alluded to it a year later in a column on racing at the Pimlico track, declaring, "I say it's Spinach. What a name for a horse!" (11/2/29:64–66). Sixty-six years later, in the 1994 anniversary issue, Robert Weber kept the joke alive by attributing the line to a little boy in a Japanese teahouse: "I say it's seaweed, and I say the hell with it" (2/20–27/94:77). The semiotic conflict between words and images in the spinach joke has infinite flexibility.

"I say it's seaweed, and I say the hell with it."

The spinach joke continued to tickle *New Yorker* humorists' imaginations sixty-six years after White wrote it. Robert Weber, 2/21/94:77.

Old cartoons' clumsy designation of speakers as "He," "Old Gentleman," "First Professor," or "Apprentice" gradually diminished from 1925 to 1927, with a few exceptions through 1929.[1] Pressure against such labels came from the art committee's requirement that the drawing contain as much information as possible, including the identity of the speaker. The two-line caption lived on, but it and the drawing acquired new relationships to each other as the *New Yorker* cartoon developed.

Alan Dunn, who drew the third idea drawing in the turning-point issue of August 7, 1926, also advanced the new relation of image to text. His first idea drawing for the magazine announced mastery of the genre. The dark one-third-page image conveys a romantic scene of youthful longing: a young woman sits on a fire escape and stares at the moon while the glow of city lights brings the skyline into silhouette, with loneliness just barely suggested by the single plant

"The next selection, entitled 'Moonbeams and You,' is dedicated to those of our radio audience who may at this moment be resting beside their sweethearts on the cool moonlit shores of lakes and rivers, beside the glorious ocean, or far at sea."

Alan Dunn, 8/7/26:21. Courtesy of the Syracuse University Art Collection.

on the windowsill and the oversized radio-speaker replacing a companion next to the figure. The caption evokes the same mood, but the scene it describes clashes with the depiction on the page. The radio announcer dedicates "The next selection, entitled 'Moonbeams and You'" to people "resting beside their sweethearts" (not sitting alone) "on cool moonlit shores" (not fire escapes many stories up) "beside the glorious ocean or far at sea" (not the densely populated islands of New York's urban archipelago). Dunn's cartoon epitomized the *New Yorker's* brand of sophisticated humor: invoking neither snob appeal nor opposing sneers, it invited the audience to exercise intelligence and wit. The *New Yorker* announced the importance of this piece by running it just above an important casual by E. B. White, "Hey Day Labor" (8/7/26:21).

Among the most prolific *New Yorker* artists in the magazine's history, Dunn seems to have had no bone to pick with high society, though he traveled in more comfortable New York circles than many of his colleagues. He grew up in a Manhattan brownstone, attended Columbia for one year, then studied at the National School of Fine and Applied Art (1918–19) and the National Academy of Design (1919–22), after which he won fellowships from the Tiffany Foundation providing housing and studio for him to paint on the foundation's grounds in Oyster Bay and travel grants to study at the Fontainebleau School of Fine Arts and the American Academy of Rome.[2] His experience as a painter, like Klein's career in animated cartoons, helps explain his facility with the visual demands of the idea drawing. The success of his first *New Yorker* effort, however, quickly diverted Dunn from fine art; lacking the steady income of a day job, he devoted himself entirely to publishing what he called "social cartoons," which he considered professionally equal to fine art. He saved his studies, or "roughs," accordingly; refused as a matter of professional pride to accept ideas from any source other than his imagination (he avoided reading other magazines for fear of inadvertently committing plagiarism);[3] and successfully defended his exemption from New York State's taxes on unincorporated businesses by demonstrating that he practiced a profession rather than ran a commercial art business.[4]

Dunn sold so many cartoons to the *New Yorker* that no one has succeeded in counting them. Although *New Yorker* staff estimated his total as 1,900 (Tatham [5]), Dunn (who meticulously tallied submissions, sales, rejections, and critiques) claimed nearly 3,000 when he suggested in 1968 that the magazine mark the accomplishment by repairing the award he received for his one thousandth, a watch that "ticked its last tock 1500 pictures ago."[5] His 181 drawings through the end of volume 5 identify the quality and import of his contributions. A master of the idea drawing's ironic relation of image and text, Dunn provided examples from 1926 onward for other artists to follow.

His choice of subjects kept his social criticism light. Radio was a favorite target, other media ranking just behind. "Just a minute, dearie, until I shut off Herbert Hoover," says one of his characters, choosing the telephone over the radio, conflating the mediated voice and the person (9/15/28:19)—a favorite joke. "Yes, we named her Mavis Dorine," coos a proud mother in an unsigned drawing using Dunn's style and themes; then she adds (while her husband looks on with disgust), "isn't it lovely? We got it over the radio" (10/1/27:26).[6] But his

"Now, Winifred, don't be specious."

Alan Dunn, 10/9/26:30.

most durable joke, which became a *New Yorker* trademark, exploited in the spinach joke and others, resulted having emotion-laden words emerge from the wrong mouth.

One strand put adult language in children's mouths. Two years before White wrote the spinach line, Dunn had a child insist, "Now Winifred, don't be specious" (10/9/26:30). Only the picture makes clear that a conversation between two males at a dance—a reminder that "mother" expected him "to dance with Miss Jones," followed by an appalled "What, that adolescent?"—involves two youngsters in a room full of their peers, including Miss Jones, who looks less than adolescent. By December, Dunn stretched the idea further, attributing adult hostility to a toddler and her associates. When Gladys wants a turn with her scooter, a comrade insists, "Oh, don't be such a bore" (12/11/26:29). Her mother responds to Gladys's conversation by warning, "Another word about my morals and I'll send you right home" (8/27/27:18). After Dunn moved Gladys to daily newspapers, where *Gladys and the Young Moderns* was syndicated nationally beginning August 29, 1927,[7] other artists played with the idea. Fourteen months after it provided the zing for the spinach cartoon, it fueled a drawing by Helen Hokinson where two little boys still in short pants consider the little girl sitting demurely on the sofa, and remark that she lacks intellect but "has won-

"*Bloomers,
panties,
step-ins,
or teddies?*"

Mary Petty's cartoons spoke for the peer society in joking about the older generation.
6/29/29:50.

derful associations" (2/15/30:22). The idea had staying power because individual artists visualized it differently. Whereas Dunn contrasted Gladys's adult
speech with the primitive crayon outline of her shape, Rose and Hokinson reinforced the incongruity of the children's vulgarity by delineating them gently.

Mary Petty reversed this idea, attributing to adults phrases for children.
Dunn's wife, Petty began her *New Yorker* career somewhat later than her husband, who declared himself her only teacher, but her twenty-nine drawings from
October 22, 1927, through February 8, 1930, show independent mastery of the
idea drawing. A stellar example came at the start of volume 5, "'Mrs. Cox, this
is my first-born'" (2/23/29:30):[8] although the caption implies a mother introducing a very young child or infant, the drawing shows an elderly woman presenting a balding man to a middle-aged woman younger than he. Still fairly
young herself, Petty particularly enjoyed making fun of middle-aged men and
women—especially insecure women taking advice from others. One nattily

dressed character, speaking cheerfully into a pay phone, announces her arrival in Harlem and asks, "what ought I to do?" (6/16/28:30). The look on her face does not imply any worry about finding herself uptown (as it might have in the 1970s) but rather suggests that she seeks adventure, even if she does not quite know how to find it. Such digs at the older generation—like her shopping-page drawing of a modish young saleswoman breezily asking a dignified elderly woman, "Bloomers, panties, step-ins, or teddies?" (6/29/29:50)—particularly flattered the peer society. As Arno's cartoons approved the peer society's values, so Petty's critiqued their parents'.

Favorite Ideas and Themes

Playing with the caption led naturally to dialect jokes. A staple of American jokelore, dialect humor connects the *New Yorker*'s comic art to nineteenth-century popular literary traditions as well as to 1920s newspaper comics. *New Yorker* dialect cartoons developed humor based on character rather than situation. Like Arno's Whoops! sisters, a few featured nearly incoherent slang, but most others toyed with regional color (in immigrant or regional accents) and social class (through slang and pronunciation). All exhibited far more restraint than the twenties' vogue, as exemplified by the Yiddish accents of Milt Gross's *Hiawatta* (1926). For example, "ain't" and "dearie" suffice to classify the chorus girl of a 1926 drawing by Eugene McNerney, but the caption extends its ridicule to the reader as well. McNerney, who contributed sixty graphic items to volumes 1–5, mainly in 1926 and 1927, here exposes venality along with a chorus girl's legs. The caption reinforces stereotypes about chorus girls' ignorance and selfishness, what they see in college men, and vice versa: "He ain't stingy," the friend of the half-dressed dancer urges, "an' he's gonna drive us down to Princeton for the Yale-Harvard game" (11/6/26:27). The scenario encapsulated in the line invites the educated *New Yorker* reader to feel superior to the chorus girl, no matter how attractive or beautifully undressed. The picture specifies that she already makes money off her body, so why should she resist the friend who offers her a socially desirable date? Yet the remark also implies the girl's reluctance to accept the offer, complicating the joke: criticism of the girl for having the nerve to think such a man unworthy of a date reflects back on the reader—and the man and her friend—for condescending to her.

As the twenties progressed, however, class politics became less subtle. Mary Petty ridiculed a pair of schoolgirls in uniform whose language undercuts their

"Mais non Madame, your watch is perfect. All it needs is a little erl."

A staple of American jokelore, dialect humor in the 1920s *New Yorker* reversed nineteenth-century comic traditions. Nancy Fay, 2/23/29:22.

efforts to show off their sophistication: one has a Brooklyn accent ("What's he got—an awfice?"), and the other is inarticulate ("No, he's got like a loft" 9/15/28:33). In fact, a drawing by Nancy Fay suggests the smug view that class will always out: her handsome tuxedo-clad worker in a jewelry store slips from an elegant "Mais non" to Brooklynese in a single statement, advising a customer that her watch needs only "a little erl" (2/23/29:22). The *New Yorker*'s dialect cartoons reversed the traditions of nineteenth-century American humor, which valorized vernacular speakers as heroes of a popular culture that values common sense over book learning. (Helen Hokinson, on the other hand, urged more cartoons without any captions at all.[9])

Some cartoons reversed course and razzed upper-class characters, especially stuffy ones, as the magazine's class-restrictions loosened toward the end of the decade. Arno mocked one of his dowagers as she stands with her small grandson, calls a Coney Island vendor "my good man," and orders "Two weenies" (9/15/28:29). A full-page dialect joke by Garrett Price shows that the *New Yorker* found humor in any socially incongruous speech, no matter who spoke it: an American's elegant dress cannot cover his stupidity in asking a count whether "they no spikka much English in your country" (10/26/29:35). Whereas heroic dialect speakers as Huckleberry Finn or Jim promoted a democratic vision equating natural language with natural virtue, the *New Yorker's* dialect speakers—of whatever class—expose their inadequacy.

The social conservatism of *New Yorker* cartoons coexisted with liberal politics, however. Although the *New Yorker* failed to cover the "Mongrel Manhattan" described by Ann Douglas in *Terrible Honesty,* I see no evidence in the 1920s for Thomas Grant's claim that Ross infected the magazine with racism ("Feminist" 157–58). Cartoons joked about the contemporary interest in African aesthetics, and many explicitly satirized racial prejudice. The cover for April 27, 1929, by no less an insider than art director Rea Irvin envisioned a happy reversal of racial and class hierarchies by contrasting two figures at a fashion show. An African woman in flowered dress and lace mantilla aristocratically parades before a dumpy white matron, a performance that puts the brown woman in the center and the white woman on the margin. More important, bearing and beauty define the African as the true aristocrat. Nose in the air, headdress breaking through the upper border into the title, profile framed by the halo of a round window in the background, she fills the visual field, towering above and displacing the dowdy matron, so mousey in her grey suit and hat. The model so dominates the cover, in fact, that she limits the matron to a space where only her head and one shoulder fit. The design avoids serious social critique but ridicules racism by attributing it to the old guard and portraying its reversal as aesthetically attractive.

Cartoons inside the book did undertake such satire. "The Last Ku Kluxer," an early drawing by *Judge* regular Frank Hanley, imagines a comic reversal of fortunes when African Americans will be well dressed and Klan members reduced to begging (3/28/25:20). The cartoon acknowledges New Yorkers' resistance to the Klan, which thrived almost everywhere in the United States outside New York and Boston during this period (Douglas 316). Late in 1926, Reginald Marsh satirized the Afrophilia of liberal racists in "'Miranda, I thought you'd be interested in this'" (12/4/26:35). This drawing of a woman talking to her African-American maid is filled with signs of the employer's cultivated taste, but the caption implies the irrelevance of white taste to black lives. While the

"Miranda, I thought you'd be interested in this... by your people, you know —such significant solidity... such a surface... how do you do it?"

New Yorker cartoons scorned pseudoliberalism as well as conventional racism. Reginald Marsh, 12/4/26:35.

maid stands uncomfortable and silent near the left edge of the drawing, wedged between the grand piano and a Queen Anne desk, the employer sits comfortably, with plenty of space around her, just off center to the right. A Picasso-esque still life, grandfather clock, and abstract sculpture in the background all testify that her money is old but her tastes up to date, while her hands—exactly in the center—point to the featured item in the drawing, an African statuette, placed slightly to the left. As she leans earnestly toward the maid, the matron's posture exposes the pretense of appealing to the maid's interest as her claim to the maid's attention, implying that the praise for the aesthetic accomplishments of "your people" is as empty as the center of the drawing. Employers' condescension toward maids also boomerangs in cartoons by Garrett Price and Peter Arno, who continued this critique of racism in 1927 and 1928 with similarly ironic relations between the caption and art (Price 12/17/27:21; Arno 5/12/28:19). As New Yorker artists and readers grew more fluent with the conventions of the idea drawing, ironic tensions grew between the verbal and graphic renderings of the speaker.

"Niggers all look alike to me."
"Yeah, no individuality."

Claims that the *New Yorker* was racist fizzle in the face of satirical cartoons like this attack on prejudice. Alan Dunn, 5/7/27:26.

A few cartoons explicitly advanced the liberal agenda. Six months after Marsh's drawing, Alan Dunn deflated racist smugness by depicting a large delegation of white politicians—all of them with identical features, glasses, and clothes—who complain as their open car passes 135th Street in Harlem. "'Niggers all look alike to me,'" says one unidentifiable member of the group; another replies, "Yeah, no individuality" (5/7/27:26). Sympathy for the economic and social limitations of dark skin came through in a poignant cartoon by Eugene McNerney four months later. The dialect of "'She passin', boy?'" expresses an African-American viewpoint without ridiculing it, as two well-dressed men discuss a woman they know as she rides by in a chauffeured convertible. The punning response, "Yassuh. And in passin' is how yo' got to note her," declares her subversion of racial politics amusing (9/24/27:34). The appearance of these cartoons in a magazine directed at a white, elite audience underscores James Weldon Johnson's claim in *Black Manhattan* (1930) that "New York, more than any other American city, maintains a matter-of-fact, a taken-for-granted attitude towards her Negro citizens" (Johnson 157). It also explains the Raeburn Van Buren cartoon of two African Americans buying a ticket for a sightseeing tour of Chinatown (2/1/30:11) as a comic parallel to the white tours of Harlem.

The *New Yorker*'s policy on racial themes reflected a contemporary understanding of good taste. Angell rejected an item for "Talk" about a redheaded bootblack with "potential qualities as a side-show feature,"[10] yet a "We Stand Corrected" column carried a letter complaining that Gardner Rea's cartoon "Dirty Work at the Union League" (9/24/27:30) misrepresented its employees as white (10/29/27:60). The lengthy complaint, complete with history of the club's support of black regiments, demonstrates the *New Yorker*'s attitude toward race: a rather typical middle-class tolerance, well behind the avant-garde celebrated by Carl Van Vechten and his crowd, but hardly racist.

Overt racism does mark some cartoons by today's standards. Black figures were often tribesmen or servants; minstrel masks predominated. A 1928 spot drawing by Julian De Miskey showed a well-dressed uptown couple—she in a cloche hat and fashionably slender chemise dress, he in a plaid jacket, striped tie, and jaunty straw boater, both of them smiling broadly in an abstract rendering of blackface (8/11/28:32). The terrified African warriors running away from the smiling pink elephant in Constantin Aladjalov's 1929 jungle cover offer a certain—and certainly comic—ambiguity by implying that they're fleeing a hallucination come to life. But it's not at all certain whose nightmare this is, nor what is the cause of the not-so-great white hunter's surprise, the elephant's emergence from the jungle or the warriors' abandonment of the hunt. On the other hand, the dismaying visual parallels between the warriors' faces below and monkeys' faces above render the humor stale and offensive for readers today, even though primate features, like the minstrel mask, were graphic conventions particularly in vogue in the period that saw the Monkey Trial. Just as Al Frueh's "Little-Known Event in the Advertising World" (1/21/28:19) and "A New Perfume is Created" (7/14/28:22–23) portray virile tribal types with monkey faces, his white males are similarly (though less politically) stereotyped as portly middle-age bumblers. Compared to *Judge,* however, the *New Yorker* had quite a liberal and sophisticated slant on race. Not one of the *New Yorker*'s early cartoons expresses the smug contempt of *Judge*'s "Frosted Chocolate" by H. J. Peck, showing a well-dressed African-American couple drinking root beer at a bar with a grinning blackface bartender and surrounded by semiliterate signs for "water-mellin flip" and "plantation <S>undy" (*Judge* 5/5/23:11). Nor did the *New Yorker* of the twenties ever indulge racial representations such as E. W. Kemble's illustrated joke about "sanctified milk" (*Judge* 1/7/22:5) that gave black folks the job of amusing white readers.

Cartoons about courtship, marriage, and gender roles lampooned the peer society's liberal attitudes as much as their elders' conservative ones. Earnest faces mock free love in a "Talk" layout appropriately titled "Companionate Marriage: To Be Or Not To Be?" (Hokinson, 2/18/28:22). The long legs and shapely bodies of Shermund's female characters exude sexuality, but her cartoons sneer at courtship explicitly and implicitly. In drawings that contrast women's soft hats and skirts with their harsh judgments, Shermund's women usually find men wanting. "I think Henry'd make a marvellous husband," an attractive, well-dressed young woman explains to her stylishly coiffed friend, who sits on the edge of her chair waiting for the rest of the assessment while the speaker stares earnestly at a large picture, presumably Henry's. "He's so kind to animals" (10/1/27:23). Thus she implies not only that Henry can't tell a dog from a woman and that marriage is for the birds but also that husbands and wives constitute a lower species. Other Shermund cartoons joke about the difference between marriage and love. Hence a manicurist, a member of the practical lower class, advises her demure client to have a large wedding: "then you have something nice to remember" (11/24/28:66). As in most of her cartoons about courtship, Shermund drew these two women as age peers and placed them in opposite but otherwise similar positions across the table from one another, suggesting a bond across the class lines normally separating the well-bred client, with her bobbed hair, cloche, and pearls, from the manicurist, also attractive, but whose heavily made-up eyes and slang "dearie" mark her as lower class. Not the cute flappers of Fish or Held, Shermund's attractive modern women—sleek of body, strong of dress and opinion—reject men in word and deed.

Men fared little better when Shermund put them in the picture than when she left them out. Two women ignore the man between them as they gossip about a nearby couple, and their comment about that man, "He was quite a bachelor—but he's married now," implies that the state has unsexed him (12/31/27). One of Shermund's rare narrative cartoons takes the point further. Chosen for reprint in *The New Yorker Album, 1925–1950,* the nine scenes run boldly across two pages text as they track the conversation between a December-May couple, she slim and beautiful and silent, he portly and balding and voluble. The joke hinges on talk—a pretty funny idea for eight panels without dialogue.

Barbara Shermund, 7/1/28:30–31.

His gesticulations show the intensity of his conversation, which she has followed mutely, but only the last drawing has a caption, implying that he had nothing worthwhile to say until his announcement, "You're a very intelligent little woman, my dear" (5/19/28:30–31). By looking straight out of the drawing, the woman invites readers to share her bewilderment at this declaration, which exposes his vanity and ridicules his values (like children, women should be seen but not heard?), and thus suggests the degree to which Shermund's ideas spoke directly to at least one segment of the *New Yorker*'s audience. The increasing boldness of her antimale feminism in 1928 demonstrates that claims to the *New*

"You're a very intelligent little woman, my dear."

Yorker's misogyny are absolutely unfounded in this period, when the art committee of Rea Irvin, Katharine Angell, and Harold Ross approved and enjoyed this radical feminist humor.

Of course, gender jokes ran in both directions. In addition to Arno's famous undignified matrons, Leonard Dove portrayed a woman subway rider whose packages drove her seatmate into the wall while he insisted, "No——no inconvenience whatsoever, Madam" (1/14/28:23), pointing out the injustice of etiquette. The same issue had an Arno cartoon of a group of men in a steamroom, one clutching his towel as he tried to get rid of his woman caller (20), and a Shermund drawing of an older woman stretched out on her chaise as she complained to the doctor, sitting worriedly beside her, about the distressing amount of activity in her mind (19). Misogyny *may* have emerged more explicitly as a theme in cartoons and stories from the 1930s, a period often collapsed into the '20s but which my analysis suggests should remain distinct. Specifically, the theme usually hinges on Thurber's cartoons, many of which focus on the war between the sexes; research has not determined, however, whether they dominated the magazine, despite the intriguing possibility that they reflected the changing mood of the peer culture as members confronted the Great Depression and their movement from youth toward middle age. In any case, Thurber did not publish cartoons in the magazine until 6:1, and extant examples of his graphic humor from the twenties suggest he still felt some idealism about love then. The "Embrace Series" that he gave as a wedding present to E. B. and Katharine White in 1929 came with a note pointing out his efforts to "catch . . . the mad delight, the pathos, the fun, and the beauty of love."[11]

The most consistent target of race and gender jokes was the older generation—a bias inherent in the magazine's peer audience. As the twenties progressed, and more members of this generation married and had children, cartoons on family life and parent-child interactions gradually displaced drunken revels. A drawing signed "Ginny W" depicted a schoolgirl pressed into service to clean up booze after a bridge game (11/9/29:33). But for the most part, older folks were simply funny, especially if they imagined themselves equal to their younger counterparts. This idea underlay many of Hokinson's drawings—including her cover of a matron dancing for the joy of spring and her cartoon of another matron buying a funny Christmas card because "I want to indulge in a caprice" (11/9/29:88). Both men and women cartoonists enjoyed ridiculing the follies of older women. A large drawing by Alice Harvey on the shopping page, for instance, showed a matron in a her slip nervously chewing her nails while eyeing a dress that the young saleswoman holds out: "Oh dear, that one goes in at the waist, doesn't it?" she asks, adding (accurately), "I can't go in at the waist" (8/10/29:44).

Mass media joined generation and gender gaps as a favorite topic for *New Yorker* cartoons. Alan Dunn tweaked lower-class aficionados of the illustrated newspapers in a drawing of pudgy, baseball-hatted reader of the *Graphic* who complains, "The trouble wit Coolidge is he don't seem to read the editorials" (5/7/27:32). I. Klein's "News" offered a one-panel allegory: a photographer dressed in a costume made of screaming sensationalist headlines (complete with a newsprint dunce cap) aims his camera at a posed scene of a frightened man holding in his lap an equally frightened woman whose sheer nightgown is slip-

"Is there anything in the 'Times'?"

Garrett Price revised this drawing several times to meet the art meeting's specifications about how and where the newspapers should be strewn. 11/16/29:29.

ping off her shoulders, while an ax murderer stands behind them, weapon poised for business (7/2/27:28). The drawing combines old-fashioned tableau (reminiscent of John Held's woodcuts) and contemporary imagery (primarily the headlines and camera but also the top hat, evening gloves, and cane waiting for one of the men to doff his present costume for this one); such details as the dunce cap's reflection in the mirror underscore the irony of the simple title "News." But perhaps the most important idea drawing on the subject, judging both from its full-page position in the front of the book (just before "Profiles") and from the art committee's several requests that details be redrawn, is Garrett Price's rendering of an attractive couple lounging in their bathrobes, the woman half-buried under pages and sections of Sunday newspaper strewn around the room when the man asks, "Is there anything in the 'Times'?" (11/16/29:29). Her posture and tilted head suggest a casual involvement with the photo section in her lap; his face, slightly masked by shadow, declares disinterest as he looks away from her and toward the window. Price's ink wash, with its suggestions of Gibson-style portraiture, gives the characters and their situation an elegance that high-lights the incongruity of the newspaper mess, and the man's remarks in the caption, though it has just a single line, invites the reader to imagine her reply, "No, nothing much."

Leading up to this comic contempt for news, I. Klein's series of newspaper parodies began March 3, 1928, and ran for twenty installments in volumes 4 and 5. Distantly related to Ralph Barton's photo-section burlesques in volume 1, caricatures of the week's news makers, Klein's series featured fictionalized events modeled on real ones. Klein's smaller drawings and longer captions than Barton's brought art and text into balance and thereby ridiculed journalism rather than individuals, events, or types. Each installment contained four images incongruously matched to their captions and events. The series parodied news-paper images and rhetoric, exploiting readers' familiarity with journalistic prac-tice.

The first installment set the narrative pattern, though the graphic style soon changed from detailed, rounded crayon shapes to more abstract ink lines. "Seven Cent Fare: Exclusive Advance Pictures of Tense Situation" presented extravagant solutions to the potential problem of higher subway fares (3/3/28:32). Two fetching chorus girls push each other in a wheelbarrow to illustrate one alterna-tive, in "Why Use the Subways?," while "Would Swim to Brooklyn" points out limitations of another, in the story of Patrolman Delaney's rescue of an "impul-sive citizen" from the East River. The joke in the caption, which identifies the principals of this incidents as "Patrolman Delany, Citizen, Grover Whalen. Statue of Liberty in distance," offered local readers an inside joke about local pol-itics and provided out-of-towners an accessible joke about politicians and jour-nalists.[12] This joke also sums up the spirit of the series: exploiting contempt for news with local humor in a silly mood. Although fares remained a nickel from 1913 to 1948 (when they rose to a dime), and although subway companies went bankrupt in 1923 because the mayor rejected fare increases, Klein's cartoon does not target transit policy. Rather it lampoons representations of the news. As a re-sult, "A Seat for Every Pupil: Allocation of $41,000,000 Will Eliminate Part-time School Day" borrowed the politically hot topic of the double shifts required by insufficient classroom space as an occasion to make jokes about poor driving, domestic murder, lawsuits by estranged lovers, and mob killings: "Salvatore

Gigo, 6, yesterday wounded playmate, Joseph Lotto, with father's machine gun. 'Too much spare time,' said Salvatore, 'is the cause of my present embarrassment'" ("Sues for Education" 9/15/28:24). As the series progressed, however, subjects became less topical and drawings more comical; the final installment in volume 5, a month before the fifth anniversary, offered little of substance about its professed topic, "International Harmony News: Beating Swords Into Ploughshares Keeps Many People Busy Now" (1/18/30:18). The series' silliness made lower-class media, rather than lower-class people, the target of the joke.

Not that *New Yorker* cartoons refused to bite the hand that fed them. Cartoons on advertising and commerce called a plague on both houses, although (or perhaps because) advertising employed many *New Yorker* staff and freelancers either before or while they associated with the magazine. Commercial art by Peter Arno (for Miltiades Egyptian Cigarettes), Gluyas Williams (for McCreery's Department Store), and Julian De Miskey (for Faultless No-Belt pajamas) appeared in the early *New Yorker*; Phillip Wylie and E. B. White left the field before joining the staff. More to the point, the *New Yorker* targeted advertising professionals as readers. An ad series directed "To the Advertising Profession of America" in the summer of 1928 flattered "you men who, within one short generation, have brought an obscure profession to its present high plane . . . to the greatest good of all" (6/2/28:37). In light of New York's role as America's advertising capital, cartoons about ads amounted to variations on local color humor, and admen came in for special ridicule as familiar local types. Klein portrayed them as lunatics (8/7/26:20), Perry Barlow as viewing the world through commercial lenses: his copywriter relaxes by a pond graced by swans with a murmured "Grace, poise, charm, and—ah—floatability" 6/5/26:25). Admen's professional protocols also rubbed off on their children, as in J. H. Fyfe's drawing of the "Advertising Expert's Son," who asks a buddy, "Will you let me have your reactions to this lollypop, Harold?" (2/25/28:22). Alan Dunn imagined a glum group at a desk marked "ADV. MGR" getting their comeuppance from a businessman's double entendre: "Have you gentlemen ever considered changing your appeal?" (2/23/29:28).

The concept of commercial brands got a lot of ribbing. No fewer than three drawings from the issue of October 22, 1927, played with the idea. Arno's bearded lady lost her beard because "she mistook her Dunhill lighter for her Dunhill lipstick" (25). Klein represented the merger between Doubleday, Page and the Doran Company as a scene played out by their colophons, with Pegasus galloping overhead and dropping a laurel wreath onto the gods emerging from

WHEN THE TRAFFIC COP YAWNED

Gluyas Williams, *Life*, 10/25/23:1.

lightning below (30). Variations of the inside joke, all three cartoons depend on readers' familiarity with specific brands and commercial rhetoric. As Dunn pointed out in a Kindl cartoon featured on the shopping page, itself a by-product of increased commercial activity, advertising sells brand associations, not functional commodities. Hence his middle-aged shopper goes up to the pharmacist in a drugstore requesting, "Some Pond's Extract and a Borzoi book, please" (3/2/29:60), and an Alice Harvey character cautions her maid at breakfast by reciting an ad jingle, "Remember, the toaster knows" (1/25/30:20).

The high point of jokes about advertising claims and personnel came in Gluyas Williams's twenty-three full-page drawings in volumes 1–5, including

his twenty "Industrial Crises." Related to Irvin's Social Errors idea, the series began with two drawings, "The Doorman Who Forgot The Name of the Oldest
Member" (3/13/25:18) and "The Housewrecker Discovers He Has the Wrong
Number" (6/26/26:12), both of which extended themes and comic devices already present in Williams's cartoons for *Life.* "When the Traffic Cop Yawned"
(*Life* 10/25/23:11), like his subsequent "Deserter" (*Life* 11/6/24:7), celebrates
the deviant individual—the traffic policeman whose inadvertent motion instantly halts traffic (note the grotesquely slanted bodies in the tableau), the girl
scout who abandons her quasi-military responsibilities in a parade to indulge
fantasies of love and madness at the movies. When the *New Yorker's* deservedly
famous "Industrial Crises" began with "Unfortunate occurrence in the general
offices of a well-known cigarette manufacturer" (10/1/27:17), deviance shifted
from the social to the commercial arena. The calamity is a violation of the advertising claim for Old Gold cigarettes (in the *New Yorker* and elsewhere): "not a
cough in a carload." The drawings' style reinforces their idea of deviance: the formal design, with shapes sharply defined in black and white, contrasts with the
frantic emotions implied by the tableau. When the series concluded with "A
Face Appears in One of the Italian Windows at Alice Foote MacDougal's"
(9/7/29:28), no less an authority than Dorothy Hoover, the editorial assistant for
art correspondence, declared it "just about the funniest drawing I ever saw."[13]
The longevity of Williams's Industrial Crisis cartoons, among the *New Yorker's*
best-known early drawings, enabled the series to parody not only specific advertising claims but also advertising culture itself. In the 1920s commercial discourse forged its contemporary role as the bedrock of Americans' common
culture, providing materials for modern humor.

   One strand of idea drawing took a different tack, rendering the caption literally instead of contrasting image and caption for ironic effect. Although literalism began in the fall of 1925 with such ideas as Irvin's "Tomato Surprise," which
imagines a menu item as a dramatic event (10/10/25:11), funnier examples came
later—for example, his drawing of a frenetic pianist, "The Professor Plays
Chopin's 'Minute Waltz' in Forty-Seven Seconds" (12/15/28:30). Literalism had
its strongest run, however, not in conventional gag cartoons but in the layout
humor that began late in 1926 and peaked between 1927 and 1929.

   Layout decisions putting the fold or turn of page to comic advantage began
in 1926 and grew during 1927. This most innovative form of *New Yorker* humor
has gone entirely unnoticed, probably because the drawing interacts with copy
as a spacial element of the page, a comic idea not easily reproduced in cartoon

H. O. Hofman's drawing of a hunter, dog, and bird occasioned an early experiment in layout as a comic device. 11/27/26:26–27.

anthologies. An early example appeared November 27, 1926, just three weeks after Spud Johnson's contribution to the parody issue teased Ross as exclaiming, "We gotta be playful in makeup":[14] a hunting scene by H. O. Hofman puts an attractive woman hunter on the bottom left page and the duck she's tracking across the fold on the top right (11/27/26:26–27). The layout exploits the fold and the left-to-right direction of the book to claim and direct the reader's attention as it develops and then resolves suspense. Staff found the concept funny enough to repeat with other subjects, including a bridal procession so long that its participants stretched across the bottom of four pages (Hokinson, 6/4/1927:20–23). Literalism also brought humor to department illustrations. Johan Bull's sports caricatures for a 1926 football column included the silly "Lawler's Feet Could Not Follow Him" (11/13/26:26), a drawing probably split to cross a fold but much more comically made up on a single page. Making

LAWLER'S FEET COULD NOT FOLLOW HIM

Layout enhanced humor in departments. Johan Bull, 11/13/26:40.

comic use of space and time in the single-image drawing, layout humor transferred recent innovations in film and animation to popular print culture.

And Then There Were None

Pantomime cartoon series contributed to layout humor more broadly, adding narrative conventions to space and time as comic elements. Emphasis on the single-panel gag cartoon, the most famous genre of *New Yorker* art, has obscured a genre that the art committee considered important enough to include in almost every issue: the narrative cartoon. The *New Yorker* published 245 multi-image graphic narratives in volumes 1–5, of which the vast majority—some 190—were pantomimes: stories told frame by frame through images alone, without dialogue or captions. A handful of the art committee's favorite artists drew most of them. Otto Soglow contributed nearly half the total himself (74), followed by Al Frueh (46), Gardner Rea (15), Rea Irvin (14), and Julian De Miskey (7). The interrelation of word and picture elsewhere in the magazine made pantomimes' silence all the more deafening. After all, newspaper cartoons had incorporated dialogue since July 7, 1895, when Richard Felton Outcault inaugurated *The Yellow Kid,* the first cartoon to substitute dialogue inside the drawing for a caption below it (Becker 10–13). Movies incorporated dialogue into their narratives through "intertitle" frames even before "talkies" arrived in 1927, when Al Jolson starred in

This early pantomime narrative played with modernist ideas about representation of mental states. Rea Irvin, 10/31/25:16–17.

The Jazz Singer. In this context, the *New Yorker's* use of pantomime cartoons has nothing to do with the state of comic art or its technologies but reflects aesthetic and editorial preference instead—a retrograde joke. Unlike idea drawings, whose many visual details construct a complex social humor, pantomimes feature an abstract, deceptively simple style that focuses on two essentials of storytelling, plot and point of view. The process made popular humor from the materials of the modernist project.

A few narratives played with the familiar modernist issues of interior reality and mental states. In Rea Irvin's "A Quiet Evening with a Book" (10/31/1925:16–17), twelve drawings across two pages trace a man's rising drunkenness by distorting the representation of him and his surroundings: straight lines become swirls and flat surfaces bend as the protagonist's vision—and ours—becomes destabilized. Otto Soglow joked about the power of the imagination in a six-frame story about a man's dream of a fabulous multicourse restaurant dinner, from which he awakens bewildered by his expanded belly (6/11/1927:18–19). Soglow returned to this theme of ideas made real a few other times during this period (e.g., 12/8/28:58, 1/4/30:21), but for the most part the genre avoided explicit expressions of the modernist literary manifesto.

The *New Yorker* ridiculed modernist ideas while also exploiting them. I. Klein, 3/10/28:30–31.

Indeed, as theme, modernism was a joke, as when I. Klein burlesqued dadaism in "The Connoisseur And The . . . / . . . Fried Eggs" (3/10/28:30–31).

More typical were jokes about narration itself. Pantomimes often stretched stories into anticlimactic jokes about plot, as in Frueh's early cartoon about a father and his grown son who traverse the countryside in thirty-four frames on three pages en route to the dad's confession, "There isn't any Santa Claus"

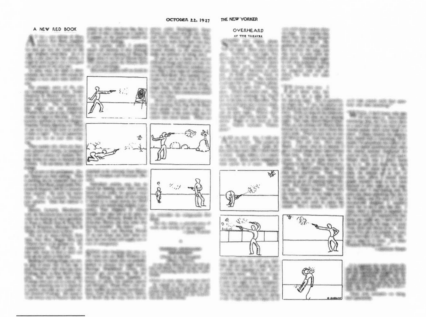

Otto Soglow, 10/22/27:26–27.

(6/13/25:11–13). Otto Soglow perfected this idea in much shorter tales that likewise gave absurd answers to the question "What's happening?" Many of Soglow's cartoons follow the pattern of his story of a woman who for five panels just sits in her bathtub, then exits the tub with two small dogs (10/20/1928:38). The joke is on us, for seeking connections—even absurd ones, such as the possibility that she gave birth to those dogs while soaking—between the individual frames of the tale.

Pantomime cartoons seldom reappeared in cartoon anthologies, probably because many layouts bound them to the magazine. Whereas Frueh's narrative cartoons usually filled a page or two, Soglow's shorter strips appeared amid text, where they acquired various shapes—stepped down across the page or laid out in other patterns—that controlled the narrative pace by imposing pauses on the reader. Soglow's became the dominant form as his pantomimes outnumbered Frueh's by a ratio of two to one beginning in 1927, when layout humor peaked. An untitled drawing of a man engaged in target practice illustrates how this kind of narrative rhetoric suspends and then frustrates expectations (Soglow, 10/22/27:26–27). The strip shows a sharpshooter performing a series of difficult tricks, but the layout makes it hard to follow the story in a single movement

Otto Soglow, 2/11/28:25.

from beginning to end. Images run in pairs across and down two pages of text, like a flight of steps, requiring readers to trace the story down, then across, then down, then across the fold, then down and across and down again. Pairs of panels frame the action, emphasizing the tricks themselves, not the progress from one trick to the next; thus the layout invites a comic contrast between the progress of the narrative and lack of progress in the plot. In fact, the layout delays not only our anticipation of the ending but also our arrival there, where the sudden, climactic finale violates the loose pattern of the story and its promised end. Instead of a dazzlingly difficult finale typical of performers, for his last trick the sharpshooter shoots himself in the head, surely not by accident. The force of the shot knocks him into the air, reinforcing the finality of this unfunny end.

An early example of the black humor that became popular in the 1960s, Soglow's apparently simple strip plays in sophisticated ways with generic expectations of plot and mood. Other pantomimes repeated the joke and reinforced its dark rhetoric, evidently enjoyed by the art committee. A few months after this grim tale of target practice, another of Soglow's pantomimes showed a circus performer actually succeed in sawing a woman in half (2/11/28:25). Gardner

Rea ("Down But Not Out: Dan, the Ex-dip, Makes Good" 12/3/27:32–33) and Julian De Miskey (whose grim story of entrepreneurial failure ended with a "success" wreath on a grave, 6/26/26:16) also contributed to this strand of grim humor. Published at the same time that e. e. cummings composed his most important work, these narratives—as made up by *New Yorker* staff—explore how line breaks shape reading, and thus how reading constructs significance. In this context, it would be hard to find a more compelling application of modernist principles than Soglow's pantomimes. As *New Yorker* layout humor played with the flexibility of time in relation to space, only a few years after Einsteinian physics received wide public attention, it demonstrated that sophisticated humor relied less on representations of class than on knowledge and ideas shared by artists and readers.

The pantomime cartoon asserted a purely graphic wit, a strong contrast to the emphatically linguistic genres of the *New Yorker*'s verbal humor. The opening department was, after all, "The *Talk* of the Town," and a surprising number of prose pieces featured puns, dialect, and mock-oral dialogue. As modern painters influenced literary experimentalists such as Gertrude Stein (Steiner, *Pictures*), so those narrative experiments came back into visual culture through the *New Yorker*'s comic drawings for popular audiences.

In addition, pantomimes support W. J. T. Mitchell's arguments for the non-semiotic dimensions of the visual image (*Iconology*; *Picture Theory*). The *New Yorker*'s pantomime narratives suggest a more radical conclusion, however, than Mitchell's claim that painting and writing are mutually reinforcing sister arts more similar than different. In the hands of *New Yorker* artists and editors, adding the time element implied by narrative sequence to the static graphic image eliminates the need for words altogether. Thus the early *New Yorker* characterized art not as "mute poetry," in the tradition of *ut pictura poesis,* but treated sister arts of drawing and writing as siamese twins.

Collaboration Between Editors and Artists

Once *New Yorker* artists mastered the premises of the idea drawing, the art committee and editorial staff focused on helping them fulfill its potential. Waggish layout represented ways that staff collaborated with artists in producing humor; series were another; asking artists for revisions was a third. Thomas Craven exaggerates the collaboration as a homogenizing process, beginning with control over ideas and subjects (103); the results varied too much in style,

"Down there, and
first door to the right."

a.SoGLoW

The *New Yorker*'s John Chapin Mosher wrote the line for this installment of the early magazine's longest-running cartoon series. Otto Soglow, 3/9/29:20.

theme, and tone to support the claim. But the art committee did expect artists to satisfy *their* sense of humor and demanded that artists as well as writers precisely articulate comic ideas.

Ideas for cartoon series usually originated with artists, but editors forwarded their own and readers' ideas for continuing them. Artists could reject these suggestions, as Gluyas Williams declined an "Industrial Crisis" of a train wreck featuring a B.V.D. manufacturer clad in flannel underwear.[15] At the other extreme, series relied on editorial activity. *New Yorker* staff researched the names, locations, and other details of subjects for Aaron Birnbaum's series of unsung New Yorkers during this period, including the twenty-five caricatures for "Our Distinguished Doormen" (10/27/28 to 4/13/29) and "Our Conscientious Cops" (6/8/28 to 10/19/29).[16]

Otto Soglow's manhole series followed a middle course. Details of collaboration over this series, the longest in the early period, show that staff followed the artist's lead, and readers followed suit. Lasting thirty installments over thirteen months (12/15/28–1/11/30), the series used only a single image—an open manhole on an empty street—as the background for implied conversations between Bill and Joe, two sewer workers whom we never see. Soglow's ink-and-wash manhole drawing, with its curving lines and abundance of white space, provided a blank slate, literally and figuratively, for absurd suggestions about the underground space and the people who work there. Does it contain a Christmas tree? ("Where can you buy tinsel, Bill?" 12/22/28:18), a toilet? ("Down there, and first door to the right" 3/9/29:20). Can insurance solicitors seek a sale even there? (1/5/29:20). A few captions call attention to the incongruity of subterranean workers' having their "head[s] in the clouds" (5/18/28:29) or getting sunburned (6/29/29:16). But as Joe and Bill spent a year discussing the status of women, whales' reproductive habits, personality types, and polite locutions for pregnancy, most of the captions played with readers' assumptions of sewer workers' inferiority—in knowledge, abilities, and sensibilities. When one of them describes how "she looked at me with the eyes of a wounded deer" (12/21/29:23) and another mentions receiving a telephone call "the day she got her interlocutory decree" (1/4/30:18), it's clear that the joke is on the snobs. No wonder the last caption ended with an emphatic "And That's That" (1/11/30:18).

Although Soglow apparently supplied the original dialogue—"Do you do much reading, Bill?" (12/15/28:26) and "Where can you buy tinsel, Bill?" (12/22/28:18)—later lines came not only from John Chapin Mosher, Wolcott Gibbs, and James Thurber (staff members who published their own prose humor in the magazine) but also from Cole Porter, John O'Hara, and Frank Sullivan, as well as dozens of readers who continued to submit captions well into 1930.[17] Captions submitted but not used—such as Carl Rose's implication that Joe shops at Brooks Brothers[18]—indicate that readers particularly enjoyed the series' critique of social class.

Readers' pleasure in this critique doubtless sharpened as the stock market faltered throughout 1929 before finally crashing in October as the series wound down. Economic conditions did not apparently influence the decision to end the series, though they did inspire a few published drawings and many more rejected submissions. Leonard Dove's cartoon of an investor who declares his support "for putting the Stock Exchange in its place" appeared so quickly that it probably anticipated Black Tuesday (11/2/29:19). A few weeks later Klein poked fun at wealthy New Yorkers' newfound sympathy for the down-and-out with an old-fashioned he-she joke: a woman giving a panhandler both a coin and a sympathetic "The stock market, I suppose?" learns that he "always was a bum" (12/14/29:51). But the committee declined cartoons incorporating apple sellers and jokes about suicide, among other disturbing and widely communicated consequences of the Great Crash.[19]

The most common collaboration between the art committee and artists involved revisions to the caption or the drawing. Requests for both increased, rather than diminished, as the art committee drew confidence from the *New Yorker*'s success. The art meeting sometimes rewrote the caption, or asked the artist's permission to send the idea to a writer for assistance, as when Philip Wylie wrote the goofy dialogue for Peter Arno's Whoops! sisters and E. B. White wrote the famous spinach line.

Beginning in 1927, however, the art committee became more activist in requiring precision in drawings as well as captions. Ironic one-line captions succeed best when drawings identify the speaker; otherwise the reader may miss the joke. In 1926 and 1927 the art committee seems to have required only that either the caption or the drawing imply the speaker, except (as in Alice Harvey's early cartoons) when a caption applies to any of the figures in the drawing. Nonetheless, Ross became infamous for requiring artists to open a speaker's mouth, and commentators amused or offended by the policy's apparent literal-mindedness have cited it to prove Ross's amateurishness (Flanner, in J. Grant 12; Kramer, *Ross* 127–29). Marsh's early "Upper Crust" drawings, among others, indicate that the requirement for open mouths, not a vestige of early ignorance, evolved after 1927 as idea drawings made identifying the speaker critical to the humor.

Cartoons from the issue of October 1, 1927, more than halfway through volume 3, prove how historians have exaggerated the requirement: not one has its speaker's mouth open because precise drawings and well-chosen captions do the job of identifying who speaks the line. Arno's two-line caption for a squabble between a wealthy couple needs neither old-fashioned "He" and "She" designations nor an open mouth to indicate who says what. The word *sniff* gives the first line to the woman, a slender thing in ruffles, who lies across the mattress of their canopy bed, handkerchief at her nose, weeping over having given him "(*sniff*) the best years of my life!"; the second line confirms that the man with the overstuffed shirt protruding from his tuxedo, who has turned away in a position of rejection, has the last word, as he asks, "who made 'em the best years?" (10/1/27:12). One-line captions accomplish the same end a few pages later in Perry Barlow's subway scene of a child curious about the ex-convict asleep in the car (16) and Gardner Rea's cartoon of a dowager congratulating her retainer on the birth of his son (21). By contrast, Alan Dunn's half-page drawing of two men

"Yoo hoo!— and a quarter pound of butter."

Alan Dunn

Layout intensified the comic idea of this long, skinny drawing, which ran in a single column along the left margin. Alan Dunn, 4/7/28:29.

watching street construction does not identify who says what in its two-line caption, nor does it even require that both figures face front; the conversation exchanges absurdities between physical peers, shown in profile and from the rear, whose identity as speakers does not matter (19). Dunn seldom needed to open his characters' mouths because his compositions identified the speaker without such detail, as in the drawing of a speck of a figure who leans out the window of the umpeenth floor of a skyscraper and shouts down to a speck of a figure on the sidewalk below, "Yoo hoo!—and a quarter pound of butter" (4/7/28:30).

When captions applied more subtly to the drawing, increasingly common in 1928, articulating the comic idea required precise identification of the speaker. A half-page Arno cartoon from the third anniversary issue illustrates the issue: the drawing shows a hostess, her mouth clearly open, telling a guest, "We love to see old faces" (2/25/28:24). The conventional remark becomes a double entendre in context: as the hostess leans down and puts her face next to her guest's, the contrast and her remark emphasize her guest's advanced age. Adding to the pun is the faux pas by which the hostess converts graciousness into an insult—humor that would have fizzled if the reader had to puzzle over who said it. Although this example shows literal use of the line, open mouths more commonly served ironic captions. The open mouth emphasizes role reversal when one of Shermund's young women asks her beau whether he would "rather have . . . brains or character" (2/25/28:14). Despite the emphasis historians have given to the requirement for open mouths, even in the late 1920s artists typically avoided the issue altogether, arranging figures to indicate the speaker. Helen Hokinson, who enjoyed the humor of figures drawn from behind, turned one figure's back to the reader and gave the other an inquiring expression appropriate to the question in the caption (2/25/28:41). Klein used body language and composition to differentiate between two pancake demonstrators: declarative posture of the figure in the foreground identifies her as the speaker (2/25/28:17). The need to identify speakers had less to do with small-minded literalism by Ross or the art meeting than with precise comic expression.

The art committee did become more finicky as the twenties went on, however, and requests for revision increased accordingly. These make clear that cartoons through 1928 privileged the artist's comic sensibility, but those from the end of the twenties involved more collaboration between artists and editors. Perry Barlow redrew his idea of a child pretending to be Lindbergh flying off to Paris after the art committee suggested making the airplane more prominent, having the child hold it, and adding a door to the nursery in the background—all changes incorporated into the finished drawing (8/11/28:15).[20] Most of Garrett Price's drawings in 1929 underwent at least one revision, as they asked him to invent a new caption, take an item out of someone's hand, add more newspapers around a room.[21] Even Irvin had to satisfy the committee's comic sensi-

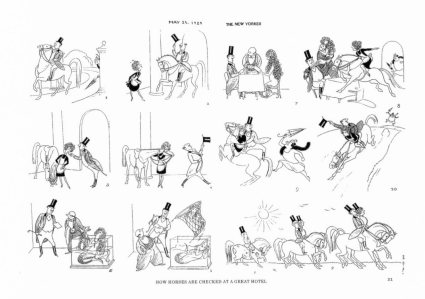

Rea Irvin revised these drawings substantially, adding a new first drawing and reversing the last one to symbolize the reversal in the man's life, in response to suggestions from Katharine S. Angell. 5/25/29:18–19.

bility and aesthetic perfectionism, though he did not follow every recommendation Angell made for "How Horses Are Checked at a Great Hotel" (5/25/29:18–19).[22] When Ross asked for a "more desperate character," however, the face in Gluyas Williams's "Industrial Crises: A Face Appears in One of the Italian Windows at Alice Foote MacDougal's," received black hair and a mustache (9/7/29:28).

Revisions occasionally addressed issues extrinsic to humor. As hemlines dropped along with stock values in the fall of 1929, Angell warned the art meeting that women's new silhouette would make artwork on hand obsolete[23]— deflating their investment in cartoons and especially in covers, which cost one hundred dollars or more. Although formally assigned to fiction and poetry, Angell had considerable clout over the handling of New Yorker art by this time, and her authority over cartoons continued expanding until, late in 1931, she also controlled scheduling of series cartoons.[24]

In the midtwenties artists took revision requests in stride even when the ultimate verdict was "no," but the art committee's demands rose at the same time that the economy worsened and other magazines closed or lost their caché. By late 1928 artists began resisting a procedure that called for extensive work without the assurance of a check at the end. John Held threatened in November to take his woodcuts and maps to magazines that would pay a higher price and not quarrel about taste.[25] In the summer of 1929, Isidore Klein complained directly to Ross about his growing pile of rejected revisions, pointing out that obliging artists to redo their work without a parallel obligation for the art committee to buy it amounted to a "policy of exploitation" out of character for a "liberal magazine like the New Yorker."[26] That fall Alice Harvey called the art meeting's bluff: when asked to redraw a cat "in order to achieve a better and more 'catlike' feline,"[27] she declared the cat exactly the creature she intended and invited them to reconsider or release the idea for submission elsewhere—whence they decided to buy the drawing.[28] This resistance eventually led the art committee to adopt a new system in the fall of 1931 whereby artists submitted and revised rough sketches and prepared a formal drawing only after approval of a "rough."[29] The quest for perfection, *New Yorker* staff understood, depended on artists' willingness to collaborate. Success depended on the editors' attracting the most suitable work of the most appropriate artists, whom they cultivated through a combination of editorial policies, interpersonal relations, and comic vision—their own and others'.

By 1931, the *New Yorker*'s comic vision was so distinctive that Ross's old *American Legion* magazine, reduced from a weekly to a monthly, sternly instructed Alan Dunn not to submit his *New Yorker* "rejects" although those from *Collier's* or the *Saturday Evening Post* would do.[30] Today's readers take for granted the ironic rhetoric of the idea drawing, which seventy-five years of familiarity have naturalized.

Integrating word and picture, or letting the picture speak for itself, the *New Yorker* reoriented the verbal and visual dimensions of the comic drawing. It also unified a great variety of comic art into a coherent visual humor. Not a monolith but a mosaic, the *New Yorker*'s comic art represented economic and social politics along a spectrum that created comic tension between the serious graphic elements of the *New Yorker*'s publishing business— the official elitism of Eustace Tilley, department headers, and advertising art—and its idea drawings. Here, in freelancers' work, the art committee strove for diversity of styles—from elaborately detailed maps by John Held to abstract suggestions by Otto Soglow, from the Four Hundred's trivial tribulations as Rea Irvin imagined them to the suffering of the unemployed as Reginald Marsh recorded it, from Dunn's satire of racism to Shermund's celebration of androgyny, and from Arno's beautiful drunks to Harvey's harried mothers and Barlow's bumpkins. For all their differences, these artists shared what defined *New Yorker* art: an invitation to the reader to discover the joke.

CHAPTER 6

Comic Storytelling

We are coming rapidly to the time when New York will be a city of character—when memories will cling about this street corner and that, when all over the gleaming town of spires and piled stones there will hang an aura of things past. And this is true because a great many good writers are taking the city for their theme: examining its temperament, its history, its people as a people: New Yorkers as something different from Philadelphians or Parisians.

Asper, 1928

Since 1937, when Bernard DeVoto distinguished modern American humor from the braggart strains of the tall story and the wit of newspaper columns, *"New Yorker* humor" has meant Little Man humor, particularly as practiced by Thurber, White, Benchley, and Perelman. Later efforts to define the magazine's comic prose more accurately did not catch on. Norris W. Yates pointed out in 1964 that the *New Yorker* borrowed the classic figure of the inept but lovable man from newspaper comics and silent film even before the *New Yorker* was born, noting that the term *"New Yorker* style" extends beyond the magazine to any prose humor marked by "compression, the *mot juste,* informality, suavity, and irony" (222–28). Nor did these spring fully developed from Ross's head. With the exception of his acquaintants from *Stars and Stripes, Judge,* and the Algonquin-Thanatopsis networks, writers came on board the *New Yorker* one by one, and the magazine's comic prose reflected the material available to the editors (or amenable to editorial development) at any given time. The *New Yorker's* prose humor developed as individual writers succeeded in meeting editorial goals.

The pages of the 1920s magazine show that familiar writers contributed differently and less prominently than their reputations have suggested. S. J. Perelman did not begin his long and important association with the magazine until 1931 (Toombs 85). Ross's buddy Tip Bliss helped fill empty pages before he left in May 1925 but appeared in print only three times thereafter.[1] E. B. White signed verse as often as prose in volumes 1 and 2, and James Thurber broke into the magazine as a poet (2/26/27). Among the celebrated examples of *New Yorker* humor that Enid Veron included in her anthology *Humor in America* (1976), only Ring Lardner's "Large Coffee" dates from the early period (9/28/29:26–27); the others represent later stages of the magazine's development: White's "Dusk In Fierce Pajamas" just before the tenth anniversary (1/27/34:16–17), Thurber's "Day the Dam Broke" from the early 1930s (*My Life and Hard Times,* 1933), and so on. Jesse Bier's discussion of "Interwar Humor" in *The Rise and Fall of American Humor* (1968) likewise compresses a huge period in the life of the *New Yorker* and reinforces misogyny as *New Yorker* humorists' dominant theme (Bier 208–84, esp. 222–27)—even as he privileges writing between hard covers and ignores women writers other than Dorothy Parker.

More important, the contents of volumes 1–5 link the *New Yorker*'s preferences in prose humor to the sensibilities of many writers not often associated with the magazine. Djuna Barnes poses as a comic Sufferer who transforms physical travails into narrative triumphs—one of Mark Twain's favorite postures—for a report on her recent visit to Africa: obsequious hucksters everywhere turn her quest for adventure into a pitch for a shoe-shine until she concludes, "Why *does* one leave Paris?" ("Reproving Africa" 5/5/28:26–28). The mock-oral materials traditional to American vernacular humor reappear in John O'Hara's Delphian Society narratives, Arthur Kober's backstage monologues, and the various "Overheard" telephone calls and subway conversations. Stanley Jones's 1927 "Social Evasions" and 1928 "Making It Easier" series invited members of the peer society to laugh at the etiquette of their youth while celebrating subversive practices for interpersonal and bureaucratic encounters. These pieces urbanized dialect narratives and ironic monologues—conventions that American humor developed in rural settings for vernacular narrators—and applied them to New York's literate scene.

Explicitly literary humor ranged from burlesques of popular genres—such as Hemingway's "My Own Life," a spoof of Frank Harris's autobiography (2/12/27:23–24)—to the genre that became known as the "casual," which the *New Yorker* invented by crossing fiction with the informal essay. Ross credited

Katharine Angell with naming the genre, but she had a lot of help in developing it. Fiction staff members Wolcott Gibbs, Filmore Hyde, and John Mosher wrote their own casuals as well as edited those of freelancers, who included not only "Talk" staffers White and Thurber and Algonquinites Benchley and Parker, but also Frank Sullivan and Corey Ford, Katherine Sproehnle and Alice Frankforter, Josie Turner and other writers whose humor broadens the misogynous Little Man school of *New Yorker* humor that scholars have mistaken for the whole.

Prose humor during the *New Yorker*'s early years underwent at least as many changes as other comic contents of the magazine. The miscellaneous collection of short prose pieces and verse in the first issue justified Ross's apology for looking like a humor magazine. Except for their unifying New York theme, the sketches could have run in *Life* or *Judge*. On a single page, F. P. A.'s "Short Story Scenarios" offers capsule plots as a free service to needy writers (2/21/25:19), a proud but dizzy mamma introduces her children in a three-hundred-word monologue by Clarence Knapp ("She Presents the Flock"), and the unsigned "Fifth Avenue at 3 P.M." surveys the scene and snippets of conversation from it. In contrast to these plotless sketches, the front of the book featured two full-page items, about one thousand words each, of narrative humor. Morris Markey's burlesque history "Story of Manhattankind" (signed "Sawdust") conflated Indians and communists with puns about dangers to New York "in the hands of the Reds" (6); inside jokes on local history range from Peter Stuyvesant's notorious anti-Semitism to Mayor Hylan's loyalty to the nickel subway fare. Together with "Say It with Scandal," an unsigned satire on newspaper editing set in the near future, after mergers created a *Times-World-Tribune* and a *Mirror-News-Graphic,* these examples point to the *New Yorker*'s prime problem at its start: it aimed at an audience of writers, probably the authors' and editors' friends.

"Say It with Scandal" satirized not only the new tabloid press's tendency to fictionalize and sensationalize the news but also the impoverished journalistic imaginations that instituted "Krazy Kracks" at *Judge* after Ross left. "The man who does Hearts Bereft is gloomily figuring out a three-letter word meaning Japanese sash," the author sneers, emphasizing that the journalist lacks the verbal felicity even to play the new crossword puzzles, and then directs his scorn toward a more enterprising staff member, "the octogenarian who dopes the Kute Kracks and sells them to himself at one dollar a krack" (8). The *New Yorker* instituted a policy against stories about newspapers and writers early in 1929,[2] but in 1925 newspapers provided the combination of characters, events, and institutions the magazine needed to imagine sophisticated, urban local humor—largely because the staff imagined themselves and their friends as their readers.

The Search for Subjects

"The Story of Manhattankind" ran seven installments, but the series fizzled out after the first. Lame jokes about neighbors (3/7/25:6), landlords (3/14/25:14), and other urban frustrations could not equal the humor of Herb Roth's illustrations.[3] Ross seems to have recognized the failure of mock history as an element of the local humor formula, pushing the series from the front of the book to the middle and reviving it only twice after 1:5.

Mock-oral humor, on the other hand, quickly became a staple of *New Yorker* prose, urbanized as snippets of conversation in the crowds—a thematic, but not technical, leap from its origins in the southeastern tall tale and northeastern fable. In addition to the conversation captured in "Fifth Avenue at 3 P.M.," the first issue offered two other items exploring the comic potential of urban speech. The two-inch column titled "Spiritist" captured a hawker's claim, "I have pierced the hideous shroud of Death" (15); on the same page ran Corey Ford's "Highlights," his first of three impressionistic renderings of city life.

Modernist in their focus on sensory input and reliance on a continuous present, all three of Ford's "Highlights" followed the same formula: an introductory paragraph setting the scene in the present, dialogue, an ironic summarizing sentence. Set specifically in New York locales—at an East Side boxing match (2/21/25:15), city streets on a rainy night (2/28/25:23), and a Broadway opening (3/21/26:26)—all offered local color and irony, the second installment most dryly of the three:

autos like a thousand flashing scales, darting, glinting . . . "the price of a meal, buddy?": "Sorry, just gave my last cent to feller. . . ." [original ellipses] . . . . .

It comes again from the bushes, a call of agony, the voice that cries out of nightmares. Two passersby halt; then turn and walk rapidly away . . . . waiting for the cop . . . latter day Samaritans. (2/28/25:23)

Forty years later Ford dismissed his "arty" efforts as "something the present *New Yorker* would never dream of printing" (116). These modest beginnings nonetheless initiated the *New Yorker*'s version of mock-oral humor. The updated genre relocates Americans' longstanding comic pleasure in written versions of oral stories and common talk, a tradition that Walter Blair called "A Man's Voice, Speaking," into a modern, urban context of diverse voices, women's and men's.

Three *New Yorker* forms replaced the standard nineteenth-century frame tale: dialogues portraying "New Yorkish" situations, dialect pieces depicting local types, and interior and dramatic monologues revealing the speaker's character. Together these mock-oral genres defined *New Yorker* prose humor as a contemporary, urban scion of America's most distinguished comic tradition. Mock-oral writing's focus on the present moment and, thus, its use of present tense also links it to the twenties' modernist literary experiments, giving *New Yorker* humor currency as well as familiarity, bridging high literary culture and low.

The genre that began with Ford's snippets expanded later that spring into full-fledged dialogue, a complete story without narration. Knapp's "Straw Hat Salesman" (5/23/25:20) showed the form's ironic potential early on in a tale of reverse salesmanship: the customer persuades the salesman not to sell him a straw hat because they look funny (5/23/25:20). An alternative strand, exemplified in Charles G. Shaw's "On the Wire," explored social matters of courtship, friendship, and class. The telephone conversation between "A Young Man" and the African American who answers the phone, insisting that Miss Jones "done move' long time ago" reframes who has the upper hand after the beau's bewildered "But I spoke to her only yesterday" establishes his credentials: "well, if you all spoke to huh yestuday, I guess it's all right. . . . I'll connec' yuh" (5/30/25:23). Over the summer of 1925, dialogue became so important that it appeared in "Talk" as well as sketches for the back of the book. Some served basically as comic fillers, but one dialogue during the summer showed how overheard talk, even without a gag or punch line, could give *New Yorker* humor the flavor of local people, places, and situations. "At the Thé Dansant Sweetly While Dancing" presents a conversation between two "ennuiers," easily identified as a man asking the questions ("do you like dancing? . . . Whiteman? . . . polo? . . . gin? . . .") to which the woman replies consistently: "I simply adore it . . . him . . . it . . . ") until "a meddling stag" cuts in on them (6/20/25:23). This slice of New York life soon became a favored type.

Ironic mock-oral dialogues began in earnest late in the fall of 1925, with the publication of "At the Matinee" (11/21/25:27), signed *B. L.,* probably Baird Leonard, who published poetry in the *New Yorker* over her name but was obligated to *Life* for prose humor. Just six quotations totaling a half-column, "At the Matinee" generates humor by displacement. With remarks such as "Shall we go out this way and fall over four people, or out that way and fall over five?," the piece makes banal conversation rhetorically significant, focuses on the audience instead of actors, and privileges the time when the curtain is down. The matinee setting, which characterizes the speakers as matrons older and less fashionable than the couples and groups at evening performances, plays into the snobberies of the peer society. The timing of the piece, appearing a week before Ellin Mackay's cabaret article, underlines that the *New Yorker* had turned the corner in identifying its audience by November of 1925. Equally important, "At the Matinee" exemplified the *New Yorker*'s strategy for drawing readers through the service departments and ads at the back of the book: the makeup department wedged the piece between the end of "Sports" and the beginning of "On and Off the Avenue." In all these ways "At the Matinee" offered a modernist humor of indirection, inversion, and juxtaposition.

This strategy suited perfectly the serendipitous quality of overheard talk, which became a mainstay of *New Yorker* humor. Indeed, not ten pages after "At the Matinee" came a longer, fuller example of overheard talk, M. D. Beuick's "Concerto Americano" (11/21/25:39), excerpting conversation at the symphony. Beuick's piece contrasts the ungrammatical speech of the ushers ("Sure; call 'em Sir and Madam. It don't do no harm"), the affected superiority of the audience ("Ah! Maestro Stransky. Bravo"), and sounds from the orchestra and audience ("Tra-tra-ra—bum-bum-boom"). Overheard talk found its way into the back of the book from the Ritz Hotel in Paris, the Forest Hills tennis tournament, Schrafft's, notable concerts, Womrath's, Liggett's Grand Central Fountain, a telephone party line—anywhere and everywhere New Yorkers went.[4] In addition to the two dozen items in the "Overheard" series from 2:32 to 5:5, dialogue and represented speech also shaped fully developed narratives. E. B. White's "He" for example, presents a pair of women juggling two simultaneous conversations (2/4/28:19). In one they gossip about their friend's marriage; in the other, they comment on their snack and the bill for it. The title points to the irony that White adds to the "Overheard" formula: "He" concerns *them,* both female. The *New Yorker* required mock-oral writing to "ring entirely true as conversation," as Angell explained to Lillian Hellman in rejecting several of her monologues, without even "the suggestion of being written rather than spoken."[5] The traditional American pleasure in the incongruity between oral language and written representations called for superior writing skills to escape literacy and thus create that incongruity—a sophisticated trick perfect for an educated audience.

Dialect humor had a slower start, perhaps because its conventions called more attention to craft. The reluctance, surprising in light of the magazine's early class-conscious cartoons, underlines how the *New Yorker*'s literate style diverged from nineteenth-century vernacular conventions; jokes celebrating the triumph of common sense over book learning cannot comfortably coexist with those flaunting the peer society's college educations. The disinterest is all the more notable in light of Michael North's argument in *The Dialect of Modernism* that dialect writing inspired modernist writers' stylistic experiments.[6] Nonetheless, at a time when scholars began examining issues of dialect (Williamson and Burke), and Milt Gross set wildly popular mock-oral tales in broken Yiddish-English on the Lower East Side, the *New Yorker* found traditions of dialect humor largely irrelevant.

In the early months the editors allowed a few unfortunate examples of African-American dialect, a dominant American dialect tradition, before replacing it with vernacular from the outer boroughs, especially Brooklyn and the Bronx, but the process took more than a year. Tip Bliss's "Busonally Conducted" (6/27/25:10), its title conflating *bus* and *personally,* offers a grievous example. In this display of an incompetent tour guide's patter along the length of Manhattan, thick African-American dialect renders the speaker so inarticulate that it kills its own comic ideas. The sketch makes a small point of reviving Mark Twain's famous joke from *The Innocents Abroad* in describing Grant's Tomb ("Grant's dead. Thass his Tomb . . ." [original ellipses]), but the genuinely funny nub of the speaker's scam transforms his contemptible narration into an ironic monologue of social satire. Wrapping up the tour from Harlem to Chinatown (a reversal of the contemporary white fad of uptown slumming), the guide scares his group about the dangers of the Chinese ("Most these Chinese would stick a knife inta yuh if they got the chancet, but you don't need to be scared because they's plenty cops here"). As the peer society titillated itself with visits to Harlem clubs, so he holds out the decadence of their stop at a "genuiwine opyum den," but at "the end of this most instructive an' intrustin' trip," he announces, almost as an afterthought, that return transportation (to uptown safety) will add fifty cents to their tab.

Subsequent dialect pieces replaced jokes about race with jokes about literary forms. Nat N. Dorfman's "If Humorists Wrote Our Historic Incidents" (10/31/25:31) does not entirely succeed, but the idea of retelling Paul Revere's ride as a parody of "darkey stories"—an implied sneer at the local color dialect writing of the last generation—has some merit. More interesting was Fred G.

Steelman's "The New Yawker" (10/24/25:31), which considered the Brooklyn chauvinist as poet laureate: "London Bridge ain't got a look in / With the Williamsburg or Brooklyn." By 1928 the editors preferred dialect pieces revealing character to those about situations—Angell rejected a Mr. Dooley parody, presumably in Irish Chicago-ese, from Donald Ogden Stewart on the ground that *New Yorker* readers were too young to recognize it.[7] But editors had less to choose from in 1925 and still stumbled in choosing it.

Dialogues with foreign speakers fit the format much better, and these became more prevalent in 1926. Nettles's "Telephone Booths" provided an early example of how dialect (even poorly constructed) gains humor from the contrast, implied or demonstrated, with conventional representations of speech: "Say, listen, hoperator, foist ya don't ring de pahty, then ya ring de wrung pahty, then ya give me de Hatlantic hand Pecific Kosher Butchaires" (6/27/25:13). A year later, Florence Helm's "'Allo! Allo!' (An Appreciation of the New York Telephone Company)" subordinated its comic sneers at incorrect English speech to a clubby awareness of the travails of international travel, such as the woes caused by the Parisian telephone system (5/1/26:56–57). Frenchified English had enough comic appeal that a featured piece by Lewis Galantiere in the fall of 1926, "Mister Poincaray, Meet Monsiou Mellon!: An Imaginary Dialogue" ran half in heavily accented English, half in bastardized French (10/2/26:27–28). By contrast, the *New Yorker* kept cool toward the rage for Yiddish-English dialect, despite full-page ads for Gross's *Nize Baby* (1926). Philip Wylie's "Against Dialect" decried the Yiddish-English his friends adopted for all-purpose joking, and imagined it coming from politicians (9/11/26:30), though a few weeks later one of Al Frueh's pantomime narratives told "The Story of Mankind, Or, Iss Diss a System?" (10/23/26:32). As a compromise, perhaps, dialect figured mainly in cartoon captions, where visual characterization shaped ethnic or class humor more precisely; in verbal humor, slang replaced dialect as the primary class marker and the chief signifier of mock-oral writing.

These alternatives to dialect began in 1926 and continued through the end of volume 5. Some took the form of dramatic scripts, such as William Rose Benét's "He Saw Nothing Abroad; Or, the Tourist's Shameful Return," a dialogue between a Traveler and an American Friend, which poked fun not only at ordinary speech but also at its written representations:

—Lowtherebill;binbrawdeyehear!
—Yupshoorav

—Baggenay?
—Yeahaddagraytime!

(9/25/26:52)

Phonetic spellings call attention to the visual joke behind dialect humor. The difficulties of reading such renderings also affected some nineteenth-century representations—the Sut Lovingood stories of George Washington Harris, for example, and the misspellings of the Phunny Phellows—where the writing also impeded silent reading. But of course, oral effort returns the visual symbols to speech, and less than a column rewards the reader with the joke at the end, where the friend scorns the traveler's interest in cultural sights over people and sports.

To this formula Arthur Kober added the idea of comic contrasts among accents in crowds, as in "Overheard: At Pier 57." Snippets of conversation mark different character types at the West Side piers when a ship brings vacationers home from Europe: a guard from Brooklyn ("Hey, wait a minute. . . . Which one of youse has got de pass?"), a romantic wannabe waiting for her friend ("Oh, what a lovely boat! Believe me, next time I go across I'm going on that vessel"), a woman who heckles her husband but gushes to her friends ("Well, open it, booby, open it. Oh, it was too precious"). And then comes a bystander: "Oh, for Gossakes, look! . . . Why, it's Nazimova! My Gawd, don't she look exotic? She certainly is the exoitickest looking woman I've ever seen. . . . Oh, for Pete's sake, look over there. Don't you reckanize her from her pitchurs? It's Edna Ferber. Yeah, she wrote a book—you know, a novel" (9/3/27:45-46). The New Yorker's dialect speakers remain outsiders and inferiors like Huckleberry Finn and Jim. But nineteenth-century humor celebrated the incongruity between dialect speakers' low social standing and high moral standards; substandard speech mocked social and linguistic superiority. By contrast, the New Yorker's desire to target the Stuyvesants rather than the Sweeneys shifted the allegiance of dialect humor toward the values of the educated peer society and asserted *their* superiority.

Monologues diffused this class-based humor by emphasizing individual consciousness. The New Yorker's fondness for monologues, especially interior monologues, enabled it to bridge literary modernism and popular humor, and these sketches ran the gamut of social classes and character types. Together these monologues updated and urbanized the tradition of American humor of "a man's voice, speaking." From the start New Yorker monologues fell into two distinct groups. One group belonged to the mock-oral tradition. Focusing on narration itself, these monologues featured nonstandard language, including stream of consciousness and other conventions of interior monologue as well as radio rhetoric and dialect. Mock-oral monologues began early but diminished during the exploratory period from the middle of 1925 through the end of 1926, resuming in earnest during volume 3. The second group emerged separately and focused less on speech than on storytelling, a consequence of their origins in the personal experience narrative. An oral folk genre rather than a literary one, personal narratives blend the storyteller's particular experiences and insights with traditional formal, stylistic, and social elements (Stahl 268). Whereas the mock-oral monologue focuses naïvely on the present, often a continuous present, and leaves interpretation of the story to the reader, the personal experience narrative recounts the past, usually a troubling experience, and offers meaning from it. Authentic personal narratives recount factual events and seek listeners' confirmation of their meaning, but the *New Yorker* merged this factual genre with the fictional tradition of the comic lie. The result: ironic first-person narratives that became the *New Yorker* casual.

Radio monologues gave mock-oral narration a modern spin, exploiting the difficulties and conventions of a new (and newly commercialized) medium. Radio's caché, emphasized in the *New Yorker's* many back-cover ads for Atwater and other brands, offered a fresh humor of linguistic and social superiority. Between 1921 and 1926, American radio ownership increased from one in five hundred homes to one in six, with higher penetration in urban areas and among high-income families (Sterling and Kittross 81)—that is, the *New Yorker's* audience. As early as 1:9, the *New Yorker* announced, "The radio, it is known, is developing a real school of American humor," and gave the mock-oral "Jim Announcing" as proof (H. L. B., 4/18/25:20). Jim's initial "Good evening, laz-en-gemmum" identifies him immediately as a vernacular speaker, probably unreliable in the class context of the *New Yorker,* while his butchery of broadcast-host patter ridicules him and the program format both. He declares every component of his show "very wunnerful," yet accompanying details undercut each declaration:

The very wunnerful array of talented artists assembled here to entertain you this evening are really the rankest kind of amateurs. . . .

The first number on this very wunnerful program will be a solo by Miss Eva Ganderhook, little known universally. . . . Unfortunately, Snippy Eva, as she is affectionately nicknamed around this very wunnerful studio here, has a slight attack of bronchitis or something which causes her to kinda slip up on the high notes. . . . (20)

Although "Jim Announcing" sneers at lowbrow radio programming, it reserves special scorn for radio's invisibility and commercial sponsorship. The announcer is constituted in words, H. L. B. points out, and these may well be false. Our narrator surely lies when he identifies himself at the beginning: "J I M announcing. I am 31 years old, married, two chi———, pardon me just a moment, my mistake. Ha! Ha!" A similar statement at the end, imitating the broadcasting convention of signing off, reinforces the implication of his unreliability, as do his criticisms of another announcer named Jim, who runs an exercise program that our Jim declares a fraud: "Just between you and me, laz-en-gemmun . . . The jingling you hear is not money rattling around in his pockets, it's his wife jangling the keys when she opens the cellar door to go down and shovel coal in the furnace while that faker of a Jim lies in bed and hollers his orders over the phone" (20). In declaring radio responsible for a new variety of American humor, H. L. B. put new wine in an old bottle.

Radio monologues fizzled as a genre less because they used old comic ideas than because they exploited a short-lived novelty. Two months after "Jim Announcing," Nettles's "Radio Sans Static" could still make fun of radio's troubles with tuning and banal programming (6/20/25:10), and in 1926 "Talk" could compare it to remote newspaper photography, complaining that radio "sounds exactly as the pictures look" (5/15/26:9). But the medium professionalized rapidly, and before the end of the decade, Parke Cummings's "The Game," a mock-oral rendering of a football game, turned the tables, using radio rhetoric to sneer at print. "Oh! . . . My! . . . O-o-o-o-oh! He's through! . . . No . . . Yes . . . "—with these and other examples Cummings contrasts radio's play-by-play, with its spontaneous overflow of powerful emotions, with the morning newspaper's inverted pyramid, whose recollections in tranquility destroy the game's excitement and suspense by disclosing the outcome at the start (11/30/29:65). Although primarily a *New Yorker* verse writer (forty-six of his sixty items were poems), Cummings understood a key feature of live radio and monologues—indeed, of all oral genres—the open end. And the *New Yorker* apparently recognized, in abandoning radio monologues, that magazine humor requires more literary genres.

The casual emerged in 1927 to fill this need, but first the *New Yorker* tried and abandoned another old device of mock-oral humor, the frame tale, in which a literate first-person narrator records the narrative of a dialect speaker. The aptly titled "A Rather Unusual Essay" by Algonquinite Marc Connelly borrowed this formula twice over. The introduction to "A Rather Unusual Essay" frames a

THE MEN'S CLUB KEEPS ABREAST OF SCIENCE

Radio was a favorite topic of *New Yorker* humorists. Frueh exercised his powerful imagination in this futuristic drawing, the year after radio was commercialized and long before the development of television or video phones. Al Frueh, 7/2/27:16.

story called "Mr. Radio," which itself frames a mock-oral monologue by Mr. Radio. Or, from the inside out, Connelly's sketch embeds the first-person confessions of Mr. Radio within the first-person account by a man named Marc, whose efforts to "write a 'piece'" form the third-person introduction to Marc Connelly's "Rather Unusual Essay" (12/11/26:29–30). This structure constitutes the joke—alas, the only one in the sketch. The tale of Mr. Radio's sudden emergence from the loudspeaker (looking rather like Rumpelstiltskin in James Daugherty's illustration) puts his confessions at the center: he vows to reform programming and throw out "unfunny comic entertainers . . . un-social flag wavers . . . brassy advertising dodges . . . invitations to morons to entertain you" (29). But he concludes with the familiar disappointment: "It had all been a dream" (30). The flatness of this story, one of four written by Connelly in 1926 of his fourteen for volumes 1–5, underscores the limitations of the frame tale in the absence of a dialect narrator, and identifies the problems facing the *New Yorker* in adapting mock-oral traditions to educated urban subjects and audiences.

Three solutions remained, and the *New Yorker* adopted them all. First, monologues with or without dialect could continue in settings revealing particular
characters and situations, a solution already identified in Arthur Kober's "The
First-Nighter" (12/11/26:101–103), a woman recounting her experience at the
opening of *Seventh Avenue*. Kober's piece appeared eighty pages behind Connelly's Mr. Radio sketch, and this monologue genre gained momentum in volume 3, when Kober became a frequent contributor, though John Chapin
Mosher, Jack Cluett, and others also worked in the genre. Indeed, Katharine Angell liked it enough to contribute four pithy remarks as "Taxi Driver Philoso-
phy" (K. S. A., 10/8/27:32). A second solution was to focus on interior
monologues, such as those of the museum attendant and floorwalker in Zelda F.
Popkin's "Reflections of Silent New Yorkers" (10/30/26:38–39), the first in her
four-part series featuring mock-oral stream of consciousness. This genre appealed less broadly, though it shaped E. B. White's two "Thoughts" sketches
(6/18/27:16; 12/24/27:15–16) as well as Florence W. Ross's "Thoughts While
Waiting for Five O'Clock" (12/10/27:48) and Thurber's "I Burn My Bridge Behind Me" (12/1/28:31–32). Finally, the monologue could be folded into other
first-person narratives, especially the personal narrative, a solution that became
"the casual."

The focus on segments of experience, defined by time and place, in the *New
Yorker*'s mock-oral narratives reflects not only the power of nineteenth-century
comic traditions but also the influence of films. The histories of film comedy and
American literary humor followed different paths, of course, especially before
1927, when the first "talkies" played in New York, but many *New Yorker* writers
from the twenties lived in both camps. Robert Benchley, Dorothy Parker, Herman Mankiewicz, John Chapin Mosher, and Donald Ogden Stewart all ran back
and forth between New York and Hollywood, where the commercial film industry relocated in the 1910s after originating in New York. Added to this specific context is the larger influence of film on the repertoire of narrative
possibilities and conventions, which led contemporary cultural critic James
Truslow Adams to claim that film helped set what he called *The Tempo of Modern
Life* (1931). He argued that film had become a metaphor for life and that the
close-up had become the reference point for framing and interpreting human experience. He pointed out that the close-up separates a single event and particular elements of it from the comprehensive narrative stream, and thereby
rearranges the proportions from which meaning arises: it emphasizes digression
over the main narrative, wrenches the subject from background and setting, exaggerates individuals at the expense of the group, or divorces the face from the

body. Thus the close-up disrupts causal relationships and substitutes "crudely emotional" appeals for "intellectual attention," and Adams saw its influence extending beyond film: "For the last two or three decades this technic of the close-up [has appeared in areas of life] which seem far removed from the screen, notably in newspapers, magazines, and even education. As a result, we are tending to look at our world, with its interests and problems, more and more as a series of close-ups than as a causal continuum" (Adams 325–26). Leaving aside the tendency to blame a new communication medium for disappointing cultural developments—as in old worries about comic books and more recent ones over television and the internet—Adams suggests a connection between the close-up and *New Yorker* humor that explains its divergence from the American humor before it.

Overheard talk, dialogues, and monologues all borrow the technique of close-up, isolating bits of experience and framing them as representative of modern life. Even the casual, with its more expansive narrative, nonetheless compresses larger events into a smaller slice of narrative time, though in fact many tales present only the speaking voice rather than a set of events extended over time. With its emphasis on "a man's voice, speaking" (though some early narrators were women), the *New Yorker* casual reinvented the mock-oral tale as a literary close-up of modern types. But these twentieth-century close-ups differed more in degree than in kind from their nineteenth-century predecessors: the vernacular speaker's monologue forming the inner narrative of a classic frame tale already presents a story in close-up. As the *New Yorker's* mock-oral humor played into contemporary interest in the close-up, however, the intense concentration on a moment's experience that had already mutated from film into literary explorations of consciousness gave *New Yorker* humor a particularly modern, sophisticated edge.

Voices Above the Din

Although Ford's "Highlights" pointed the way toward urbanized mock-oral humor, his more immediate contribution to the magazine was his "Fugitive Art" series. These eleven burlesques targeted the art and art criticism of dadaism beginning with "Bearding the Leyendecker," an analysis of subway graffiti complete with Ford's own illustrations in the issue of May 2, 1925, the week before Fleischmann declared the magazine dead. "Every subway station shows this craving for Expression," he proclaims as he describes notable examples from

Park Place and Brooklyn Bridge in lower Manhattan to 179th Street in the Bronx (5/2/25:20): "there is a really fine Paris Garter Man on exhibit at Grand Central that you would swear was Abraham Lincoln. Beard and all. It must be admitted that it is strange to have Abraham Lincoln saying 'Oh, Minnin!' out of the corner of his mouth but you must make allowances for changing times and customs" (20). The deadpan critique concludes that New Yorkers "also have quite a little knack for poetry, as far as that goes, and this is sometimes pretty far" (20), but nothing else undercuts the irony. A second installment, "Blotters: An Absorbing Medium," reworked a joke that Ford published in *Judge* six months earlier, "The Absorbing Adventures of Professor Blotter" (*Judge* 12/27/24:7), but with "Laundry Art: Study in Wash" already in the queue for the next week, the series' possibilities may have helped persuade Hanrahan and Fleischmann that the magazine deserved a second chance. By the June 6 issue, when retrenchment consolidated reviews into one "Critique" section, Ford's series began expanding. The seventh installment, "Shattered Glass: A Fugitive Art in New York" effused silliness for three-quarters of a page, featuring "Artemus J. Teeter, Harvard '09 A.B., Columbia '11 A.M., Daylight Saving Time": "In the course of his talk Dr. Teeter showed the Society a number of interesting things, including . . . his prize window entitled: 'Fly Ball! an impression of L. Schmalz's Delicatessen and Groceries, at Twilight.' Here we have an effective rendition of glass, treated in the angular manner of one accustomed to the Cubistic School of Expression" (6/6/25:16). By the time that "Tenement Art: Lines" filled a full page with interpretation of "the arrangement and treatment of clothes lines, ropes and aerials" (6/13/25:24), Ross and Irvin had decided to claim Ford's sense of humor as the *New Yorker*'s. Inviting Ford to fill the inside cover with the "Making of a Magazine," they trusted his comic imagination enough to expect the first installment in one day (Ford 120), and the series debuted just two weeks after "The Art of Tatooing" (7/25/25:11).

The importance of "Making of a Magazine" (see chapter 2), which attracted advertising and established Eustace Tilley as the eponymous New Yorker (Ford 119–20), led Ford to mention the "Fugitive Art" series only in passing, as the impetus for Ross's commission. As a result, the series is virtually unknown; not even the entry on Ford in *American Humorists, 1800–1950* cites it (see Day). But "Fugitive Art" deserves recognition on two counts: because it shows that Ross commissioned "Making of a Magazine" on the strength of current achievement, not (as Ford implied) because of their 1924 association at *Judge,* and because it targeted the peer society perfectly. A sophisticated parody of contemporary art criticism, "Fugitive Art" expected readers to know about dadaism and primitive art, and thus would have had no place at *Judge,* with its audience of old ladies in Dubuque and former subscribers to *Leslie's Illustrated Weekly.* Still more important, "Fugitive Art" helped make Ford the dominant comic voice of the *New Yorker's* first year.

Ford published thirty-six items in the critical forty issues between 1:11 (5/2/25) and 1:50 (1/30/26)—fifteen of them in addition to "Making of a Magazine." He averaged one full page a week, usually with his own illustrations, though he missed five weeks in the summer of 1925, presumably while writing "Making of a Magazine," illustrated by the new staff artist Johan Bull. As testimony to his importance, Ford wrote a special birthday installment, "The Anniversary of a Great Magazine: Looking Back Over the Vast History of THE NEW YORKER With Mr. Eustace Tilley" (2/20/26:28–29), which alluded to notable cartoons by Al Frueh and Reginald Marsh and made inside jokes—about an Andrew Johnson profile leading to his 1843 impeachment, for instance, and "*The New Yorker's* vigorous editorial policy" averting "a calamity" akin to the 1903 fire at the New York Public Library (2/20/26:28).[8] The high spirits of Ford's birthday piece contrasted with the "reasonable amount of solemnity" announced in "Notes and Comment" (15). In the summer of 1926, when he enjoyed among the highest rates the *New Yorker* paid for casuals,[9] he followed this success with a seven-part series on "The Bleakest Job in New York" before turning his attention toward *Vanity Fair* and other opportunities. Ford's three series gave the *New Yorker* a consistently ironic humor on contemporary topics in a local setting. Indeed, in the eighteen months before E. B. White joined the staff, Corey Ford defined the *New Yorker's* prose humor.

Ford specialized in burlesque rather than deadpan, but at least one of his characters anticipated the *New Yorker's* signature Little Man, a comic Sufferer whose 1930s avatars include Thurber's Walter Mitty and S. J. Perelman's victims of advertising and modern technology. Often taken as a character type unique to *New Yorker* humor, the comic pose of the Sufferer dates back at least to Mark Twain's early sketches, according to John Gerber, and in the twentieth century it also marked the humor of Charlie Chaplin's Little Tramp, who debuted in the *Kid Auto Races at Venice* (1914), and of Caspar Milquetoast, H. T. Webster's *Timid Man* (1931). Historians of modernism cite the cultural dislocation following World War I to explain the appeal of antiheroic characters among 1920s artists and audiences, but rhetorical practicality is a factor too. Humorists from Twain to Garrison Keillor have recognized that the Sufferer's pose has staying power (Lee): an inferior character can continue to evoke a blend of ridicule and sympathy as long as the slings and arrows of outrageous fortune continue the attack. Avatars of the braggart, by contrast, lose their comic reasons for being after one comeuppance. Unlike film and cartoon Sufferers, but very like Twain's, *New Yorker* Sufferers express their interior experience directly to their audiences. First-person mock-oral narration limits the tale's miseries, if only because the speaker survived to tell the tale, and its direct communication invites the reader to collaborate in the narrative creation of pleasure from pain.

Ford's Sufferer bemoans his fate in "The Tie That Blinds," a back-of-the-book piece from May 16, 1925, in which the speaker confides his failure to resist buying a necktie so loud "They might as well have draped it over the front of the store and hired a German band to play beneath it, for all that hid it" (29). He chronicles his increasing mortification as "Destiny" leads him into the shop, inspires the clerk to show him the tie (despite his request for "Something sombre . . . Preferably black"), and prompts him to demonstrate its inappropriateness by trying it on—until suddenly, he has paid for it and agreed to look at socks to match. "Destiny, that's all," he concludes. "Destiny, and that way that clerks have with me. Between them, I'm so much clay" (29). At least part of the humor here comes from the contrast between the minor events Ford describes (and claims as true) and the grand context of fate he has constructed for them in his imagination and in his narrative (which we know is false). If the original incarnation of the *New Yorker*'s comic Sufferer was Ross's harried editor, besieged by carpenters, switchboard, and secretary, in the opening "Of All Things" in 1:1 (see introduction), Ford's ran a close second—fully eighteen months before E. B. White labeled the type in "The Little Man" (11/6/26:22–23).

A blend of local color and character humor, White's "Little Man" reports the narrator's surprise at an unexpected change in the typical New York scene outside his rear window. Details that characterize White's narrator as a mock-oral speaker rather than as a writer shift the emphasis from tale to telling. When he reinforces the sameness of the daily scene by repeating "Things don't change much" four times in six paragraphs, he gives the phrase the oral quality of a refrain. When he notes that the story involves a Maltese cat, he declares it a detail "I have forgotten to mention," in the manner of an oral narrative sequenced in time, not space. When he notes how the dog leaped "ineffectually . . . just as he had done for months" at a drawing of the cat, he acknowledges his audience by adding, "as I told you." When he describes how, on one special night, he climbed up that vine to give the girl a kiss, like Jack climbing the beanstalk, magic transforms everything. "Things that were loud grew louder. Things that were fast grew faster. . . . the dog leapt with impossible leaps . . . The cat on the piano lashed its tail, turning the pages of music so fast no one could possibly have seen the notes" (23). And only in the last paragraph, when the narrator remarks that the event so thrilled him that he did not mind awakening the next morning with sore throat and fever, does he reveal that he, like so many narrators of dramatic monologues, misunderstands his story: the event occurred only in his mind.

Although White's speaker is not the victimized Little Man conventionally associated with *New Yorker* humor, the story illustrates a number of features about the *New Yorker* genre known as the casual, a term coined by Katharine Angell, apparently to distinguish it from the formal essay and other nonfiction forms. Like "The Tie That Blinds," "The Little Man" is a first-person narrative, reporting an ostensibly factual experience that occurred in New York City. Thus the casual imitates the folklore genre of the personal experience narrative while translating oral storytelling into print. As Sandra K. D. Stahl points out, personal experience stories enable individuals to transform troubling events into narrative triumphs and to collaborate with listeners in identifying what the experiences mean. Stahl's description also suggests why *New Yorker* writers found the genre appealing:

The character presented in . . . [the] story is protected by the humor and the entertaining style of the storyteller. . . . In effect the narrator tests personal values—practical, moral, social, aesthetic—with every story repetition. The willingness to bring forward values for the scrutiny of the audience makes the narrator vulnerable: but like Achilles or Siegfried, the teller proves heroic not by hiding that vulnerability but by courageously accepting responsibility for the story . . . . Existentially, the personal experience narrator not only acts or experiences but "thinks about" his action, evaluates it, learns from it, and tells the story—not to express his values, but to build them, to create them, to remake them each time he tells his stories. (Stahl 274)

Writing fictional personal experience narratives allowed *New Yorker* writers to develop a comic genre suitable for a literate urban audience. First-person narration and self-revelation preserved key elements of traditional, mock-oral humor but reversed the tall tale's relation of teller to listener. Whereas the tall talker typically gulled listeners with a string of small lies built into a climactic moment of exposure—of the teller's lies and the listeners' naivete—the *New Yorker* narrator worked realistically, the teller alone the object of humor. Against the aggrandizement of the tall talker, the irony of the *New Yorker* narrator renders him little indeed. The personal experience narrative thus integrated the mock-oral modes of traditional American humor into the self-conscious modes of modern prose fiction.

By the time "The Little Man" appeared in 2:38, White had already published some three dozen items in the *New Yorker.* His career with the magazine began in 1:9 with "A Step Forward" (4/18/25:21), a parody of advertising jingles that hinted at the kinds of kick lines he would later write for newsbreaks, and he followed up three weeks later (between submissions to F. P. A.'s "The Conning Tower" in the *World*) with "Defense of the Bronx River," which ran in the issue of May 9, 1925, when the future of the magazine was on the line, and which most critics hail as his first contribution. Unlike "The Little Man," which focuses on character, "Defense" concentrates on scene. The two reflect the first shift in the *New Yorker's* early prose humor: from narratives of place to narratives of character.

Frank Sullivan's eight casuals between 1:6 and 2:45 also participated in that shift. The usual date claimed for Sullivan's *New Yorker* debut is January 1926 (as in Erkkila 479), but two pieces actually ran in 1925. Sullivan's first contribution, "Ten, Twenty, ThirT" aims to explain New York's new system of taxi fares, a topic of current interest (3/28/25:11–12). The licensing system established in 1923 failed to standardize taxi fares and operations, resulting in the 1925 decision to create a Taxicab Commission controlled by the police ("Taxicabs," *Encyclopedia of New York City*), and Sullivan's piece takes New York's byzantine fare calculations as a springboard. Our narrator, introducing himself as "the foremost alegebratician of my time," has a sure formula for calculating the fare. Arm yourself with paper, pencils, and a gun; divide the license numbers of the car and driver by six, "multiply the first of the two rate figures by sixteen and reduce the results to quarts . . . and divide the result between the chauffeur and yourself" (11)—and when the cabbie complains, "take out the revolver . . . [,] shoot him dead, and pay him exactly eighty cents" (12). This absurdity transcends the topicality that 1925 readers surely appreciated, even as the narrator—no Little Man, he!—remains undaunted by the travails of urban life. Traffic rules and parking problems remained favorite topics of cartoon, verse, and prose humor in the *New Yorker,* applying ingenuity to frustration on paper, if not in fact.

Sullivan's other early pieces also focused on atmosphere. "The Sport of Kings" (8/22/25:7–8), timed to coincide with the Saratoga racing season, offered a first-person tour of New York society at play out of town. In the winter of 1926, on the other hand, "The Costume Balls" burlesqued the society page, turning irrelevancies and errors into insults:

Among the prettiest of the debutantes present was Mrs. Hawthorne, grandmother of the Duchess of Margate. . . . She came as Mary Queen of Scots from the neck up. . . .

From the waist to the knees she was Paul Revere. . . .

Mrs. Hawthorne was awarded first prize, a safety razor and a pair of cuffs, by the committee on awards, which consisted of Whitney Warren, Condé Nast, Ambrose Glutz, Frank Crowninshield, Neysa McMein, Whitney Warren, Condé Nast, Neysa McMein and the late Dr. Elwood Speering . . . . [sic] (3/13/26:13–14)

Hyperbolic detail and a slightly mad spirit link Sullivan's forays into various genres: the mock-historical account in "Down the Ages with the Social Center," with Julian De Miskey's illustrations of Columbus atop his mast and Galileo jumping for joy in his cell (3/6/26:13–14), the burlesque travelogue of "The Nice Cool Sewer," with its breathless enthusiasm for "a trip through the famous sewers of New York!" (6/5/26:21), and the parodic journalism in "The Iron Man of Wall Street: An Interview with Pilate Noogle," a mogul who can arrange a Wall Street panic at his convenience and who attributes his success to "an old proverb of W. C. Fields, 'Never give a sucker an even break'" (9/25/26:20–21). Each parody frames its subject as a variant of New York's madness.

Sullivan approached comic extravagance differently in "How I Became a Subway Excavator" (1/23/26:13–14), his third casual, which extended the madness from the city to the narrator. The tale exemplifies what became known as "dementia praecox" humor, which Robert Benchley defined in a 1934 column for the New York *American* as characterized by "defective judgement," "deficiency of ethical inhibitions," and "silly laughter." Frustrated by interruptions from the blasting for the West Side IND subway, the narrator investigates the excavations below his apartment, finds the brutality thrilling, and henceforth embarks on a new career dedicated to breaking windows and trapping taxicabs. His transformation from ordinary chap to excavator fulfills a prophecy by his friend Prnszlumxszki (!), an aficionado of the joys of excavating. "It'll get you yet," he promises, with "the gleam of the fanatic," and indeed it does, but our narrator has nothing of the victim about him as he concocts new recipes for blasting powder and plans to capture taxis. On the contrary, he ends his narrative triumphant, having successfully snagged a "particularly fine specimen . . . a male Luxor, bedecked with all the magnificent plumage of that most gorgeous species," completing his "menagerie" in preparation for a performance destined to be "a sure fire hit": when the cabs run over the night watchman. Five exuberant illustrations, unsigned but probably the work of Al Frueh, convey the cheerful lunacy of Sullivan's narrative.

Published shortly before the magazine's first anniversary, "How I Became a Subway Excavator" broke new ground for *New Yorker* humor, transforming whimsy to mania, but Sullivan did not repeat the achievement soon. A year later, his last casual for volume 2, "Amy, the Central Park Cow," sneered at women who seek self-actualization over domestic bliss. Amy's credo summed up its satire: "Better a cow with ideals, whose milk is a trifle sour than one of these flaccid, flabby, spineless, contented creatures. The ambitious cow lives for her art" (12/25/26:15). The possibility that the narrator has "serious mental ills" affects the story less than his loss of opportunity to "stroke her sleek hide," now that Amy has determined to leave the city "to join the navy and see the world" (16). Even Frueh's amusing illustrations cannot quite rescue the fable.

By contrast with the hyperbolic humor of Ford and Sullivan, Dorothy Parker brought a wry, contemptuous irony to her early casuals. "A Certain Lady," her prose contribution to 1:2, presents "My friend, Mrs. Legion," a native-born New Yorker whose vulgarity (her name implies both ubiquity and commonness) outweighs her "appreciable edge on the parvenus who are Manhattanites only by migration" (2/28/25:15). This particular Mrs. Legion has plenty of certainty— "she can dismiss any subject with a single sentence" (16)—but no distinction. She misunderstands fashion as a process of "sedulously effac[ing] all traces of individuality," and "the Legion school of conversationalists" is, quite simply, a gaggle of gossips. But after demonstrating the lady's ethnic and racial prejudice, ignorance of the arts, and antiquated views on sex, Parker declares Mrs. Legion "Heiress of the ages" (16). Thus Parker invites *New Yorker* readers—women and men—to share her own superior values and style, and Perry Barlow depicts Legion as backward and nondescript with his illustration of an attractive, well dressed woman seen only from behind.

As early *New Yorker* prose struggled to adapt mock-oral conventions for an audience of young urban professionals, a few writers saw the potential of targeting humor at their elders, rather than social inferiors. Staff writer James Kevin McGuinness took this tack in "Modom," which plays with the social knowledge of insiders and outsiders. The story hints at first that the wealthy old men who buy Modom's couture for their young mistresses have succeeded in passing the women off as their wards, but finally exposes that the joke is on them, and us, because the girls are her shills, and she splits her profits with them (4/18/25:8).

By 1926, when Parker's next stories appeared, she pared narration to the bare minimum. Rendered as narrated dialogues rather than overheard speech, these tales blend the ironic distance of omniscient storytelling with the frame tale's conventional contrast between speakers. Parker updates and urbanizes the gentleman and vernacular narrators as the social combatants of her dialogues. In setting up comic tales between socially imbalanced pairs of men and women or older and younger generations, her prose humor reinforces the favored themes of the idea drawing. More important, however, her contrasts enable the powerful speakers (always male or older) descended from the frame tale's foolish gentleman narrator to damn themselves through their talk, while the weaker ones (usually female or younger) invite our sympathy.

Parker's "Dialogue at Three in the Morning" (2/13/26:13) ran just three weeks after Sullivan's "Subway Excavator," but the tales' moods could not have differed more. Against the excavator's zesty attacks on boulders and taxis come the defensive recriminations of a drunk woman talking herself into near-suicidal depression. From its first word, Parker's story scorns the woman as "plain"; her slightly ungrammatical speech exposes not only her drunkenness and anger but also her working-class background, pride in making her own way, and overwhelming feelings of victimization. Her male companion offers warmth and friendship, notwithstanding his description as "the man with the ice-blue hair," but he fails even to capture her attention, much less to correct her impressions of insult and injury. The bleak humor here lies in Parker's reversal of conventional courtship talk, of love or quarrel, and the story ends with the implication that the cycle of drinks and recriminations will continue without resolution—as ironic a conclusion as anyone could conceive, even for a "Dialogue" that proves a monologue.

Parker's humor lightened in the fall of 1926, but she continued the contrasts implied in the first dialogue. The bleakest of the three, "The Last Tea" contrasts the smooth self-interest of "the young man in the chocolate brown suit" with the propriety of "the girl with the artificial camillia" (9/11/26:23–24). These descriptions emphasize the pair's artificiality and bring readers into the scene as he brags about his wild night out and praises his new girlfriend, leaving the girl to salvage her pride through a transparently false tale of social opportunities. That she holds her tears "until she was out in the dark street" (24) marks a small victory for dignity against her loss of love. A broader tweak at men came in "Oh, He's Charming," where a popular male writer reveals less sophisticated literary taste than the modestly educated woman who admires him despite his hauteur (10/9/26:22–23). Parker invites readers to enjoy the comeuppance from his unfamiliarity with recent books by Sherwood Anderson and Theodore Dreiser, or even the reputation of Ring Lardner—a rich joke for the cognoscenti to share the year after *Dark Laughter* and *An American Tragedy* were published, and ten years after *You Know Me Al*. Lighter still, "Travelogue" turns the tables with a dialogue of a man unable to tell a woman about his travels because she interrupts him with her own stories every time he tries to talk (10/30/26:20–21). While these tales confirm John Updike's claim that "Dorothy Parker was an expert on the lovers' quarrel, . . . [with] a thorough education in the self-wounding perversity of the human heart" (111), they also point to parallels between the *New Yorker*'s verbal and graphic humor, which similarly played with relationships of unequal power.

Ben Hecht's early contributions show more clearly how *New Yorker* editors began shaping their prose material. Angell headed the fiction department beginning in the fall of 1925, but Ross often dealt directly with his friends among the contributors. These included Hecht, who brought the Colyumist tradition to his earliest pieces. "The Sacred White Cow" complained about newspapers' abuse of quotations from prominent citizens on issues of public morality (4/18/25:8); and subsequent pieces decried Heywood Broun's professional difficulties (6/6/25:12) and humans' essential hypocrisy (6/13/25:17). What Carl Van Doren said in 1923 about Hecht's newspaper column applies equally well to his early *New Yorker* writing: "he throws no verbal handsprings," but merely "talks about himself and his opinions" (314). Just about the time Angell arrived, after four more pieces, only one of them amusing—"The Wife Beating Wave" credits bridge and crossword puzzles with the prevention of domestic violence in the postwar period (6/27/25:9)—Hecht disappeared from the *New Yorker.*

Sixteen months later, "The Caliph Complex" showed that Hecht and the *New Yorker* staff had learned in the interim one way to write a casual: to treat a contemporary social practice to heavy irony but only mild satire, as critique from inside, through first-person narration. Hecht feigns breathless enthusiasm over the peer society's rage for uptown entertainment. "My set has discovered something too marvelous for words," he gushes at the start. "Negroes!" Then he adds, emphasizing the irony of his naïve pose, "Oddles and oodles of negroes. Big ones and little ones" (12/4/26:30–31). The piece goes on with such mock-explanation for three full columns, its sarcasm mimicked by Julian De Miskey's illustration of a dignified, steatopygous couple (slightly bored) in minstrel blackface and evening dress—a visualization of the self-congratulatory tone with which Hecht asserts the "truly democratic yet regal gesture" of white folks visiting Harlem:

we sit down at a table right next to male and female darkies as if we were all just human beings in one room together. The thrill of this pretense is much superior to the one we used to feel in the chop suey joints sitting next to Chinamen. After all, you can't get away from the fact that there are Mandarins and Chinese civilization and Confucius and all that sort of thing. . . .
Unlike the Chinamen, they appreciate the true depth of our democracy. . . .

Heavens, as if anybody could ever suspect us of being colored just because we like colored folks! (30)

Hecht moves his critique past several sources of superiority—proof of liberality, proof of intellectuality, proof of taste "in the exotic"—before reaching the nub in the last sentence. There, he slams "my set" with the ultimate irony of their fad: that they join the crowd in the search for (dramatic pause) "distinction" (31).

In addition to illustrating the *New Yorker*'s progress in defining topics and comic strategies for prose humor, "The Caliph Complex" also hints at the magazine's attitude toward fashionable Afrophilia. Appearing in the same issue as Reginald Marsh's sneer at the white woman who, showing her black maid a primitive sculpture, exclaimed, "your people . . . how do you do it?" (12/4/26:35), "The Caliph Complex" suggests that the *New Yorker* did not so much ignore Africanist movements as suspect their white supporters. No evidence exists that African-American writers submitted their work or were rejected during this period, though correspondence in the archives indicates reluctance to cover black revues.[10] Yet the *New Yorker* gave "The Caliph Complex" front-of-the-book placement and an illustration by Julian De Miskey, by implication joining Hecht in his disdain for the racism of the slumming crowd. Staff member Fillmore Hyde published illustrated verse on a related issue earlier that year. "Moral Problems" ridicules prejudices by putting them in verse, but the contrast between low birthrates for "effete" white women and how "Infants over-rich in pigment / Follow one upon another" leads to a troublesome conclusion: "Now if things like this are true,/ What are moral men to do?" (F. H., 4/24/26:16).

Eighteen months later, Dorothy Parker's "Arrangement in Black and White" extended Hecht and Hyde's attack on false liberality with the story of a woman at a party in honor of a famous gospel singer (10/8/27:22–23). Parker identifies the woman only by the fashionable clothing she wears, implying that she dons and doffs attitudes with similar frequency and ease. Thrilled to meet a celebrity, the woman professes not to understand "why on earth it isn't perfectly all right to meet colored people," yet she praises her host for his generosity, "giving this perfectly marvelous party for him, and having him meet all these white people, and all" (22). When she adopts a benefactor's posture herself, asking, "Isn't he terribly grateful?" the voice of genuine liberalism answers, "I hope not," and Parker's carefully ironic prose exposes the condescension in the woman's boldest acts of equality:

The woman with the pink velvet poppies extended her hand at the length of her arm and held it so, in fine determination, for all the world to see, until the Negro took it, shook it, and gave it back to her. . . .

She spoke with great distinctness, moving her lips meticulously, as if in parlance with the deaf. (23)

The woman runs on with stereotypical nonsense, on the one hand praising blacks as "easy going, and always singing and laughing and everything" (22), and barely avoiding racial epithets, on the other. Not surprisingly, the story ends with such two-facedness, as the woman applauds her own open-mindedness by exclaiming, "Oh, wait till I tell Burton I called him 'Mister'!" (24).

Parker, whose racial politics included supporting Communist causes and willing her papers to the National Association for the Advancement of Colored People (T. Grant, "Dorothy Parker" 379, 382), seems in "Arrangement" to have expressed the *New Yorker*'s politics as well. Like Hecht's "The Caliph Complex" and various cartoons on racial themes, "Arrangement in Black and White" sneers at pseudoliberal racism. In the process, the story suggests why African-American writing and entertainment seldom appeared in *New Yorker* departments other than "Books," which could treat accomplishment regardless of race.

Hecht's subsequent contributions failed to sustain the success of "The Caliph Complex," as the *New Yorker* more clearly distinguished between "colyum" writing and casuals. The process took most of the decade, as a summary of Hecht's later work suggests. "A Literary Debacle" (12/18/26:32–33), "The Female Bridge Menace" (6/25/27:19–20), and "A Plea for Bad Plays" (9/22/28:25–26) all strove for irony without reaching it, and six weeks after "A Plea," Hecht concluded his contributions to volumes 1–5 with "The Philoolooloo Bird," an amusing "Reporter At Large" piece on the audience for prize fights at Madison Square Garden (11/3/28:40–44), written much earlier but saved by the staff for boxing season.[11] Because Hecht generally spoke in his own voice, rather than adopting a comic persona or pose, his casuals lacked a central element for success, though Angell encouraged him to write "light humorous stuff if you feel in the mood."[12] But by the end of the decade, Ross was exhorting his staff to "get clear on the fact that all the departmental stuff in the book is FACTUAL, all the non-departmental stuff *fictional,* and that the two kinds of stuff have no place other than in their regular one."[13]

Robert Benchley had no such difficulty, perhaps because his humor tended toward hyperbole rather than irony. By all accounts, Benchley mastered the madcap persona by 1910, while still an undergraduate at Harvard, when "Through the Alimentary Canal with Gun and Camera" established him as an earnest dealer in non sequiturs (Solomon 24). Ten years later he had sufficient comic material from *Vanity Fair, Harper's,* and elsewhere to collect as *Of All Things* (1921), illustrated by college friend Gluyas Williams. Though Dale Kramer claimed that Ross's Algonquin buddies failed to supply material for his new magazine (75), Benchley contributed fifteen pieces, including three "Profiles," to volume 1 and seventeen more to volume 2.

He signed most of his 1925 pieces as "Search-Light," probably because *Life* owned his byline, but the pseudonym allowed him to experiment with a voice other than his well-known madcap persona. The deadpan social satire of these pieces also suggests a willingness to explore political humor. "Fez and the Dark Age" (4/4/25:11–12), for instance, ridicules a young Arab poet's admiration of New York, which he knows only from film and misperceives because of his youth and his Islamic lens. After observing that "All the men work. All the women make good wives. There is no drinking of wine" [11]), the poet leaps to an absurd conclusion: "To this I dedicate my life! Some day Fez-el-Bali shall be like New York!" (12). Benchley criticizes American decadence more directly in "The New Conquistadores" (5/2/25:7–8), which contrasts speculators in Florida real estate with an earlier generation of invaders. Returning to New York by ship after spending so much money on land that he couldn't afford a train ticket, the narrator hears in contemporary talk—about land values and the new $300,000 church in Deland—parallels to an old report he has found. In it, Spanish colonial leaders take pride in announcing a new Cathedral "built by Christian natives" and donated to the University of Salamanca, though they concede at the end, "We had to shoot many infidel natives who did not understand why we wanted to build so fair a church in a land that was not ours" (7–8). The parallels between past and present equate today's "believers in Jacksonville" with yesterday's believers in God, and declare both enthralled to Mammon.

Though for most of 1925 Benchley maintained the gloomy spirit of this piece, which appeared the week before Fleischmann determined to kill the *New Yorker,* he abandoned it for a lighter spirit just before Christmas of 1925, when he began signing his own name to four stories in as many weeks. "Up the Dark Stairs—" (12/19/25:7–8), his first signed piece, contrasts conventional journalism with the literary newspaper writing that Benchley calls the "O. Henry-Irvin Cobb tradition," with burlesque accounts of a police rescue, a funeral, and an international monetary conference, all of them beginning with the evocative "Up the dark stairs" (as in "Up the dark stairs at 17 Downing Street"). Here he subordinates critique to the display of comic imagination—especially verbal play—priorities that link the most successful prose humor of volume 1.

Despite their difference in tone, Benchley's signed and pseudonymous casuals follow the same narrative formula: they begin with a piece of news, real or fictional, and build an elaborate fantasy on it—often gilding the lily by parodying a serious form. These became more broadly comic as the *New Yorker* approached its first anniversary, enhancing the mood established by Ford and Sullivan. "Sex is Out" (12/26/25:16) begins with the scientific claim that "there is no such thing as absolute sex," but even before reciting his facts ("If 60% of your cells are masculine . . . ") he exposes his own unreliability and that of his ostensible source, and ends by claiming absurd consequences—the execrable dialogue and songs of theater robbed of its classic plot device, Mary's desire to leave Fred for Roger. The more spirited but less good-natured "Uncle Calvin's No-Waste Games" lampoons Coolidge's Christmas message to America's children with a monologue in which Uncle Calvin introduces a series of games—calculation of the national debt, washing and drying dishes, typesetting the *Congressional Record*—and then goads the teams from the sidelines (1/9/26:17). The satire extends beyond its contemporary relevance because the humor comes from the wooden comic villainy attributed to Uncle Calvin.

The momentum of early fall brought other talents on board. A regular contributor unknown today, Joseph Fulling Fishman debuted a few weeks before Ellin Mackay published her cabaret piece; his series of futuristic chronicles sardonically reports the decline of various institutions. An amusing antinostalgic perspective for a magazine targeted to the young set, the series began with "Future of the Films" (10/24/25:32–33), which probably inspired editors to suggest that he apply the idea to other industries, resulting in "The Future of Hotels," which tweaked the industry by predicting such deviations from current practice as "Guest desiring to sleep late not awakened by maid rattling key in lock" (12/12/25:45), and similar ironic prophesies in "The Future of the Sleeping Car" (1/23/26:28) and "The Future of the Subway" (1/30/26:42–43). Fishman's "Newspaper Crime Report 1950" took a different approach, however, presenting a journalist's report of criminal success followed by a military expert's evaluation of the police strategy (2/13/26:29). The sketch envisions crime and police efforts as an urban war, complete with tank convoys—not a funny idea to anyone familiar with urban crime in the 1980s and '90s but apparently amusing in a city where crime remained low until the 1960s.[14]

The difference between these pleasant local items and Fishman's "Millions of Prizes" demonstrates the divide emerging in 1926 between the front and back of the book. In contrast to his short, somewhat formulaic local sketches, "Millions of Prizes" offered a distinctive narrative voice and an elaborately developed comic idea sustained over three columns (2/27/26:13–14). "Millions of Prizes" not only burlesques the contemporary contest craze but also parodies the first-person success story, a newly developed genre of magazine writing, as our narrator earnestly describes his "puzzle-solving plant," its elaborate irrelevancies intensified by Al Frueh's illustrations. The drawings, especially "Experts in the Missing Letter Department at work," visualize the hyperbole in Fishman's conception, suggesting that to the artist and editors, at least, Fishman's piece belonged to the same manic narrative mode as Ford's and Sullivan's writing. Perhaps more important, Frueh's drawings emphasize the incongruity between the narrator's deadpan explication and the byzantine system he describes. This comic contrast between manner and matter, a classic device of American tall tales, here serves an industrial subject, imitating a written report rather than oral talk.

The first anniversary issue proved the distance traveled since 1:1. "The Modern Music Jag" filled the featured page after "Talk" with W. J. Henderson's critique of contemporary classical music and an illustration by Peter Arno of a violinist taking a hand-saw to his strings as a matron crowns him with laurel. The speaker's informed dislike of Schönberg and Copeland's music makes his criticisms funny to a knowledgeable reader as they swerve from reduction to exaggeration. "The process was just like the Cubist painting trick," he notes. "Break good tunes up into little pieces and shake the pieces up in a hat" (2/20/26:21). Corey Ford's "Anniversary of a Great Magazine" followed a few pages later, leading into Elinor Wylie's "Sundae School," a parody of sentimental fiction dripping with metaphors and adjectives as it describes a group of young Manhattanites concocting drinks at tea-time:

It was five o'clock of a fine cool February evening, and seven delicate veils of twilight, colored blue and violet like the flames which dance upon the surface of burning brandy, had already descended athwart the frosty pinnacles of high Manhattan. . . .

"Will you have an Alexander, Peter, or do you prefer an eggnog to your tea?" asked little Allegra Goodheart, for such was the maiden's pretty and appropriate name, leaning towards a youth whose fiery red hair lent a somewhat ferocious aspect to his intelligently simian countenance. (2/20/26:29)

The sketch runs on in this vein as Wylie parodies Proust with descriptions of various drinks—Alexander made with strawberry jam, for instance, or a blend of rum, Hildegarde, chutney, and condensed milk—while offering society banter on whether women deserve blame for the "decline of decent traditional drinking." Thus Wylie sets up for the punch line: that, because of her traditional upbringing, Allegra's "pretty teacup of pearly pink lustre-ware" does not contain tea but (she blushingly admits) plain whiskey and water. In place of the early issues' snobbery, the featured casuals of 2:1 target the elite through insiders' knowledge—of music, the Eustace Tilley series, drinking practices, and literary conventions.

The back of the book, by contrast, had become the place to introduce new contributors and entice readers to ad columns. Newman Levy's story of a robber turned prohibition agent makes a first-person local story of the old joke wherein a bandit takes a bank job because that's where the money is ("Billings Buys a Button" 38). Robert Jay Misch's "Hades Notes" (52) describes boating on the Styx under the heading "More Foreign Letters," a literal play on the injunction "Go to Hell." More successful, the "Night Club Idyll" by E. Paramore (Edmund Wilson's former roommate[15]) revived the tradition of George Ade's *Fables in Slang* (1899): the Serious Young Man from Dubuque, offended by the ignorance of the Young Lady Who Showed Her Ears, the Woman Who Didn't Need Brassières, and the Flapper Who Still Wore Stays, runs off with the Coat Room Girl, who turns out to be a girl from home. The sneering, euphemistic portrait of a wealthy Jewish merchant in "Thrift" (66) provided East Side local color that bordered on ethnic slur, though the absence of a byline suggests some discomfort with running it.

Inside Jobs

As the editors became clearer about what kind of humor should appear in the *New Yorker*, they began writing it themselves. John Chapin Mosher from Angell's staff and Fillmore Hyde from Ingersoll's both debuted in volume 2. The opportunity to augment their editorial wages appealed to staff, and helped the *New Yorker* recruit writers, not just editors, to the staff. Most important, it enabled the *New Yorker* to shape prose humor from the inside.

Fillmore Hyde, the "Talk" staffer who introduced Katharine Angell to Harold Ross and now wrote "Notes and Comment," worked much the same burlesque vein as Corey Ford, but specialized in comic anticlimax. Hyde's first casual, "The English Author Who Consented to Be Interviewed" begins with three suspenseful columns leading up to an interview that does not, ultimately, take place. The English author refuses to be interviewed, spurns the $100,000 offered for his opinion of America, then gives his opinion anyway, finally abandoning his rented room in fury and littering it with "scraps of green paper" after the $100,000 check arrives (5/1/26:16). Reversals mount: the narrator's story of the author's consent recounts his refusal; the English author's recantation becomes the American editor in chief's comeuppance. The editors endorsed this madcap mode with illustrations from Julian De Miskey, whose stick figures reinforced its silliness.

"The English Author" set the mood for the summer, including the outrageous "Prehistoric New York As I Knew It." Also illustrated by De Miskey and ostentatiously signed by "Fillmore Hyde's Grandmother" (7/3/26:13–14), the piece burlesqued nostalgic recollections (and perhaps inspired the 1928 occasional series "A New York Childhood," featuring memoirs by Elmer Rice, Babette Deutsch, Gilbert Seldes, Ernest Groening, and others). In the spirit of Corey Ford, Grandma's recollections include her Cro-Magnon grandfather, "known as Old Crow," and the marriage of Pitecanthropus Erectus to Miss Neanderthal.

More interesting was a blend of hyperbole and comic inferiority in Ford's third series, "The Bleakest Job," which began in late May of 1926. A spoof of newspaper and magazine features, the seven installments revive Eustace Tilley to head the Bleakest Job Committee and expose "the loneliness and heartache that masquerade behind the gaudy tinsel of Business" (5/29/26:20).[16] Beginning with Mr. Adolph Prossey, the man who cleans Central Park's statuary, a man "so tender-hearted that when he bathes a female statue he heats the water before he dashes it over her back," the series ends by expanding its targets to include contests themselves (Tilley wins the prize as the ultimate sufferer for having to interview so many people in dreadful circumstances) and Sinclair Lewis's rejection of the Pulitzer (Tilley refuses his prize because he already has a *New Yorker* subscription and because "all prizes, like all titles, are dangerous" [7/31/26:24]). The silly spirit of volume 2 received a boost from Robert Benchley, who missed only four issues between 2:6 (3/27/26) and 2:23 (7/24/26),[17] including two mock-oral frame tales in the nineteenth-century tradition, "Louis Dot Dope" (presenting Benchley in his dimwit pose, 4/3/26:15) and "Kamp Koolidge" (featuring a campfire yarn from "Old Cal, the grizzled trapper," 6/5/26:25).

The peak of the silly summer of 1926, however, came in Fillmore Hyde's "Ritz Carlton" series, which invited the peer society to laugh at the Four Hundred. This series differed from earlier ones by offering a novella in eleven parts, running monthly from 2:26 ("A Hard Day with the Ritz Carltons: An Upper-Class Tragedy," 8/14/26:13–14) to 3:18 ("The Ritz Carltons: A Happy Day,"

6/18/27:14–16).[18] In contrast to the experience of August 1925 when editors took advantage of low circulation to experiment almost unnoticed, this series began boldly toward the end of the summer, exuding confidence that the magazine had followed readers to the Hamptons. The novella's targets range from drawing-room and sentimental fiction to society journalism, beginning with the first installment, how Mrs. Carlton's day ran from bad to worse, then got worse still: she began with a sprained thumb from playing bridge the night before, and now her pearls need restringing, but the restringer has gone on vacation, the chauffeur has the day off, her daughter's bathing suit has reappeared on another young woman (despite Madam Poilu's promises not to make another), and so on. The travails continue in this vein throughout the series, emphasizing that the rich have their troubles too. Indeed, Mrs. Carlton requires constant medical ministrations for the stresses in her life. Mere mention of the possibility of summer activities away from their Southampton summer house shocks Mrs. Carlton into insensibility. Fortunately the doctor stands ready when Ritza marries Ritz Tower (a distant cousin of her father) and Mrs. Carlton, after remaining vertical for the event, finally collapses, "her pearls rattling against the balustrade" (6/18/27:14–16). At this signal, the doctor emerges from the orchidery, ready to catch her and put her in the awaiting ambulance. All's well that ends well.

Hyde's travesty of the troubles of the rich underlines how well *New Yorker* editors, and Hyde in particular, had come to know their readers by the middle of volume 2. After Ellin Mackay's cabaret piece in 1:40, Hyde checked around drawing rooms and newsstands, and learned that the magazine appealed primarily to "the speakeasy set" (Kramer, *Ross* 95). A send-up of high society populated by characters so literally pillars of society that their names are hotels—Ritz Carlton, Park Lane, and Copley Plaza—specifically targeted these iconoclasts of the peer society. As if to underline this appeal, several installments ran alongside cartoons similarly twitting high society. A Julian De Miskey drawing within the Harvard graduation segment reinforced its theme that the rich don't need intelligence: two women at a polo game remark that a player standing nearby "has no right to look so dumb" because "he isn't so terribly rich" (5/28/27:17). Far from pandering to the Stuyvesants whom advertisers targeted, the *New Yorker* twitted them from a rung slightly lower on the social ladder but substantially higher on the intellectual scale.

The Elsie Dinsmore parodies by Phyllis Crawford writing as Josie Turner[19] picked up where Hyde's series left off. These came six weeks after the "Ritz Carlton" series ended, in the same issue featuring Turner's *New Yorker* debut sketch,

"The Bridle" (5/28/27:82). At the back of the book, Turner's piece extended an idea Oliver Claxton introduced three weeks before in "The Decline of the Gesture," which mourned the loss of "The Ogle," "The Bow," and "The Wink" (5/7/27:21). Turner takes a different approach with "The Bridle," claiming that she and her friends define it as "a self-conscious recognition of wicked admiration" despite Webster's description, "indignant Toss of the head." Together with her next two casuals, also mocking obsolete manners, "The Passing of the Flounce" (7/23/27:47) and "The Decline of Leering" (7/30/27:23–24), "The Bridle" exemplifies the dynamic process by which *New Yorker* readers became *New Yorker* contributors. Because new writers often began as readers inspired by recent pieces, the *New Yorker* had more coherence than its diverse contents and contributors might suggest, giving the false impression of editorial doors closed to outsiders.

The wry hilarity of the Dinsmore parodies differentiated them from the "Ritz Carlton" burlesques. The original five episodes ran between July 1927 and January 1928 (3:24 to 3:50), with later installments in 4:49 and 5:27. Two factors kept the series going: widespread familiarity with Martha Farquharson Finley's original series of twenty-eight novels for girls (published 1867 to 1905, during the childhoods of *New Yorker* readers and their parents), and the flexibility of a comic idea in which New York sophisticates, including her daddy, dupe a Candide-like innocent.[20] Turner's series hinges on Elsie's dutiful obedience in absurd contexts. In "Elsie Dinsmore's Weekend" she ends up almost as drunk as her father, who falls out of his chair after an afternoon of orange juice and bootleg liquor, and follows up by romping with the maid (and probably with his hostess too); yet Elsie commends him for kissing the maid farewell in thanks "for being so kind to us" (7/30/27:24). Later episodes detail other examples of his abusing her innocence to conceal his sexual escapades. By mocking Finley's sermons on filial obedience and parental authority, Turner's series emphasizes the generational break represented by the peer society.

By today's standards, Turner's ideas wear thin after the third episode, "Elsie Dinsmore Goes Shopping," when the father's pretext of buying underwear for Elsie justifies a day of leering at nearly nude models (12/17/27:23–24). The series' continuation suggests that staff expected readers to enjoy Turner's reminders that the social and literary conventions of their parents' generation were comically irrelevant. Three years later Ross praised the Dinsmore stories as "among the funniest we ever printed" because they "had a lot of incident," and encouraged Turner's work on a parodic Little Lord Fauntleroy series with a remark that no misogynist would add: "I have always had high hopes for you—you're one of the few feminine humorists."[21]

Tall Tales Get Shorter

Although Turner's focus on social rules looked back to Hyde's travesty of elite society, her tone looked ahead to the quieter humor of John Mosher, a second *New Yorker* staffer turned writer. Burlesques dominated prose during the summer of 1926, but in the same period the ironic mode of Dorothy Parker began to get support from prose by Mosher and E. B. White, whose ironic first-person narratives united the mock-oral traditions of tall talk with the travails of the Sufferer. As Katherine Sproehnle and James Thurber joined them in mining this ironic vein, it counterbalanced, then displaced the broad burlesque of Ford and Hyde.

John Mosher's record as a writer for the early *New Yorker*—four dozen casuals, regular film reviews, and the occasional "Profile"—points to the inadequacy of his reputation as the infamous "rejecting machine" of Thurber's *Years with Ross* (27). Thurber's ridicule has drowned out other praise: Dale Kramer credited him as a pioneer of the *New Yorker* short story (*Ross* 243), and Katharine White pointed out that every reader of unsolicited manuscripts culls little from the slush pile (qtd. in Kinney 305). Mosher's *New Yorker* prose in volumes 2–5 demonstrates a sharp sense of humor and an early understanding of how to invite laughter at elites. In 1929 John O'Hara (whose work Mosher found in the slush pile) put Mosher's humor in a class with Parker's and Woollcott's.[22] Mosher's periodic appearances in the illustrated page following "Talk" indicate that Angell, Ross, and others agreed.

His first casual, "The Man with a Box" (3/6/26:18), deserved its star treatment opposite a layout by Helen Hokinson and a few pages behind Sullivan's "Down the Age with the Social Center" (13–14). Mosher transfers the old American tradition of the frame narrative to a tale of urban travail. An accountant who has lost his job and his apartment has been living in the family box at the opera, but plans for a new opera house now threaten him with homelessness. The narrator adopts his friend's anxiety as his own as he describes the problem: "Had I any influence? Certain improvements he longed to have introduced. A kitchenette and a private bath. 'A private bath,' he cried, 'would mean everything to me. . . .'" Well, almost everything: as our narrator leaves the friend's box to play bridge in another, he hears a sigh, "But I shall never be in a position to keep any pets." Despite its structural similarity to the tall yarn, this tale features a Sufferer in place of the conventional braggart. But this mock-oral tale does end at the peak of incredulity, giving the interior storyteller the last word as his tale of woe invites sympathy for his plight rather than awe over his exploits.

Mosher continued this realistic mode of urban fantasy without the narrative frame in later stories, but alternated between hyperbolic and minimized situations. Like Benchley, Mosher often based his casuals on news stories, but Mosher gave wry comments, not absurd details. "The Prize Problem" relates how Sinclair Lewis's decision to decline the Pulitzer Prize, announced May 6, 1926, led ten-year-old Miss Smeed of Waukegan, Illinois, to reject her Sunday School's award for best attendance (5/29/26:15). His later fantasies contrasted more boldly with his deadpan style. When "Bon Voyage, Say We" describes reactions from passengers on the Staten Island ferry after its captain hijacked their boat and set sail for Paris (7/10/26:13–14), Mosher jokes about New York's rum-runners, noting that the passengers calmed down after the ship passed the three-mile limit. "The little skiff made friends at once with the various craft loitering about the limit," he reports, and the passengers' higher spirits (and blood alcohol levels) enabled the group to enjoy their voyage at last.

Mosher's more ironic narratives detail comically small events, some with large consequences. In "The Best Dressed Man Has Amnesia," freedom from his responsibilities inspires the hero to buy a silk cap with a lining so loud that the homeless on the street give him wide berth (7/31/26:24). After the threadbare poet in "Opening an Account" buys a new wardrobe but fails to qualify for credit, his mortification drives from his head all the rhymes that he needed to earn a living (8/7/26:25). Mosher's urban fantasies unfold with such fastidious social detail that if Hero and Leander lived in New York City, as he imagines in "Liebestod," she would learn of his death from her maid, secretary, and publicity agent and then devote herself to determining an appropriate approach to public mourning (9/4/26:22). In 1926 Mosher's prose helped *New Yorker* humor combine broad comic conception and ironic realistic narration.

Mosher also helped the *New Yorker* reorient local color writing. Like its Southern counterpart, *New Yorker* local color humor asserts regional distinctiveness through eccentric characters, customs, and speech, a tradition that Walter Blair traces to the Reconstruction, especially notable in the writing of Joel Chandler Harris and George Washington Cable (Blair 124–47). And like its New England cousin, *New Yorker* local color promotes gendered values, though not typically the feminist values that Josephine Donovan has linked to Harriet

Beecher Stowe and Sarah Orne Jewett. But *New Yorker* humor rejected both the rural verities of simplicity and nature that the older types celebrated, and their preference for folklore over literary wit. Indeed, whereas nineteenth-century regional humor offered a rear-guard defense against expanding national literary traditions, *New Yorker* local color writing co-opted them through parody and popularization.

Katherine Sproehnle's casuals helped shape the *New Yorker's* local color prose with a dozen reports on women's experiences in New York City. Her first, "Worry? Nonsense" (5/15/26:30), takes up a favorite New York frustration: dealing with the police after a burglary. The patronizing attitudes of New York's finest add insult to injury. "Lady, you wouldn't let a little thing like a robbery that happens fifty times a day in New York worry you—" soothes the officer who answers the telephone at her precinct, as our narrator explains why "there's no use" trying to get help from the police. "Why little girl," assures the detective who takes the report that all her clothes are missing, but brushes off her desire for an investigation, "all you have to do is tidy up what's left." When he adds that he'd even help "come and spend tomorrow with you if it weren't my day off" (as he leaves through the door that the burglars destroyed), she responds to his insincerity with sarcasm: "I didn't know you cared" (5/15/26:30).

Sproehnle followed up that summer with several front-of-the-book sketches of woman Sufferers. Although "Bringing Up a Bond" features a woman whose ignorance set her up for mistreatment by an investment broker (6/26/26:19), for the most part Sproehnle avoided the pose of the empty-headed ditz for a role "talking back to the culture," as Nancy Walker put it ("Talking"). "Passionate Letters to Public Utilities," for instance, shows an urbanite desperately exercising intelligence along with feminine wiles in begging the milkman to leave cream instead of Grade B milk, the gas company to turn on the gas, and the newspaper delivery man to restore her daily *Times* instead of rotating her subscription among the *Graphic,* the *Herald-Tribune,* and the *World.* Sproehnle knows urban frustrations, and her writing speaks to the initiated when she promises the milkman, "This is the last thing I shall ever ask of you" (7/24/26:21). Wrapped around an I. Klein drawing of working-class men in a cafeteria crowded with white-collar workers, Sproehnle's humor joins Klein's in a mock-realism addressed to urban insiders. The "Passionate Letters" series probably would have continued past a second installment except that the correspondent died—"of suppressed emotions," of all things—while complaining to New York Telephone (7/31/26:20). Sproehnle's work did not reappear in the magazine until the following spring, but in her first summer Sproehnle offset burlesque silliness with a wry, realistic humor akin to Hokinson's series of urban quests.

The epistolary vein that Sproehnle initiated proved especially rich for women humorists, who wrote more than half the epistolary narratives in the early magazine. In volume 3 Sproehnle followed "Passionate Letters" with "Financial Letters" (4/23/27:30) and "The Yacht Complex," the latter an exchange in which Sproehnle waxes ecstatic over the news that a boat with seven staterooms (including one for the maid) is being offered at a reasonable price for quick sale (8/13/27:15). Perhaps more interesting in terms of gendered narrative choice, poet Margaret Fishback's first casual also took epistolary form. Fishback followed her half-dozen "Why I Like New York" items in the fall of 1926 with "Dead Letters," containing proposals to the I.R.T. subway company on allowing riding on the platforms and to John D. Rockefeller on opening the concrete area between his house and his father's to roller skaters, among other suggestions (10/30/26:65–66). The genre also inspired the *New Yorker* prose debut of poet Margaret Widdemer, whose "Personal-Touch Department" contains a pair of letters between Widdemer and the subscription department of the *Atlantic Monthly*: in this mock-drama of contemporary commerce the *Atlantic*'s Christine Lowell claims that she "cannot bear to say 'yes'" to the Stencil Department's demands to place Widdemer's address stencil in the "Discontinued" file, to which Widdemer replies that *she* cannot bear to say yes, either, considering that she can save "four dollars toward my bootlegger's bill" by reading the magazine at the library, but hopes to reciprocate Christine's kindnesses some day (10/26/29:112). The idea of personal letters sent to impersonal institutions was a durable joke from 1926 to 1929, when the professionalization of mass marketing made the topic timely, but epistolary humor expanded early to include letters between lovers as well as business relations.

Courtship letters created richer fictions than commercial correspondence. The humor of the latter hinged on authors' signing their own names to the letters, contrasting the realism of the signatures and commercial situations with the absurdity of their rhetoric. Letters involving courtship, on the other hand, created fictional personas—for the addressee, if not also the author. These narrative differences had large consequences. In the hands of women writers, this epistolary variation characterized the female writer as dizzy, insincere, or aggressive; men who used the form became victims.

The two letters in "Circumstances Alter Cases," Nancy Hoyt's debut, expose

a young woman's venality as she writes to her two fiancés. To the first, Miss Ot-
tillie Starr acknowledges "regretfully" his concerns about "how sordid a marriage might become on an insufficient *dot*"; to the second, she turns effusive and
enthusiastically accepts the offer of a ring, yet she advises against ostentation in
favor of more understated elegance—perhaps a small, square (and sightly more
expensive) emerald in lieu of a diamond (1/22/27:21). The *New Yorker* endorsed
this piece, the first of six contributions by Hoyt between January and April of
1927, by placing it near the front of the book and asking Alice Harvey to illustrate it.

Male writers apparently found the genre less appealing, and used it differently. Leonard Hall's "Love on a Quantity Basis" played with rhetoric, using the
language of marketing in the context of courtship: a suitor offers a girl "Neck-
ing Up to Date," and she requests a guarantee "that your product will maintain
its quality over a period of time" (6/13/25:14). Mosher's "Commercial Correspondence" followed Sproehnle's lead in "Yacht Complex" by offering a personal
response to a pseudopersonal form letter (1/7/28:50–51), but a year later Wolcott Gibbs demonstrated how letter form can reorganize time and information
to make a sad story hilarious.

In "Facsimile of a Letter" (2/23/29:84–85), Gibbs gradually widens the gap
between the emotionally charged events of his tale and the repose of his telling,
and humor grows as the gap expands. The letter to girlfriend Ella establishes a
structure of increasing suffering as the writer enumerates the illnesses and injuries he acquired in her quest for fun: exhaustion from racing to the top of the
Statue of Liberty, pneumonia from taking the Hoboken ferry in a December
rain, concussions from falling on his head while skating and from her hitting
him with a snowball containing a "little piece of brick." Noting that her responses to his afflictions ranged from laughter to lecture, he concedes that "it
was practically suicidal for me to try to kiss you last night in the taxi" and concludes that he was lucky that she declined. Whatever inconvenience I suffered
from the temporary loss of my sight is nothing compared to what I would have
gone through for the rest of my life had you chosen to favor my suit. In fact, after knowing you for slightly less than three months, I am convinced that it is
only because my ancestors lived lives of terrific hardship, in continual conflict
with the Indians, that I am still able to creep about the streets" (85). The sketch
mutes the cliché of the speaker's insight arriving just as his vision goes, emphasizing instead the welcome reversal of a head injury's ill effects. But this outcome
intensifies the contrast between the narrator's evident calm and the intense ex-

periences he describes—a contrast that increases along with his injuries and keeps the story comic. By the start of volume 5, when Gibbs's letter appeared over his own signature, blurring the fantasy of the story with the reality of the author, the Sufferer had assumed the author's identity and become the victim in the war between the sexes, but his bloodied head remained unbowed.

The high point of epistolary humor in the early *New Yorker* came in Frank Sullivan's "Moderately Heartrending Letter" (3/23/29:17–18). A four-column attack on a Third Avenue laundry, Sullivan's letter proclaimed his own humiliation and the laundry's cruelty and ingratitude in response to a note (submitted with the outrageously false sentiment "Respectfully yours") announcing, "We called for your laundry but found no one home. Please notify us when to call again." The sketch exaggerates the disproportion between the laundry's formality and the customer's informality (Sproehnle's conceit) by contrasting the laundry's terse communication with Sullivan's extended invective. "You and your fair words and your everlasting promises to put more starch in my collars," the rant begins, and it ends with plea for guilt: "Lord knows what ever made me ever expect that you would be different from any of the other hand laundries. . . . Things that didn't need laundering at all, I'd sent over to you, so that you'd have enough to make ends meet" (17). An urban figure caught in an urban dilemma, Sullivan's letter writer gets the last word, even though the laundry still has his handkerchiefs. Published five weeks after Gibbs's letter of the battered boyfriend, "A Moderately Heartrending Letter" offered lip service to moderation, showing the parallel advance of the *New Yorker*'s ironic and hyperbolic voices.

Ford and Hyde continued publishing in the *New Yorker,* but the decreasing frequency of their work diminished its overall impact, especially in contrast to the greater number of writers playing with the ironic possibilities of first-person narration. Changing tastes and new opportunities also figured in the shift. Not Ford but White wrote the house ad series in the spring of 1927, early in volume 3; White's protagonist Sterling Finny, victim of one trauma after the next in the new therapeutic ethos of advertising, stood in ironic contrast to Eustace Tilley, the ever triumphant jack-of-all-trades. Of Ford's sixty-five items in the first five years, fifty-four appeared in volumes 1 and 2, and the irregular appearance of his seven casuals for volumes 4 and 5, despite their importance as front-of-the book features often graced by his own comic illustrations, signaled Ford's declining import to the *New Yorker* as he became a regular (as John Riddle) for *Vanity Fair* (Day 148). For his part, after the "Ritz Carlton" series ended, Hyde signed only eight more items—all but one of them verse—and moved out of the editorial inner circle to a role more nearly freelance. In fact, on July 13, 1927, Ross offered him fifty dollars per week (at least ten dollars less than E. B. White's salary) in exchange for four or five "Talk" items and two or three art ideas, with the option of attending editorial meetings to get ideas for casuals and other pieces for which he could earn more.[23] Having known Ross since his tramp journalism days (Kunkel 136), Hyde surely recognized the offer as the standard Ross signal to find work elsewhere. After *The Ritz Carltons* (1927) appeared in book form with illustrations by Rea Irvin, Hyde disappeared from view until he resurfaced in 1930 as an editor at *Newsweek* (he ended his career at New York University Press, where he became director and editor in 1953, "Fillmore Hyde"). The different reasons that Hyde and Ford moved away from the *New Yorker* remind us that a magazine's contents reflect personal circumstances as well as editorial policy.

The diminished influence of Hyde and Ford after the summer of 1927 also coincided with the rising influence of Thurber and White—and Alice Frankforter, Arthur Kober, and John O'Hara—a host of other writers more interested in narration than in parody. Thus *New Yorker* humor shifted its focus away from extravagant satires of class and society toward a quieter humor of individual feelings and relationships. While the new values corresponded to modernist literary interest in interior reality and self-expression, early in 1929 Angell explained the redirection as "steering away from what Mosher calls 'our old mad days of whimsy.'"[24]

CHAPTER 7

Ironic I's Are Smiling

The literary quality of The New Yorker *is as surely, and as exclusively, Katharine Sergeant's as the flavor of the art is Irvin's.*
Ralph Ingersoll, 1961

The *New Yorker*'s prose humor grew more distinctive as writers focused on characters rather than the city. "Talk" writer James Kevin McGuinness hit upon the difference as early as his internal monologue "The Renting Agent Muses" (10/31/25:15), and over the next five years staff and freelance humorists joked about city life through a range of local types. In playing with these, *New Yorker* humorists also experimented with their own personas and with comic narration. In particular they toyed with comic frameworks borrowed from the tall tale: the way that first-person narration frames traumas with implications of escape, if not triumph; the way that humor of bloodied and bowed urbanites invokes a classic contrast between the hugeness of the city and the paltriness of the individual. Intensifying the humor of narrative play, the editors interspersed journalism and fiction without highlighting differences between them; the genre of "the casual" arose as an alternative to the formal essay, but it grew on the cusp between fiction and fact. The ironic narrator, the personal narrative, the semifictional persona, and other experiments with lies and narration updated comic storytelling for an educated audience of readers. Folk tales have an audience of listeners, whom mock-oral stories also imagine. Whereas tall tales played with fantasy and realism and local color humor smiled in memory, *New Yorker* humor invited readers to recognize accurate contemporary situations, feelings, and types.

Narrative Experiments

White's early prose recapitulates the casual's shift from city to self. After his brief "Step Forward" played with advertising rhetoric (4/18/25:21), "The Defense of the Bronx River" made a joke of local geography, pointedly observing that the river "rises in Valhalla and flows south to Hell Gate" (5/9/25:14). Then, following nearly a dozen items, including his "Definitions" verse series and two entries for "Why I Like New York," White published his first long narrative, "Child's Play" (12/26/25:17), which the editors honored by placing across from Benchley's "Sex Is Out" and a Hokinson matron painting lamp shades and boxes. The narrator's comment that his experience at a Childs restaurant might qualify as "one of those 'smart backgrounds' THE NEW YORKER is always talking about" indicates that already Angell and Mosher were cultivating him (White's name appears on undated contributors' mailing lists from 1925–26¹), but even with this steady progress, "Child's Play" presented a breakthrough. Never reprinted, "Child's Play" appeared a month before Sullivan's excavator piece, and though Elledge exaggerates in claiming that "no event in the young life of *The New Yorker* was more auspicious" (106), the incident inspiring the story certainly had that significance for White himself. Two dozen years later he told Max Eastman, "My life as a humorist began in a Childs restaurant when a waitress spilled buttermilk down my neck. That great smear of white wet coming down over a blue serge suit, and her words, 'Jesus Christ!' were the turning point in my career" (Eastman 343).

The double entendres running from the title to the last line show that White carefully wrought his narrative to transform life into humor. The subtitle promises only an anecdote "In Which the Author Turns a Glass of Buttermilk Into a Personal Triumph" (12/26/25:17), but the waitress's exclamation as she spills the milk, "In the name of John!," recreates slapstick as baptism by buttermilk, and elevates victimage into heroism. Quite literally refusing to cry over spilled milk, our narrator takes pride in his ability to keep his temper, his dignity, and his sense of humor, all of which coalesce as he seizes the rare opportunity "to lie heroically." He not only refuses to blame the waitress who anointed him but also—underscoring his accomplishment—leaves her a tip, pays for the buttermilk, *and* forgoes the quarter change from a dollar. In refusing his change, he proclaims his triumph. Borrowing a line from comic strip pugilists, he puns, "Let that take care of the buttermilk."

This *New Yorker* humor rejected hyperbole for reduction. The careful word choices and felicitous images of "Child's Play" convert slapstick to understatement. The man, the milk, and other objects become as mixed up in his sentences as on his person. "I was buttermilk," he remarks, and after ten minutes of cleaning he became "a smear." While he remains calm, everything around him moves at top speed. The waitress brings "fifteen paper napkins"; one spread on his chest looks like "a boiled shirt," a garnish for an edible suit. A woman at the next table natters on, criticizing his cleaning efforts and advising him on preferred methods; the waitress trots back and forth with towels and apologies, and the narrator realizes that he has the best role and best audience any New York actor could want. But unlike Benchley, who imported a theatrical scene into his casual on the facing page, White devised a drama of feelings, not action. Understatement controls theme and tone of "Child's Play," its prose humor built with the care of poetry.

As a turning point, "Child's Play" maintained a certain understatement itself, however. The *New Yorker* passed its first birthday to humor by Ford, Benchley, Sullivan, Mosher, Parker, and Woollcott. Marc Connelly added to the broad mode when he debuted with "The Traveler: An Idyll" (4/17/26:17–19), his nod to the Algonquinites, though he refused to transfer his copyright, even for first serial publication. White contributed only a single item (and that in verse) until "Always" ran in the back of the May 8 issue. But then White's ironic, casual style gathered momentum both for himself and the *New Yorker* as four of his sketches ran in the five weeks between 2:12 and 2:16 in the spring of 1926.

In May, the *New Yorker* introduced White's sketches of less fortunate souls shortly before burlesque humor reached its peak with Hyde's lampoon of the Ritz Carltons and Ford's jokes about bleak jobs. A tale of urban despair, "Always" describes a man arriving in Union Square, New York's labor center, wearing a "four-day beard," trousers that "trailed off to nothing between knees and ankles," and shoes fitting his feet "as easily as a spoon in a coffee cup" (5/8/26:31). With the song "Always" in the background—"Now that my blue days have passed . . . . Not for just an hour, not for just a day, always"—the increasingly ironic narrative follows as the man surveys job openings posted on nearby buildings, implying that unlike the singer's, *his* misfortune will continue without end. "Lower Level" (5/22/26:20) reinforced this mood two weeks later, with the story of another lost urban soul, this one providing train passengers with the "balmy feeling" of having their thoughts verbalized. When "the soul" offers an old joke for the second time, however, it seems likely that "the merry company . . . of the tunnel" outside Grand Central will soon see their spirits, like the humor, sink lower, the train and society declining together. These sad stories, never reprinted, offer humor as a mood, inviting readers to think about incongruities between art and life.

The sole upbeat tale in the bunch, "Garter Motif" (6/5/26:33), identifies the difference between White's sense of humor and Ford's. Like "The Tie That Blinds" (5/16/25:29), White's story describes a consumer in battle with a Manhattan haberdashery. Whereas Ford adopts a pose of mock-resignation to his fate when confronted by a loud tie and a timid clerk, White exercises "caprice in the presence of a haberdasher": he rejects the suggestion that he buy blue garters, despite the appeal of a quick and unembarrassing purchase, and asserts himself boldly instead, declaring, "Never! Let me have pale green" (33). Both stories communicate the intimate significance of an outwardly minor experience, but Ford's speaker begins in braggadocio and ends shamefaced, while White's narrator exchanges his original inferiority for a newfound, if insignificant, strength. Even though these tales stand apart from the vernacular mock-oral tradition, their first-person intimacy connects them to the comic continuum Blair called "a man's voice, speaking." Ford's piece diverged somewhat from his typical humor of exaggeration to a more modest humor of reduction, where White's narrator starts, yet the modest triumphs of White's persona testify to the value of the Sufferer's pose, which makes small gains comically great, if only by contrast.

In fact, the *New Yorker* began turning away from class-conscious humor even before Hyde's "Ritz Carlton" series began, as evidenced by White's "Hey Day Labor" (8/7/26:21). Never reprinted, this story sympathizes with the lower classes, as does the cartoon running above it, Alan Dunn's first *New Yorker* drawing ("The next selection, entitled 'Moonbeams and You'. . . "). The tale criticizes racial prejudice, as well. The narrator of "Hey Day Labor" grows increasingly respectful of day laborers as his romantic fantasy of a day on a Mack truck delivering coal to Brooklyn yields to the reality of hard physical work. In particular, his comeuppance tweaks the idea of class-crossing as tourism. The "souvenir-hunting instincts" that inspire him to pocket a piece of coal soon "proved redundant" because "by sunset there was so much coal in my neck and ears that one piece in my pocket made no difference" (8/7/26:21). More important, he discovers the false premises of class prejudice. "It was beginning to be clear to me that the term 'unskilled labor' is somewhat loosely applied," he concedes near the end, just before he disappears into a coal chute, and the recognition reaffirms his initial sense of inferiority to the black man sitting next to him at the East River hiring site. "The man I sat next to was better dressed than I, and, on the whole, handsomer. He was black in every particular, even his eyes—which were full of little pieces of coal—and he seemed to be in perfect condition. An African, he had come black into the world (which I had not), but his original darkness had been immeasurably intensified, and his cheeks had the gloss which you can get from anthracite but not from Palmolive" (21). The African demonstrates his superiority not only by his attractiveness as a man and his fitness as a laborer (traits that reverse but affirm class distinction) but also in his scorn for the job that our narrator finds so romantic. Whereas the African disdains even to call one truck driver a man—"That ain't a man at all: thassa sickness!"—our hero finds the truck itself "magnificent," noting (in the manner of Tom Sawyer and other Mark Twain heroes awaiting comeuppance) its "imperious grandeur" and imagining it as "the great ancestor of those swoop-nose French cars that I see pictures of in the more important magazines" (21). Indeed, the soft hands that inspire our narrator to seek day labor signify his soft-headed romanticism. Freeing his spirit from the binds of white-collar work means taking the Williamsburg Bridge on a journey of reverse economic mobility, from Manhattan to Brooklyn. Years later this kind of writing inspired Ross to proclaim, "I have never seen you use an unnecessary word. I am willing to take an oath [to] this effect."[2] White's prose style—as evocative and compressed as poetry, with serious themes beneath the humor—became the *New Yorker's* trademark, though the same qualities describe Mark Twain's best work. But White appropriated them for members of the peer society, who would have no truck with folk wisdom.

The *New Yorker* checks waiting for White on his return from Europe on August 7, 1926, likely paid for "Hey Day Labor" and four other casuals in the six issues between 2:26 and 2:32. White's influence accelerated after he began part-time writing for "Talk" in October 1926: fifteen more casuals appeared the four months before the second anniversary. These ranged widely in joke and tone, but all relied on first-person narration by a social inferior. In addition to "The Little Man" (11/6/26:22–23), which revealed its narrator's feverish delusion, "Petite Dejuner" offered straight deadpan, as an American in Paris indulges his longing for shredded wheat only to have it frustrated by French waiters' ignorance of how to serve it, so that he finally "poured out a platterful of red wine and ate the biscuits dry" (9/18/26:26). By contrast, "A Lady of the Chorus Watches Dorothy Stone" (10/30/26:29) was a hybrid. In the chorus girl's resentment of social inequities ("Wonder where Dorothy Stone would be if her old man sold linoleum. . . . It's the breaks"), the piece crosses the modernist interior monologue with the vernacular mock-oral narrative.

White's writing contributed to a trend toward unhappy endings in the winter of 1926–27, which he tweaked in the ironically titled "Elevated"

(12/4/26:107). Barely a quarter-column, the squib adopts the first-person plural of "Talk" and builds its joke on a groan-inspiring pun. When the trainman announces that the train will skip Fourteenth Street, and our wit thanks him "for elevating us beyond our station," he assures us that the deviation might have surprised passengers but is nonetheless "in keeping with THE NEW YORKER's editorial policy"—that is, causing "the splendid old structure" to tumble down. Whatever inspired "Elevated," White's personal narratives soon balanced darkness with an absurdist light.

His "Baby" series, for instance, plays with the conceit that people who love their pets treat them like children. "Before Baby Came" details White's declining relationship with his roommate after the arrival of his bird Baby, who now claims all his time and interest (1/22/27:15). The series kept its ironic edge as two installments stretched into five over eighteen months (a sixth came fifteen months later). Baby's precocious interest in the sounds and sights of his environment extends to the lining of his cage—he prefers the narrator's rejected manuscripts to other paper and even, White notes, "has his eye on this one as I write, the mischievous tot" ("M'Baby Loves Me" 2/5/27:30). Baby also rescues White from an annoying insurance salesman ("Baby's First Steps" 6/22/29:16). The installments' irregularity suggests that White returned periodically to the subject rather than developed it as series, but the fabulist use of Baby remained even after Baby acquired a wife in "Bye Low Baby" (3/17/28:25–26).[3] As in earlier pieces where the canary inspired a discussion of profound ambivalence, so here Baby explains that he appreciates his wife but misses the uncertainty, even the loneliness, of bachelorhood. Resigning himself to parenthood, Baby finds consolation in hoping "maybe one of the fledglings will take after me" (26). The exaggerated conception of this piece contrasts with its delicate ironies.

White's darker stories kept despair in check by focusing on characters other than himself—many of them not even human. Baby prefigured the more famous animal characters of White's mature fiction, including Wilbur, the pig of *Charlotte's Web* (1952), and Margalo, the bird of *Stuart Little* (1945), though the animal characters in White's early *New Yorker* stories lack the rich characterizations of his novels. Little known because never reprinted, these stories include the mock-journalism of local lifestyles in "Interview with a Sparrow" (4/9/27:31) as well as the philosophical discussions of moths' Darwinian struggles in "Treasures Upon Earth" (5/2/8:22) and flowers' similarities to humans in "The Care and Feeding of Begonias; Or, the Manly Art" (7/7/28:23). Earnestly pseudoscientific, the latter informs us, "Begonias are mammals—that is, the young are born alive and are fed at the breast," who experience the same emotional challenges as humans. "Begonia plants thrive on love alone, the same as anybody," the narrator instructs. "Each plant soon learns for itself that one's early dreams come to nothing, that ecstasy can never be perpetuated in captivity, and that the happy begonia plant is the one who finds pleasure in small things" (23). These sad sentiments would make the humor very dark if an allegory equating humans and begonias were not absurd.

White's humor stamped the year from August 1926 to August 1927 as clearly as Corey Ford's marked the same period in 1925–26, although White mainly wrote discrete casuals rather than series as Ford did. Indeed, twenty-four examples of White's prose humor ran in the first half-year (twenty-six issues) of volume 3, including not only the Sterling Finny ad series collected as *Less Than Nothing* (1927) but also a large group of uncollected narratives that helped direct the evolution of *New Yorker* humor. A few exploited topical issues. "Mate-of-the-Month Club," for example, took its cue from the rising battle between the Book-of-the-Month Club (launched a year earlier) and the more recently founded Literary Guild[4] with a promise "to take the burden out of selecting a good woman by having it done for you by a committee of five experts, who know all about it" (4/2/27:30). During this same period, however, White settled into writing fictional personal narratives by a comic alter ego—a shy writer who sometimes observed others, but more often reflected on himself as a source of amusement.

The initial stories in this mode did not specify White as the first-person narrator. From "Child's Play" (12/26/25:17) through "Renting the Leviathan" (10/2/26:50–51) and "The Little Man" (11/6/26:22–23), first-person narrators characterize themselves in tales of comeuppance that do not equate speaker and author. In the winter of 1927, however, narrators became identifiable as E. B. White, a comic confusion that other *New Yorker* humorists also exploited to push the boundaries of comic realism and offer lies as fact. Not only the title of "Howdy, King; Howdy, Queen [In Which the Author Is Presented at the Court of St. James']" but also its details identify the speaker as "Mr. E. B. White," in this instance revealed as obsessed with proper dress and subject to "conniption fits . . . in funny places." The Court of St. James' becomes one such place when, after all his concerns about the right clothes, the queen honors him by noting how well his pants fit. "'Fit?' I repeated. . . . And then, sure enough I threw one" (6/4/27:28). With White himself as the speaker, the stories supplemented humor of situation with humor of character, contrasting the speaker's expertise as a storyteller with his ineptitude in life. White experimented with this combination of incident and narrative pose throughout the spring and summer of 1927.

The results varied in mood. "An Evening on Ice" is a melancholy interior monologue in which a "woebegone spectacle of a dismal man standing, ice-skates under his arm, in front of a silver polish booth" suddenly determines to "change my
life and give it the richness it deserved" (3/19/27:30); in the self-deprecating
"America," he describes accomplishing on one typewriter what George Antheil
did on eleven pianos—express America in a single composition—though he
concedes that "it isn't very good reading" (4/23/27:23–24). For all their variations, as a group these sketches brought literary modernism to the mock-oral
traditions of "a man's voice, speaking," with ironic first-person narratives of intimate thoughts.

Interior monologues revealed a vulnerable speaker. "Thoughts—While
Minding a Sleeping Infant Belonging to Someone Else" (6/18/27:16) and
"Thoughts While Skating 240 Laps at the Ice Club" (12/24/27:15–16) show
him frantic with contemplation. That incongruity itself drove the humor,
though both pieces also contain amusing remarks. "Things That Bother Me"
goes further, substituting thought for action as the speaker recounts troubling
ideas that first came to mind in "the days of my extremity" but continue to assert themselves: why the opening in the change booth at the Elevated "is too
small for a thought or a wish to get through," why he worries about whether his
letters get stuck in the mailbox when "nothing I write is important in the least,"
why he cannot connect with the person facing him eye to eye from the train on
the opposite track. His disproportionate concern over these small matters, with
their suggestion of mental imbalance, gives way to a passionate need to escape
from urban isolation and make contact with the girl in the next train. "A tele-
pathic shaft glints between us, shooting out from me to her, flashing back from
her to me. . . . I want to break the glass and shout, 'I love you!' if only to still my
fear that she might go to her grave thinking I had met her—in that bright moment—less than halfway" (5/21/27:19). The narrator justifies his preference for
mental life over public affairs as appropriately modest: "People say I should concern myself with larger affairs," he explains, "—with heavy wars, matters of government, and planetary devices. But I find to my regret that the small occasions
in a day are what chiefly constitute existence; and anyone who pretends that his
life embraces larger issues is probably just talking big" (5/21/27:19). By substituting small thoughts for tall talk, White led *New Yorker* humor in reversing
America's chief convention of comic prose.

The similarity between these sentiments and White's definition of humor for
Max Eastman makes clear that White speaks for himself here. Recalling the humor behind "Child's Play," White told Eastman, "Humor is a final emotion like

breaking out into tears" (343). This tension explains White's concern with narrators teetering between triumph and disaster, and kept *New Yorker* humor on
the edge with what we might call the "larger affairs" of modernist literature.

Staff Development

The *New Yorker* nurtured talent both by inviting successful freelancers to join
the staff and by fostering imaginative writing by staff. This practice gave the
magazine an editorial coherence that belied openness to new talent. In the summer of 1926 Angell and Ross recruited White for the staff and published Fillmore Hyde's "Ritz Carlton" series, but the magazine's success as an advertising
vehicle added new challenges. The second anniversary boast that the *New Yorker*
ranked fourth in advertising lines brought pressure to print more text, especially
prose humor, which cost less than verse and cartoons and allowed more variety
than journalism. The editors turned to department writers: writers who could
strike the right mood in fact pieces could write fiction to supplement their income, add to the editorial mix, and meet the magazine's need for coherence. If
she was "Angelina," Angell withdrew her own work after contributing two
back-of-the-book items: a pair of epigrams on dating ("The Men I Hate to Go
Out With" and "The Men I Like to Go Out With" 1/2/26:33) and "Poor Fish"
(6/26/26:34–35), a story of fly fishing that contrasts a woman's idea of fishing
(the triumph in landing two fine trout) with her male companions' ideas (the joy
of fleecing each other at poker and getting very drunk). "Talk" writers Russel
Crouse and Spud Johnson joined Oliver Claxton in filling the need for prose humor between the summer of 1926 and Thurber's move from managing editor to
"Talk" writer a year later.

Department writers succeeded in varying the subjects of comic prose. Russel
Crouse, known to humor scholars as Corey Ford's coauthor of the 1922 comedy
Hunky Dory (Day 150), specialized at the *New Yorker* in local color pieces akin to
"Talk," historical anecdotes in a comic vein. The six installments of his first series, "They Were New Yorkers" (3/12/27–10/22/27), revived an amusing past
for contemporary readers to appreciate as their own. With a nod toward his polyglot audience, Crouse borrowed the Yiddish for "may he rest in peace" to introduce the man behind the slang for a suicidal leap, "to do a Brodie": "If old Steve
Brodie, *olav hashalem,* knew the traduction that now and again falls upon his noble
name today there is little doubt that he would return, with an ectoplasmic brown
derby cocked over his eye, and take his plunge again. For there are those in this
doubting era who would relegate Mr. Brodie and his bridge to the legendary

status of Horatius and an earlier aqueduct" (3/12/27:22). "That Was New York," Crouse's second series, added visual humor to the mix, complementing historical anecdotes of familiar names and places with old illustrations, including some by Thomas Nast. Although the series deviated from Ross's policy that departmental writing be fact, and everything else fiction,[5] "They Were New Yorkers" reinforced the *New Yorker*'s identity as a vehicle for local humor—in a more ironic, low-key vein than the inaugural issue's "Story of Manhattankind"—and underscored how desirable Ross and Angell considered this anachronistic vein of historical journalism, which continued intermittently through volume 5.

Willard "Spud" Johnson of "Talk" had only modest impact on the development of prose humor in the twenties (his signed work ran only from 2:13 to 3:9, when he left the magazine, and he failed to sell more writing to Angell before 1930), but his twenty-four pieces during 1926–27 nicely directed realistic fantasies toward the peer society. In addition to "Another English Author Comes to New York" (2/26/27:47–48), which imagined how Shakespeare and Anne Hathaway would respond to modern New York's theater and publishing scenes, Johnson played with monologues and personal narratives. A tale of many reversals, "How Pauline's Heart Was Broken" recounts the speaker's habit of steeling himself in his finacée's absence against expressions of sexuality everywhere around him—neighbors' lovemaking (audible through the walls), movie plots, advertisements, dinner companions' groping—and how his unfortunate restraint when she returns from two months in Europe ultimately causes their breakup (11/13/26:29). But by the time Johnson imagined in "Wanderlust" a runaway subway car who thought "it would be so romantic to go to Chicago" (4/16/27:87), he clearly had run out of ideas.

Oliver Claxton's casuals lasted a year longer than Johnson's, though they stopped in 1928 while Claxton remained on staff, presumably because better material was available. By 1928, in fact, *available* had become the house euphemism for "unacceptable," as editors returned manuscripts and drawings with professed regrets that "we did not find your manuscript available at this time."[6] Claxton's casuals reached out to the peer society with a mirror for their experience and a good ear for the personal narrative.

Claxton also mastered the pose of the Sufferer. The speaker of his first casual, "Let's Picnic," reports how politeness enables him to survive the boredom and annoyance of a summer picnic. Detailing how he schlepped the Victrola across the lawn, extracted children's feet from the sandwiches, endured local gossip, and tried to avoid saying anything wrong, the plotless piece plays with the contrast between his dry recitation and his purported suffering as it targets the reader's familiarity with such travails (7/31/26:17). He followed it up with "Laugh and the World Laughs With You," an example of dementia praecox humor that also begins with a summertime pitfall familiar to comfortable New Yorkers, the weekend at a friend's country house. To "tune . . . up" as a raconteur in the time before dinner, our narrator opens "an appalling tome" called *The World's Best 1001 Humorous Anecdotes,* whose old jokes so intoxicate and infuriate him that he loses all self-control in the sudden need to recite them to anyone nearby. Tensions escalate as he throws the book at his hosts' little boy (whose wailing had evoked a dreadful punch line), shuts up his beloved Miss Gamp (who tried to tell a story at dinner), and leads his host and the other guests to choke him. He recovers enough to leave three days later, but the story his hostess tells as she accepts his apology triggers this response: "I stretched her dead on her doorstep and took my way back to town" (8/7/26:19). Claxton's broad humor, like his ironic narratives, toyed with incongruities between outer behavior and inner thoughts, but they ended with the narrator's triumph.

Thurber, Algonquinites, and other first-rate humorists bumped Claxton to the back of the book in the fall of 1927, where he remained through the publication of "Do You Believe In Signs?" the next spring. That he continued writing "The Current Cinema" for another five months before handing it off to Mosher makes clear that the *New Yorker* continued to respect his abilities. And his last casual, an amusing column almost entirely in dialogue tweaking people who take advertising seriously *and* those who (think they) don't (4/28/28:87), indicates that Claxton still had funny ideas for casuals. But evidently the *New Yorker* no longer wanted them.

It did, however, want artists, and welcomed efforts by graphic artists who wanted to experiment with verbal humor. Openness to such work created a sense of community between readers and contributors while inviting new artists to the roster. The award-winning political cartoonist Rollin Kirby, for example, published only two drawings in the early *New Yorker* (and those not until volume 5),[7] but he published a dozen poems and a set of song lyrics between July 1926 and May 1927—two years before his drawings appeared. Thus Kirby's verse not only filled early pages but also provided an investment in future art. Artists contributing prose included Carl Rose, who ratified Lipstick's defense of taxi drivers (3/12/27:30–31), and Rube Goldberg, who appeared as a writer twice during this period (in the silly "Are There More Than One Otto Kahn?" 4/9/27:22–23, and "The Red-Light District" 11/3/28:22–24). Targeting the peer society enabled the *New Yorker* to convert readers into contributors and to develop *New*

Yorker humor—graphic, poetry, and prose—by cultivating individual humorists, one at a time. The tone of *New Yorker* humor shifted, like a boat, in response to the contributors aboard.

Thurber, White, and the Little Man

Ross did not expect writers to solve the *New Yorker's* problems in March of 1927, when James Thurber arrived on the heels of the second anniversary issue, keeping Thurber in the managing editor's post for five months before moving him to "Talk" rewrite and an office with White. Peter Arno acknowledged his importance with a teasing panel of an aunt asking a child, "'And what does my boy want to be when he grows up—a great engineer like Uncle Thurber?'" (10/15/27:20). Thurber first appeared in the magazine as a poet[8] but soon turned almost exclusively toward prose, unlike White, Hyde, and Wylie, who continued writing prose and verse.

Thurber played first with parodies of newspaper rhetoric, sneering at commercialized fame. The imitation news clips in "News of the Day," for example, include the story of eleven-year-old Marjorie Morrison, who cleverly converts her parents' murders into vaudeville bookings worth sixty thousand dollars (4/2/27:34). Media inflation underlies the nubs of "Polo in the Home," which offers step-by-step advice for holding a polo match in your New York apartment (9/17/27:29), and "The Literary Meet," which treats reading as a sporting event (9/24/27:20). "Breakfast with the President (As the HERALD TRIBUNE Might Report It)" and other pieces from the winter of 1927–28 lampoon journalism more directly (11/12/27:28). Like cartoons about the rich, parodies of journalism contributed to the superior tone of *New Yorker* humor.

So did literary parodies. Thurber took on the modernist trinity of Gertrude Stein, James Joyce, and Ty Cobb in "More Authors Cover the Snyder Trial," the latter a snipe at the parody itself as he shifted from style to style:

[Stein:] He says he did. He says he did not. She says she did. She says she did not. She says he did. He says she did. She says they did. . . .

[Joyce:] Trial regen by trialholden Queenscountrycourthouse with tumpetty taptap mid socksocking with sashweights by jackals. . . . .

[Cobb:] Stealing home from a bridge game is a clever stunt, if properly worked. (5/7/27:69)

Years later Thurber claimed surprise "that Ross put his approving R" on this piece, citing his ignorance of high literature (Thurber, *Years* 31), but Stein and Joyce received too much attention for Ross to have missed them, either in Paris or New York. Thurber's biographer Harrison Kinney singled out this piece in 1972 when he asked Katharine White how the *New Yorker* could have accepted such poor writing, noting that she replied, "The magazine was desperate for material" (Kinney 355). But parodies take aim at literary knowledge as well as literary style. Like Thurber's parody for the Christmas issue, "A Visit from Saint Nicholas [In the Ernest Hemingway Manner]" (12/24/27:17–18), such humor flattered the cultured, up-to-date readers who got the joke.

Thurber turned from ridiculing others to making fun of first-person speakers like himself in August of 1927. A transitional piece, "My Trip Abroad" (8/6/27:26), merges personal narrative and theatrical farce in a comedy of multiple doors and mistaken impressions. Unable to find the cabin containing his own wife (as opposed to someone else's), our narrator never quite gets around to describing his tour of the Continent while telling of his various mishaps en route. Contrasts abound: between his deadpan account and other characters' outrage, between his understatements and his misery. And the piece ends, appropriately enough, in anticlimax, when he finally gets to Paris: "I shall always remember a little church in Paris in the moonlight. It was there, three weeks later, that my wife first spoke to me again." Next week "The Thin Red Leash" (8/13/27:60–61) added local color to the mix and further linked speaker and author. Daily taunts in an aggressive dialect heighten the contrast between West Side stevedores and our narrator, "a tall thin man" with a tiny dog on a "thin red leash"—until a deus ex machina appears in the form of "a monstrous man, evidently an artisan who lifts locomotives from track to track when the turntables are out of order" and certifies Scotch terriers as "damn fine dogs . . . . Hellcats in a fight" (61). Comedy reigns as he confers the dog's virtues and his own strength on the narrator. Appearing one year after White's "Hey Day Labor," these stories joined Mosher's and Claxton's in ironically transforming personal pain into symbolic and narrative success, which came to define the *New Yorker* style.

Early in 1928 Thurber put his own spin on the Sufferer: the Little Man cannot transcend his problems even rhetorically. The turning point came in a story so lost that even Harrison Kinney's thousand-page biography omits it. "Cross-Country Gamut" (2/11/28:40–42) introduces Thurber's first henpecked Little Man, the earliest avatar of Walter Mitty, who eleven years later retreated from his wife's nagging into heroic fantasies so enthralling that he never noticed the car running over him ("The Secret Life . . . " 3/18/39). Thurber's last casual for volume 3, "Cross-Country Gamut," is a personal narrative by a man so distracted by fears of inadequacy that he can barely function. Here he tells how he "ran the gamut of human emotions" by attending the opening of Eugene O'Neill's newest play, *Strange Interlude,* whose nine-act performance (all afternoon and evening, with a dinner break) presents a daunting set of problems, each compounded by his wife's criticism. After he worries—and excites his wife's irritation—about being judged crazy for wearing a tuxedo in the afternoon, for looking young among all the old men in evening dress, for applauding too enthusiastically after the show, he achieves the "last great emotion of the gamut, Peace, Pity and Comprehension" when the next morning's reviews declare the play "simply great" (41)—which his wife dispels with a simple "Pish" (42). The anticlimax at the end of "Cross-Country Gamut" leaves the Sufferer without even rhetorical triumph, certifying the Little Man's deep failure, yet first-person narration provides a comic frame, keeping him connected to us, instead of lost to his thoughts as in Mitty's third-person account.

The Little Man's comic tribulations also intrigued E. B. White during the winter of 1927–28, and his versions also invoked the structural controls of the personal narrative. But whereas Thurber envisioned comic victimization in sexual terms, White saw mere challenges to self-esteem. White's early incarnations of the Little Man overlay the comic ineptitude of Sterling Finny, whose problems dramatize his need for the right product, with interior monologues and accounts of insecurity and longing—as in "Shrine," a sad tale of a lame girl's prayers for a cure (8/6/27:31), and "Critique," in which a cowboy's failure to rope a steer after an energetic chase earns him the comment, "Take him away . . . he's lousy" (11/5/27:30).

White's sketches from this period test the boundaries of comic framing, shrinking the distance between speaker and author and following an anticomic structure that moves from bad to worse. Comic structures typically end with the protagonist's success, so this reversal brings a dark mood to the tales' verbal wit. Thurber may have inspired them: the first of White's classic Little Man stories, "Tombs Are Best" (8/13/27:14–15), ran in the same issue as Thurber's "Thin Red Leash." More important, the first-person tale describes our narrator, "Mr. White," as nearly twenty-nine years old (the author had recently turned twenty-eight), and De Miskey's illustration provides a good likeness of the author.

The story's humor pits the literal fact that White is author and narrator against the allegorical story he tells of his metaphorical (or rhetorical) entombment. A Mr. Esau Dank of Rosyturn Mausoleum offers to sell him a tomb, speaking in "liquid tones . . . as though he had a mouthful of embalming fluid." When White declines his offer of cigarettes, "Mr. Dank put the coffin-nails back in his pocket" (14). Dank buries him in the mausoleum map and prospectus so that White's question about cremation comes "from beneath my shroud" (14).

After both agree that they "don't like cremation" and the salesman declares, "Your best bet is a nice coffin," White jumps up, throws off all the paper, and delivers the final puns: "Put me down for one," he tells Dank; "I'm going to move in with the kiddies the first of October," he reports to us readers (15). The narrative links success and death in a single conceit; jokes about lower prices for upper floors invite comparisons with New Yorkers' quest for the perfect apartment.

White continued exploring bad-to-worse humor over the next several months. In "Now That I'm Organized" (11/5/27:19–20), the hypochondriacal White becomes the ineffectual White. The twelve compartments of his new desk organizer allow him to spend his entire day arranging his work without doing any, marking his progression as an executive from inefficient to incompetent. But not all the bad-to-worse tales from this period ended sadly. "How to Drive the New Ford with Two Beautiful Illustrations" lacks the promised drawings (ha! ha!) but not the instructions, although it concludes by suggesting "that you move over and let somebody drive who knows how" (1/21/28:18). The focus on "you" rather than "I" in this narrative keeps the humor away from the edge, while the interior monologue drives it closer to despair. White's "Thoughts While Skating 240 Laps at the Ice Club" (12/24/27:15), for example, contrasts the silliness of the narrator's talking in circles to himself as he skates in circles around the rink. But his thoughts become increasingly frustrated when he recognizes that shyness will not let him approach the girl he's watching but rather will keep him locked in fantasy. "You're so observant you ought to write," he muses, "I suppose you'll go home and write a piece called 'Thoughts While Skating 240 Laps at the Ice Club.'" The story, like the skating, ends without progress. The monologue does not run in a circle, because he quits skating, yet White's "Thoughts While Skating 240 Laps" reenacts the narrator's thoughts while skating 240 laps as he imagines writing a story with the same title. The story's structure of frustration reinforces its theme for a humor of melancholy.

Similarities between White's and Thurber's dark humor during this period led biographer Scott Elledge to conclude that they influenced each other (133–34). White evidently initiated the darker mode, and experimented more fully during this period with its narrative dimensions. It seems likely, however, that mutual influence resulted not only from the writers' sharing an office and a transformative period in their lives as writers and husbands—Thurber moving toward divorce, White away from several romances and toward marriage to Katharine (Kinney 368–73; Elledge 148–57)—but also from their sharing the same attitude toward humor. When Thurber told Max Eastman, "Humor is a kind of emotional chaos told about calmly and quietly in retrospect" (Eastman 342), he echoed White's definition of humor as a "final emotion" as well as Wordsworth's famous definition of poetry as "the powerful overflow of spontaneous emotion, recollected in tranquility."

Comic Exuberance Resumes

Though Thurber and White's dark mood characterized the end of volume 3, it did not dominate the prose humor of volume 4, which began with the third anniversary issue, February 25, 1928. Many factors led to the brighter mood, but different proportions of writers' work ranks high among them. White increased his contributions to "Talk" but published just twenty-two casuals in volume 4, including his untitled parody of newspaper features (11/17/28:22–23)—substantially less than the ten-part Sterling Finny series and twenty-six casuals he published in volume 3 or his twenty-five casuals for volume 2. Thurber likewise directed his energies elsewhere. He published only six casuals in the five months from 4:2 to 4:19, and none at all from July through Thanksgiving (4:19–4:40); then his pace accelerated, and six stories appeared in the last three months of volume 4. Thurber's public silence in the spring of 1928 occurred during a busy editorial period, when he handled fiction and "Talk" correspondence as well as "Talk" rewrite.[9] Thus he shaped the magazine's humor from the editorial side as he let writers know that "We are always eager to be tried" and suggested eventual success "for anyone who can write fairly well and has an idea once a fortnight."[10] But his acceptances and rejections did not replicate in other writers' humor the dark mood of his own.

While Thurber and White had less presence in volume 4's fiction department, Frank Sullivan had more—more than Thurber or White, and more than he himself had published in the *New Yorker* previously. Sullivan wrote fifteen casuals for volume 4, compared to eleven in all of volumes 1–3, and these sustained a comic spirit that in 1924 *Vanity Fair* critic Vivian Shaw called the "cuckoo school of American humor": a combination of inappropriate phrases, incompatibles, and incongruities bordering on "unintentional dadaism" (16). Such later casuals as "Should Admirals Shave?" (2/25/28:16–17) and "How to Deal with Grommet Trouble" (7/14/28:19–20) maintained the exuberant spirit in his *New Yorker* writing. More to the point, Angell and Ross solicited this kind of humor so insistently that Sullivan compared them to "two hungry little robins, ever yawping for food."[11] And their so-called "clamorous demands" continued after Donald Ogden Stewart joined Sullivan in reasserting a broad comic sensibility that offset experiments with irony.

The insistent lightness of Stewart's humor suggests editorial interest in pulling back from the more literary writing of Thurber and White. A practitioner of cuckoo humor celebrated for his *Parody Outline of History* (1921), Donald Ogden Stewart, who had recently returned to New York, was writing for *College Humor* when his first casual appeared in the issue of December 10, 1927, near the end of volume 3. Ross had apparently contracted for biweekly casuals and a drawing account: twenty-four appeared within eleven months, but he ran a deficit of four hundred dollars, the price of two full-length pieces, by August.[12] Stewart's contributions over the first six months took broad swipes at timely topics, its humor residing in overall conception and occasional remark rather than in meticulous irony and detail. "Some Interesting Stories About Lincoln" made its humor by failing to live up to the title's promise, running from irrelevancy to digression (2/11/28:21–23). Specializing in a pseudoinstructional rhetoric, Stewart portrayed himself as an incompetent expert, an ideal persona for burlesque. His "How" series parodied service journalism and self-help instruction. "How I Got My Rabbits to Lay" combined an Easter theme with contemporary interest in theories of child-rearing as members of the peer society (including Stewart) began having children (4/7/28:27–28; McNutt 471). More ambitious, in "How We Introduced the Budget System Into Our Home" (6/2/28:23–24), the incompetent narrator procrastinates for three columns until his last evasions ("Any budget caught smoking will be instantly expelled" [24]) nail his ignorance. Such remarks put Stewart squarely in the cuckoo school, but his reliance on topics of current interest, rather than on the character of his narrator, left some sketches flat. "How We Solved the Servant Problem," for instance, begins parodically by identifying reasons for the shortage of domestic help but soon falls into an uninteresting whine over the problems of the rich (6/16/28:21). Topicality gave Stewart's writing its contemporary appeal, but many pieces seem dated today.

Cuckoo humor aside, even Stewart's comic technique was not modern: in fact, his deadpan narration for absurd situations revived the traditional technique of the tall yarnspinner. Thus his first casual, "The President's Son," began with a classical bit of understatement leading up to and away from a great lie: "I am the illegitimate son of one of the presidents of the United States" (12/10/27:24). The joke evidently warranted a reprise two months later, when Stewart submitted a letter to the editor in which he followed a lengthy complaint about a recently announced pretender to the Russian royal family with a startling confession:

> The time has come when I can no longer keep silent, and so I reluctantly take my pen in hand to tell you that young "Mme. Tchaikowsky" is not what she claims to be. She is not the Grand Duchess Anastasia. And the reason I know of what I speak is that I am the Grand Duchess myself. . . . And if you don't believe it you can ask Ferdie Yakimov who the girl was who yelled "Yoo-hoo" to him that night outside Sergeyev's drug store. . . .
>
> This will no doubt be a surprise to the many people who have become accustomed to calling me "Don" Stewart, and I assure you I have had many laughable moments myself when I think about it. ("Introducing Anastasia" 2/25/28:19)

After explaining how Anastasia survived execution and escaped on a false passport with the name of a mad monk, Donald Ogden Stewart, the story hints at E. B. White's inspiration for *Charlotte's Web* (1952), as Stewart explains how a spider's determination and success in building a web inspire Anastasia-Don to remain in America and find success. The *New Yorker* sketch remains in the world of the tall yarn, however, as Stewart challenges anyone to prove him a liar: "If you want proof," he says of the current pretender, "you can look and see if she's got a map of Moscow tattooed on her left shoulder blade showing the proposed subway *as of 1910*" (20)—the perfect unprovable boast of the tall teller. Stewart abandoned his aspirations to become, in James C. McNutt's words, "an uncorrupted Mark Twain" (472) when he quit writing for the *New Yorker,* but the kinship between these and Twain's early sketches gave the *New Yorker's* urbanity some classic overtones in 1928.

Ironic I's

Ditto for Arthur Kober, whose forty-three sketches in volumes 2–5 helped reshape the monologue as an urban genre for revealing character through dialect. His first *New Yorker* appearance coincided with the beginning of Fillmore Hyde's "Ritz Carlton" series, midway through volume 2. Kober's collage of advertising parodies, "If Others Adopt the Idea" (8/14/26:50), represented a very small start, but its series of ad parodies demonstrated his skill at imitating styles. With his next contribution, "The First-Nighter" (12/11/25:101–3), he found his forté, however, and his mock-oral monologues and other types of overheard talk appeared regularly almost every month thereafter. While Hyde tweaked the vapid lives and values of the rich in the overwritten prose of burlesque, Kober featured lively, mock-oral writing, specializing in working-class dialect and theater slang. Thus he expanded the *New Yorker*'s cast of local types beyond the peer society. As White and Thurber toyed with the comic limits of the personal monologue, Kober presented recognizable local scenes and experiences through a range of characters, most of them women, whose dramatic monologues exposed personality and motive in a friendly, even affectionate way. His mock-oral casuals celebrated the comic distance between author and persona during the same period that Thurber and White experimented with compressing it.

Kober's mock-oral speakers ranged across the working classes. His earliest pieces, appearing in volumes 2 and 3, took pleasure in contrasting varieties of speech and character. Such contrasts formed the basis of two Broadway local color portraits as well as his four contributions to the "Overheard" series. "Stage Directors," published just before the second anniversary, depicted five distinctive types as they advised their actors: Verbose, Effeminate, Artistic, Temperament [sic], Calm (1/15/27:49–51). A year later, near the end of the "Overheard" series, he applied the same formula to the production hierarchy in "The Dress Rehearsal," monologues that suggested individual priorities, if not different realities, among five principals: the producer ("I want you should phone that damn shop and tell them where the hell's that backdrop?"), technical director ("The concert border, ya sap"), stage director ("I think that's practically set now, don't you, Mr. Bodnick?"), actor ("Well, that's the makeup Frank Keenan taught me when I was just starting, and I used it ever since"), and friend ("Well, Herman, you got a marvelous piece of property, but it needs just a little fixing") (1/28/28:14–15). Kober's other Broadway monologues lack explicit contrasts between speakers, but the characters' distinctive modes of speech imply differences among the harangues of "The Music Director" against incompetent and temperamental performers (10/8/27:30), the comments on a wife's voice and gestures in "The Stage Director Spends an Evening at Home" (12/3/27:54–55), and the sports metaphors of "The Opening Night: A Former Football Coach Directs A Broadway Play" (11/10/28:29–30). Shop and other contextualized talk constituted an important variation on slang in Kober's 1927 monologues, and his backstage view of Broadway gave an ironic undertone to volume 3's graphic images, especially Arno's, of its glamour.

In 1928, however, Kober turned away from the backstage crew and focused on characterizing other unglamorous New Yorkers, mostly women, whom he represented with affectionate but unsentimental realism and slight but persistent irony. The least attractive and most stereotypical of these characters appeared a month apart in the spring of 1928: the overbearing Aunt Hattie Phelps visiting her sick nephew Harold in "The Comforter" (4/14/28:46–48) and the fast-talking agent seeking investors for a new play in "The Promoter" (5/12/28:30–31). He had more sympathy, however, for less powerful figures, and gave uneducated young women particular depth. Four stories from volume 4 show these efforts at their best, although Kober began exploring this type of mock-oral humor earlier, featuring lower-class women such as Agnes, an elevator operator at Gimbel's. Though not a continuing narrative, these pieces rely on similar, sometimes overlapping characters to ridicule the speakers' self-absorption, naïveté, and dialect, while respecting them as bona fide urban types: working girls in search of mates and good times.

Kober balances ridicule and respect by muting the girls' dialect and stressing their efforts at respect. The title of "The Pick-Up" (2/25/28:36), his story for the third anniversary issue, refers to both setting and theme: the narrator chatters nervously to her roommate Helen while waiting for her date, a man she met without formal introduction the day before. Aware that relationships easily turn sour—she opens her monologue by cautioning Helen, "If I take a loan of your hat tonight, I don't want you should throw it up to my face the next time we have a fight or somethin'"—the speaker worries that her date will consider her cheap. She claims that she accepted a ride from him "oney" because she had a sprained ankle, and justifies his having put his arm around her almost as soon as she got in, "being as how he asts my permission" (36). While she reveals her bad judgment and sexual eagerness, she also exposes her naïveté and vulnerability, which give her concerns a wistfulness that his sudden arrival dispels—to her pleasure and, by extension, ours. Her dialect of New York's outer boroughs underscores her status as an outsider for whom a millinery wholesaler's son with two years at City College and a business school diploma represents a step up the social ladder.

Less sympathetic narrators exhibit more obtrusive verbal mannerisms. A coarser speaker reveals herself in "Just a Pal" (3/31/28:42–44) when she defends her decision to take her roommate's place on a date and then strands the guy at Carnegie Hall because she hates concerts. The narrator's vulgarity extends from her manners to her taste, reinforced by her thick dialect. "If I'da known it was for a concert, I would of let him sit there and wait all night for Florrie," she insists to her friend Agnes, noting with outrage that when she decided to leave after the intermission "that stiff had the nerve to sit there and let me go home alone" (42, 44). And she insists through the end that she cannot understand why neither Florrie nor Paul appreciated her efforts to help out. "Geez," she exclaims, "you'da think I din do her no favor by bein' bored stiff by that paluka the way she carried on" (44). Her lively talk offsets her defensive assertions of virtue to keep the piece amusing. Kober's dialect writing advanced the *New Yorker*'s program of comic realism, inviting the peer society to respect lower-class aspirations as well as smile at their vulgarity.

Kober gave mock-oral monologues psychological and ethical depth by developing sincere but ignorant speakers as he continued exploring women's narration in volumes 4 and 5. The eager adviser of "Going Abroad?" (4/21/28:36) makes few grammatical errors, though she says "ast" instead of "ask," but her constant requests for her mother's approval (every exchange ends with a variation on "Don't you, mother?") mark her as very naïve. Kober balances amusement and respect even more impressively in "The Art Lover," in which an American innocent lacks education but demonstrates native taste. Though she describes every painting she likes as "sweet," inarticulateness does not prevent her from recognizing the most important painting on display at the Salon, even if she cannot believe that it sold for twelve hundred dollars rather than twelve hundred francs (6/23/28:44–47). Here, as in "Just Walking" (8/3/29:24) and "Is Shirley Insulted?" (12/7/29:37), volume 5 tales of young women struggling to interpret the ambiguous intentions of men, Kober matched the psychological realism of the dialect narrative to characters and situations equal to it. Kober's best narratives indicate that precisely modulated irony, more than any other device, distinguished *New Yorker* prose humor from other types.

Kober showed much less sympathy for his male characters—and for most of his characters in volume 5. A predatory fellow makes "Handin' Her a Line" an unsavory story of deceptive courtship practices, even though Kober revised it (at Angell's request) to make it less "unpleasant" (4/13/29:77–78).[13] Amusing Bronx-Jewish dialect does not entirely offset the mean spirit of "The Promotion," where a wife bemoans the promotion that went to "Poikins" instead of her Moe (3/16/29:44–47), and "The Show-Off," a dialogue over petty injuries for which Moe's lodge brothers now plan and justify his comeuppance (3/30/29:25–26). And so on, except for the women speakers of "Just Walking" and "Is Shirley Insulted?"—both sympathetic insights into women's experience.

Kober's comic writing for this period expanded the *New Yorker*'s interest in "a man's voice, speaking" to include women's voices, and invited the peer society to sympathize with social problems beyond their own. Remembered primarily as Lillian Hellman's husband from 1925 to 1932, Kober wrote for the *World*,

Evening Sun, and *Morning Telegraph* during the twenties and followed S. N. Berhman as a press agent for the Shubert brothers before beginning a career as a Hollywood screenwriter in 1930 (Pinsker, "Arthur Kober" 238). Kober's reputation as a humorist, much underestimated, rests on his depression-era mock-oral stories of the Gross family in the Bronx, a *New Yorker* series eventually republished in several books, beginning with *Thunder Over the Bronx* (1935), with an introduction by Dorothy Parker.[14] Yet Kober also exerted considerable influence on *New Yorker* humor in the twenties.

Like Kober, John O'Hara wrote mainly in the mock-oral vein and became a regular contributor almost as soon as his first acceptance check made the *New Yorker*'s preferences clear. All but one of his fourteen pieces for volume 4 and twenty-four in volume 5 feature monologues or overheard talk; and even the exception, two documents presented in "Memo and Another Memo," allow the implied character, an executive compiling his Christmas shopping list, to speak for himself (12/14/29:77). Together O'Hara's thirty-eight sketches reinforce and extend the early *New Yorker*'s emphasis on the ironic voice, while their frequency signals their importance: one in every three issues of volume 4, one in every two issues of volume 5.

Indeed, O'Hara's name appeared almost as frequently as Thurber's in volumes 4 and 5, and only three casual writers—Thurber, White, and Kober—signed more sketches than he in volumes 3 through 5. O'Hara's biographer Matthew Bruccoli has noted the difficult relations between the writer and various editors, but publication statistics articulate how much *New Yorker* valued O'Hara's comic prose, even though Ingersoll turned O'Hara down for a reporting job in December of 1927, and Angell and Ross repeatedly declined his ideas for "Talk" pieces and "Profiles" (O'Hara 26, 34–43). Bruccoli's dismissal of O'Hara's casuals as "exercises" lacking in literary significance or stylistic distinction (58) misses the point of their publication as *New Yorker* humor. Also to the point is Dale Kramer's erroneous claim that O'Hara held a staff position in 1928, a mistake that underlines how well his work fit (Kramer, *Ross* 193). In fact, O'Hara bragged to Ross in 1934 that he "contributed more pieces to The New Yorker than any other non-staff man" (O'Hara, *Selected Letters* 97).

O'Hara's earliest sketches develop irony between narrative manner and matter. The woman reading and critiquing her classmates' news in "The Alumnae Bulletin" (the title refers to both the speaker's remarks and the text she reads) ends by dismissing the text as irrelevant (5/5/28:101). Thus O'Hara implies not only the irrelevance of *her* remarks but also her insincerity in disclaiming interest in such gossip and one-upsmanship. O'Hara also experimented with telephone conversations, including a dialect piece, "Spring 3100," in which the accent of the man who answers the phone "Twennyfustreet stationhaw. Looten Bgrm spng" keeps the conversation going through twelve turns before the two parties understand each other well enough for the caller to get the right number (9/8/28:56). Unlike Kober, who used dialect to characterize individuals, O'Hara used dialect to create comic problems.

O'Hara contributed two monologue series to the early *New Yorker,* each extending the reach of mock-oral humor. The first, beginning in the fall of 1928, gave the magazine its first extended run of social satire. Narrated by Mrs. Carl Uhlein, program chairwoman of the Orange County Afternoon Delphian Society, it begins by ridiculing the charitable pretensions of the Delphians, suburban women seeking to occupy themselves while their husbands work in the city and their children attend school, but eventually satirizes their social intolerance and political ignorance. From the first installment, "A Safe and Sane Fourth and the Part Played by the Orange County Afternoon Delphian Society" (9/15/28:79–82), first-person narration exposes the group's charitable agenda as an excuse for serving the members' own needs. For example, the Safe and Sane Fourth Committee reports that its bridge benefit to discourage the sale and use of firecrackers had a net profit of $48.85, while close attention to the lengthy account reveals not only that the event cost three times as much but also that the women seek to limit fireworks to the country club, "and I am sure that those [children] who are not members will be invited also" (82). From this beginning O'Hara goes on to attack the leaders' subversion of the democratic process. The speaker in "The Hallowe'en Party" dominates the meeting ("I am sure Madam President will appoint a committee of three or four who have cars to . . . get pumpkins" [84]) to ram through an elitist program ("I believe in sending my children to public school . . . But all the same I see no reason why we should be compelled to sit through a Hallowe'en program with the riffraff" [85]), and O'Hara emphasizes her insincerity when the piece ends with no chance for a response when she asks, "Any questions?" (85).

O'Hara redirected the mock-oral monologue from personal ridicule to political satire, when he took up the Pennsylvania strikes in "The Coal Fields" (10/20/28:85–88). Despite her pompous title, "Report on Actual Conditions in the Pennsylvania Coal Fields," the speaker *actually* says little about conditions in the fields, though she says much about hostesses and social events. After a wonderful set of parties in Scranton, but the wrong kind of coal, she moves her mission to Pittsburgh, where she finally meets miners while escorted by Mrs.

Clarence J. Yocum, wife of an "assistant to one of the vice-presidents of the Allegheny County Coke & Coal Company" (87). Someone that far down the organizational ladder should side with labor, O'Hara implies, but Mrs. Yocum and her friends have allied themselves with the oppressors, and our speaker joins them. Admitting that miners' "conditions were frightful," she blames the "rack and ruin" of the homes on poor housekeeping and decries "the arrogance of some of the coal miners in refusing to leave their homes when they were evicted" (87). Double entendres call attention to her self-deception, when she reports her hosts' expectations: "Mrs. Yocum said she hoped I would give an honest and true account of conditions because most of the investigators had gone away with only one side of the story, making the miners martyrs when they were no such thing. Quite sordid, I assure you" (87–88). O'Hara repeatedly reinforces this irony, as when she exclaims, "The things Mrs. Yocum told me were almost unbelievable" (87), and when she concludes with false modesty, "if I have in any way given you an idea of how things really are, then my trip was not in vain" (88). Later installments in the series retreated from such intense satire but continued the ridicule of Babbitry.[15] The *New Yorker* abandoned its prejudice against advocacy when events warranted and a humorist rose to the aesthetic and political challenges.

O'Hara's second series, the Hagedorn & Brownmiller monologues, satirized capitalism more broadly as the stock market faltered. Beginning with "The Boss' Present" on December 1, 1928, the Hagedorn & Brownmiller series ran concurrently with the Delphian monologues with cheerleading speeches to the (male) office staff of a paint and varnish manufacturer in Yorkville.[16] Various speakers constitute the series, including the head bookkeeper, Irv Rosenthal ("Mr. Rosenthal" 7/20/29:24–25) and the Boss, known only as F. W. ("The Boss Talks" 8/3/29:43–45). But most monologues unmask the unctuous personality of Mr. Woodring, the company brownnose and F. W.'s longtime assistant, who never fails to remind the staff to appreciate that "F. W. is one of the best little bosses in the world" (12/1/28:58), to devise meticulous hierarchies of approval and reward, or to reproach Mr. Cleary, the college-educated son of a retired executive. Woodring's harangues identify Cleary as a representative of the peer culture and expose himself as a hopelessly out-of-date member of their parents' generation (7/20/29:25). When Rosenthal concedes that the times have changed and people do business in speakeasies and on the golf course as well as in the office, his admission (which also allows O'Hara to reveal Cleary as heir to the company presidency) clarifies how the Hagedorn & Brownmiller series fit into *New Yorker* prose humor. The series hit the *New Yorker*'s rhetorical target from both sides. It made fun of sycophants and the older generation, and reveled in youth as liberated from archaic prohibitions and conventions.

Both of O'Hara's series attacked bureaucracy, an increasingly important dimension of the economy and the culture in the late twenties. Woodring runs meetings with as heavy a hand as Mrs. Uhlein; though he pretends to solicit ideas about what to buy the boss for Christmas and how much to spend, the meeting for that purpose quickly turns into a rundown of the traditions and policies—everybody contributes five dollars and Woodring buys a gift, only for use out of the office—and an admission that "I've been sort of shopping around lately and have just about definitely decided what we ought to get F. W. this year" (62). But O'Hara adds to the irony of Woodring's false compliance with the group will by emphasizing his self-importance. He concludes the meeting by announcing, "We'll have at least two more meetings before this is finally settled, but I'm pretty sure you fellows will agree that it's just the thing the boss would like" (62). Mrs. Uhlein, similarly, undertakes repair of the local cannons, the (un)dress of young women at the community swimming pool, and the finance of a new fire engine for reasons of her own, which she projects onto her fellow Afternoon Delphians, who are just as compliant as the staff of Hagedorn & Brownmiller, Incorporated, but with less reason. In this context, the two sets of monologues satirize not only organizations, both capitalist and charitable, but also members' sheeplike behavior, on which power structures of vanity, wealth, and community rely.

The voices in O'Hara's series helped fill the *New Yorker,* like New York itself, with identifiable individuals of many types. O'Hara's stand-alone monologues and a personal narrative expanded his cast to include women and men, football coaches and businessmen, New Yorkers and western wannabes.[17] The wiseguy in "Unconditioned Reflexes," for example, gives stupid answers to stupid questions (*"Well, wuddia say?"* "Go to hell, and you can quote me" (8/31/29:58–61). O'Hara's pieces ran in the back of the book, but Angell and Ross indicated their importance by buying them in abundance.

Although the personal narrative "Suits Pressed" (2/8/29:28) marked a new direction for O'Hara, it reinforced this literate variation on mock-oral narration as central to the magazine. Implied self-characterization and direct communication with the reader replace the overheard talk of invented characters addressing an unseen audience. In the ironic mode typical of this genre, "Suits Pressed" presents O'Hara as a man-about-town sophisticated enough to call a tuxedo a "dinner coat" but so prone to "bad usage" that he and his tailor have a running joke in which the tailor pretends not to understand him. Instead of hinging on the tailor's pedantry or the speaker's ineptitude, however, the story turns on miscommunication with a third party, the tailor's beautiful, exotic daughter. When O'Hara comes to claim a "dinner coat" from the shop and the tailor puzzles over the request, the daughter responds by sneering, "Oh, Pop, wotsa matter with you? *Dinner* coat. Doncha know it means 'Tuxedo'?" Her comment reveals not only what the narrator notices—the father's worries about getting old and his humiliation that "his daughter knew something about men's clothes that he didn't know"—but also something he does not acknowledge: the girl's efforts to press her own suit with the eligible, fashionable young man by breaking his relationship to her father. Her accent and behavior outweigh her beauty as she reveals herself unable to speak or love well, but the tailor salvages his relationship with his client along with his self-respect by telling O'Hara, "Maybe you call it a Prince Albert cutaway I know what you mean," and "Suits Pressed" closes by reasserting the bond between them. "We laughed together" (28), the narrator recalls, and he ends the tale with their joint activity and the word *together.* Jokes about the characters' sophistication keep the story light as O'Hara demonstrates sophisticated comic writing: dialect to create characters and first-person narration to build tensions between them. O'Hara's narrative experiments, like those of other *New Yorker* prose humorists, united American traditions of comic storytelling with the agenda of literary modernism.

Non-narrative Genres

Charles G. Shaw's writing sustained New York's upper-class topics in volumes 4 and 5 while Kober and O'Hara attended to the hoi polloi. A longtime *New Yorker* contributor whom Ross had published at *Judge,* Shaw consistently asserted the local viewpoint of the peer society, beginning as early as his epigrams for 1:1, "From the Opinions of a New Yorker":

New York is noisy.
New York is overcrowded.
. . . .
New York is unhealthy.
. . . .
I wouldn't live outside New York for anything in the world.

(2/21/25:14)

In a similar realist, congratulatory vein, Shaw's two dozen pieces for volumes 1 and 2 took up theater, overheard talk, and other experiences of the "Man About

Town" (9/11/26:31). Shaw never became a front-of-the-book writer, despite two featured casuals in 1926, "Two Rooms, Bath And Kitchenette," illustrated by Helen Hokinson, in which the man-about-town suffers his girlfriend's disorganization when he arrives for cocktails (3/20/26:15–16), and "Furnished Bachelor," in which one Roger Wren and his apartment suffer a Monday morning hangover (11/27/26:29). After experimenting with other genres in volume 3, including a short-lived biographical series, "Through the Magnifying Glass,"[18] Shaw returned to evocations of the city in volume 4 with his ten-part "I Knew the Town."

Shaw's series ran in the back of the book beginning April 7, 1928 (67), where its nostalgia distinguished native New Yorkers from parvenus. Thus it belonged to the *New Yorker*'s strand of occasional congratulatory features, such as volume 1's "Why I Like New York," characterizing the city and its residents as unique and therefore uniquely deserving of their own magazine. Each "I Knew the Town" column begins with a string of recollections—"I knew the town when chorus girls wore spangled tights and a 'first night' was a real event of the season" (5/12/28:86). These certify the speaker's authority and implicitly contrast the good old days with today, a theme that Shaw first invoked in the dual dialogue "Speaking of Prohibition" (7/4/25:19). In debunking the idea of progress, however, "I Knew the Town" gives nostalgia an ironic twist entirely appropriate to sophisticates too young (and unwilling in any case) to look back with longing. Installments appeared every few weeks through June, then stopped until September, but by then the idea had caught on, and other writers began sharing their recollections. Frank Parker Stockbridge, probably a reader,[19] set the ball rolling on October 27, 1928, when "And *I* Knew The Town (With a Nod To Charles G. Shaw)" ran two columns, almost twice as long as Shaw's (73–74); other cognoscenti quickly followed suit. The series' smugness invited deflation, of course, and F. P. A. obliged a month after Stockbridge with "I Never Knew the Town (With a Kiss to Charles G. Shaw)" (11/24/28:48). With such recollections as "I never knew the town when there wasn't a subway problem and when American womanhood wasn't affronted twice daily" (48), Adams debunks a nostalgic view of New York with realist observations that ring true today.

The preference for public topics and monologues implied by Shaw's series marked a shift away from personal experience stories in volume 4. Genres as distinct as W. E. Farbstein's news charts and E. B. White's casuals helped turn the tide. Together they identified *New Yorker* humor as attitudes defined by contributors, not a program defined by editors.

W. E. Farbstein provided consistent, explicit satire of journalism and news-worthiness in a series of forty-five charts running almost biweekly between 4:6 and 5:50. Farbstein distilled genuine news stories[20] into pseudoobjective data sets that mocked newspapers' definition of news and narrative reporting. For example, "Spring Championships: Our own chart based on the very newest press reports," the genre's debut, lampooned the twenties' fad of setting records of dubious significance by listing oddball feats: peach packing (260 boxes in a day by R. T. Lewis of Live Oak, California), sitting on a bed of nails ("seven years' stretch" by "Unnamed Sadhu" from Benares, India), and fasting (55 days by a Mrs. Leontough of Toronto, who died thereafter [3/31/28:28]). The chart's presumption of objectivity gave Farbstein's barbs a funny deadpan irony, and in similar fashion over the next two years he offered a host of other dubious, but evidently true, details.

Farbstein's charts tapped the same vein as the "News of the Weird" column featured in American alternative newspapers of the 1990s while also calling attention to the journalistic values underlying such information. The rising importance of statistics in bureaucratic life gave a special zing to such charts as "Paternity Champions of the World: Records of amazing fatherhoods, collated from recent and authentic press reports" ("average number of progeny per [listed] father: 613.8" 1/12/29:64), and "Pride of the Cities: An Authentic List of Communities of International Preëmince, if We Are to Believe the Daily Press," noting statistics for Glasgow and Wipperfurth, Germany, but ignoring New York and Paris (1/11/30:25). Farbstein continued to poke fun at representations of the social world even when, in his last contribution to volume 5, "True Stories" (2/1/30:66), he wrought current events into verse. The *New Yorker* appreciated these charts so much that Farbstein, who also published in *Life* during the twenties, was still producing them in 1940 (e.g., "Slicing It Thin: A Listing of a Few Individuals Who Have Recently Demonstrated a Nice Concern for Fractions" 6/1/40:40).

Though its incongruities and absurdities remain glorious today, Farbstein's non-narrative humor fit particularly well with the ethos of the 1920s. Its form echoed modernist interest in pastiche. Its content strained the boundaries of the believable. Its rhetoric debunked the authority that the press increasingly asserted during the 1920s. Working from Pittsburgh,[21] Farbstein gathered details from newspapers around the globe for a humor grounded in local fact but accessible to outsiders—a significant factor as the *New Yorker* started its own syndicate and began planning for national circulation. Such humor had a local edge in

New York, however, because newspaper writers and editors formed a major segment of the *New Yorker*'s audience and contributors. Nonetheless, Farbstein's emphasis on the world outside New York helped redirect *New Yorker* humor from the confessional mode of volume 3 to the more public approaches of volumes 4 and 5.

Lightening Up

The turn toward public topics gave E. B. White's 1928–29 prose a lighter spirit than his preceding group of monologues. He still focused on tribulations of various sorts, and continued writing in the first person, but only five of his fifteen fiction pieces for volume 4 recounted (ostensibly) personal experiences. Most of his comic victims and their problems stood at several removes from himself. He displaced personal emotions onto moths and begonias in his fables; he used third-person narration in his Little Man story of "Philip Wedge," a man socially crippled by his fears (1/12/29:15–16). And in "Open Reply to Mrs. Mendelson" (12/22/28:14), he exaggerated his problem—how to reply to Mrs. Mendelson's offer of laundry service to a nonexistent Mrs. White—without minimizing his ability to resolve it.

White's personal narratives from volume 4 end with the hero standing bloody but unbowed. "Memoirs of a Dramatic Critic" (9/29/28:23–24) even concludes on the relatively happy note of many a tall yarn. After the narrator confesses to his humiliations and triumphs as interim drama critic for the *Armature Winders Plain Dealer* (first he lacked a suitable companion for an important opening, then he found one, only to have his boss commandeer the tickets), he reports his highest glory: when people even less connected with Broadway than he mistook him for a celebrity. Only the narrator of "The Color of Mice" (9/22/28:19–20) seems doomed to failure despite a brief moment of triumph when, alas, his pants fall down. The tale recounts his troubles when he succumbs to a haberdasher's suggestion that he buy a new belt in a gray color that his wife warns might attract mice or battleships—as indeed it does. Though he escapes both by giving away his belt (and losing his pants), he takes refuge in the nearest haberdashery, where the cycle of humiliation will doubtless resume: he needs trousers, but the clerk offers to show him underwear, ending the story on an ominous, ambiguous note of circularity.

White also leavened the mood of volume 4 by turning his attention outward, beyond himself. In the spring of 1928 he wrote a variation on legalese for "The

Subway Trouble Explained" (4/7/28:25), explaining the politics surrounding a proposed seven-cent fare in sentences almost as byzantine as the issue. An equally broad conception animates the untitled parody of newspaper features from the New York *Sun, Times, World,* and *Graphic* (11/17/28:22–23).[22] During this period White sustained his trademark first-person deadpan by speaking about subjects other than himself. A professional poet-watcher narrates "Poets Are Being Watched" (2/25/28:22), which jokes about the new idea of tax deductions by imagining how they would apply to poets' expenses, such as the cost of taking loved ones to dinner or traveling the continent in despair. Public topics also drove two dialogues: an imaginary conversation between the erudite boxer Gene Tunney and his slangy son ("Tunney's Little Man" 8/11/28:20) and a dialogue about New York City between two men aboard a ship bound for Europe ("Getting Away" 6/23/28:12).

About half of Thurber's dozen prose pieces for volume 4 also contributed to the more genial mode of the volume. His interest in parody during this period resulted in several burlesques: "Helps for Entertaining Count Deterding (Compiled by His Secretary)" (4/14/28:32–36), "Advice to American Ladies" (6/16/28:28), and "Our Own Modern English Usage" (1/5/29:22–23). The first of nine installments aimed at Fowler's reference book, "Our Own Modern English Usage" offers foolishly precise rules for *whom,* adverbs, and infinitives, and thus revived the elaborate humor of "The Making of a Magazine," though much of it seems tedious today.[23] Thurber also played with broad humor on miscellaneous topics in volume 5. A personal narrative, the pseudonymous "Burglar Proof— Maybe," signed *James Grover,* features the memoirs of a highly successful burglar who ends up in a cell with former colleagues from both sides of the law (9/14/29:72–80). "This Week's Miracle," written while he and White saw *Is Sex Necessary?* (1929) through publication, parodies publishers' notices (4/6/29:25–26). "Two Ships Bring Americans of Note and English Author" (6/8/29:18) extends its burlesque to illustrations and layout. The mock-newspaper account uses irrelevant illustrations along with typography reminiscent of the *New York Times,* recycling photographs of only two faces for each of the five notables in the article. More incongruous, the photos depict the Flora and Sterling Finny mannequins from E. B. White's 1927 house ad campaign, not live people. A final visual joke comes in the last image, which shows the mannequin's head quite obviously detached from the body. Kinney declared "Two Ships" an "obscure casual" (Kinney 429), but it joins "The Roaring Talkies" (8/24/29:19), "Little Joe (Suggested by the Latest Gunman Fiction, and Several Other Things)" (9/7/29:24–25), and others in a substantial, if previously unrecognized, playful strain of Thurber's humor.

Good-natured humor emerged from Thurber's more ironic pieces as well. Despite its lurid title, "How It Feels to Kill a Man" (3/10/28:27–28) stands squarely in the nineteenth-century line of tales of vernacular speakers who deflate literate narrators' romantic notions; the theme dates back at least to A. B. Longstreet's *Georgia Scenes* (1835). In this instance, structured as a dialogue rather than as a framed narrative, Thurber's alter ego discovers that the crime-stopping New York City police have less dramatic lives than he imagines. By contrast, "The Spirit of Saint Louis" introduces the contemptible Mrs. Burch, who earns everyone's scorn with her empty chatter on the train ride from Missouri to New York (12/8/28:27). Thurber consistently created unpleasant women during this period, in "Not Together" (3/3/28:73), "Quiet Please" (2/9/29:79), and other tales, but their publication in the magazine one at a time dissipates the misogyny of the group.

Thurber's biographer reports that Ross worried about Thurber's humor "going grim"—particularly in "Menaces in May" (5/26/28:30–36; Kinney 217). Humorous mainly for its exaggerations of gloom, "Menaces in May" shows the extent to which Ross and Angell trusted a few valued writers to communicate with *New Yorker* readers. The third-person story describes the emotions overwhelming a writer who misses his wife, inexplicably absent but due back soon. On the street, in the subway, he feels menaced by the random urban chaos leading to violence and death, and can feign courage only by whistling because he feels so alone and so afraid. By contrast "Camera vs. St. Bernard" (6/30/28:17–18) and "I Burn My Bridge Behind Me" (12/1/28:31–32) constrain the Little Man's vulnerability through the reassurance of first-person narration. First-person narrators master troubles through rhetoric if not in fact.

Third-person stories prevailed in Thurber's writing for volume 5, lifting these constraints in tale after tale and giving grimness full rein. "What Every Wife Should Know: A Study of Claustrophobia" (10/12/29:23–24), "The Psyching of Mr. Rogers" (4/27/29:22), and "What Life Did to Us: One Man's True Confession" (2/1/30:17) all parody genres of popular journalism, but they trade exuberance of form for bleakness of mood as they depict heroes trapped in marriage, driven insane by domesticity, and cowed by daily life. This strand reached its peak in the seven installments of Thurber's Monroe series, which alternated tales of male and female defeat from December 1928 through January 1930.[24] Every story ends with John Monroe's humiliation, despite these variations, and his suffering increases as the series goes on. In contrast to the classic end of Fillmore Hyde's comedy, with a marriage celebration, the Monroe series ends as John Monroe crawls into bed alone, abandoning with a resigned sigh the quest for happiness. The ironic title of this episode, "The Middle Years," implies that the end can come at any time; it also alludes to Henry James's story by the same name and thus implies that Monroe, like James's protagonist, finally understands that lost opportunities never return. Monroe had hoped to take advantage of his wife's absence and a new acquaintance's flirtation to attempt an affair, but he finds one reason after another to delay, including a dalliance with James's *Golden Bowl,* before finally abandoning the idea. Now he understands the stakes, which James articulated in *his* "Middle Years": "A second chance—*that's* the delusion. There never was to be but one. We work in the dark—we do what we can—we give what we have. Our doubt is our passion and our passion is our task. The rest is the madness of art" (James 165–66). In place of Fillmore Hyde's caricatures, as wooden as the institutions whose names they carry, Thurber's characters come from life, and invite us to understand their experience as the madness of comic art. Thurber's mood as his marriage to Althea failed[25] coincided with the growing economic depression, fostering at the end of volume 5 a gloomy outlook often attributed to the early *New Yorker* as a whole, as in Thomas Grant's claim that Little Man humor signifies a backlash to the 1920s feminist movement ("Feminist" 158). But the pages of the magazine demonstrate that Thurber's mood was his own, not the *New Yorker's.*

Reprinted or read as a group, Thurber's stories reinforce each other's misogyny and gloom; together with similar stories by White, Perelman, and others, they have implied that Little Man humor was more representative of *New Yorker* humor than it actually was, especially in the 1920s. Publication in the magazine isolates the gloom as well as frames it with other comic writing and art. These counterbalances disappear in reprints. A case in point is Enid Veron's version of Ring Lardner's "Large Coffee" (9/28/29:26–27) in *Humor in America* (1976). She offers the tale as an example of "The Little Soul" and how he "becomes suicidal over the impossibility of dealing successfully with hotel room service" (202), but the original version in the *New Yorker,* accompanied by Otto Soglow and Leonard Dove cartoons, asserts a much broader humor, which Ross pronounced "A MASTERPIECE FROM THE MASTER."[26]

The *New Yorker* version uses typography to emphasize a parodic editor's note, less distinct in Veron's edition, and identify the story as a tall tale. While the tone of the editor's note establishes the authenticity of the diary at the start of the piece, absurd details expose it as a fraud. The occupant of Room 657 is found in a state "worse" than dead? The police found the diary and "used parts of it as curl papers for Grover Whalen"? "A blunt instrument, probably another hotel" crushed Mr. Lardner's head? By the time the editor closes his preface with melodramatic warnings about "men and women who, like the writer thereof, have been battered and broken by an insensate world" (26), the astute reader should have recognized the signals of the comic lie, despite the realistic diary form. These narrative winks also render the end of the story less despairing than Veron claims. To be sure, the diarist bemoans "the worst"—the only clerk to ever get his breakfast order right has left the hotel (27)—but he also declares his plan to "lean out the window" and offer himself to the ménage à trois he's been watching all summer across the courtyard as "a fourth for strip bridge" (27). Thus the tale ends on the cheerier, if equally preposterous, possibility that he died by accident or after making an obscene advance. Regardless, this version of the story establishes it as an editor's tall yarn, not an example of a "little soul . . . driven to desperate straits" (Veron 202). By making the editor a liar and the interior narrator a fiction, Lardner exchanges a realistic frame for a parodic one—a context enhanced by magazine publication. Moreover, by making both narrators writers, he abandons the traditional contrast between writing and talk for a contrast between types of writing—both lies masquerading as truth. If the editor's claims are lies, the interior narrator's suffering hardly matters.

Other comic Sufferers likewise diverged from Thurber's. In 1929–30 White's Sufferers enjoyed better relations than Thurber's with both women and the universe, probably because White was falling in rather than out of love during this period. The worst fate suffered by any character in any of White's ten casuals from volume 5 occurs in "The Doily Menace," where the speaker confesses to a lifelong "trouble with doilies"—hardly a real (much less crippling) affliction, despite its origin in a childhood belief that doilies had some connection to sex (7/20/29:15). Except for "Frigidity in Men" (9/28/29:23–29), an excerpt from Thurber and White's *Is Sex Necessary?*, where White poses as an expert in sexual behavior, White's remaining casuals for volume 5 characterize him as a silly comic victim in much the same mode as "The Doily Menace," alternating between internal and external events.

Even White's nightmares during this period lack terror; they evoke dismay as social critique, not as a response to personal misfortune. For example, "Dream Children: A Reverie (By Arrangement with Charles Lamb and 24 Other Newspapers)" tells two stories at once (4/20/29:20–21). One tale involves the narrator's comeuppance: he introduces an anecdote to illustrate how children love to read about their elders in newspapers, but the incident actually shows that such reading has blurred generational roles: childhood conversation and activities have given way to commercial rhetoric. (Fifty-five years later Joshua Meyrowitz made a similar argument about television in *No Sense of Place* [1985].) In the typical manner of tall stories framing one tale within another, this comic story of domestic life encloses a nightmare vision of changes in the newspaper industry amid the syndications, mergers, and advertising practices of the late twenties. Yet the narrative frame constrains—even domesticates—the satire in which commercial language displaces social discourse.

This critique of media trends joined the *New Yorker*'s ongoing ridicule of advertising, newspapers, and radio. A distant relative of his 1927 Sterling Finny house-ad series, White's elaborate unsigned, untitled parody of newspaper features ran as a two-page spread in the issue of November 17, 1928 (22–23). The spread, which imitated visually the collage of articles and images on newspaper pages, incorporated visual jokes and textual parodies. Type fonts ridicule the *Times* and *Sun* specifically, and photographs interject incongruous images: a photo labeled "Angelo Patri" depicts the Sterling Finny mannequin, and "Antics of Arabella" presents exercise demonstrations by two girls identified as "W. C. Fields and John Gilbert" (23). The *New Yorker* had ridiculed journalism's self-importance and claims to truth as far back as Ford's "Making of a Magazine" series, and White's collage shows the durability of this burlesque strand alongside his more ironic "Romance of the Publishing Game" (2/23/29:18–19). The *New Yorker* generally steered clear of stories from journalists' standpoint but occasionally made room for a congratulatory piece by an old friend, as when F. P. A.'s "'The Lore She Brought Me'" listed such truisms as "the business office and the editorial office hate each other" and "there are no dull stories; there are only bored reporters" (9/21/29:31).

Like its mockery of high society, the *New Yorker*'s humor about mass media avoided serious social satire and joked about its subject from the inside. Newspaper writers, artists, and editors populated its audience as well as its pages. So did admen. An advertisement for the Philadelphia *Evening Bulletin* in the issue of March 31, 1928, just after the third anniversary, indicates that the *New Yorker*'s advertising staff knew that their media-buying clients constituted a special segment of the magazine's audience. In their private lives they purchased retail goods, but in their professional lives they purchased national advertising. The campaign for the *Evening Bulletin* ran monthly, eventually joined by ads for the *Pittsburgh Press* (e.g., 9/15/28:45) and the *Chicago Tribune* (2/2/29:37), which together praised "men who, within one short generation, have . . . Aided in the transforming of small manufacturers into giants of world commerce" (6/2/28:37). The campaign went on to include not only broad claims about the papers' reach into "homes of wealth" and "prosperous residential districts" but also charts and other statistical proof. Graphic and verbal humor about advertising—a topic of broad interest in the twenties—tweaked the *New Yorker*'s friends.

Women Too

Comic Sufferers in the upbeat spirit of 1928–30 included the heroines of Alice Frankforter's casuals, who triumph (if only by endurance) over life's daily travails. Unknown today, Frankforter was among the few women regularly signing *New Yorker* fiction during this early period. Her twenty-six casuals ran in one of every three issues from the middle of volume 4, when "Portrait of a Lady Bathing" (8/18/28:51–52) appeared, through the end of volume 5 (where my statistics end, but probably not her contributions). Her 18 casuals for volume 5 rank her ahead of Gibbs (17), Kober (14), Sullivan (13), White (10), Benchley (8), Mosher (7), and Parker (3); only Thurber (24) and O'Hara (24) published more prose fiction than Frankforter in volume 5. Frankforter's publication record demonstrates how much the editorial staff valued her work ("Going South" actually ran twice in the issue of 11/23/29!), while her progress from the back to the front of the book suggests that they actively cultivated her contributions. They valued her in monetary terms as well, according to a document from 1929 or 1930, which identifies Frankforter's rate at six cents a word, less than half of the fifteen cents paid to Benchley and Parker or the eleven paid to E. B. White and Corey Ford, but just a little less than the seven cents paid to Groucho Marx and slightly more than the nickel per word paid to Charles G. Shaw, Wolcott Gibbs, and John O'Hara.[27] Like O'Hara, Frankforter began her *New Yorker* career in the back pages with a series featuring a distinctive point of view. Much as Helen Hokinson drew captioned cartoon narratives of young women battling urban gauntlets ranging from haircuts and taxis to the passport office and boulevard traffic, Frankforter offered a woman's eye view of the peer society's social scene.

Most of her stories portray a young woman struggling with a social situation in which she feels out of her element. An ingenue named "Miss Sloop" figures in two stories, where she finds herself one-upped in conversation by older women who have visited Europe often and by the horsey set's enthusiasm for broken bones incurred in the line of pleasure ("The First Trip" 9/14/29:26; "Boot and Saddle" 12/7/29:30–31). Frankforter generally chose genres that set her heroine's experience directly before the reader, avoiding both the personal narrative and third-person narration.[28] The Sloop pieces and a few others take the form of dramatic scripts with scene-setting statements, such as this dinner-table exchange:

> MISS BIRD (*a fine, breezy young woman in a red evening dress, shouting across the table*)— You must come out Sunday, Miss Sloop. The Flying Dutchman would give you a good ride. Only (*with great solemnity*) he doesn't like ditches. He sometimes refuses at ditches.
> MISS SLOOP (*reflecting that she doesn't like ditches either, so maybe they could refuse together*)—How sensible of him! (12/7/29:30)[29]

More commonly, however, Frankforter used scene-setting statements in the second person, giving the heroine's experience the immediacy of the present tense and endowing the prose with that hallmark of interpersonal communication, "you." The heroine, never identified by name, becomes a stand-in for the author—and speaks specifically to the female reader, whom she invites to see herself in her place.

The heroine's first ride in an airplane results in "The wish that your pilot were more the type of Lindbergh" ("The Airplane Ride" 4/13/29:21). A winter invitation for a day of sports in the country leads to "Your longing for the days when hostesses sent written invitations and you had time to think up something that a child of three wouldn't detect as a weak-kneed, crawling lie" ("Sports D'Hiver" 3/2/29:72). Frankforter's technique exploits the intimacy of first-person genres such as the personal narrative with the opportunity to render mental life (Joyce's stream-of-consciousness masterpiece, *Ulysses* [1922], was already well-known), yet at the same time, she maintains some of the ironic distance of the third-person report along with the ability to set the character within the scene. "Symphony Concert," for example, begins by alternating exterior and interior impressions: "The black georgette and imitation pearls. The reflection that while you don't know much about music you have a natural liking for the best. The arrival of your escort, who says with happy enthusiasm that you'll enjoy the program tonight because of Brahms. The vague murmur indicating that your feeling about Brahms lies too deep for words. The secret uneasiness because the only musical compositions you recognize without prompting are Dvořak's 'Humoresque,' the 'Caprice Viennois,' and the 'Lohengrin Wedding March'"

(2/23/29:74). This unusual technique, Frankforter's signature style, intensifies her characters' comic pain—specifically identified as the reader's.

Her protagonists represent the New Woman on the move, literally as well as culturally. A substantial group of stories takes place en route by ship, train, and plane, showing a solo woman traveler content with her own company as she triumphs over trial by transport. "Going South," a shipboard piece, sums up the prospects of travel for Frankforter's New Woman: "The high adventure. The possible romance. The carefree exhilaration, undimmed by any thought of dull old ladies . . . or the possibility of your ever needing to open the box of Mothersill's" (11/23/29:56). Ever optimistic, Frankforter's heroine courageously seeks experience despite previous suffering.

Her courage occasionally flags, but she perseveres undaunted by toothache ("Nuit Blanch" 1/26/29:48–49), contract bridge (1/12/29:28–30), or Christmas ("Nuit de Noël" 12/22/28:14–15). "Spinster Wail" shows our heroine receiving her comeuppance for the "secret conviction that maternity has a weakening effect upon the brain and that any woman who has earned a living can take care of a baby with one hand tied behind her" (11/17/28:105) as she struggles with the basics (11/17/28:104–6). But the end finds her in "merciful escape" as she realizes that she now has the answer to "that much discussed problem—Why College Women Stay Single" (106). By implying that smart women avoid motherhood, Frankforter aims her humor directly at the New Women of the peer society.

Indeed, Frankforter's stories have little use for men, though her characters tolerate them. A day of sports for which our heroine feels well dressed but otherwise ill-equipped ends with a ski accident providing (along with snow down her neck and up her sleeves) a excuse to rush back to town, an escape neither diminished nor enhanced when her skiing partner, "a serious young man," insists on escorting her ("Sports D'Hiver" 3/2/29:75). On the other hand, nearly every story ends with Frankforter's protagonist making a "merciful escape," from women as well as from men. She describes her college reunion as an event so tedious that "for the first time in your life you are longing for the speeches to start" ("College Luncheon" 1/4/30:32). In these stories, all's well that ends well. And her heroines feel well off by themselves.

A more jaundiced view of both women and men came from Parker's late fiction, though she published just seven stories in the two years after "Arrangement in Black and White" (10/8/27:22–24), most to pay off her *New Yorker* contract after Morris Markey and others took over the book department. Together with Thurber's Monroe series, these tales of drunkenness and depression present some of the magazine's bleakest humor during the late twenties, though with the publication of *Enough Rope* (1926) Parker had already established herself as, in Nina Miller's words, "the most luckless and sardonic woman lover on literary record" (763). The four pieces from 1928 insist upon this cynicism, although Parker declares herself a character in only one of them. But the other women suffer even more than her own persona. In her customary vein of overheard talk, "A Terrible Day Tomorrow" depicts an anonymous couple who begin their evening together determined to have just one drink but lose their resolve and civility as one round turns into half a dozen (2/11/28:14–16). The couple in "Just a Little One" likewise drink themselves through the gamut of emotions from flirtatious to defensive, maudlin, and mean (5/12/28:20–21). By the end, the woman is so drunk that her initial (feigned) reservation about drinking quality liquor—"You'll stay by me if anything happens, won't you? . . . Don't let me take any horses home with me"—actually comes true, as she begs her companion, "Let's go out and pick up a lot of stray dogs. . . . And a horse. I've never had one single horse, Fred. Isn't that rotten?" (21). As these stories portray lives controlled by drink and irony built on lies, they draw humor from banal dialogue summed up by empty promises of one last drink.

Even Parker's drunken dialogues acquired a broader humor in volume 5, however. Leading off the volume, "You Were Perfectly Fine" gradually reveals just how drunkenly unfine the man had been the night before; humor grows from contrasts among her repeated assurances, her offhand reports of his boorish behavior, and his progressive uncertainty over whether he did the deeds or she fabricated them (2/23/29:17–18). Conventional irony marks "The Cradle of Civilization," in which dissolute New Yorkers proclaim the French Riviera "a darned good little dump," though unfortunately French: "They're so damn dumb, they make me sick," the woman complains. "Why, they don't even speak English in the post-office" (9/21/29:23–24). Parker revived old jokes and gave them a hostile edge by depicting characters very like her readers and letting them damn themselves. But her characterization of herself at the end of volume 5 stuck with the self-deprecation of the comic Sufferer. "But the One on the Right—" follows the structure of a dinner party, each course marking a new stage in the speaker's misery over the man seated to her left, yet the story ends happily because just as his conversation incites her to violence, the man on her right notices her, and together they plot an escape (10/19/29:25–27). Small insults cause deep pain in Parker's satiric courtship dialogues for volume 2 but by volume 5 her fiction brightened, differentiating between other Sufferers and her fictionalized self.

Another comically jaundiced view of human relationships in volume 5 came in the ironic tales of Wolcott Gibbs, whose "Facsimile of a Letter," already noted, describes a nearly fatal courtship (2/23/29:84–85). In "The Colonel's Leg," Gibbs describes his niece's relentless quest, beginning with kicks and pinpricks and ending with false claims of attempted murder, to determine exactly what fills Colonel Justinian's trousers (3/9/29:19–20). Gibbs's ridicule of the authoritarian older generation continues when guests at a Colonel Driscoll's country house rebel against the gardening chores assigned to them. They subvert his orders by trimming the hedges to resemble a roller coaster, painting the maple trees like peppermint sticks, and giving the sheep a poodle cut ("The Summer Labor Problem" 7/1/29:17–18). Indeed, the inhabitants of Gibbs's New York behave so badly that in "Sea Change" Edgar Guest abandons his sentimental view of humanity when confronted by the population of Central Park ("Sea Change" 6/29/29:17–19).

A counterbalancing absurdity often arose from Gibbs's darkest narratives, mostly from volume 5. Probably the most extreme example occurs in his war drama, "Chevaux 40, Hommes 8," whose silly script ends with everyone dead (7/20/29:19–20). But what other conclusion could he invent for a parody of recent war literature (including *What Price Glory?* and *All Quiet on the Western Front*), considering the number of *New Yorker* readers and contributors who knew trench warfare firsthand? (Gibbs, born in 1902, passed the war in high school.) So, after drunken British soldiers discuss *Peter Rabbit's* literary merits and German conscripts ruminate on the irony of turning bakers into killers, Gibbs calls for stage action that underlines the difference between the audience's experience and the characters'—while making fun of such drama: "At the conclusion of this remark, Gus dies of starvation and Fritz [his comrade] is quietly eaten by a large rat. The tent blows away. On this ultimate irony the curtain falls and everybody goes home" (20). His personal narratives, by contrast, veered from the absurd to the depressive. His first signed casual, "On Working That Line Into the Conversation," describes a comic comeuppance too extreme to take seriously: the speaker runs from the room in shame and jumps into a snowbank, where friends find him two weeks later (2/25/28:60–61). Whereas the silly end to this tale creates a lighthearted frame for his pose of ineptitude, the financial desperation and spousal abuse of "Long Distance" invite scorn for the narrator's naïveté (6/9/28:19). Gibbs's narrator does not understand the significance of the men who visit Helen during Peter's absence, the bruises on her body, or the baby's unanswered cries. Gibbs fails to identify their fifty-dollar phone call to California as a distress signal, even though he knows that Peter has not worked for several months, the sofa lacks springs, and their apartment looks out on the Elevated tracks, and even after Helen advises Peter, "Tell them the baby's just fine and you're making lots of money and I'm still pretty." In fact, when the call reaches the maid instead of his mother, Peter's recriminations over Helen's "smart idea" go over the speaker's head, as does Helen's reply, which closes the story with hints of murder or suicide while silently condemning the speaker's impotence. Six months before Thurber's first Monroe story (but three years after Nick Caraway demonstrated a similar innocence in *The Great Gatsby* [1925]), "Long Distance" showed the *New Yorker's* willingness to sacrifice laughter for rue.

Gibbs's first-person narratives also gave parody an ironic twist. Advice literature came in for special tweaking. "Aviation for Amateurs" covers what to wear, how to get to the airfield, and what to do in the cockpit before confessing, "I don't know a damn thing about it except what I read in the papers. I've never been up" (6/16/28:64–65). A self-help article, "What Examining Desks Has Taught Me," offers keys to success as an extortionist, with such advice as "there is probably no desk anywhere which doesn't contain *some* little thing which would be of interest to the neighbors" (10/20/28:96–97). A pair of mock reviews, "Glorious Calvin (A Critical Appreciation)" (2/9/29:17) and "The Master's Touch" (11/9/29:23), skewers President Coolidge's (so-called) personality along with movie and book criticism. "The Peepshow Season in Retrospect" decries the pornographic shorts in the arcade at Moe's Grotto on Sixth Avenue as inferior to such old-time favorites as *A Night in a Turkish Bath* and *Glimpses of the Chicago Fire* (9/21/29:25–26).

Toward the end of volume 5, nearly all his casuals ridiculed media rhetoric. "Pal, a Dog," makes fun of the *Saturday Evening Post* (10/26/29:29). "Hurrah for Mrs. Porsena," described as a "slightly cockeyed epic" on the Harvard-Yale game, lampoons sports columns with a tale about the mother about Harvard's injured football captain; in a spectacular save, she ran onto the field to score the winning touchdown and field goal (11/23/29:27). "The Cartoon Situation" recommends that everyone use and relabel a single image (12/28/29:18). Although he joked about current issues in both local and national politics, his humor aims more at media rhetoric and practitioners than at their subjects. His parodies play with writing as a means of expressing oneself or controlling others—the theme behind "The Facts of Life" (11/3/28:79–80), an antiromantic letter by which Bob from Harvard woos Ellen from Vassar. "It isn't altogether pleasant to reflect that in the last analysis love is only a biological device to keep the world populated," he concedes, hoping to pull her away from her roommate's Victorian romanticism, "but just the same I believe it can still be quite lovely" (79). Humor about writing qualified as inside jokes at the *New Yorker,* whose audience specifically included writers.

By his own account Gibbs was hired as a copy editor in 1927 (not 1928, as recorded by Brendan Gill [116]) after his aunt Alice Duer Miller threatened to exclude Ross from her parties unless Gibbs got a job.[30] Not until June 1928, however, did his prose begin appearing regularly enough—about every three weeks—to help define *New Yorker* humor. Gibbs's 31 pieces in volumes 4 and 5 nonetheless place his contribution on a par with freelancers Kober (26), O'Hara (38), and Frankforter (26) and staff members Thurber (26) and White (32).

By volume 5, the *New Yorker* had refined its prose preferences so precisely that writers could not peddle their rejections elsewhere. Fairfax Downey, who had published 13 items between 1925 and 1927, complained at the end of 1929 that he considered writing for the *New Yorker* a "hazard": "if a piece done for your field misses," he wrote Katharine White, "it's just about dead."[31] When Elmer Rice took offense in 1928 at the rejection of three pieces that he claimed "were definitely ordered," Angell countered that only one writer had ever declined to work under the magazine's policy of not contracting articles in advance of submission.[32] Contributors varied enormously in their willingness to have their work heavily cut and edited, however. Arthur Kober withdrew a piece rather than sign the edited work.[33] F. Scott Fitzgerald so resented the magazine's requirements that he dismissed out of hand the opportunity to write a "Profile" of Ring Lardner.[34] "*New Yorker* offers o.k. but uninteresting—," he wrote his agent Harold Ober, who also represented Stephen Leacock to the magazine, in November of 1929. "As for Mrs. Angell (whoever she is) I will gladly modify my style and subject matter for her, but she will have to give me her beautiful body first, and I dare say the price is too high" (Fitzgerald 173). The editors' insistence on their prerogative to choose what appeared in the *New Yorker*'s pages and to tailor manuscripts to that context means that what they did publish represented a conjunction of their goals and the authors'. Thus *New Yorker* humor encompassed Rice's eleven-part melodramatic satire, *Voyage to Purilia* (5:34 to 5:44; rpt. 1930), a novel as long as anything William Shawn ever published, as well as Fitzgerald's mock-oral narrative, "Salesmanship in the Champs-Élyséees," which appeared in the last issue of volume 5.

Playing into New Yorkers' familiarity with Paris, "Salesmanship in the Champs-Élyséees" imagines a Frenchman's view of the American expatriate (2/15/30:20). Its pseudo-French dialect identifies the speaker as ironic at the start ("To work for the Company Automobile is a *métier* exacting"), and we quickly learn why: he entertains himself by making fun of customers and proving the salesman always right. He understands that the American who enters the showroom wants to buy a car, will return to inspect the model he wants, and will write a check on the spot. But the American does not understand that no Frenchman will sell to him "without making a proper study of his sincerity and his character and the extent of his desire for the car," that the American's resistance to this practice makes him impolite—and that "the impolite will end himself by being able to get no car at all." No Little Man, no Sufferer, not a misogynist, not even an American, Fitzgerald's ironic narrator nonetheless sums up the achievement of *New Yorker* prose humor at the end of five years: an urban wit of character, situation, and narration for educated New Yorkers. *New Yorker* humor featured the ironic voices of men and women speaking, pushing aside admiration of rural verities and vernacular values for demonstrations of intelligence, sensitivity, and style—even when inadequate to the tasks at hand. In concentrating on urban characters and their lives, mental and physical, in New York or abroad, *New Yorker* humor removed mock-oral narration from the traditions of the tall tale (which toyed with readers' ignorance) and nineteenth-century local color humor (which played with nostalgia) and moved it to modern forms that flattered educated readers with the power of wit.

CHAPTER 8

That Other
New Yorker Humor

Comic Verse

In The New Yorker, *the unknown writer was on equal footing with the established
one; the editor sought good writing, not great names.*

E. B. White [1951]

Critics and scholars who overlooked comic verse and defined *New Yorker* humor
mainly as prose fiction and graphic art helped misrepresent the magazine as
misogynous. The *New Yorker* published some 1,700 poems in its first five years,
and the genre attracted dozens of poets—many of them women. In contrast with
the 6,000 comic drawings published during the same period, poetry was a lesser
genre, and even poets occasionally missed it. Only late in 1930 did William Car-
los Williams learn of the magazine's interest "in poetry as poetry,"[1] yet it had already published serious poetry by such major writers as William Butler Yeats
("Death" 4/27/29:21) and Louise Bogan ("For an Old Dance" 2/1/30:17), as well
as comic works by David McCord (seven poems, including four in the "Intellectual Diversions" series), Margaret Widdemer (four poems), Elinor Wylie (four
poems) and Wylie's coterie, who constituted a miniature peer society: sisters-in-
law Laura Benét and Rosemary Carr Benét, brother-in-law Stephen Vincent
Benét, husband William Rose Benét, and sister Nancy Hoyt.[2] Light verse from
serious poets helped identify the *New Yorker*'s target market as the educated consumers of the peer society; the market for verse thus attracted literary humorists
as consumers *and* producers, as readers *and* writers. This reflexive relationship,
not an acquisitions process closed to outsiders, explains the coherent attitudes

and themes of *New Yorker* humor—in large measure coherent across gender and genre.

Editor Katharine Sergeant Angell White shaped *New Yorker* verse even more fully than its prose, and archival correspondence shows how deftly she worked to attract and sustain the kind of poetry she sought. When poet Newman Levy complained to her just before Christmas of 1929 about a check for less than his usual rate, she gave with one hand and held back with the other. "The New Yorker has been paying me a dollar a line and more since my piece that appeared in Volume I, No. 1," argued Levy, by day an attorney with Greenbaum Wolf & Ernst on Madison Avenue, as he tried to pull rank by claiming relationships older than hers with both the magazine and Ross: "This thing irritates me, especially as Ross and I went out of Judge together years ago under his slogan 'A living wage for authors.' Shall I return your fifty dollars or do you want to send me twenty-five more?"[3] White's response not only asserted her own authority, deflecting the appeal to Ross with a polite statement of policy—"The New Yorker feels that there is a genuine distinction in buying short and long verse, especially when the long verse is of the ballad or narrative type which is usually easier to write than short and compact poetry"—but also reminded Levy that poets worked in a buyer's market that she controlled. "Verse is an expensive product for us to use," she informed him, "and we have to draw the line sometimes at buying long poems at a very high rate, whereas we can use them at a slightly lower rate." Nonetheless, she made up the difference to a dollar a line; although she refused to increase his rates to $1.50, as he challenged, she reaffirmed the magazine's commitment to, and dependence on, its contributors. "We want you to contribute, however, and we want you to be as happy as possible about it."[4] White recognized that poets, like artists and prose writers, had to choose the *New Yorker* before the magazine could choose them.

Similar exchanges throughout the first five years of the magazine identify verse as important comic content, not mere filler. Correspondence asking poets to accept editorial preferences in word, rhyme, format, title, and other substantive elements (as well as financial ones) makes clear that verse cost the *New Yorker* considerable time, money, and editorial effort. But because light verse seldom found its way out of the magazine into anthologies and other books, it remains little known today. Indeed, most *New Yorker* poets have reputations even more obscure than Levy, whose claims to fame include *Opera Guyed* (1923), issued in fine bindings and illustrated by Rea Irvin, and two items in the 1979 *Oxford Book of American Light Verse*. That anthology includes several other writers associated with the early *New Yorker*. Arthur Guiterman, Dorothy Parker, David Mc-Cord, and Elinor Wylie are there, but only one poem, E. B. White's "Marble-Top" (1/15/27:21, also rpt. *The Lady Is Cold* [1929]), actually appeared in the magazine before its fifth birthday. Though invisible outside the pages of the *New Yorker*, comic verse nonetheless helped define *New Yorker* humor for educated, local readers—especially women. As a result the *New Yorker* attracted poets such as Jacqueline Embry from as far away as Louisville, Kentucky; Martha Bensley Bruère and Mary Ritter Beard judged her *New Yorker* couplet "Burnt Lady" (12/8/28:34) important enough to reprint in their landmark 1934 anthology of women's humor, *Laughing Their Way*. And Embry doubtless spoke for other poets, men and women, when she expressed gratitude for Angell's criticisms of "Hic Jacet—Petrel" (10/12/29:33) by exclaiming, "God's little gift to Poetry—that's what *you* are."⁵

The poem that Levy and White quibbled over is almost certainly his "The Flying Dutchman of Central Park West (A Ballad of the Traffic Rules)" (1/4/30:36). Its sixteen stanzas lament a crosstown gauntlet still recognizable today, and include one quatrain repeated three times as a refrain:

> Oh, the roads run south, and the roads run north,
> And they twist and turn in a devious way,
> And the luckless wight who ventures forth
> Will ne'er see home again that day.

Levy's doughty wight endures one crisis after the next as he tries to escape the West Side in a yellow cab:

> The driver stepped upon the gas,
> When, lo, his frighted eyes did meet—
> As though to say, "Thou shalt not pass"—
> An arrow reading "One Way Street."

Levy elevates comic blundering to epic dimensions as the hero and his cabbie sidekick battle streets and signs, and the ballad ends with the pair raised to mythic status as tragic heroes, doomed for eternity by bureaucrats:

> They say that now on stormy nights
> Hard by the brazen Boliva
> With muffled horn and darkened lights
> There speeds a silent ghostly car.

The predictable story line and jaunty doggerel make this ballad amusing, even to readers in the provinces, who by 1930 represented a considerable number. The *New Yorker*'s circulation rose even as the economy deflated; Ray Bowen reported that national circulation increased "by leaps and bounds" in the eight months between October 1929 and June 1930,[6] increasing 56 percent from 77,500 in 1929 to 121,000 in 1931 (Kramer, *Ross* 211).

The six or eight poems in each issue of the *New Yorker* in the late 1920s underline White's point about expense. Verse cost more than cartoons or prose in the same space. In the period that Levy's poem cost $50 for 1⅓ columns (plus perhaps $10 for Bobritsky's illustrations, which expanded the piece to two columns but were reruns from 4/24/26:28), the magazine paid about $50 for two columns of prose and $50 or $60 for a quarter-page drawing. (Verse illustrations, Angell hinted to Julian De Miskey, aimed to supplement artists' incomes.[7]) Journalism cost less than fiction or humor: "Profile" biographical pieces of three to five pages paid $150 in 1928,[8] substantially less than the $75 the famous Stephen Leacock earned for "The Repatriation of the Minstrel" (10/6/28:28),[9] two columns of deadpan prose recommending the formation of a charity to send home "all the mournful minstrels" of whatever color or origin who long to return to old Virginny, Old Erin, Annie Laurie, or wherever. In January of 1929, Ross raised Howard Brubaker from $50 to $60 for the weekly half-page gossip and anecdote department "Of All Things," which he had written since 1:1; this 20 percent increase came with a note about the organization's "loosening a little bit financially,"[10] and given the small world in which *New Yorker* contributors traveled, Brubaker's raise may have prompted Levy to seek one too. The repetitions in "The Flying Dutchman" could have justified payment of $64 at $1 per line, but White's refusal to pay for narrative verse at the same rate as more challenging poetic forms demonstrates that comic poetry received as much editorial thought as prose and art.

Only star poets received substantially higher rates than Levy, however. In 1929–30, William Butler Yeats earned $1.50 a line, Dorothy Parker, $2, E. B. White, $1.25, James Thurber $0.80.[11] Elinor Wylie earned $85 in October of 1928 for a pair of poems, "Hughie at the Inn" and "Mary at the Fair" (11/10/28:35), at a newly increased line rate of $1.25.[12] Quite out of Wylie's league, Levy's poem would have cost $96 at $1.50 per line; in this context, payment of $50 for "The Flying Dutchman" shows a genuine commitment to verse publication in general and to Levy in particular. White's offer of a face-saving sum, with hints that future work might prove too expensive to acquire, underlines that she knew what she was doing.

She had done so for nearly five years already. When Katharine Sergeant Angell joined the five-month-old *New Yorker* in the summer of 1925 (Davis 55), the
magazine was struggling to outlast its subscribers' out-of-town vacations. At
this point, verse had declined as a significant part of the *New Yorker's* editorial
mix, but not for lack of editorial interest. A letter from late in 1924 solicited
contributions for the first issue of the magazine by detailing contents other than
departments and art: "A large part of the magazine will consist of more or less
casual stuff, short, and in tone satirical, philosophical, ironic, sentimental, or
name it and take it. This includes verse."[13] And the magazine did begin with
verse prominent.

Early acquisitions drew on well-known humor writers, like Levy, from *Life,
Judge,* and *Vanity Fair.* Arthur Guiterman, famous since 1909 for his "Rhymed
Reviews" in *Life* and before that for his editorial verses in the *New York Times* on
Theodore Roosevelt and the Spanish American War (Terrie 166), inaugurated
the *New Yorker* with his verse series, "Lyrics from the Pekinese," which ran in the
first number and in fifteen issues thereafter. A satire on society verse as well as an
example of it, the series featured ten-line stanzas (two quatrains and a couplet)—
three per installment—critiquing high society from the point of view of a lap-
dog. (A picture of the dog, pen in hand, clarified the title—a play on Elizabeth
Barrett Browning's *Sonnets from the Portuguese,* which Guiterman had edited in
1910 for publisher Paul Elder.) The series began by ridiculing the new cross-
word puzzle craze and theater critics in rhymes that avoided doggerel by irregular line-lengths and run-on lines, as in the beginning of a lyric on the New
Woman:

> Our ladies don't mean any harm,
>   But their swift innovations
> One cannot but view with alarm:
>   Their domestic relations
> Are shocking; their language,—oh hush!
>   They are bobbing their tresses!
>
>   (II, 2/21/25:21)

Guiterman contributed a dozen poems to volumes 1–5 outside this series,
though he and Ross evidently disagreed about a series on Manhattan statuary,
which Guiterman proposed in April 1926.[14] A founder of the Poetry Society of
America, whose members included George Santayana, Edwin Markham, and
Gertrude Atherton (Terrie 167), Guiterman brought more stature to the new

magazine than it conferred upon him. Nonetheless, according to his biographer in *American Humorists,* Guiterman had published more than 120 poems in the *New Yorker* when he died in 1943 (Terrie 168).

The second issue brought another series by a notable humorist, Baird Leonard's "Metropolitan Monotypes." A columnist for the *Morning Telegraph,* Leonard also wrote a long-running weekly satire of a society woman, "Mrs. Pep's Diary," for *Life.* Leonard's work remains unknown today and even her 1941 obituary in the *New York Times* failed to note her association with the *New Yorker* (1/24/41:17, col. 4), but her contemporaries ranked her among the best humorists of the day. In "The Newspaper Colyumists" for the September 1923 *Vanity Fair,* Gilbert Seldes proclaimed her superior to F. P. A., the dean of newspaper wits, because she mastered the pose of the *"faux naïf"* (46). She did not carry this pose over from her *Life* series into the *New Yorker,* however. Rather, she adopted the sharp eye of the sophisticate for the thirty-six "Metropolitan Monotypes" she published in the early *New Yorker,* along with two dozen other poems and sketches, and probably the book reviews signed "B. L.," as well.

"Metropolitan Monotypes," half-page free-verse characterizations of local types, debuted in the issue of February 28, 1925, in a prime spot in the front of the book, sharing a page with Morris Markey's "Story of Manhattankind" and facing a profile of Alice Roosevelt Longworth ("Princess Alice"). A rhetorical formula shapes the free verse. A pair of italicized lines begin the poem and frame it again at the end: "It takes all kinds / To make a town like ours." The phrase not only identifies the series theme but also establishes its ironic tone, setting New York City above the homogeneous small towns elsewhere and granting dubious distinction to the unstylishly eccentric. A second component of the formula introduces the "monotype" of each poem in the third and fourth lines, with the formulaic "There is, for instance, / The Woman Who Is Here on a Bat" (2/28/25:8). With this loose formula, thirty-six installments of "Metropolitan Monotypes" tweaked a range of individuals over the next five years:

> The Aesthete, who
>
> .   .   .   .
>
> [will] try to pick a fight with some poor soul whom he sees first
> About the artistic integrity of the pre-Raphaelites
>
> > (2/26/26:22);
>
> The Ritzy Radical, who
>
> .   .   .   .
>
> . . . has always sympathized with the Lucy Stoners,

But retains her husband's name simply to avoid getting two of every kind
of circular in the morning post.

(9/15/28:27)

And so on, criticizing one type after another through "The Undergraduate"
(1/12/29:20), when the series suspended publication, resuming a year later with
the more positive character of "The Welcome Guest," whose self-sufficiency,
good manners, and pleasant habits make her easy to satisfy and do not strain the
household, even though "She is seldom a relative" (1/25/30:20). Spud Johnson
underlined the importance of "Metropolitan Monotypes" as an exemplar of early
New Yorker humor when he made Ross its subject in the private 1926 parody issue.[15] There he captured the nub of the joke: a humor of character that contrasts
the poet's cleverness with the subject's failings. Thus Leonard's series inverts the
ostensible focus on the subject as well as substitutes the urban scene of the peer
society for the rustic settings typical of American character humor. As free verse
linked the character sketches to the literary avant-garde, so the *New Yorker* situ-
ated its verse humor far from doggerel poetry.

Indeed, Leonard's other *New Yorker* poetry looked inward, where the jaundiced view of character dominating "Metropolitan Monotypes" translated into
complaints from a comic Sufferer. Although this first-person pose of inferiority
divides the Little Man school from misogynous *New Yorker* prose, verse by
Leonard and others demonstrates that the Sufferer provided a voice for other
genres and genders too. Leonard's "Shop Talk," for example, vents her frustration
at having great ideas disappear before she can write them down (1/16/26:24).
And she rewrites William Ernest Henley's "Invictus" for a less-than-heroic
woman in the twenty-four "Lines in Neither the Manner Nor Spirit of Thomas
à Kempis":

> I never was a girl to shine
>   Beneath the bludgeonings of chance,
> And how I dwindle, peak and pine
>   In the fell clutch of circumstance!
> . . . .
> What centuries will bring to pass
>   Or level off or neatly hide
> Is splendid comfort for a lass
>   Who's contemplating suicide.

(7/30/27:13)

Baird's version of the Sufferer shows rhetoric triumphant over fact—an amusing reversal of life and art. Her "Lines on the Back of a Nurse's Chart," a lament in twenty-three singsong iambic tetrameter couplets, offers a metaphorical flip side to the nurse's commentary about her patient. The first ten couplets praise the nurse for tender ministrations, but her faults (and lines devoted to them) gradually outnumber her virtues. The final quatrain summarizes the score:

> Yes, Lady, when I'm down and out,
> For your sweet ministries I shout,
> But when I start in getting well,
> I meanly mumble, "Get the hell—!"
>
> (10/27/28:32)

Like the male victims of *New Yorker* personal narratives, Leonard's Sufferer proves her wit superior to life's travails.

By numbers alone, Guiterman and Leonard shaped the *New Yorker*'s earliest verse humor, whereas the more celebrated Dorothy Parker contributed relatively little. Despite her reputation as a founding *New Yorker* insider, Parker published just four items during the magazine's first year, two of them verse, "Cassandra Drops Into Verse" in (2/28/25:5) and "Rainy Night" seven months later (9/26/25:10). Parker's first *New Yorker* poem reverses conventional ideas about city and suburban life. In a monologue to her mate, Cassandra envisions the escape to suburbia as a return to Eden—which can only result in a second expulsion:

> But oh, my love, if we made the flight,
>   I see the end of our pastoral plan. . . .
> Why, you'd be staying in town each night,
>   And I'd elope with the furnace man.
>
> (2/28/25:5)

Parker ridicules the expectations of suburban bliss by veering between doggerel rhymes and romantic language—"dwell," "'mid brooks and bowers," "soul communion." In fact, the *New Yorker* ran doggerel only for parodic purpose. (Of course, Guiterman's Pekinese lyrics exemplified *dog*gerel at its extreme.) Among other efforts at local color verse that followed over the next two weeks, silly rhymes like Arthur H. Folwell's "Ten Little Subway Guards" (3/7/25:12) and Levy's "Song of the Traffic Rules" (3/14/25:18) ridiculed subjects that readers would recognize. (Levy's fondness for the traffic theme might also explain why White wouldn't pay more for his 1929 version.)

The greater importance of prose humor and art perhaps allowed the *New Yorker* to choose verse more carefully, because early issues contained just two or three poems each. An exception was 1:6, which had seven, including the unsigned "A Waitress in Childs's" (3/28/25:31). This bit of local color in free verse features a Little Man who finds himself nonplused by the sexuality of a socially inferior woman. The lyric deflects attention from the subject to the speaker. His criticisms of her indelicacy ("Like a brewery truck on wire wheels") and grooming (she has a "Faint flush that seems a bit too steady and hair that glows a bit too golden") reveal his own inadequacies of presence. She dominates him physically, and the poem describes a tableau that comically contrasts their inverted social and physical positions:

> And you bend above me suddenly to catch my order,
> And just as suddenly I cease smiling and analyzing you,
> And start, and stammer an order I do not want, and mop my face when
>   your blue eyes have left me.
>
> (3/28/25:31)

Her physicality unmans him; from this irony he makes a poem instead of a relationship. The poem contrasts his superior sensibility with his inadequate sexuality, her social irrelevance with her sexual potency, and the uncoupled pair with each other. The poet plays with social hierarchies by challenging *and* accepting them. The sophistication of the humor thus comes less from an assertion of social rank than from an appeal to educated readers to appreciate its wit.

This kind of ironic lyric grew more frequent that fall, but in the meanwhile the verse highlight of the number was E. E.'s "The New England Poets See a Ghost," parodies of Robert Frost, Amy Lowell, and others—including Edwin Arlington Robinson:

> There isn't any doubt about the matter
> At all. If you believe in transmigration,
> Well then, so much the worse for you. But listen.
>
> (3/28/25:16)

With quality such as this, readers may not have cared that verse disappeared for the six weeks between June 13 and August 1, or that it fell to just one or two poems per issue until September 19, 1925. Subsequent years proved that these fluctuations followed a seasonal pattern: poetry dipped every summer to about half the usual number in mid-June (about issue number seventeen) and returned to normal in September or October (about issue number thirty). The chief reason for this pattern in the first few years was probably the summer decline in newsstand sales, which corresponded to a fall in advertising pages. The squeeze in revenues and editorial space that prompted Hanrahan's suggestion for the first summer—to hold the best material for fall, when readers and advertisers returned—made continued sense for verse as a costly and difficult acquisition.

Seasonal patterns emerged later, of course; in the first summer lack of poetry appeared a deficiency, and the editors acted accordingly. A call for contributions dated August 1, 1925, specified, "The New Yorker wants the best short light and serious verse that it can get."[16] A follow-up letter a month later, after Katharine Angell rose from part-time manuscript reader to full-time editor of fiction and poetry, promised that "Clever couplets and quatrains on current affairs will be given particular attention."[17] Submissions increased enough by mid-October (1:35) to publish at least six poems each week through the first anniversary.

By the third anniversary the weekly rate rose to eight poems, half of them by women, and women signed all seven poems in the issue of July 23, 1927. Women had accounted for a small minority of the poets in volume 1. By my count they signed only 31 of its 199 poems, barely 15 percent, while twice that number (65) ran anonymously, probably because staff members wrote them. Volume 2 had twice as many poems, but women signed a similar proportion: just 58 of 390, though relatively fewer (96) went unsigned—an indicator that the *New Yorker* had won more respect from poets. The pattern began shifting in volume 3, as poems increased to an average of 8 per issue, and the magazine attracted contributions from such major poets as Elinor Wylie and Christopher Morley in addition to versifiers such as Patience Eden, Margaret Fishback, and Margaretta Manning. Women signed slightly more than half the poems in volume 3 (205 of 388), and nearly 60 percent thereafter: 226 of 383 in volume 4 (57.5 percent), and 201 of 344 in volume 5 (58.4 percent). Though the total number of poems declined somewhat in volume 5, the genre had grown important enough that only three poems ran anonymously. Acquisitions now encompassed serious poetry as well as light verse, finally fulfilling the goal of the first summer's call for poetry. Unexpectedly, however, verse had become the comic genre specifically articulating women's themes and views.

These effects accumulated over time. Few women responded immediately to the call for verse in the summer of 1925. Baird Leonard alone contributed twenty of the thirty-one poems by women in volume 1, seventeen of them after the summer call, which gave increasing importance to "Metropolitan Mono-types" in the second half of volume 1. On the other hand, the call resulted in po-ems from a number of new contributors, demonstrating the *New Yorker's* recovery from near-death even before the publication of Ellin Mackay's cabaret piece in late November. A month earlier, Margaret Widdemer published her first poem, "Catty Portraits" (10/24/25:37), whose speaker ridicules her critical self along with other female felons; soon after came "In Praise of Predecessors" (12/5/25:23), verses of gratitude to the women who taught her lover his superior "manner and voice and touch." While character poems took on social conven-tions, such as Helen Rockwell's sneer at the disingenuous drinker's claim "I *hate* the taste but I like the effect" ("To a Constant Nymph" 12/26/25:29), local color verse cast these characters in familiar scenes. Dorothy Homans blended ridicule and affection for the eccentric in "The Last Command—Battery Park" (9/19/25:26), in which a retired seaman with "a sense of duty and a conscience" watches the ships go out and imagines himself still at sea. The imminent dem-olition of Madison Square Garden evoked a sentimental mood in Homans's sec-ond poem, "The End: 1890–1925," accompanied by a gloomy half-page illustration by Paul Bissell:

> Harlequin is dead, Diana gone,
> Only the doves, the poets, and the moon
> Are left to mourn.
>
> (8/8/25:11)

These early poems did not coalesce, however, into patterns of humor akin to those developing in graphic and prose forms. Part of the difficulty lay in the ab-sence of repeated contributions from individual poets other than Leonard and Guiterman. Despite her promising start, for example, Homans published only two other items to the early *New Yorker,* a contribution to "Why I Like New York" in the important issue of September 12, 1925 (18) and, nearly three years later, a casual illustrated by Julian De Miskey, "Wanted—An Arcadia (An Open Letter to the Mayor)" (5/19/28:62–63).

Volume 1's poetry received a boost when Dorothy Parker published "Rainy Night," a serious lyric that helped extend the boundaries of *New Yorker* verse hu-mor to encompass the conceit. As John Donne insisted "Death, thou shalt die," so Parker shunts guilt feelings off to hell. A woman so tearful that she claims "I am sister to the rain" admonishes the "Ghosts of all my lovely sins" to leave her pillow, cross the River Styx, and return to Hades, where they can prepare to greet another of their number. Meanwhile she will remain on earth to sin anew and "tell of their siring":

> Ghosts of dear temptations, heed;
>   I am frail, be you forgiving.
> See you not that I have need
>   To be living with the living?
> .   .   .   .
> Roam with young Persephone,
>   Plucking poppies for your slumber
> With the morrow, there shall be
>   One more wraith among your number.

Parker's verses joined Guiterman's in rewarding the educated reader, but otherwise they stood apart from the run of poetry in volume 1, which brought mainly society and light verse from a new group of male contributors.

The writers in this male tradition specialized in often-elevated doggerel on local topics, especially the physical world, with a heavy dose of sarcasm or ennui. Though he disappeared after tossing off five poems and two casuals in eight weeks, A. van Steenbergh expressed an irreverence that also marked *New Yorker* prose and graphic humor. "In the Subway" mixes the pleasures of familiarity with the discomfort of embarrassment along with internal and end rhymes:

> I grasped her.
> I clasped her.
> .   .   .   .   .   .
> We reeled together out of the train,
> And I hope I never see her again.

(10/24/25:27)

More elaborately, the string of Hudibrastic couplets of "In Washington Square" cheerily violate the sentimentality of the poem's opening by turning it ironic:

> The finish to a perfect day
> It is, to watch the children play;
> .   .   .   .
> To see them in their dirty dress
> So innocent of gentleness.
> O children, . . .
> .   .   .   .

How scarce perceptible a void
'T'would leave were you to be destroyed.

(9/12/25:35)

Such contempt for children asserted the peer society's focus on its own generation, which (rather like the baby boomers two generations later) celebrated its
own youth and resisted settling into parenthood. In this spirit, van Steenbergh
abandoned the superior posture of the adult for the inferiority of youth a few
weeks afterwards in "The Predicament," when a spokesman for "we men of
greatest charm" worries that their moment of physical perfection has passed:

Conceive our diaphragm
    Incomparably placed,
Our well developed ham,
    Our nicely rounded waist.

.   .   .   .

Conceive our fiery eye
    As less disposed to burn
And you'll not wonder why
    It fills us with concern.

.   .   .   .

In fact the point of view
    Increasingly we hold
There's nothing we can do
    To keep from growing old.

(10/31/25:31)

At a point when prose fiction and graphic humor struggled uncertainly to find
appropriate subjects and viewpoints, the most successful comic verse directed
attention inward, away from the city and society, toward writers' private
thoughts.

Poems in this period balance intellectual or poetic expertise with social or
verbal irreverence. Fred G. Steelman, who also had a limited run in the fall of
1925 as a poet on local subjects, hit this balance just right in "The New
Yawker," which merged the stereotypes of the Brooklyn booster and the unim-
pressable tourist in rigid six-line stanzas of mock-oral dialect rhymes:

Take, for instance, Piccadilly,
Old Fifth Av'noo knocks it silly;
As for bridges, you just wanna make me laugh;
London Bridge ain't got a look in

With the Williamsburg or Brooklyn—
Wait a minute, I ain't even told you half.

(10/24/25:31)

In addition to the main comic incongruity of dialect prose, which contrasts writing and speech, mock-oral verse adds another: the shape of the stanza and sound of the rhymes. The mix of high and low elements often appeared as a mixture of fancy language and doggerel rhymes, as in Steelman's "The New York Girl," in the next issue (10/31/25:35). Stuck at the end of the book department on the last page of text, this quatrain rewards the reader who finds it; *diaphanous* rhymes with "laugh on us" and *extensive* with *expensive* to suggest the paradox of expensive yet scanty garments. Though too expensive to serve primarily as filler, verse epigrams such as this transformed leftover space into comic capital.

Two editorial programs already capitalized on epigrams, the newsbreak and "Why I Like New York," and by mid-fall Angell and Ross added verse components too. Epigrammatic humor offers a performance of wit; verse epigrams thus joined other early "Talk" and prose pieces in self-conscious displays of cleverness. E. B. White's contribution to the genre differed precisely because his modest subjects and language kept the focus on them, rather than deflecting attention to himself. Not yet a staff member, White had already made the mailing list for the contributors' advisory letter, and led this verse genre with his five-part "Definitions" series in October and November. Here he teased out paradoxes, defining "Critic" as one who "scarcely saw the play at all / For watching his reaction to it" (10/17/25:8) and "Commuter" as "a man who shaves and takes a train / And then rides back to shave again" (10/24/25:33).[18] A derivative series on "The New York Girl" opened the topic to verse epigrams by many hands—a sort of "Why I Like New York" in rhyme. Inaugurated by Steelman the next week, the series lasted nine poems, but the absence of signatures suggests that staff wrote them (perhaps Fillmore Hyde, who followed Steelman, 11/7/25) in an effort to stimulate submissions; the series died nonetheless on January 9, 1926. An attempt to attract women poets to the series with a quatrain twitting "The New York Man" as "always cynical, though pleasant" (1/16/26:27) likewise failed to take off. On the other hand, definitions continued to attract versifiers, but White retained title to the "Definitions" headline, making it unavailable for other epigrams, which ran untitled.

Staff writers contributed much of the early verse, unsigned pieces in particular. Fillmore Hyde provided some thirty-two signed poems, though *New Yorker* history credits him primarily for writing "Talk" before E. B. White arrived. Hyde's verse belonged to the same burlesque spirit as his 1926–27 prose series "The Ritz Carltons." His early poems drew their fun from local people and places. "Doctor Straton," for example, criticizes the controversial fundamentalist preacher for overstepping his bounds ("Why doesn't he / Kindly let the keyhole / Of decent folk be?" 1/30/26:37),[19] and "A Room for Rent" versifies the negotiations between landlord and prospective tenant, ending comically in a stalemate (7/24/26:14). In contrast to these rhyming ditties, Hyde's later pieces kept pace with the growing sophistication of verse humor. Octosyllabic couplets (known as "society verse") elevate the prosaic subject of "Steam": "It makes the locomotive puff, / It certainly is useful stuff" (12/11/26:54). Hyde exploited that incongruity between matter and manner even more fully in "The Esquimau's Dream," the ballad of a quest for cultivated society doomed by a snowstorm (2/15/30:81).

Increased emphasis on verse in the fall of 1925 soon attracted other poets to the magazine. The avant-garde poet Maxwell Bodenheim (1892–1954) contributed five items (three in prose) to the *New Yorker* between January and July of 1926, including "Rhymes from a Coquette's Diary," which unmasked her beau's pretensions: a boy who'd "won a Ph.D. / just crammed with facts and learnings" finally revealed to her one night "More ordinary yearnings" (1/23/26:30). February brought long-desired success in an occasional verse series on local themes. A sign of the *New Yorker*'s triumph in surviving its first year, "If I Were King" began on the last number of the last page of volume 1 with unsigned rhymes inveighing against sidewalk vendors (2/13/26:45); ten months later, the series boasted twenty-five installments, twelve of them by new contributor Parke Cummings. The poems indulge fantasies of power. Doing away with arguments between idealists and realists (Cummings 4/24/26:20), vain women who flaunt their slender shapes (Angell 5/1/26:36), and a host of other social ills. Equally important, beginning in July "If I Were King" spawned a half-dozen verses on the related theme of "If I Were Queen," including two by Katharine Angell, who promised, in mock-Elizabethan style,

> I would estop the estimable
> Ladies who are only able
> To discourse on bulbs and seeds
> Or Garden Clubs or pests and weeds.

> (9/18/26:58)

New versifiers also brought ideas of their own for series, most notably "Down-Town Lyrics" by Burke Boyce, which extended to thirty-four installments between "Chanson des Rues" (8/14/26:15) and "The New Subway" (11/3/28:26). By that time, Boyce had begun his second series, "Pavement Portraits" with a verse on "The Chestnut Man" (12/17/27:34). Like cartoon and prose series, verse series identified appropriate themes and approaches, and thus invited new contributors to participate in the editorial give and take.

None of these new contributors brought more to the magazine than E. B. White. For all his fame as a prose stylist, White apparently aimed to be a poet. White debuted as a *New Yorker* poet with his October 1925 "Definitions" series but had begun publishing comic poetry three years before, when his sonnet praising the winner of the 1922 Kentucky Derby ran in the *Louisville Herald* May 14, 1922 (Hall 222), followed by poems the next year in F. P. A.'s "Conning Tower" column in the *New York World*. Verse accounted for half of White's published writing there and in the *New Yorker* before he joined the "Talk" staff late in 1926. He continued writing poetry throughout his career, and private manuscripts in his personal papers identify it as his genre of choice for intimate communications with his wife throughout their lives together. More publicly, in 1929 he won F. P. A.'s gold watch for "The Twentieth Century Gets Through," a poem in "The Conning Tower" (*World* 12/4/29:13). With sixty poems in volumes 1–5, White advanced the *New Yorker*'s comic verse as much as it shaped his own career.

"Lines in Anguish," one of his more overtly ambitious poems, lampooned Coleridge's "Dejection" ode (12/11/26:113), but much of White's verse wrought humor by putting trivial topics in rhyme. The very titles of some poems comically contrast high manner with low matter—for example, "Eastern Standard: The Time of My Life" (9/25/26:26)—and their verses follow suit. Each quatrain of "Hot, Carnivorous Retort to Health Food Menu," for example, reasserts the title's theme:

> And rather than pollute with fruit
> My simple, childlike maw
> I'd go, eftsoons, to pasture lots
> And eat cow raw!

(6/19/26:52)

A few years later, White managed a more complex comic trick in "To a Hot Water Bottle Named Jonathan," where each stanza alternates a interior monologue *cum* lament with a grandiose apostrophe to the title object:

> Small is the solace in being dead,
>   With never a love at my side;
> I think I had rather get well instead,
>   So Jonathan, do not slide!

(2/18/28:28)

Although White's posture of the comic Sufferer in these poems links his prose and verse humor, a more important component of his verse is the contrast between the physical and the cerebral. The elevated phrasings of these poems, as in "Clinic Joust" (3/5/27:30), comically transform physical topics into imaginative material. Like Parker, White brought comic point of view and technique to *New Yorker* verse, in contrast to the more familiar local color or character humor.

By 1928 White's poetry took a lyric turn that gave it more in common with the verse of the women poets than with the men's verse on local places and scenes. Although "Intimations at Fifty-Eighth Street" begins with the fountain at the Fifth Avenue Plaza, the poem's ambitions extend beyond the local scene. The poem, which provided the title for *The Lady Is Cold* (1929), imagines that spring air gives life to the environment—not only the fountain, air, and clouds, but also the human watching them:

> The lady is cold in the fountain,
>   The sitter is cold on the ledge,
>   . . . .
> The earth is but held in solution,
>   And March will release before long
> The lady in brazen ablution,
>   The trees and the fountain in song!

(2/11/28:23)

This verse humor comes not from the subject or versification but from its conceit: that spring revives city and country alike, and thus urban creatures (including the bronze figure in the fountain) should come to life as well. As White developed them, conceits made humor of otherwise sad themes, such as the ineffable love that his "Sonnet" compares to frost, which "Painted your portrait on my secret soul" (2/2/29:19).

The shift in focus from exterior to interior themes paved the way for publication of serious poetry as well as light verse. By January of 1929, for example, White's poems mourning his and Angell's decision to remain friends rather than have her divorce her husband began appearing in "The Conning Tower" (Elledge 156–59). The next month saw them in his *New Yorker* "Sonnet" as well. Over the next year White continued publishing such whimsical verses as "Poet: Or the Growth of a Lit'ry Figure" ("Before he reached the age of thirty / He sold his pipe and bought a QWERTY," 4/6/29:26) and "The Driving of the Rivet: A Ballad of the New Hotel Pierre at Fifth Avenue and Sixty-First Street" (illustrated by Julian De Miskey, 2/15/30:21). But he balanced these lengthy narrative poems with the coded rhymes of "For Serena, Who Owns a Pair of Snowshoes," the private humor of the newlywed (2/1/30:20). In addition`to its significance in his own life, however, White's poetry helped define the progression of *New Yorker* verse humor from the epigrammatic local rhymes of 1925 and the character humor of 1926, to the 1927 and '28 modernist contrasts between interior states and exterior realities, and the more serious expressions of 1928–30.

Other poets joined White in steering *New Yorker* verse humor in these directions. During the second year, between February of 1926 and 1927, before White or Thurber took on editorial responsibility, Angell and Mosher discovered in the slush pile of unsolicited manuscripts four new poets who quickly became prolific contributors. Together with Dorothy Parker, who contributed more actively in 1927, these four poets—Patience Eden, Margaretta Manning, Margaret Fishback, and Elspeth—published nearly 40 percent of all the poems by women in volumes 1–5, and nearly 20 percent of all verse in volumes 2–5.[20] And their poetry directed *New Yorker* verse humor toward the topics that interested them most: problems of love, work, and self-fulfillment.

The first new voice belonged to Martha Banning Thomas, writing as Patience Eden, whose run of seventy poems in the early magazine began in March 1926 with "Poet Reduced to the Cliché" (3/13/26:17). Its three stanzas present a comic Sufferer frustrated over the inability to find a compelling way to describe blonde hair; the poet, not identified as man or woman, resolves the problem by quitting. The next week, Eden addressed the high spirits of the peer society in "A Lady Bored," describing a woman whose purity in moments of dullness parallels her capacity for wickedness (3/20/26:18). Eden specialized in striking metaphors on women's concerns. She resolved the mystery of the nice girl's naïveté in "To Hold Up Its Stocking":

I've often wondered at her smile,
  Adhesive . . . Bleak . . . refined,
But now I know—*a nice girl wears*
  A garter on her mind!

                                        (5/22/26:22)

With equal wit, "Footnote on a Flapper" transforms resentment into metaphor, charging a dancer's fancy footwork with trampling her heart (6/5/26:58). A few poems on less conventionally gendered topics also kept the love theme going. "The Confessions of an Old Coupe" presents the fantasies of a "battle-scarred, doctor's Ford" for a "Lady-Lim[ousine]": he has planned an accident requiring the doctor to attend to her beautiful young owner, leading the humans to marry and put their cars in a single garage (8/7/26:12). Her "On Saying Goodbye to a Favorite Roadster," on the other hand, sentimentalizes her farewell to Hannibal to the point of self-parody (1/22/27:65). She took a harder stand on men than on cars, however, and the singsong couplets of "Toast to Your Smile" contrast iron-ically with the serious theme of unrequited love (12/10/27:25). In 1928 Angell welcomed Thomas's proposal for publishing free verse under a second pseudo-nym, Mary Shane,[21] but no such work appeared in the magazine by the end of volume 5. A few other poets published more verse than Eden, but her consistent appearance in the front of the book signaled the editors' high regard.

Five months after Eden's debut, the important August 1926 issue containing Alan Dunn's first drawing and White's "Hey Day Labor" also introduced the early *New Yorker*'s most prolific poet, Margaret Fishback, who published 115 po-ems and 26 casuals by the end of volume 5. Almost unknown today, though Nancy Walker mentions her briefly in *A Very Serious Thing* (5, 10–11), Fishback had enough of a contemporary following that E. P. Dutton collected her first four books of poetry in *One to A Customer* (1937), with three printings in three months. "The Fire Alarm" (8/7/26:34), Fishback's *New Yorker* debut, typifies her approach: she put familiar topics into rhymed stanza forms and elevated them to social or philosophical import. As a result, her poems often have feminist impli-cations even though the topic has ostensibly little to do with gender. In "The Fire Alarm," for instance, the siren reverses social hierarchies while the stanzas themselves revise verse formulas (the effect of turning two iambic pentameter quatrains into ten-foot couplets, though editors, not the poet, may have con-densed them to save space):

The man who works the siren. . . .

    . . . .

Must feel great satisfaction when he sees the costly clutter
Of high and mighty limousines parked humbly in the gutter.

(8/7/26:34)

With its blend of high and low subjects and social significance drawn from banal details, such iconoclasm marks much of Fishback's verse. Natural scenery mixes with gasoline prices in her "Guide for Motorists," a poem that the editors edited heavily—a sign that they admired the comic idea but not its expression (9/11/26:88).[22] The assumption that *New Yorker* readers drive cars extends to "A Manhattan Cocktail"—in this case not a fashionable drink but a mixture of sublime skyline with the "reek of Armenian cookery" (10/30/26:47). The 1941 *Current Biography* claims that contemporary readers enjoyed Fishback's take on fashions, men, and other topics of perennial interest to women (282), but her early *New Yorker* verse addressed urban topics of wider interest—such as the mock-heroics of a dime store bulb in "A Short History of a City-Bred Hyacinth":

A simple bulb she was before
　　She started on her bright career,
Despatched by Woolworth's ten-cent store
　　To bring her day of beauty here.

(2/12/27:67)

Fishback's virtuoso performances of French stanza forms also belong to this line of humor, most hilariously in triolets on such banal subjects as "A Warm Bench" (3/26/27:89) and "The Pigeon Surplus" (9/17/27:58). The eight-line, two-rhyme triolet, evidently one of her favorite forms, totaled 13 of her 111 poems in volumes 1–5; these often featured long titles that start the poem off with amusing excess and create a funny contrast with the short stanza. She establishes the comic context of "Triolet on the Appearance of Spring in Twenty-Seventh Street" even before the first line, and the verses and title acquire ironic significance for any reader who has mistakenly drawn a deep appreciative breath on a busy New York street:

The smell of Spring gets in the air;
I look for crocuses but there
Are only ash cans, row on row—

(4/2/27:40)

Primarily back-of-the-book material, Fishback's poetry rewarded readers who persevered to the end.

In contrast to Fishback's pleasure in elevating the mundane, Margaretta Manning typically reduced elegant scenes through pithy language. Manning and Fishback thus wrought in verse the key incongruity between image and text that *New Yorker* artists were working out in the idea drawing during this same period. Beginning with "Metropolitans" in July 1926, Manning signed the earliest of her thirty-four poems with initials only, probably because she often had two pieces running in the same issue. This dialogue imagines Eve rejecting Adam's plans for a bucolic life in Eden with a dismissive "There's not a single night club there! / I don't know what I'd do!" (7/24/26:18), and later poems likewise featured a tart woman's view. Her first signed poem was an untitled lyric by a jilted woman speaking to her erstwhile lover, a painter. The first two stanzas contrast her virtues with her successor's failings, but she chastises him more for his taste than his inconstancy. How could he abandon her, a refined woman whose cerebral virtues he appreciated in declaring her "'As exquisite as Dresden ware / As rare as Cloisonné,'" for an inferior "girl" defined by physical tastes?—"a girl who eats / French pastry—and who shows it" (12/25/26:21). The rhymes of the last stanza answer the question by comparing attractions of money and art:

> I fail to see
> What picture she
> Would sensibly enhance
> Though I'm not sure
> They've no allure
> Who can finance romance
>
> (12/25/26:21)

These poems raise women's issues in the broader context of the lyric, which focuses on subject, speaker, and point of view. In the context of prose jokes about male Sufferers, however, Manning's verse underscores the *New Yorker*'s interest in its women readers, to whom the editors offered a humor of wit.

While poems about courtship took for granted a major concern of the twenty-something members of the peer society, Manning's verse humor also took up the more general concerns of that generation. "Upon Re-Reading 'The Mauve Decade'" contrasts relatively staid Georgian morés with the dissipations of the peer society (1/29/27:57). And "Marriage á la Mode" fantasizes about a ceremony "quite romantic, / . . . in a translantic / Plane" (10/13/28:119). References to "moods al Pirandello" and "Justine" ("Dressing Table" 9/8/28:21) and jokes in French ("Petite Sauvage" 11/17/28:33) emphasize the poet's membership in the sophisticated elite that *New Yorker* humor imagined as its readership. The women's issues in Manning's verse arose within a general humor of verbal play, which displayed her erudition and flattered readers'. Considering this match among contributor, magazine, and audience, the disappearance of Manning's verse after 4:39 makes little sense, yet neither the magazine's archives nor biographical sources explain it.

The fourth new poet of the summer of 1926 expressed a complex combination of misandry and man-hunger, creating an arch persona that contrasted comically with the feminine elegance of her literary signature. She signed herself simply *Elspeth* (for Elspeth MacDuffie O'Halloran), and her thirty-five poems in the early magazine offered herself as a comic survivor of the love wars. "Insured," for instance, takes a potshot at marriage by equating the wedding ring with symbols of superstition:

> I haven't smashed a mirror
> > Since I was four.
> I keep a horseshoe
> > Over my door.
> . . . .
> Here is my rabbit's-foot,
> > Close at my hand,
> And on my finger
> > I wear a gold band.
>
> > (3/5/27:93)

This poem does not attack men or marriage but laughs at the power of marriage as a social convention among people too sophisticated for other expressions of conformity. "Lenten Thoughts," by contrast, suggests she hardly met a man she didn't like—and that the season's deprivations have sharpened her appetite:

> For better, for sicker,
> I'd marry a vicar
> . . . .
> I'm seldom obdurate
> To any young curate.
>
> > (3/12/27:79)

Elspeth's display of sexual interest, like her acceptance of marriage, makes herself the butt of the humor, moderating her social critique.

In this context, Elspeth's particular contribution to *New Yorker* verse humor in the twenties lay in bringing sarcasm and wit to conventionally sentimental topics. A sardonic pair of poems in the issue of December 17, 1927, marks the end of a romance. In "Last Word," a woman sarcastically agrees with her beau's proposal that "We are but friends with friendship as a tie," but adds another layer of irony by using Shakespearean sonnet form. Thus the classic English love poem reasserts the speaker's desire for love while conceding its end, and the final couplet flashes anger:

> You have forgotten if you ever knew
> How to say simply what is merely true.
>
> (12/17/27:34)

Two pages later, the exuberant verses of the second poem, "To a Young Man Who Is Afraid He Is Polygamous" transform familiar excuses and the clichés of inconstancy into charges of inadequacy. "Are you fancy-free and wild?" she asks, "*Would to God you were, my child!*" (36).

Elspeth's humor relies on ambivalence, mediating desire and dismissal, and the tone unifies the broad range of her topics and treatments. A modernist contrast between outer talk and inner thoughts animates "A School Marm Greets Her Class" (10/22/27:91), for example. The poem converts the old saw about how the apple doesn't fall far from the tree into a joke about propriety, as Elspeth juxtaposes the teacher's cheery corrections to her students with snide thoughts of their parents—and contrasts her solitary role with their family groups. Her two poems on death published ten pages apart in the front of a single issue in spring 1928 express ambivalence through reversal. "How could you bear to leave it," the speaker asks in "To a Young Suicide," before reversing the premise of suicide and the ideal of afterlife: "The sight and sound of things, / So good—so good! . . . What could you hope to find more fair / In death?" (3/24/28:20). The dirge rhythms of "Lady in Mourning" augment the irony by which a poem about mourning ends with "love and laughter":

> And down by the stream
> Forever after,
> She walks in a dream
> Of love and laughter.
>
> (3/24/28:30)

These examples emphasize not only that early in its fourth year the *New Yorker* began publishing serious poetry as well as light verse but also that its verse and prose shared a sense of humor defined not by situations or characters, as in nineteenth-century American comic writing, but by speakers' expressions of irony and paradox—that is, of modern consciousness.

E. B. White admired Elspeth's poetry enough to recommend her to Angell as an occasional book reviewer,[23] but Elspeth did not pass muster in this role, despite similarities between her poetry's and Dorothy Parker's. For her part, Parker found inspiration or motivation in the *New Yorker's* increased commitment to poetry. As the number of poems grew to eight and twelve per issue toward the end of volume 2, Parker began actively contributing hers—even before contracting with Ross for book reviews and other regular submissions. Thus volume 3 opened with nine poems by Parker in the first ten weeks, beginning with her six-part series "Songs Not Encumbered by Reticence" (2/19/27:28). Nine months later, after signing her contract for book reviews and other work, she followed up with three installments of "Songs for the Nearest Harmonica" (11/12/27:28). Parker's presence reduced the gap between serious poetry and comic verse, identifying her ironic poetry as humor, as well as steered *New Yorker* verse toward an audience of women.

Poems in Parker's "Songs Not Encumbered" series vent intense expressions of women's suffering, as the title implies. In the first song, "The Enemy," a jilted lover taunts, "Let another cross his way— / She's the one will do the weeping!" before conceding, as an afterthought to herself and us, that her predecessor presents a similar threat to *her* (2/19/27:28). More damning, "Fulfillment" proclaims womanhood the ironic consummation of a girl's development: "For this my mother wrapped me warm," she sneers, comparing the security of childhood with the risks of adult life, "That I might . . . / . . . hear a whistle, and drop my wits, / And break my heart to clattering bits" (2/26/27:24). Though she takes pleasure in reaching the state described in "Healed," in which the former lover looks unremarkable or unattractive, Parker's verses laugh at the innocence by which Tennyson claimed in part 27 of *In Memoriam,* "'Tis better to have loved and lost / Than never to have loved at all" (3/19/27:28). As she points out in "Afternoon," for example, Memory and Peace cannot compare with men as companions by the fire or in bed (3/12/27:28). And "The Second Oldest Story" points out that women at least suffer from genuine injuries to the heart, while men collapse from the pain of a simple pinprick (3/26/27:26). The mixture of invective with wit in "Songs Not Encumbered" characterizes the speakers as strong of spirit even in the face of romantic doom.

Parker continued this sardonic self-mockery throughout her *New Yorker* verse of the early period. "Swan Song" suggests that old age offers so many insults and so few opportunities that a person may as well jump in the river (4/2/27:23). Her presumably cheery "Thought for a Sunshiny Morning" does not offer a seasonal rhyme about spring but rather the gloomy thought that she can compensate for stepping on a worm: "'Aha, my little dear,' I say, / 'Your clan will pay me back one day'" (4/9/27:31). Unrequited love dominates three of the five "Songs for the Nearest Harmonica" in the issue of January 7, 1928. Bitter past experience does not prevent her from seeking love again in the ironically titled "Wisdom"; "Surprise" results when she leaves the man before he can leave her; and "Post-Graduate" points out that Sorrow teaches the same lessons as Hope and Love. The other two poems broaden her themes, however. She criticizes the double standard in "Penelope"; imagining herself as Ulyssees's wife, she recounts her trials and concludes, "They will call him brave." In "For R. C. B." probably referring to her good friend Robert (Charles) Benchley, she points out that "Many people care" about life's problems but insists, "we don't, do we?" (1/27/28:21). Parker sustained this mordant view of relations between the sexes through her last poems from this period, four dramatic monologues collected as "The Beloved Ladies," with Salome, Ninon de l'Enclos, Guinevere, and Lesbia as ironic speakers ignorant of their unhappy ends (12/14/29:27), but her poetry had its greatest impact on the direction of *New Yorker* verse humor in volume 3 (1927–28). She published only four poems in volumes 4 and 5 (1928–30), when her attention turned to book reviews and prose.

As other poets reiterated Parker's favorite themes, *New Yorker* verse humor increasingly emphasized women's views on women's lives. For example, Parker and others spoofed the courtship advice already dominating mass market magazines and advertisements in the twenties. Parker's variation on this theme, "To a Favorite Granddaughter," the third of her "Songs Not Encumbered by Reticence," ticks off the undesirable types on a comprehensive list of men—"Never love a simple lad; / Guard against the wise," and so on—before concluding that biology is destiny for both sexes: "Should you heed my words, my dear, / You're no blood of mine!" (3/5/27:26). Ruth McClellan's brief "Advice to Girls," which appeared six months later, envisions a similar cycle of hope, passion, and disappointment:

> If a maid would marry
> Let her ask not when or why

But say her prayers at bedtime
And lunch off humble pie.

(9/3/27:35)

Not limited to a couple of poems in 1927, this theme resurfaced variously
throughout the twenties. The thirty-two lines of Fishback's "Short Inspirational
Talk for Young Women" make their point by overkill and reversal: following
conventional advice about how to "sympathize with every ill" and "listen, wide-
eyed to each myth / He elects to tempt you with" comes an admission of the te-
dium involved. Speaking directly to her readers, Fishback concedes,

> . . . you know you'd be
> Much more advantageously
> Occupied, in sewing seams,
> Reading books, or dreaming dreams.

(2/23/29:93)

Such comic laments stand apart from the tradition of comic suffering because
the speakers' resignation transforms complaints about men into declarations
about women. In this context, women's complaints about men do not so much
offset the critique of women by Little Men, most egregiously in Thurber's Monroe series, running contemporaneously in the pages of the *New Yorker*. Rather the
women's complaints refocus the men's as just half of the peer society's ongoing
war between the sexes.

Few poems specifically advocate feminist issues, but their speakers imply
feminist values through speakers' assertion of equality with men. The octosyllabic couplets of Fishback's "Be Yourself, Lothario" come close to a manifesto,
rejecting monogamy in favor of what the twenties termed "companionate marriage," or free love:

> Don't rob me of the sweet despair
> Of fearing you have slipped away
>
> .   .   .   .
> But it would be so much more fun
> For both of us, if neither one
> Of us would ever have to be
> Restricted by monogamy.

(12/10/27:107)

Though it provides background rather than subject, the agenda of the New Woman also figures in Fishback's poem about apartment hunting, "The September Trek" (9/24/27:99). "Sentimental Lines to a Young Man Who Favors Pink Wallpaper, While I Personally Lean to the Blue" represents contemporary arguments about gender roles with the obliqueness of euphemism: the verses contrast the couple's modern attitudes—their preference for companionate over conventional marriage and their reversal of gendered color preferences—with their traditional sexual politics. After the speaker declares herself willing to accept his preferences, she suggests that they compromise, and initiates the process with a kiss:

> Dear, I love you. Don't you see
> That's the biggest thing to me?
> Let me kiss you darling, do?—
> Now do you prefer the blue?
>
> (10/29/27:97)

As the last line implies, her apparently spontaneous, gracious gesture of conciliation is just old-fashioned feminine sexual coercion. With a wink at her audience, Fishback invites us to enjoy a joke at the expense of both the speaker and her lover.

While men expressed frustration and resentment over women, the women displayed exasperation at themselves as much as at men. Indeed, women's attacks on courtship and the opposite sex have less vehemence than the men's because they focus on their own feelings rather than their lovers' behavior. Among the eleven poems by Chicagoan Dorothy Dow in 1927 and 1928, "Undefeated" makes fun of the speaker's inability to learn from bitter experience:

> . . . all too soon
>   I shall believe
> Again that love
>   Can never grieve.
>
> (12/10/27:62)

This theme, also developed by Dorothy Parker, points to the chief difference between the women's humor and the men's: an ambivalent "can't live with 'em, can't live without 'em." The attitude keeps the humor lively despite its consistency. Frustrated but not bitter, the women speakers of the *New Yorker*'s love-weary humor are not harridans retaliating against men. They're combatants in the sex wars, ready to continue the fight. Or, like Margaret Fishback in "Inventory" (3/16/29:105), they aim to solve the mystery of why women who can count their blessings still want men. But they count their blessings quietly, often in the inferior postures invoked by *New Yorker* prose humorists.

Elinor Wylie addressed that ambivalence head-on in her posthumously published "Anti-Feminist Song for My Sister" (2/16/29:22). Privately composed for Wylie's sister Nancy Hoyt, the poem underscores the importance of interpersonal contacts among authors, editors, and friends in the *New Yorker*'s acquisition process: a *New Yorker* contributor herself, Hoyt brought the poem's attention to Katharine Angell, knowing Angell's editorial preferences.[24] The poem creates comic ambivalence with a singsong rhythm that undercuts the argument that men aren't good for much, but at least they pay the bills:

> Each of us, born every minute
>   Still wears fern-seed in her shoes
> Love of man, we always win it;
>   Peace of mind, we always lose.
>
> Drawing cheques is still our pastime;
>   Paying checks our private hell;
> .   .   .   .
> Yes, we've had our fairly thick times
>   Paying for the cakes and beers;
> It's more fun to be the victims
>   Than the bloody conquerors.

The poem views the battle of the sexes as a stalemate. The allusion to P. T. Barnum's sucker "born every minute" characterizes "love of man" as a bad bargain for women. But the last stanza points out, with its references to the feminist agenda of economic independence, that the alternative is worse, by noting that self-sufficiency comes at a very high price—insolvency—while dependence compensates with social, financial, and physical pleasures. For the professional women of the peer society who read the *New Yorker,* this argument invited laughter at their own pretensions.

Although Wylie's poem addresses the same insincere feminist that Baird Leonard ridiculed in "Metropolitan Monotypes" as the "Ritzy Radical" (9/15/28:27), Wylie also reinforces the stereotype of female spendthrifts. By contrast, Hoyt's earlier "These Vanities" left extravagance ungendered. After listing expensive items appealing to women and men, Hoyt concludes:

So since we have not the money
To get necessities,
Dearest, let's do without them
And just buy luxuries.

(3/12/27:34)

Wylie took up gender roles and expectations more specifically in a pair of poems, "Hughie at the Inn" and "Mary at the Fair" (11/10/28:25), her last *New Yorker* work before her death on December 16, 1928. The two poems consist of dramatic monologues urging the title characters to abandon romantic dreams for realistic actions. Hughie receives his lesson from his "tapster," Mary from a gypsy. Countering the myth of the romantic hero, the tapster points out that heroism ends in death, both literally and figuratively: "A stab in the back; a serpent in the breast; / And worst that murders best." He characterizes the hero as a victim of aspirations to glory and "cruel chance gone mad," but certainly not of deceit at a personal level, before he offers worldly advice: "Be provident, and pray for cowardice / And the loaded pair of dice." Mary's advisor, by contrast, urges her to see that troubles as well as wishes can die, and the gypsy reassures her that her lover's deceits need not foreclose her future. Though her lover gave her a worthless ring, and she has lost her virginity, her heart, and any chance to marry him, Mary still has good looks and opportunities to trade on them. The gypsy says,

> Mary, you have made your bed
> Out of briars and withies
> No one lies where you are laid
> For a score of prithees;
>
> . . . .
>
> Mary, wait another year;
> Turn your mattress over;
> You shall see it change, my dear,
> To a field of clover;
>
> . . . . . .
>
> You shall find a lover.

Individually, these poems ridicule romance as a lower-class fantasy, and so reinforce the superiority of the *New Yorker* reader, male or female. But as a pair, the poems also mock the double and differing standards for men and women, and the bromides offered them as solace.

Poems by James Thurber, Margaret Fishback, and Patience Eden in the issue of April 9, 1927 (3:8) enacted these gendered differences. Thurber's "Portrait of a Lady (From Infancy to Murder Trial)" depicts Evangeline Wordworth's transformation from cute "'ittle Vannums" to Mrs. Oscar L. Guckler, then "Slain Man's Wife / Accused Mate" and finally "The Guckler Woman" (4/9/27:99). The free-verse list of names implies that women change from cute to dangerous as predictably as they go from childhood to maturity. Turn the page, however, and this misogynous fantasy becomes the object of ridicule in Margaret Fishback's "Triolet on the Deplorable Lack of Reliability of a Certain Season" (4/9/27:100). The prolix, ironic title hints at Fishback's comic strategy: she discusses variability in the rigid context of an eight-line form that fixes the sequence of lines and rhymes. Manner and matter clash to ridicule the clichés of female fickleness and spring's inconstancy:

> Do not trust the wiles of Spring
> She's a flirt and gay deceiver,
> Eager just to have her fling,
>
> .   .   .   .
> Here today, then on the wing,
> Leaving her insidious fever.

Humor here comes from reversal, imagining spring as a woman who leaves men in a state of unrequited passion and flattering men who might take misogynist clichés at face value. By contrast, a poem earlier in the same issue, Patience Eden's "Rueful Rhymes: On the Bus" (4/9/27:36) provides a classic example of verse that is light in topic and tone. Each of her three stanzas imagines an interior monologue for one urban female bus-riding type: "a grubby young person," "an old lady in furs" and "a lovely, lacquered and slender being." Eden's poem features local color characters, not the female self-hatred often attributed to Dorothy Parker's Algonquin quips (T. Grant, "Feminist" 158), though not characteristic of her *New Yorker* verse. Indeed, the examples of Eden, Fishback, and others illustrate that women's comic verse ranged from high wit and satire to lyrics and light verse. And whereas Thurber imagined women as murderers, the women often gave no thought to men.

Fishback takes on the New York woman as a particular type: independent, ironic, witty, and proud. Her sonnet "Brass Tacks" contrasts two lovers, one offering sincere expressions of love, the other a bum's rush, and the closing couplet sums up the speaker's preference for the truth that she calls "more than plain":

"And so I chose the two-room flat / What with this and what with that" (3/19/27: 87). As in this example, the typical speaker in Fishback's verse is an unmarried woman who has chosen to remain single rather than marry badly. Thus the humor of her "Lines on Helping a Poor Blind Man" has nothing to do helping a disabled person avoid Manhattan traffic but rather with blind love:

> . . . some day he is sure to find
> That love is not a thing designed
> For golden anniversaries
> And grim responsibilities
> .   .   .   .
> Oh, may my equilibrium
> Hold out until the time has come
> When he can see that there is more
> In weddings than he bargains for.

(12/8/28:124)

Even when Fishback's speaker has not chosen solitude, she retains her fortitude. The triple pun on *sap* in "The Sap Also Rises" spoofs Hemingway's novel, sustains a theme about spring, and ridicules her former lovesickness. Her spirits, like the flowers, have begun the blooming process, and a complete cure will follow soon (4/13/29:90). Fishback's wit characterizes her speakers as smart and effective women, fully equal to their romantic challenges.

Not all comic poetry on women's woes came from women writers. The ex-mayor of Saratoga, New York, Clarence Knapp had contributed a woman's monologue in prose, "She Presents the Flock," to 1:1, and soon specialized in prose pieces in horse-racing vernacular featuring women characters and verses in a genre known as sob ballads: rhymes of drunken remorse. Little-known today, Knapp was a *New Yorker* insider. He knew Ross well enough to complain that Frank Sullivan hadn't returned home to vote for his 1927 reelection and to seek Ross's sympathy that "you and the crowd" had lost their source for press passes and motorcycle escorts.[25] But his fourteen sob ballads between December 31, 1927, and January 11, 1930, not his connections, put Knapp on Ross's list of preferred writers at a flat rate of forty dollars per poem.[26] He anticipated the series somewhat with his "Old-Fashioned Dances for an Old-Fashioned Girl," subtitled "From THE NEW YORKER's own up-to-date Sob Songs," shortly before the second anniversary (1/8/27:73). Unlike Dorothy Parker's "Songs," Knapp's ballads follow a fixed formula. Two sixteen-line stanzas narrate a story whose turning point comes in the eight-line refrain, recited first by the protagonist as the plot advances, and again to reiterate that event. The first recitation creates mock-melodrama, while the second parodies vaudeville and burlesque musicals. Like John Held's mock-archaic woodcuts and Julian De Miskey's "Memories" series, Knapp's sob ballads joked about present social values by invoking past forms.

"Old Fashioned Dances" introduced this basic comic contrast of the series by describing how the Charleston and fox-trot stimulated a young man's passions and inspired his sweet partner's yearnings for the staid steps of old. When the "Sob Ballad" series began in earnest nearly a year later under a drawing by H. O. Hofman of a fashionable couple drinking champagne, the contrast expanded across generations, as a girl at a fashionable New Year's Eve party swears to abandon all sophistication in favor of writing letters to mom and dad (12/31/27:28). Under a mock-sentimental frieze of weeping men and women by Peter Arno (later reduced to two weeping molls and a foamy stein of beer), the next installment conflated the modern cabaret with the barroom of vaudeville westerns, as a traveling man stops a drunken youth from stealing a kiss from a showgirl in response to her protest, "Ain't there at least one gen'lman here . . . ?" (6/30/28:15). The hypersentimentality continued through 1928 with melodramas of long-lost love reclaimed ("Your Letter Today Made Me Cry" 7/14/28:28; "A Story I'm Going To Tell You" 9/1/28:19) and of violence and victimization ("He Was Good to His Wife and His Kiddies" 1/5/29:19). Early in 1929, however, contemporary themes replaced the archaic ones, making the contrast more subtle as readers recognized the form. "Naughty Mens Comed Into My Playroom," for example, gives the refrain to a little girl who hid in her toybox while police raided the speakeasy in her parents' apartment:

> "Naughty mens comed into my playroom
>   They breaked up my doll house and things.
> My picture-books too are all teared up
>   And they stepped on my dolly that sings.
> When I cried to them please not to do it,
>   They said, 'She's jus' tryin' to hide
> Some booze.' An' *so* hard they pushed me
>   I falled down and hurted my side."
>
>   (2/9/29:20)

Later ballads lampooned advertisements for self-help books ("The Ring To You

I Am Returning" 4/20/29:22), clerks who declared themselves exiled Russian noblemen ("I Spoke as No Gentleman Should" 7/13/29:25), pastoral yearnings of Greenwich Village sophisticates ("Tonight of a Village I'm Dreaming" 6/15/29:22), the romantic dreams of working-class moviegoers (10/5/29:30), and the Great Crash of 1929. Although suicides in the news prompted White to reject a sob ballad on that theme, Knapp took up her suggestion for a ballad about a woman who decides to "stick by her Sugar Daddy . . . even though he could not longer give her the sable coat, etc."[27] The protagonist of "I'm Not Weeping Because He Is Ruined" scorns her aunt's suggestion, "If your lover has lost all his riches, / Soon another you're certain to find" and insists,

> "I'm not weeping because he is ruined,
>   No—his lost wealth I'm not thinking of.
> .   .   .   .
> Why, my jewels, my sables, and autos
>   Are all his for the asking to sell."

(1/11/30:21)

By the end of volume 5, *New Yorker* verse declared its sophistication by parodying sentimentality, not by feigning ennui.

The war between the sexes dominated *New Yorker* humor in all genres and media in part because of its centrality in the lives of the target readership, the peer society of unmarried men and women in their twenties. These privileged members of the New York scene ranked between the bohemian Villagers and high society, giving their mating rituals the aura of local color. Verse on local topics specifically reached out to the peer society's favorite activities, as when each of the nine stanzas of Christopher Morley's "Epigrams in a Cellar" celebrates a different wine by name and vintage, mostly in iambic pentameter quatrains (12/31/27:65). Current events also provided topics, as in Baird Leonard's "Lines Inspired by Certain Misdirected Legislation," which notes the superiority of pornography to the run of junk mail: "obscene matter now and then / Might better suit the best of men," she observed, if only the post office did not prohibit it (1/8/27:25). Verse represented a particularly viable genre for women's humor because lyric poetry thrives on obliqueness, wit, and irony—typical strategies of American women humorists, as Nancy Walker, Zita Dresner, and Emily Toth have shown. Epistolary fiction and dramatic monologues—prose genres that also attracted a large share of women writers—also value these strategies. Men's versions of the war between the sexes dominated graphic and narrative humor, and thus pushed women's genres to the margins of *New Yorker* history, but Katharine Angell, who acquired both fiction and verse, made certain that women readers also had gender jokes to laugh at.

Layout formulas identified three main treatments for verse. Featured verse appeared in the front of the book, often on the mixed contents page following "Talk," adjacent to the featured casual, or alongside the half-page "Of All Things." Secondarily, verse provided serendipity in space following "Profiles" or theater reviews in the front of the book. Lesser poems ran among monologues and other back-of-the-book casuals in the single or double columns between the Fifth Avenue and book departments—features directed to women readers, though the more numerous male writers of prose and poetry appeared in this spot more frequently than their female counterparts. Finally, verse joined prose casuals in filling out pages in the back of the book. By avoiding jump pages that filled the back of the book with editorial leftovers, Irvin's design for the magazine invited the reader to search out gems in the last pages of the magazine. Indeed, the absence of a table of contents *required* readers to browse the back pages to find the book, sports, and shopping departments (an experiment in listing pages of service departments lasted just a few weeks, presumably because it discouraged browsing among the back pages, where each six-column spread had four columns of ads).

As early as the summer of 1925 verse mattered enough that editors solicited poetry, cultivated poets, and featured their work alongside cartoons in the front of the book. Most of Patience Eden's sixty-seven poems between 2:4 (3/13/27) and 5:51 (2/8/30) received such important treatment. "Musings on the Moon" ran under a ⅔-page drawing by Peter Arno (2/19/27:29) and "A Studio Tea" next to a cartoon by Helen Hokinson and a story by Gilbert Seldes (2/19/27:29). Even when verses ran in the back of the book, they fit neatly enough into the *New Yorker*'s serendipitous makeup that they seemed a pleasant discovery, not afterthoughts buried amid the ads. Consider, for example, Eden's "All Is Not Lost!," which sought some comic sunshine in the deepening economic gloom a few weeks after the stock market crashed:

> The strong die young,
> The weak survive,
> The wicked prosper gaily:
> The pure are hung
> (or hanged!) alive,
> And cutthroats flourish daily.

. . . .
My dreams have died,
Hope lags behind,
Yet—mark this up as thrilling—
My dentist tried,
But could not find
A tooth that needed filling!

(1/4/30:78)

Eden's doggerel has an ironic cheerfulness quite different from Fishback's humor, which relies on verse form rather than rhyme. But Eden uses her jaundiced view of men to assert herself as independent in spirit, even at the cost of economic deprivation, as in "To an Uninteresting Man Who Was Once a Suitor":

And somewhere you are being you
    More thoroughly than ever,
Thinking large thoughts the way you do
    And looking far from clever.
. . . .
And here am I quite gay and nice
    Must shape a simple ballad,
And wonder if I'll earn the price
    Of dinner . . . with a salad!

(3/2/29:24)

Eden's humor skewers the opposite sex with less vengeance but perhaps more wit—some of it self-directed—than the humor of victimized Little Men. The difference lies in the starting point for the verse. Misogynous men's humor, such as Thurber's more pointed prose and verse, lambastes intolerable conventional relationships while the women's humor satirizes the conventions themselves.

The prose emphasis of humor scholarship and magazine histories reflects a cultural and economic bias toward the book, especially prose fiction, marginalizing verse and magazines in the process. So it is not surprising that individual anthologies reprinting work by Thurber, Benchley, Perelman, and Dorothy Parker credit them with defining *New Yorker* humor to a degree disproportionate with the frequency of their writing in the actual pages of the early magazine, while overlooking the 141 poems by Margaret Fishback, many of them in extremely difficult verse forms, or the sixty by E. B. White. In addition to drawing attention away from other contributors, the prose bias has misrepresented the *New Yorker* as—to quote from Thomas Grant—"an all-male preserve" characterized by "undisguised misogyny" (T. Grant, "Feminist" 157, 167 n. 1). This is simply false. The preserve, such as it was, included women journalists such as Lois Long and Gretta Palmer in the fact departments as well as women freelance artists, such as Barbara Shermund (more than 200 cartoons in the first five years—nearly one a week—plus department headers and spot drawings), Ilonka Karasz (30 of the early covers—more than 10 percent), Nancy Fay, Nora Benjamin, and Sue Williams in addition to the better-known Helen Hokinson, Mary Petty, and Alice Harvey. Among the poets in volumes 1–5, women included not only such well-known figures as Dorothy Parker (26 poems) and Baird Leonard (54 poems) but also dozens of lesser names, most frequently Ruth Lambert Jones (28 poems), Marne (25), Frances M. Frost (24), Genova Charlot (24), Frances Park (16), Dearing Ward (14), Helene Mullins (13), Dorothy Dow (11), Ruth Brown (11), Olive Ward (10), artist Peggy Bacon (9), Grace Hazard Conkling (8), Jacqueline Embry (8), Sylvia Fuller (7), Isabel McLennan McMeekin (7), Sara Henderson Hay (6), Persis Greely Anderson (6), and Irma Brandeis (6). However we account for their invisibility, and however historians choose to judge their work, it certainly won favor from the editors choosing and paying for it. And verse humor, more than any other genre in the early *New Yorker,* was a women's realm.

Its subjects and viewpoints reflect the magazine's considerable female audience, whom advertisers and editors quite deliberately targeted, and it relies on rhetorical forms suited to typical ironies of American women's humor, especially as described in Nancy Walker's historical study, *A Very Serious Thing* (1988), and fifty years earlier by Bruére and Beard in *Laughing Their Way* (1934). To be sure, female versifiers took on such universal themes as traffic and cultural decline—in "A Child's Primer of Transit" by Margaret Fishback (1/22/27:43), for example, and "Villanelle Upon an Ancient Theme" by Irma Brandeis, with its refrain, "Nothing is what it used to be" (12/18/26:81). But the women poets also enlisted in the war between the sexes, where they took accurate, if not deadly, aim at men. These works recast *New Yorker* humor of comic male Sufferers as just half of the story—whose other half exists as prose and verse complaints by women. Not surprisingly, in this context, the readers who wrote letters complimenting the magazine on its poetry included a Brooklyn woman who asked in 1929, "Isn't there going to be a book of New Yorker poetry?" Her reasons had less to do with preferences in humor than with the *New Yorker*'s editorial formula. "It seems to me the poetry I find in your pages accidentally is more vital than any

I've seen elsewhere," she went on, "and as a collection, even including the flip-
pant ones, more evenly good than most anthologies."[28] Although the magazine
did not publish such a collection, it seems not at all coincidental that *New Yorker*
poets made up a substantial portion of the section on versifiers in Bruère and
Beard's anthology a few years later, as well as most of the writers in its section on
the skit.

The roster of poets underlines the degree to which writers and artists outside
the Algonquin circle defined *New Yorker* humor in the magazine's early years. Indeed, the small dimensions of verse—literally and metaphorically—enabled the
magazine to diversify its contributors, items, and tone at relatively little cost in
space. Hence Angell and her staff encouraged comic experimentation by artists
and other part-time writers, many of them untraceable today, while others, including the distinguished editorial cartoonist Rollin Kirby and painter Peggy
Bacon, have reputations in other media. As the magazine branched out into serious poetry, the light touch of comic poets became all the more important. In
this context, it is particularly significant that early in 1929 when Angell had to
turn down Newman Levy's offer to take on a regular weekly department, she
countered with a request: "Can't you start another verse series?"[29]

The *New Yorker*'s acceptance of serious poetry late in 1928 paralleled its publication of satiric but not comic drawings by Reginald Marsh. The smaller size
and lesser presence of verse made it, rather than art, a logical genre for serious
literary experiments. "Unknown Soldier" by V. Valerie Gates offers a good
example. The poem begins with a witty idea: reversing the typical graveyard
scene in which mourners think about the dead, the poem imagines a dead man's
thoughts about his visitors. But tone and content keep the poem serious. The
speaker imagines the unknown soldier "crying for silence and rest" and contrasts
tourists' "uninformed reverence" with the genuine sorrow of mourners who
grieve for him as their own:

> little gray mothers, timid and old,
> Come softly at dusk. "My bravest one!
> Such a grand, grand grave for my little son!"

$\hfill$ (10/13/28:104)

The poem's reversals keep it from veering off toward sentimentality, on the one
hand, or ridicule, on the other. But if the overall tone remains solemn, as the
subject requires, its witty conception justifies its place in the *New Yorker*. Such

serious poetry began with regular contributors, including E. B. White and Eden, but it also responded to market factors. The late twenties were boon times for novelists, but poets' opportunities shrank as monthly magazines disappeared. The *Century* went from monthly to quarterly publication in 1929, but the *Dial*, *Munsey's*, and *McClure's* all died even before the stock market crashed. Increased submissions of poetry coincided with the magazine's first economic success, giving editors more choice and more opportunity to refine ideas submitted by artists and writers.

Poets lacked the clout, however, to exact concessions parallel to those won by artists, who in 1931 began submitting roughs rather than finished drawings for initial review by the art committee. When English teacher Harold Willard Gleason objected to Angell's second request for revisions to a poem about Broadway, "Capacity House" (5/12/28:97), he conceded, "The offerings of a freelance rest on the knees of the editors," but insisted that the poem run anonymously.[30] A letter of praise from a reader confirmed Angell's position that the desired changes did not injure the poem, but she passed it on to him tactfully,[31] and this first poem soon led to seventeen more. The publication of Gleason's work shows how carefully the staff culled the slush pile of unsolicited manuscripts for new contributors, even though the rejection rate remained high. Poems were declined for inappropriate sentimentality (in a poem about dogs, for example), or for being "too mild"[32]—or for addressing such taboo topics as "the problems of the writing trade, which we do not find such interesting material for publication."[33] More established writers might quarrel with the editors, as when William Rose Benét responded to a rejection in the summer of 1930 with an outraged "You're cuckoo!" But his claims to high art—"That's the best poem I've written in six months and I knew more about poetry before I was born than you or anyone else will know when you die"—missed Ross's reason for returning it: "We like your stuff, God knows, but this verse, damn it, is obscure."[34]

At a time when modernist experiments in literature and art widened the divide between high and popular culture, and mass media such as film and radio began shrinking it, early *New Yorker* humor offered a middle way—comic writing and art that invited educated minds to relax and play. Obscurity had no place, but neither did vernacular virtues. As a result, mock-oral genres typically criticized rather than valorized the uneducated. Yet the magazine's politics on race and gender leaned more than a little toward the left. Liberal attitudes toward sex coexisted with conservative literary values, which led to high standards in editing and an expectation that readers would appreciate elegant verse forms and literary allusions (Marion Sturges-Jones joked about the utopian futility of "A Room of One's Own" 12/8/30:50). Yet so much intellectual superiority paraded through the magazine through comic postures of inferiority: lyric poems from jilted women, personal narratives by beleaguered Sufferers. Comic art expressed similar tensions in the ironic relations between image and text. Indeed, in creating humor from ironic contradictions, the *New Yorker* fulfilled Ross's idea for a sophisticated urban humor. As editors and contributors negotiated the magazine's contents and policies, the *New Yorker* pulled back from a social ideal of sophistication based on the nineteenth-century industrial economy and expressed in the snobbish early issues of 1925. In its place came an intellectual ideal of sophistication based on the twentieth-century information economy. The peer society of college graduates who moved from across the United States to New York City (or felt an affinity to those who did) signaled the rise of a young, educated, iconoclastic audience for American humor, which the *New Yorker* defined as an ironic point of view for celebrating—and resisting—modern life.

Appendix

A New Yorker *Calendar*

Vol.:No.	*Date*	*Notable Contents and Relevant Events*
1:1	2/21/25	First issue appears 2/17 or 2/18, 5-6 weeks late
1:2	2/28/25	Dorothy Parker's first verse, "Cassandra Drops Into Verse" (5), and prose, "A Certain Lady" (15–16)
1:3	3/7/25	A. H. F.'s "Ten Little Subway Guards" (12)
1:4	3/14/25	"Talk" format settled; first newsbreak; Levy's "Song of the Traffic Rules" (18)
1:5	3/21/25	
1:6	3/28/25	Frank Sullivan's first casual, "Ten, Twenty, ThirT" (11–12); number contains seven poems; Hanley's "The Last Ku Kluxer" (20)
1:7	4/4/25	
1:8	4/11/25	Charles Baskerville wrote and illustrated "When Nights Are Bold" (signed "Top Hat"); first "Sky-Line" column of architectural criticism; John Held's first woodcut, "The Rum-runner's Sister-in-Law" (5)
1:9	4/18/25	"A Step Forward" (21), first E. B. White contribution; Howard Brubaker signed "Of All Things"; first I. Klein cartoon; "Jim Announcing" by H. L. B. (20)
1:10	4/25/25	Frueh's first Mayor Hylan drawing (5)
1:11	5/2/25	Corey Ford's first "Fugitive Art" piece, "Bearding the Leyen-decker" (20); last "New York, Etc." column (23–24)
1:12	5/9/25	Meeting of Fleischmann, Ross, Hanrahan, and Truax on Friday, 5/8/25, ends with decision to kill the magazine; rescinded Monday, 5/11/25 (Kinney 112); first Sports column (25)
1:13	5/16/25	last issue for newsstand sale on Tuesdays; "In Our Midst" folded into "Talk"; Ford's "The Tie That Blinds" (29)
1:14	5/23/25	First issue for Friday newsstand sale, 5/22; "Talk" now signed

"The New Yorkers"; Knapp's "Straw Hat Salesman" (20)

1:15	5/30/25	Held's "Shot-Gun Wedding" (5)
1:16	6/6/25	
1:17	6/13/25	Ingersoll hired by Ross as reporter 6/13/25; Johan Bull's first sports illustrations
1:18	6/20/25	Arno's first drawing (6); T. Shane takes over Movies department 6/23/25
1:19	6/27/25	Frueh's first "Mayor Hylan's People's Concerts" (1)
1:20	7/4/25	Hokinson's first drawing (1); last Marsh "Talk" spread
1:21	7/11/25	full page cartoon inside front cover; focus on Scopes trial; Baskerville's last nightlife review as Top Hat (20)
1:22	7/18/25	full-page cartoon inside front cover; final local color "Talk" spread (1st series); Hans Stengel's first "Sermon on Sin" (5)
1:23	7/25/25	Katharine Angell arrives?
1:24	8/1/25	Contributors' letter asks for verse; Lois Long's first "When Nights Are Bold," signed "Lipstick" (20); Ralph Barton's first "Graphic Section" (5)
1:25	8/8/25	"The Making of a Magazine" series begins 20 installments running through 1:46 (1/2/26)
1:26	8/15/25	First "Notes and Comment" in "Talk"; first "Why I Like New York" column; Johan Bull begins illustrating "Talk"; first "Current Press" by Prenez Garde (pseud. for Markey?)
1:27	8/22/25	
1:28	8/29/25	Contributors asked for "clever couplets," 9/2?/25; Hokinson's "'Why Don't You Come Out for the Week End?'" (12–13), first in a series of captioned cartoon narratives depicting urban gauntlets
1:29	9/5/25	Morris Markey's first "In the News" department
1:30	9/12/25	Editorial, circulation, and advertising push begins; first "Paris Letter" by Janet Flanner; Lipstick's column changed to "Tables for Two"
1:31	9/19/25	Last run for "In Our Midst"; Stengel's first "Our Sermons on Sin" (8)
1:32	9/26/25	Parker's "Rainy Night" (10)
1:33	10/3/25	Lois Long's first "Fifth Avenue" shopping column
1:34	10/10/25	
1:35	10/17/25	EBW's first "Definitions" ("Critic" 8)
1:36	10/24/25	Fred G. Steelman's "The New Yawker" (31); Joseph Fulling Fishman's "Future of the Films" (32–33)
1:37[A]	10/31/25	De Miskey's opera cover; Carl Rose's first drawing, "'Taxi sir?'" (14); Steelman's "The New York Girl" (35), first of a series; Irvin's "A Quiet Evening with a Book" (16–17)
1:37[B]	11/7/25	"The Liquor Market" becomes a formal "Talk" section; Irvin,

		"Social Errors: The Woman Who Cut Her Husband's Bootlegger" (14)
1:38	11/14/25	Held's "Johnny and Frankie Were Lovers" (5)
1:39	11/21/25	B. L.'s "At the Matinee" (27)
1:40	11/28/25	Ellin Mackay's "Why We Go to Cabarets"
1:41	12/5/25	
1:42	12/12/25	

[1:43 number skipped to compensate for error at 1:37]

1:44	12/19/25	Robert Benchley's first casual, "Up the Dark Stairs" (7–8), ill. Johan Bull; Gilbert Seldes's "Complaint" (14)
1:45	12/26/25	First "Reporter at Large," by Morris Markey; EBW's "Child's Play" (17)
1:46	1/2/26	"Talk" layouts resume, with spread by De Miskey
1:47	1/9/26	
1:48	1/16/26	Baird Leonard's "Shop Talk" (24)
1:49	1/23/26	"Goings On" moves in front of "Talk"; Frank Sullivan's "How I Became A Subway Excavator" (13–14); Maxwell Bodenheim's "Rhymes from a Coquette's Diary" (30)
1:50	1/30/26	GWG's first "Theatre" reviews; revised header illustration for "Talk"
1:51	2/6/26	Bobritsky's minstrel & flamenco cover; Covarrubias returns from *Vanity Fair* for weekly theater caricatures (25)
1:52	2/13/26	Parker's "Dialogue at Three in the Morning" (13); first "If I Were King—" (45)
2:1	2/20/26	First anniversary issue
2:2	2/27/26	Joseph Fulling Fishman's "Millions in Prizes" (13–14)
2:3	3/6/26	John Chapin Mosher's "The Man with a Box" (18)
2:4	3/13/26	Patience Eden's first poem, "Poet Reduced to the Cliché" (17).
2:5	3/20/26	Charles G. Shaw's "Two Rooms, Bath And Kitchenette," ill. Hokinson (15–16)
2:6	3/27/26	
2:7	4/3/26	
2:8	4/10/26	
2:9	4/17/26	Marc Conelly's "The Traveler"; Arno's first Whoops! sisters drawing (30)
2:10	4/24/26	
2:11	5/1/26	Fillmore Hyde's "The English Author Who Consented To Be Interviewed" (15–16)
2:12	5/8/26	Bobritsky's baseball cover; EBW's "Always" (31)
2:13	5/15/26	Katherine Sproehnle's "Worry? Nonsense!" (30).
2:14	5/22/26	
2:15	5/29/26	Julian De Miskey takes over "Talk" illustrations; Corey Ford

		begins "The Bleakest Job: The New Yorker Offers a New Symposium," ill. Al Frueh (20)
2:16	6/5/26	Zelda Popkin's first appearance, "East Side Night Life" (68–69); Hokinson's captioned narrative cartoon "Do You Need a Passport? Try to Get One" (26–27)
2:17		
2:18	6/19/26	Harvey's "'Say, lady, I'm so tired . . . '" (21)
2:19	6/26/26	
2:20	7/3/26	First Aladjalov drawing, a "Tables for Two" header; last movie reviews by Shane; "Grandmother" Fillmore Hyde's "Prehistoric New York As I Knew It" (13–14)
2:21	7/10/26	First film reviews by Claxton (also taking over "Goings On") previously handled by Pemberton; first "If I Were Queen" (unsigned, 44)
2:22	7/17/26	
2:23	7/24/26	Sproehnle's first "Passionate Letters to Public Utilities" (21); M. M.'s "Metropolitans" (18)
2:24	7/31/26	Bobritsky's proletarian cover; first Aladjalov "Talk" spread, "At the Stadium Concert"; Claxton's "Let's Picnic" (17); Shermund's "'What is that, a boy or a girl?'" (14)
2:25	8/7/26	First Alan Dunn cartoon (21); EBW's "Hey Day Labor" (21); first Margaret Fishback verse, "The Fire Alarm" (34)
2:26	8/14/26	Hyde's Ritz-Carlton series begins (13–14); Kober's first piece, "If Others Adopt the Idea" (50); Burke Boyce's first "Downtown Lyrics: Chanson des Rues" (15)
2:27	8/21/26	
2:28	8/28/26	
2:29	9/4/26	
2:30	9/11/26	Boardman Robinson replaces Reginald Marsh as film caricaturist
2:31	9/18/26	KSA's first "If I Were Queen" (58)
2:32	9/25/26	
2:33	10/2/26	EBW's first (partial) "Notes and Comment," beginning, "The only thing . . . to the echo"; record number of poems: 22
2:34	10/9/26	
2:35	10/16/26	
2:36	10/23/26	
2:37	10/30/26	Zelda Popkin's first "Reflections of Silent New Yorkers" (38–39)
2:38	11/6/26	White's "The Little Man" (22–23); privately published parody issue in honor of HWR's birthday also carries this date (NYer Box 2)

2:39	11/13/26	
2:40	11/20/26	
2:41	11/27/26	"New Books" passed from Touchstone to Alceste (Ernest Boyd)[1]
2:42	12/4/26	Hecht's "The Caliph Complex" (30–31); Marsh's "'Miranda, I thought you'd be interested in this'" (35)
2:43	12/11/26	Kober's "The First-Nighter" (101–3); EBW's "Lines in Anguish" (113)
2:44	12/18/26	Irma Brandeis's "Villanelle Upon an Ancient Theme" (81)
2:45	12/25/26	Sullivan's "Amy, The Central Park Cow" (15–16)
2:46	1/1/27	Irvin's "Surprise of the Social Season: Oil Is Struck Under the Mills Hotel" (12–13)
2:47	1/8/27	Leonard Baird's "Lines Inspired by Certain Misdirected Legislation" (25)
2:48	1/15/27	EBW's "Marble-Top" (21); Kober's "Stage Directors" (49–51)
2:49	1/22/27	Nancy Hoyt's "Circumstances Alter Cases" (21); Margaret Fishback's "A Child's Primer of Transit" (43)
2:50	1/29/27	Frueh begins regular theater caricatures (34)
2:51	2/5/27	
2:52	2/12/27	
3:1	2/19/27	Sullivan's "Tiller Traditions" (22–23); Parker's first "Songs Not Encumbered By Reticence" (28)
3:2	2/26/27	Thurber's debut, "Villanelle of Horatio Street, Manhattan" (74)
3:3	3/5/27	Hired in Feb., Thurber joins staff as managing editor; Phillip Wylie leaves staff during March; Thurber's "An American Romance" (63–64); Parker's third "Songs Not Encumbered by Reticence: To a Favorite Granddaughter" (26); Elspeth MacDuffie's "Insured" (93).
3:4	3/12/27	Russel Crouse's first "They Were New Yorkers" (22–23)
3:5	3/19/27	
3:6	3/26/27	
3:7	4/2/27	Fishback's "Triolet on the Appearance of Spring in Twenty-Seventh Street" (40)
3:8	4/9/27	EBW's Sterling Finny house ad campaign opens; Thurber's "Portrait of a Lady [From Infancy to Murder Trial]" (99), Fishback's "Triolet on the Deplorable Lack of Reliability of a Certain Season" (100); Patience Eden's "Rueful Rhymes: On the Bus" (36)
3:9	4/16/27	
3:10	4/23/27	
3:11	4/30/27	

3:12	5/7/27	Thurber's "More Authors Cover the Snyder Trial" (69)
3:13	5/14/27	
3:14	5/21/27	EBW's "Things That Bother Me" (19)
3:15	5/28/27	
3:16	6/4/27	
3:17	6/11/27	Soglow's pantomime of "man dreaming about restaurant" (18–19)
3:18	6/18/27	last installment of FH's "Ritz Carlton" series
3:19	6/25/27	Hecht's "The Female Bridge Menace" (19–0)
3:20	7/2/27	last installment of EBW's Sterling Finny series; Frueh, "The Men's Club Keeps Abreast of Science" (16)
3:21	7/9/27	Charles G. Shaw's first "Through The Magnifying Glass" (25–26), ill. Ernest Hamlin Baker; Leonard's "Rebuttal" (20)
3:22	7/16/27	
3:23	7/23/27	Robert Benchley begins "The Press in Review" as Guy Fawkes; Kober's "She's In The 'Mo'om Pitcher Game'" (26); first issue in which women signed all poems
3:24	7/30/27	Josie Turner's "Elsie Dinsmore's Weekend," first in Dinsmore series (23–24); Baird Leonard's "Lines in Neither the Manner Nor Spirit of Thomas a Kempis" (13)
3:25	8/6/27	Thurber's "My Trip Abroad" (25–26)
3:26	8/13/27	EBW's "Tombs Are Best" (14–15)
3:27	8/20/27	
3:28	8/27/27	
3:29	9/3/27	
3:30	9/10/27	
3:31	9/17/27	
3:32	9/24/27	McNerney's "'She passin', boy?'" (34)
3:33	10/1/27	Rea's first cover; DP's first book column as Constant Reader; new "Coming Events" department
3:34	10/8/27	Hokinson's "So You're Going to 59th Street!" (28–29), first in a new series of captioned narratives on urban gauntlets; Parker's "Arrangement in Black and White" (22–24)
3:35	10/15/27	
3:36	10/22/27	Mary Petty's first drawing (70); Soglow's pantomime narrative on Target practice" (26–27)
3:37	10/29/27	Parker's department renamed "Reading and Writing"; Heywood Broun begins series, "A Doctor a Day" (19–20)
3:38	11/5/27	EBW's "Now That I'm Organized" (19–20); Marsh's "Death Ave" (10–11)
3:39	11/12/27	Parker's "Songs for the Nearest Harmonica" (28)
3:40	11/19/27	
3:41	11/26/27	

3:42	12/3/27	
3:43	12/10/27	Donald Ogden Stewart's first casual, "The President's Son" (24–25)
3:44	12/17/27	Boyce's first "Pavement Portraits: The Chestnut Man" (34)
3:45	12/24/27	Benchley's first "Wayward Press" column as Guy Fawkes; EBW's "Thoughts: While Skating 240 Laps at the Ice Club" (15–16)
3:46	12/31/27	Knapp's first "Our Own Sob Ballads: I'm Going to Start in Writing Letters" (28); Christopher Morley's "Epigrams in a Cellar" (65)
3:47	1/7/28	
3:48	1/14/28	
3:49	1/21/28	
3:50	1/28/28	
3:51	2/4/28	Kober's "A First Night" (17–19); EBW's "He" (19)
3:52	2/11/28	EBW's "Intimations at Fifty-Eighth Street" (23); Thurber's "Cross-Country Gamut" (40–42)
3:53	2/18/28	Hokinson's "Companionate Marriage" (22)
4:1	2/25/28	Stewart's "Introducing Anastasia" (19–20); Kober's "The Pick-Up" (36); Gibbs's "On Working That Line into the Conversation" (60–61)
4:2	3/3/28	
4:3	3/10/28	I. Klein's "The Connoisseur and the . . . / . . . Fried Eggs" (30–31)
4:4	3/17/28	
4:5	3/24/28	
4:6	3/31/28	Farbstein's first news chart, "Spring Championships" (28); ad for the Philadelphia Evening Bulletin
4:7	4/7/48	Shaw's first "I Knew the Town" (67)
4:8	4/14/28	Morris Markey, writing as "Asper," takes over "More Books" from N. H.[2]
4:9	4/21/28	
4:10		
4:11	5/5/28	John O'Hara's first casual, "The Alumnae Bulletin" (101); Stewart's "How It Feels to Be an Actor" (23–24)
4:12	5/12/28	EBW's "Treasures Upon Earth" (22)
4:13	5/19/28	Shermund's "You're a very intelligent woman, my dear" (30–31)
4:14	5/26/28	
4:15	6/2/28	Stewart's "How We Introduced the Budget System into Our Home" 4:15 (23–24)
4:16	6/9/28:	Gibbs's "Long Distance" (19)
4:17	6/16/28	

4:18	6/23/28	Kober's "The Art Lover" (44–47)
4:19	6/30/28	
4:20	7/7/28	EBW's "The Care and Feeding of Begonias; or, The Manly Art" (23)
4:21	7/14/28	
4:22	7/21/28	Shermund's "'I don't think he's abnormal—he's just versatile'" (12)
4:23	7/28/28	
4:24	8/4/28	EBW's "Open Letter: To the Department of Correction" (21–22)
4:25	8/11/28	
4:26	8/18/28	Alice Frankforter's first casual, "Portrait of a Lady Bathing" (51–52)
4:27	8/25/28	
4:28	9/1/28	
4:29	9/8/28	
4:30	9/15/28	O'Hara's first Delphian Society monologue, "A Safe And Sane Fourth" (79–82)
4:31	9/22/28	Claxton's last "Current Cinema" column; Frueh's "Yom Kippur" (26)
4:32	9/29/28	Mosher's first "Current Cinema" column (77–78)
4:33	10/6/28	Stephen Leacock's "The Repatriation of the Minstrel" (28)
4:34	10/13/28	"I think the last 2 numbers Oct. 13 and 6 were nearly the best you've done—" Janet Flanner to KSA, 10/24/[28][3]
4:35	10/20/28	Gibbs's "What Examining Desks Has Taught Me" (96–97)
4:36	10/27/28	Ralph Barton's caricature of astrologist Evangeline Adams (29); Leonard's "Lines on the Back of a Nurse's Chart" (32)
4:37	11/1/28	
4:38	11/8/28	Elinor Wylie's "Hughie at the Inn" and "Mary at the Fair" (35)
4:39	11/17/29	EBW's parodies of newspaper features (22–23)
4:40	11/24/28	F. P. A.'s "I Never Knew the Town" (48)
4:41	12/1/28	Lebrun layout, "Broker's Office" (33–34)
4:42	12/8/28	Carl Rose & EBW's "It's broccoli, dear" (27); Djuna Barnes's text and illustrations for "The Woman Who Goes Abroad to Forget" (28–29); Arno's cover of Asian houseman
4:43	12/15/28	Gibbs, "The Extraordinary Case of Mr. Absalom" (28–30)
4:44	12/22/28	Gibbs's "The Man and the Myth" (18–19)
4:45	12/29/28	Thurber's "Tea at Mrs. Armsby's" (15), first in the Monroe series
4:46	1/5/29	Thurber's first "Our Own Modern English Usage" (22–23); Soglow's "[M-A-M-M-Y]" pantomime narrative (23)
4:47	1/12/29	EBW's "Philip Wedge" (15–16)

4:48	1/19/29	
4:49	1/26/29	Arno's last Whoops! sisters cartoon (29)
4:50	2/2/29	EBW's "Sonnet" (19)
4:51	2/9/29	Gibbs's "Glorious Calvin: [A Critical Appreciation]" (17).
4:52	2/16/29	Alexander Woollcott's first "Shouts and Murmurs" column; Elinor Wylie's posthumous "Anti-Feminist Song for My Sister" (22)
5:1	2/23/29	Alan Dunn's first cartoon signed "Kindl"; Wolcott Gibbs's "Facsimile of a Letter" (84–85); EBW, "The Romance of the Publishing Game" (18–19)
5:2	3/2/29	Patience Eden's "To an Uninteresting Man Who Was Once a Suitor" (24)
5:3	3/9/29	
5:4	3/16/29	
5:5	3/23/29	Sullivan's "A Moderately Heartrending Letter" (17–18)
5:6	3/30/29	Kober's "The Show-Off" (25–26)
5:7	4/6/29	EBW's "Poet: Or the Growth of a Lit'ry Figure" (26)
5:8	4/13/29	
5:9	4/20/29	
5:10	4/27/29	Yeats's "Death" (21)
5:11	5/4/29	
5:12	5/11/29	
5:13	5/18/29	
5:14	5/25/29	
5:15	6/1/29	
5:16	6/8/29	Thurber's "Two Ships Bring Americans of Note and English Author" (18); Last "Liquor Market" report? (15)
5:17	6/15/29	
5:18	6/22/29	
5:19	6/29/29	
5:20	7/6/29	
5:21	7/13/29	Gibbs's "The Summer Labor Problem" (17–18)
5:22	7/20/29	Gibbs's "Chevaux 40, Hommes 8" (19–20)
5:23	7/27/29	
5:24	8/3/29	
5:25	8/10/29	
5:26	8/17/29	
5:27	8/24/29	
5:28	8/31/29	
5:29	9/7/27	Williams's "Industrial Crises: A Face Appears in One of the Italian Windows at Alice Foote MacDougal's" (28)
5:30	9/14/29	Robert Benchley's first "Theatre" reviews in his own name
5:31	9/21/29	Gibbs's "The Peepshow Season in Retrospect" (25–26)

5:32	9/28/29	
5:33	10/5/29	NYer begins publishing two editions, city and out-of-town
5:34	10/12/29	Elmer Rice's "Voyage to Purilia" begins, first of eleven installments (25–29)
5:35	10/19/29	Parker's "But the One on the Right—" (25–27); EBW's "This Is the Girl I'm Going to Marry" (28)
5:36	10/26/29	Dove's 10/26/29:29; Margaret Widdemer's first prose, "Personal-Touch Department" (112)
5:37	11/2/29	
5:38	11/9/29	Gibbs's "The Master's Touch" (23)
5:39	11/16/29	Arno's cover of mother comforting child; KSA and EBW married 11/13/29 (Elledge 170)
5:40	11/23/29	Gibbs's "Hurrah for Mrs. Porsena" (27); Frankforter's "Going South" runs twice (54, 114–16).
5:41	11/30/29	
5:42	12/7/29	Kober's "Is Shirley Insulted?" (37); Arno's "We want to report a stolen car" (31)
5:43	12/14/29	O'Hara's "Memo and Another Memo" (77)
5:44	12/21/29	
5:45	12/28/29	
5:46	1/4/30	Levy's "Flying Dutchman of Central Park West" (36); Patience Eden's "All is Not Lost!" (78)
5:47	1/11/30	
5:48	1/18/30	
5:49	1/25/30	Gibbs's "Police Are Baffled" (22–23)
5:50	2/1/30	Irvin's "The Kibitzers." (14–15); Thurber's "What Life Did to Us: One Man's True Confession" (16–17)
5:51	2/8/30	O'Hara's "Suits Pressed" (28)
5:52	2/15/30	Fitzgerald's "Salesmanship in the Champs-Élyséees" (20)

Abbreviations

The following abbreviations, listed alphabetically letter by letter, appear in documentary citations.

AA	Anthony Armstrong	CMB	Charles M. Bayer
AB	Aaron Birnbaum	CR	Carl Rose
ACL	Arthur Conrad LeDuc	DB	Djuna Barnes
AD	Alan Dunn	DF	Donald Freeman
AG	Abel Green	DH	Dorothy Hoover
AHR	Alice Harvey Ramsey	DOS	Donald Ogden Stewart
AJF	Alfred J. Frueh	DP	Dorothy Parker
AK	Arthur Kober	D&P	Alan Dunn and Mary
ALM	*American Legion Monthly*		Petty Papers, Syracuse
AP	Augustus Peck		University Library,
AS	Arthur Samuels		Department of Special
AW	Alexander Woollcott		Collections
BB	Bruce Bairnsfather	DT	Daise Terry
BH	Ben Hecht	DW	Doris Wadley
C	Contributors	EBW	E. B. White; E. B.
CB	Charlotte Barbour		White Papers, Division
CF	Corey Ford		of Rare and Manuscript
CGS	Charles G. Shaw		Collections, Cornell
CH	*College Humor*		University Library
CHK	Clarence H. Knapp	ED	Elsie Dick

ELR	Elmer L. Rice	JE	Jacqueline Embry
EMB	Ellin Mackay Berlin	JF	Janet Flanner
ERS	E. R. Spaulding	JGT	James Grover Thurber
FD	Fairfax Downey	JH	John Hanrahan
FH	Fillmore Hyde	JHW	John H. Wheeler
FL	Federico Lebrun	JO	John O'Hara
FS	Frank Sullivan; Frank	JSB	Julius S. Berg
	Sullivan Papers, Division	KB	Katherine Brush
	of Rare and Manuscript	KSA	Katharine Sergeant
	Collections, Cornell		Angell
	University Library	KSW	Katharine Sergeant
FSF	F. Scott Fitzgerald		White
GCR	Gardner C. Rea	LH	Lillian Hellman
GP	Garrett Price	Life	*Life Magazine* Literary
GW	Gluyas Williams; Gluyas		Records, Rare Books and
	Williams Papers,		Manuscripts Division,
	Syracuse University		New York Public Library
	Library, Department of	LL	Lois Long
	Special Collections	MBL	M. B. Levick
HA	Herbert Asbury	MC	Miguél Covarrubias
HB	Howard Brubaker	MEW	Marion E. Weaver
HBC	Howard Baker Cushman	MGB	Mary Graham Bonner
HDW	Harold D. Winney	MM	Morris Markey
HEH	Helen E. Hokinson	MP	Mary Petty
HNM	Howard N. Morgan	N&C	"Notes and Comment"
HO	Harold Ober		section of "The Talk of
HT	Helen Thurber		the Town"
HW	Hugh Wiley	NH	Nancy Hoyt
HWG	Harold Willard Gleason	NL	Newman Levy
HWR	Harold W. Ross	NYer	The *New Yorker*; *New*
IK	Isidore Klein		*Yorker* Records, Rare
JAS	J. A. Stevenson, Jr.		Books and Manuscripts
JBM	Joseph B. Milgram		Division, New York
JC	Jack Cluett		Public Library
JCM	John Chapin Mosher	NYT	*New York Times*
JDeM	Julian De Miskey	OH	Oliver Herford

OS	Otto Soglow
PB	Peggy Bacon; Perry Barlow
PC	Parke Cummings; Phyllis Crawford
PE	Patience Eden (Martha Banning Thomas)
PGW	Philip G. Wylie
PRR	Paul R. Reynolds
RB	Ralph Barton
RBB	Ray B. Bowen
RCB	Robert C. Benchley; Robert Benchley Papers, Billy Rose Theatre Collection, New York Public Library (Lincoln Center Division)
RHF	Raoul H. Fleischmann
RL	Ring Lardner
RMI	Ralph M. Ingersoll
SHW	Stanley Hart White
SJP	Sidney Joseph Perelman
SM	Scudder Middleton
TB	Tip Bliss
TD	Theodore Dreiser
VF	Vanity Fair
WC	Warren Chappell
WCW	William Carlos Williams
WEF	W. E. Farbstein
WG	Wolcott Gibbs
WJ	Willard "Spud" Johnson
WRB	William Rose Benét
WS	William Shawn

Notes

Epigraphs

Frontispiece. HWR to EBW, n.d. [Summer 1936], EBW Box 85.
Introduction. JGT to EBW, 1/20/[38], EBW BOX 86.
Chapter 1. HWR to EBW, 5/7/43, EBW Box 85.
Chapter 2. HWR to GW, 8/7/34, GW Box 1.
Chapter 3. Qtd. in Gill 6.
Chapter 4. Angell 132.
Chapter 5. HWR to RHF, 11/4/27, NYer Box 3.
Chapter 6. Asper, "Other Books" 5/19/28:94.
Chapter 7. Ingersoll, *Point* 190-91.
Chapter 8. EBW, draft obituary of HWR [1951], EBW Box 85.

Introduction

1. HWR, "Letter to go with outline," n.d. [before Jan. 1, 1925], NYer Box 2.
2. NYer Box 2.
3. JGT to EBW & KSW, 6/2/58, EBW Box 170.
4. EBW to HBC, 10/26/59, EBW Box 69.
5. KSW to HT, draft 1, n.d. [before 3/11/75], EBW Box 182.
6. "Ross," Notes for New Yorker Book, EBW Box 86.
7. "Unfathomable . . . ," Notes for New Yorker Book, EBW Box 86.
8. Ross Obituary, notes, n.d. [12/51], EBW Box 56.
9. Ingersoll claims the date is Thursday, 2/19 (Ingersoll, *Point*), and other sources claim the 18th (three days before the cover date), but the magazine typically went on sale Tuesdays, according to 5/16/25:1, which would date the first appearance February 17, 1925.
10. NYer to C, 2/24/29, Doubleday, Doran G. [Nash, Ogden]—1928–30, NYer Box 4.
11. E.g., NYer to Jack Cluett, 3/12/28, NYer Box 136; KSW to Perry Barlow, 11/5/31, NYer Box 937.

12. HWR to EBW, [Aug. 1946], EBW Box 85.

13. KSW to FS, 1/21/[53], FS Box 12.

14. WC to AD, 6/20/68, D&P Box 7.

15. WC to AD, 4/9/70, D&P Box 7.

16. WC to AD, 12/17/71, D&P Box 7.

17. KSW to HBC, 2/18/57, EBW Box 182.

18. KSW to HBC, 2/25/67, EBW Box 182.

Chapter 1: Old and New, Borrowed and Blue

1. Cowley 184; "Hyde," *New York Times*, 1/27/70:43. Behrman reports that Robert Benchley, Robert E. Sherwood, and Gluyas Williams all worked on the *Lampoon*, though Sherwood left a year before graduation to enlist in the war (24).

2. Stewart 134; "Downey" 169; J. Grant 228; Todd 195.

3. Erkkila 478; KSW to EBW, 12/31/[37], EBW Box 86.

Lobrano, who was White's roommate in 1926 on West Thirteenth Street in Greenwich Village, became *New Yorker* fiction editor on January 17, 1938.

4. CH Winter/24:6.

5. "Hokinson, Helen Elna"; Cook B6; Horn.

6. Stewart 135, 21; Kinney 271.

7. *Judge* and *New Yorker* artist Gardner Rea graduated from Columbus's East High School in 1909 or 1910 ("Rea, Gardner" 500)—three or four years before Thurber's class of 1913. If Rea and Thurber didn't know each other from East High School (Stewart went to Philips Exeter), they probably met at Ohio State University in 1913–14, when Rea and Thurber worked on the campus humor magazine the *Sundial*. Rea helped found the *Sundial* and was editing that year, when Thurber contributed as a freshman ("Rea, Gardner" 500; Kinney 131).

8. NL to KSW, 12/21/29, NYer Box 147.

9. Prospectus, NYer Box 2.

10. JBM to HWR, 12/4/24, Correspondence—NYer Box 2.

11. HWR reported current circulation figures to OH, 7/14/28, Herford—1928–30, NYer Box 5. *Life*'s circulation exceeded 100,000 in 1928 (Mott 231–32).

12. DH to GW, n.d. [after 6/12/30], Williams—1930, NYer Box 936.

13. E.g., "The Enterprising Optimist," which hinges on tired puns as Wee Askem and Hugh Tellem discuss a "fellow who tried to sell flying fish" to Navy pilots but now sells "coat-hangers to lawyers who win suits" (*Judge* 5/17/24:31); and "Lines Provoked By the Optimist School of Poetry," thirty lines of doggerel signed as Fuillet, whose main point is "All this optimistic junk— / It's the bunk, kid, it's the bunk!" (*Judge* 6/28/24:1).

14. NYer to C, 2/21/25, Form Letters, NYer Box 2.

15. NYers to C, 8/1/25, Form Letters, NYer Box 2.

16. NYers to C, 8/1/25, Form Letters, NYer Box 2.

17. HWR to RBB, 8/16/26, Advertising—1926, NYer Box 2.

18. KSA to DB, 11/1/28, Barnes—1928, NYer Box 135.

19. KSA to DB, n.d. [several months before 11/1/28], Barnes—1928, NYer Box 135.

20. KSA to KB, 6/8/28, Brush—1928, NYer Box 135.

21. PB to ED, n.d. [1928], NYer Box 135.

22. HWR to MC, 4/29/29, NYer Box 4.

23. JSB to NYer, telegram, 4/2/29, Letters to the Editor: Commentary—1929 (3 of 3), NYer Box 933.

24. Letters to the Editor: Commentary—1929 (3 of 3), NYer Box 933.

25. "We have a startling explanation . . . ," n.d., Manuscripts, Miscellaneous—1926 (2 of 4), NYer Box 1348.

26. HWR to HW, 10/15/25, Wiley, NYer Box 2.

27. KSA to WJ, 2/5/29, NYer Box 146; WG to Ralph Pierson, 3/23/29, General Correspondence P-Q—1929, NYer Box 147.

28. HWR to RHF, 10/20/27, NYer Box 3.

29. D&P, Box 14.

30. Constantin Aladjalov returned to Paris and the Riviera every summer ("Alajálov, Constantin" 9). "Rico" Lebrun spent the winter and spring of 1928 in Europe, spending some time in Paris (FL to KSA, n.d., Lebrun—1928, NYer Box 140). That summer, Otto Soglow met up with Isidore Klein and Reginald Marsh in Paris (OS to ED, 7/26/28, Soglow—1928, NYer Box 143). Reginald Marsh, born in Paris to American artists in 1898, had also returned in 1925 (Cohen 3). Other visitors included Garrett Price in the winter and Aaron Birnbaum in the spring of 1929, and Barbara Shermund in the summer of 1930 (KSA to GP, 2/18/29, General Correspondence P-Q—1929, NYer Box 147; SM to AB, 6/1/29, Birnbaum—1929, NYer Box 932; SM to Holden, 6/18/30, Interoffice Memoranda—1930, NYer Box 935).

31. SM to JDeM, 12/12/30, De Miskey—1930, NYer Box 934.

32. I am grateful to Joseph W. Slade for these details of censorship history from his forthcoming *Pornography and Sexual Representation: A Reference Guide.*

33. HWR to EBW, 5/7/35, EBW Box 85.

34. KSA to DP, 10/16/29, NYer Box 147.

Chapter 2: Comic Business

1. KSA to WJ, 2/5/29, NYer Box 146. Johnson worked for the *New Yorker* in 1926–27.

2. WJ to KSA, 1/22/29, NYer Box 146.

3. KSA to WJ, 2/5/29, NYer Box 146.

4. Typescript, n.d., EBW Box 85.

5. "Ross Exaggeration" (5); "A Reporter in Chains" (7-8) Parody Issue, 11/6/26, NYer Box 2.

6. EBW to FS, 12/6/51, FS Box 12.

7. "Follows an attempt," n.d. [1924], Form Letters, NYer Box 2.

8. NYer to C, 2/21/25, Form Letters, NYer Box 2.

9. "New York, Etc." ran until 1:11 (5/2/25) followed by "The Outside World," an

occasional successor carrying news of El Paso, Jersey City, and Miami as late as 1:20 (7/4/25).

10. NYer to C: "The second and third issues . . . ," n.d. [between 3/7/25 and 3/14/25], Form Letters, NYer Box 2.

11. No record exists of who edited newsbreaks in 1925, but in 1926 TB edited newsbreaks after his departure from the *New Yorker* staff (NYer Box 1348).

12. On 9/27/30, HWR invited TB to write headlines for newsbreaks, B—1928–30, NYer Box 3.

13. FPA to HWR, 3/11/30, Adams, Franklin P.—1929–30, NYer Box 3.

14. WS's history with the *New Yorker* is summarized in "Comment: William Shawn" (12/21/92:4,6); HWR to EBW [Summer 1936], EBW Box 85.

15. HWR to RHF, 3/29/27, Fleischmann—Ross, 1927 (3 of 3), NYer Box 3.

16. KSA to Levick et al, 10/25/29, White, Katharine S.—1929, NYer Box 148.

17. "Contributers [*sic*] to the New Yorker: Writers," Form Letters, NYer Box 2.

18. A June 1925 list of weekly contributors in the *New Yorker* archives (Form Letters, Box 2) shows Peter Vischer's name crossed out in the same manner as names of other newly replaced department writers. Vischer, a former Cornell classmate and *Sun* editor of E. B. White (who thus far had published in the *New Yorker* but not yet joined the staff), reassociated with the F-R Publishing Corporation and its board when he married Ruth Fleischmann, Raoul's former wife and a major stockholder.

19. "The question comes up," n.d. [1925], Form Letters, NYer Box 2.

20. Ingersoll's *New Yorker* memoir points out that in 1925 fine arts critics could claim "nullification" of liability in expressing their honest criticism, but the professional shield did not extend to architectural criticism until the *New Yorker* supported its "Sky Line" critic in a suit over the Fred F. French Building (Forty-fifth Street and Fifth Avenue), which the critic described as having a nauseating design. The developer dropped the suit after seeing architects' support for the critic's claim, resulting in case law protection for architecture critics who were architects themselves (Ingersoll 198–99). Non-architects had less authority for such criticism, however, and two years later the *New Yorker* defended another suit, this time against James Thurber, on a similar charge brought by an architect named Severance in September 1927 (Stevenson to Thurber, n.d., Thurber, James Libel Case—1927, NYer Box 3).

21. In 1926 Ross sought services of attorney Macdonald DeWitt, whom he knew through *American Legion Weekly* and *Judge* (HWR to Macdonald DeWitt, 9/11/26, Correspondence—1926, NYer Box 2). Attorney J. A. Stevenson handled Thurber's 1927 case and became the *New Yorker*'s regular libel consultant.

22. JAS to KSA, 10/15/28, Lancaster, Wm. W.—1928, NYer Box 140. This folder contains various examples of libel avoidance.

23. Between Barton and Covarrubias, W. E. Hill contributed two drawings for "Great Moments from the Drama" (5/16/25:10, 5/23/25:14) before disappearing from the magazine.

24. Ms. no. 21256 (1/26/28) *Life* editorial records vol. 55; ms. no. 27459 (9/20/29), *Life* vol. 56.

25. HWR to RB, [5?/1928], Barton—1928–30, NYer Box 3.

26. Tunis took over "Sports" on 6/23, his first column appearing 7/11/25.

27. Wiley to HWR, 9/18/25, Wiley, NYer Box 2.

28. "We thank you all very, very much for a very, very, VERY happy birthday," chart published in the *New York Post,* 2/18/27, unpaginated clipping, Poster, NYer Birthday, NYer Box 3. (See fig. 9.)

29. Names Flanner drops include Shakespeare clients James Joyce, Djuna Barnes, Gertrude Stein, Alice B. Toklas, Ernest Hemingway, T. S. Eliot, Ezra Pound, Archibald MacLeish, John Dos Passos, e. e. cummings and his wife, Marion Morehouse, Hart Crane, Kay Boyle, Glenway Wescott, and Scott and Zelda Fitzgerald, and *Maison* customers André Gide, Jean Schlumberger, Paul Valéry, and Jules Romain.

30. KSA to MBL, 10/13/27, Interoffice Memos—1928 (2 of 3), NYer Box 139.

31. KSA to JF, 8/15/28, Flanner—1928, NYer Box 138.

32. "To Contributors," 8/1/25, Form Letters, NYer Box 2.

33. Originally signed "Lambda," the "Motors" department was signed Eric Hatch beginning 7/10/26.

34. HWR to ERS, 6/15/25, Advertising (1925), NYer Box 2.

35. HWR to ERS, 7/8/25, Advertising (1925), NYer Box 2.

36. N.s., Parody Issue, 11/6/26:6, NYer Box 2.

37. HWR to EBW, 5/7/35, EBW Box 85.

38. HWR to RHF, 1/27/26, Business Dept.—1926, NYer Box 2. Ad contracts were reported in the first anniversary issue (N&C 2/20/26:15).

39. 6/21/26, Copyright Matters—1926, NYer Box 2.

40. RHF to HWR, 5/25/27, Fleischmann—1927 (2 of 3), NYer Box 3.

41. HWR to RHF, 4/6/27, Fleischmann—1927 (2 of 3), NYer Box 3.

42. RHF to HWR, 2/19/27, replies undated, Fleischmann—1927 (3 of 3), NYer Box 3.

43. HWR to JH, 4/25/30, Departmental Procedures, NYer Box 4.

44. His 1926 salary was paid partly in stock (HWR to Collector of Internal Revenue, New York City, 5/29/28, Income Tax Return, 1925–1929, NYer Box 117; "Memo for agreement" 5/11/29 provided bonus of 700 bonus shares at the end of every year for each year completed as editor, provided that he serve as editor the following year, F-R Publishing Corp.: Stock and Obligations, 1927–1930, NYer Box 5).

45. HWR to RHF, 4/17/26, Fleischmann—1926, NYer Box 2.

46. HWR to RHF, 4/17/26, Fleischmann—1926, NYer Box 2.

47. HWR to RHF, 4/17/26, and RHF to RBB, 4/19/26, Fleischmann—1926, NYer Box 2.

48. FS to HWR, 7/16/31, FS Box 3.

49. HWR to RHF, 5/1/26, Fleischmann—1926, NYer Box 2.

50. RHF to HWR, 5/3/26, Fleischmann—1926, NYer Box 2.

51. HWR to RHF, 4/17/26, Fleischmann—1926, NYer Box 2.

52. LL to HWR, 3/7/27, Fleischmann—1927 (2 of 3), NYer Box 3.

53. HWR to RHF, 3/8/27, Fleischman—1927 (2 of 3), NYer Box 3.

54. RHF to HWR, 3/23/27, Fleischmann—1927 (2 of 3), NYer Box 3.

55. RHF to HWR, 3/23/27, Fleischmann—1927 (2 of 3), NYer Box 3; Gretta Palmer wrote as "Duplex," initiating the department in her own name in 2:41 (11/27/26); Palmer to HWR, n.d.; HWR to RHF, 3/3/27, Fleischmann—1927 (2 of 3), NYer Box 3.

56. RHF to HWR, 4/20/27, Fleischmann—1927 (2 of 3), NYer Box 3.

57. HWR to RHF, 4/20/27, Fleischmann—1927 (2 of 3), NYer Box 3.

58. RBB to HWR, 3/31/27, Fleischmann—1927 (2 of 3), NYer Box 3.

59. LL to RMI, [3/31/27], Fleischmann—1927 (2 of 3), NYer Box 3.

60. HWR to RHF, 4/6/27, Fleischmann—1927 (2 of 3), NYer Box 3.

61. HRW to EBW, n.d. [April 1943], EBW Box 85.

62. RHF to HWR, 5/2/27, Fleischmann—1927 (2 of 3), NYer Box 3.

63. EBW criticized the donation without mentioning the perpetrator in a letter to George H. Healey, 9/27/61, EBW Box 69; he identified RBB as the culprit in EBW to FS, 5/14/64, FS Box 12.

64. EBW to FS, 5/14/64, FS Box 12.

65. RBB to HWR, 8/26/26, Correspondence—1926, NYer Box 2.

66. "Dear ———— / Knowing that reviewers' lists," n.d. [Dec. 1924–Jan. 1925], Form Letters, NYer Box 2.

67. RBB to HWR, 8/26/26, NYer Box 2.

68. H. Baldwin to RBB, 8/27/26, Departments—1930, NYer Box 4.

69. Editorial, NYer Box 2.

70. HWR to H. Baldwin, 10/7/26, Correspondence—1926, NYer Box 2.

71. An advertisement for Benchley's *The Early Worm,* ill. Gluyas Williams (Henry Holt and Co., 1927) identifies Alceste as Ernest Boyd. RCB 21–229.

72. HRW to EBW, n.d. [Oct. 1938], EBW Box 85.

73. HWR to DP, 10/29/27, Parker, NYer Box 3.

74. HWR to DP, 11/21/27, Parker, NYer Box 3.

75. HWR to DP, 10/29/27, Parker, NYer Box 3.

76. HWR to DP, Parker, NYer Box 3.

77. HWR to DP, 10/24/27, Parker, NYer Box 3.

78. WG to DP, 3/26/28, Parker, NYer Box 142.

79. KSA to PGW, 4/16/28, Wylie, NYer Box 144.

80. Numbers 4:10–4:12 (4/28–5/12/28) went to press without Parker, as did 4:15–4:26, 4:31, 4:33, 4:36–4:38, and 4:45–5:3.

81. KSA to HA, 11/20/28, Departments—Books—1930, NYer Box 135.

82. HWR to William A. Drake, 8/19/29, D—1926–28, NYer Box 4.

83. HWR to RB, 2/4/28, Barton, NYer Box 3.

84. Ross's negotiations with Parker during this same period raise the possibility that she deliberately followed Benchley on board. He had resigned from *Vanity Fair* in 1920 in sympathy with Parker; Benchley, Parker, and Heywood Broun protested together that summer against the Sacco and Vanzetti execution (Stewart 160), and all three published simultaneously in the *New Yorker* that fall.

85. RCB's "Press in Review" appeared 3:23, 3:26, 3:29, 3:34, 3:38.

86. HWR to MM, 6/28/27, Markey, NYer Box 3.

87. HWR to MM, 6/28/27, Markey, NYer Box 3.

88. Editors included Arthur Samuels, Katharine Angell, Ralph Ingersoll, Scudder Middleton, Wolcott Gibbs, M. Levick, R. E. M. Whitaker, James Thurber, and E. B. White. Staff writers included John Mosher, Marcia Clarke, Lois Long, and Niven Busch Jr. Staff artists included Johan Bull and Julian De Miskey. Staff reporters included Reed Johnston, Hobart Weekes, Frederick Packard, Geoffrey T. Hellman, and R. A. Hague (Police Press Passes, NYer Box 147).

89. WG, 1/20/28, Interoffice Memos—1928–30, NYer Box 5.

90. "Minutes of Meeting June 24, 1926," Editorial: Decisions—1926, NYer Box 2.

91. HWR to RHF, 5/16/27, Fleischmann—1927 (2 of 3), NYer Box 3.

92. NYer to Our Artists, 1/0/34, D&P, Box 7.

Chapter 3: "The Talk of the Town"

1. Qtd. in Harriman 177–78.

2. Another colleague, Laura Mount, notable as Laura A. Hobson of *Gentleman's Agreement,* also joined the "Talk" staff, but apparently not, as Kinney (330, 311) and Kramer (*Ross,* 59) report, in the 1920s.

3. "Follows an attempt . . . " n.d., Form Letters, NYer Box 2.

4. NYer to C, "The second and third issues . . . ," n.d, Form Letters, NYer Box 2.

5. HWR to EBW, 5/7/35, EBW Box 85.

6. Gill, 116, cites a 1928 date, but Gibbs claims that he began as a copy editor in 1927 (WG to EBW, n.d. [1950], EBW Box 83).

7. The issue of July 11 had single-panel drawings instead of a spread; the last spread in this incarnation of "Talk," Peggy Bacon's "Sunday on the Coney Island Boardwalk," appeared 7/18/25.

8. "Follows an attempt," n.d., Form Letters, NYer Box 2.

9. NYer to AA, 6/20/28, A—1928, NYer Box 135.

10. This layout appeared on the page following "Talk."

11. KSA to GP, 2/18/29, Price, NYer Box 147.

12. SM to JM, 12/12/30, De Miskey—1930, NYer Box 934.

13. Ingersoll reports his breakdown in *Point* 220–22. Documents in the archives suggest that Ross attended the staff meeting of June 24, 1926, and had returned by August 16, 1926 (NYer Box 2). He suffered from an infected wisdom tooth and jaw.

14. HWR to EBW, Sunday, n.d. [Oct. 1944], EBW Box 85.

15. EBW to SHW, [Jan. 1929], EBW Box 60.

16. The EBW papers (Box 60) date this letter to 1926, but by then White had been hired by J. H. Newmark.

17. White began work 9/26/22 (EBW to JHW, 9/25/22), and by mid-March had already begun the column (EBW to JHW, 3/14 & 3/18/23), EBW Box 60.

18. JHW to HWR, 1/27/27, Bell Syndicate, NYer Box 3.

19. RHF to HWR, 10/13/27, Bell Syndicate, NYer Box 3.

20. HWR to RHF, 10/12/27, Bell Syndicate, NYer Box 3.

21. RHF to HWR, 10/29/27; HWR to JHW, 11/15/27; HWR to JHW, 11/16/27; Bell Syndicate, NYer Box 3.

22. JGT to EBW and KSW, 6/2/58, EBW Box 170.

23. White Comment [n.d.], "Talk of the Town"—1927 (1 of 4), NYer Box 1349.

24. See Dunne—1928, NYer Box 137; Marx—1928, NYer Box 141.

25. FS to KSA, 12/20/28, Sullivan—1928, NYer Box 143.

26. Global Weather Changes, Harold Ross: Various Departments—1951 (1 of 2), NYer Box 970.

27. NYer to C, "The New Yorker is committing itself . . . ," 8/1/25, Form Letters, NYer Box 2.

28. JGT to AG, 1/24/28, Green—1928, NYer Box 138.

29. JGT to R. Angus Bayne, B-BAZ—1928, NYer Box 135.

30. JGT to A. C. M. Azoy, 6/13/28, A—1928, NYer Box 135.

31. JGT to SJP, 5/2/28, Perelman—1928, NYer Box 142.

32. JGT to MGB, 11/22/28, Bonner—1928, NYer Box 135.

33. AS to RMI, 5/4/28, Interoffice Memos—1928 (3 of 3), NYer Box 139.

34. KSA to FS, 9/18/28, Sullivan—1928, NYer Box 143.

35. KSA to FL, 6/30/28, Lebrun—1928, NYer Box 140.

36. FL to KSA, 2/11/28, Lebrun—1928, NYer Box 140.

37. EBW to KSW, 6/19/30, Ideas—1930 (1 of 2), NYer Box 935.

38. EMB to HWR, 1/11/30, Complaints—1928–30 (1 of 2), NYer Box 4.

39. HWR to EMB, 1/20/30, Complaints—1928–30 (1 of 2), NYer Box 4.

40. HWR to MC, 6/5/29, Complaints—1928–30 (1 of 2), NYer Box 4.

41. EBW, n.d., EBW Box 86.

42. HWR to EBS, 4/22/29, Editorial, Harold Ross—1930, NYer Box 5.

43. Ross obituary, notes, [Dec., 1951], EBW Box 56.

Chapter 4: Comic Art

1. One example of the distortions that can result is Leah Weaver's "Cartoon Images of Women in *The New Yorker*," a content analysis based on cartoon collections without considering whether the books' contents were statistically representative of the magazine's contents in the categories under investigation.

2. My bibliographic database for the first five years contains 367 entries for Arno, 315 for Shermund, 264 for Hokinson, 181 for Dunn, 165 for Irvin.

3. KSA to GW, 1/4/29, Williams—1929, NYer Box 933.

4. ACL to DH, 7/14/[30], Artists I-R—1930, NYer Box 934.

5. Parody Issue, 11/6/26:3, NYer Box 2.

6. AD estimated his production at nearly 3,000 in 1968 ("Autobiography in the third person," D&P Box 1); AD to PB, 10/29/69, D&P Box 7.

7. HWR to BB, 2/13/29, Bairnsfather—1929, NYer Box 3.

8. SM to DF, 8/21/29, Drawings Returned—1929, NYer Box 932.

9. KSA to AP, 4/17/29, Correspondence P-Q—1929, NYer Box 147.

10. AD to MP, 8/12/26, D&P Box 1.

11. "As for art," n.d., Art, Ideas for—1926, NYer Box 2.

12. JM to Mr. Baretto, 8/21/25, Form Letters—1925, NYer Box 2.

13. "Follows an attempt," n.d., Form Letters—1925, NYer Box 2.

14. "To Art Contributors," n.d., Form Letters—1925, NYer Box 2.

15. NYer to DW, 6/25/25, Form Letters—1925, NYer Box 2.

16. NYer to C, 8/1/25, Form Letters—1925, NYer Box 2.

17. "New York, Etc" reported in early May that Held, who had been hospitalized after a mare kicked him in the head, was planning a trip to Morocco (5/2/25:24). It's not clear whether these events affected his woodcut submissions.

18. HNM to NYer, 1/27/29 and NYer to HNM, 1/29/29; Letters to Editor: Commentary, Art Correspondence—1929 (2 of 3), NYer Box 932.

19. "Heroes of the Week" did not run in 1:45, 1:48, 1:50–51, 2:4.

20. The exception is a drawing of an author and his audience at a public reading, 10/24/25:21.

21. "Letter to Art Contributors," n.d., Contributors: Correspondence—1925, NYer Box 2.

22. Most of Hokinson's illustrations appeared by the end of October. They accompanied Lipstick's "When Nights Are Bold," (8/1/25:20), Frank Sullivan's "The Sport of Kings" (8/22/25:7–8), Search-Light [Robert Benchley]'s "Murder as Bad Art" (9/19/25:21), Elmer Davis's "Our Collegiate Hilltop" (10/24/25:9–10), W. J. Henderson's "The Opera Is Here" (10/31/25:7–8). She also illustrated Charles G. Shaw's "Two Rooms, Bath and Kitchenette" (3/20/26:15–16) and Nicholas Trott's "Twenty-Seventh Annual Motor Show" (1/8/27:36).

23. NYer to Mr. Baretto, 8/21/25, Form Letters—1925, NYer Box 2.

24. HWR to Hugh Bradley, 2/7/30, B—1928–30, NYer Box 3.

25. NYer to Mr. Baretto, 8/21/25, Form Letters—1925, NYer Box 2.

26. "Traffic" (1:52, 2:1, and 2:2), "Parking" (2:10, 2:11, 2:13). "Beautifying" (3:22–3:26, 3:28–3:31), "Enlivening" (4:4–4:18, 4:20–4:21, 4:24, 4:27).

27. A fifth drawing, "The man who poured his own water at the Banker's Club," appeared about eighteen months later (3/26/27:25), almost certainly as an afterthought to the original series.

28. JDeM to EBW, 2/25/75, EBW Box 140.

29. JDeM to EBW, 3/30/71, EBW Box 140.

30. Misfiled in Complaints—1926, NYer Box 2.

31. HWR to GCR, 6/21/28, Rea—1928, NYer Box 7.

32. "As for art," n.d., Art, Ideas for—1926, NYer Box 2.

Chapter 5: Two into One, and Then There Were None

1. "He": Gilbert Wilkinson, 6/27/25:13; "Old Gentleman": Gardner Rea, 5/2/25:22; "First Professor": I. Klein, 6/26/26:8; "Apprentice": I. Klein, 9/10/27:28. Other late examples: e.g., J. H. Fyfe, "Advertising Expert's Son: 'Will you let me have

your reactions to this . . . ." 4:1 (2/25/28:22). I. Klein, "Young Author: 'I knew it!'" 4:44 (12/22/28:24); Peter Arno, "First Bootlegger: 'Two suckers got poisoned on my stuff the other day'" 4:43 (12/15/28:35).

2. Biographical Material, D&P Box 1; affidavit, AD Income Tax, D&P Box 14.

3. Dunn did do a drawing of an auction room based on an idea and caption purchased from George Kaufman, "Going, at 35—do I hear 40?," but correspondence shows that Dunn's payment was not reduced for an idea charge (HDW to DT, 1/4/33, D&P Box 7). This arrangement suggests that Dunn may have proposed independently an idea similar to Kaufmann's, because Dunn was quite adamant about his independence from assignment.

4. Affidavit, AD Income Tax, D&P Box 14.

5. AD, "Autobiography in the third person," D&P Box 1.

6. In line with *New Yorker* policy, Dunn signed only his first drawing in this issue, "I suppose they'll be tearing it up again soon" (10/1/27:19).

7. Scrapbook, *Gladys,* D&P Box 32.

8. The *Album 1925–50* erroneously included this cartoon in its section on the thirties.

9. HEH to ED, 8/21/28, Hokinson—1928, NYer Box 139.

10. Ms. filed with letter, KSA to H. Wolf Kaufman, 2/11/27, "Talk"—1927 (1 of 4), NYer Box 1349.

11. Portraits of E. B. White by Thurber, EBW Box 170.

12. Whalen, who described himself in his autobiography as "Mr. New York," oversaw parades as chairman of the mayor's reception committee (1919–53), though he became police commissioner under Major James J. Walker in December 1928 (*Encyclopedia of New York City*).

13. DH to GW, 9/30/29, Reprints—1929 (2 of 3), NYer Box 933.

14. Parody Issue, 11/6/26:3, NYer Box 2.

15. NYer to GW, 12/7/29, Williams—1929, NYer Box 933.

16. KSA to AB, 12/18/28, NYer Box 4.

17. Mosher (2/16/29:23, 3/9/29:20, 4/20/29:18, 9/28/29:26), Gibbs (2/23/29:26, 5/18/29:29, 11/16/29:24), Thurber (3/23/29:17), Porter (7/20/29:15), "Manhole Captions," NYer Box 934. The submissions by Sullivan and O'Hara, both regular freelancers, did not run, but Ross approved them along with some fifteen others identified as "pending"; by mid-November, Dorothy Hoover began sending letters that the series would run only long enough to use up this backlog (DH to H. Frank Chase, 11/29/29, NYer Box 932), but in fact it ended before then.

18. "Manhole Captions," NYer Box 934.

19. E.g., SM to C. H. Baker, 11/13/30, NYer Box 935; SM to Raeburn Van Buren, 11/26/30, NYer Box 936.

20. NYer to PB, 7/7/28, Barlow—1928, NYer Box 135.

21. SM to GP, 8/8/29, 7/11/29, 8/21/29, Price—1929, NYer Box 933.

22. Angell recommended to Ross that Irvin change five of his eleven drawings: make a new first drawing of wife waving goodbye to husband (Irvin adapted but did not exactly follow the suggestion), change drawing #5 by adding a stand of food (not

done), show the wife entering the door in the background of #8 (done), "possibly" add a mermaid in waiter's arms in the background of #9 (not done), and reverse the images in #11 (done, for visual balance and to have them ride off in the opposite direction of his former life). KSA to HWR, 4/12/29, White—1929, NYer Box 148.

23. KSA to Art Conference, 10/10/29, Interoffice Memoranda—Art Correspondence, 1929, NYer Box 932.

24. DH to MBL, 11/10/31, Interoffice memos—1931 (1 of 2), NYer Box 938.

25. JH to KSA, 11/13/28, Held—1928, NYer Box 139.

26. IK to HWR, 8/7/29, Klein—1928–30, NYer Box 6.

27. NYer to A[H]R, 10/16/29, Harvey—1929, NYer Box 932.

28. A[H]R to DH, 10/19/29, Harvey—1929, NYer Box 932. A note on her letter says *"Buy."*

29. CR expressed appreciation for the new policy to KSW, 11/7/31, Rose—1931, NYer Box 939.

30. ALM to AD, 4/15/31, Folder 8, D&P, Box 3.

Chapter 6: Comic Storytelling

1. Four, if he wrote "Passionate Love Letter," signed T. H. B. 2/27/26:43.

2. KSA to AK, 1/18/29, Kober—1929, NYer, Box 147; KSA to TD, 11/11/29, Dreiser—1929, NYer Box 146.

3. "The Story of Manhattankind" ran 1:1 (2/21/25:6), 1:2 (2/28/25:8), 1:3 (3/7/25:6), 1:4 (3/14/25:14), 1:5 (3/21/25:12), 1:7 (4/4/25:12), 1:12 (5/9/25:8). All but the second installment had illustrations by Herb Roth.

4. Kenneth Phillips Britton compared conversations in the Paris and New York Ritz Hotels in "Intercepted Conversations" 5/22/26:57; Sylvia Fuller, "Overheard at Forest Hills" 9/25/26:53; Florence Ross, "Overheard: Two Young Ladies at Schrafft's" 4/16/27:29; Arthur Kober, "Overheard: At the Gershwin Concert at the Stadium" 8/6/27:64–65); Paul G. Gumbinner, "Overheard: At Womrath's" 10/15/27:104; Jack Cluett, "Overheard: At Liggett's Grand Central Fountain" 12/3/27:52–53); W. W. Scott, "Overheard: On a Danbury Party Line" 12/10/27:58.

5. KSA to LH, 2/17/28, Hellman—1928, NYer Box 139.

6. I am grateful to Holger Kersten for pointing out this book to me.

7. KAS to DOS, 9/19/28, Stewart—1928, NYer Box 143.

8. Ford alluded to Frueh's "Solving the Traffic Problem," a new series that began the previous week, 2/13/26:8, and Marsh's "The Rum Runner," 5/30/25:16–17, among other references.

9. 1926 rates for casuals averaged $0.056 per word, but Ford's word rates ranged from $0.641 to $0.091 (the higher rate for a shorter piece), in contrast with $0.044 for staff writer John Mosher and $0.065 for critic Gilbert Seldes ("Casuals," Editorial: Decisions—1926, NYer Box 2).

10. HWR to MC, 4/29/29, Covarrubias—1929, NYer Box 4.

11. KSA to BH, 11/6/28, Hecht—1928, NYer Box 139.

12. KSA to BH, 11/6/28, Hecht—1928, NYer Box 139.

13. HWR to KSW, JCM, WG, "The piece sent in by Donald Moffett [*sic*] . . . ," n.d. [after 11/4/29], Departments: Policies—1928–30 (no. 1), NYer Box 4.

14. New York homicides reached a rate of 26.7 per 100,000 residents in 1986, up from 7.6 in 1961–65 and 5.4 in 1921–25 ("Crime," *Encyclopedia of New York City*).

15. Wilson describes Paramore with some detail in *The Twenties*, 28–32.

16. Ford's "Bleakest Job" series ran under three titles, beginning "The Bleakest Job: The New Yorker Offers a New Symposium." 2:15 (5/29/26:20), continuing "What Is the Bleakest Job in New York? The New Symposium" 2:16 (6/5/26:66–68), 2:20 (7/3/26:17), 2:21 (7/10/26:24), 2:22 (7/17/26:21), 2:23 (7/24/26:24), and ending "The Bleakest Job: Announcing the Winners of the Prize Symposium" 2:24 (7/31/26:24).

17. The list includes three pieces as Search-Light; issues lacking a Benchley contribution include 2:8, 2:18, 2:21, 2:22.

18. The series included "A Hard Day with the Ritz Carltons: An Upper-Class Tragedy," ill. George Shanks, 2:26 (8/14/26:13–14); "The Ritz Carltons: Mr. Carlton Crashes Through," ill. George Shanks, 2:29 (9/4/26:13–15); "The Ritz Carltons: They Get a Bad Scare and Ritza Learns A Lesson" 2:36 (10/23/26:23–24); "The Ritz Carltons: Mrs. Carlton Does It Herself," ill. Rea Irvin, 2:40 (11/20/26:23–24); "The Ritz Carltons: Mrs. Carlton Errs" 2:44 (12/18/26:25–26); "The Ritz Carltons: Ritza Comes Out" 2:48 (1/15/27:15–17); "The Ritz Carltons: They Catch a Lion," ill. Rea Irvin, 2:51 (2/5/27:24–26); "The Ritz Carltons: A Bit of Carelessness," ill. [Rea Irvin] 3:2 (2/26/27:23–24); "The Ritz Carltons: Summer Plans," ill. Rea Irvin, 3:6 (3/26/27:22–24); "The Ritz Carltons: A Crisis," ill. Rea Irvin 3:15 (5/28/27:16–17); "The Ritz Carltons: A Happy Day," ill. Rea Irvin, 3:18 (6/18/27:14–16).

19. A letter in the archives about another series indicates that Phyllis Crawford wrote as Josie Turner (HWR to PC, 12/18/30, C—1929–30 [2 of 2], NYer Box 4).

20. A short step leads from Turner's series to two other American parodies of *Candide*: Nathanael West's *A Cool Million* (1934) and Terry Southern and Mason Hoffenberg's *Candy* (1964).

21. HWR to PC, 12/18/30, C—1929–30 (2 of 2), NYer Box 4.

22. JO to KSA, n.d., O'Hara—1929, NYer Box 147.

23. HWR to FH, 7/13/27, Hyde—1927, NYer Box 3.

24. KSA to WJ, 2/5/29, General Correspondence, I-J—1929, NYer Box 146.

Chapter 7: Ironic I's Are Smiling

1. "Contributors to the New Yorker: Writers," Contributors: Correspondence—1925, NYer Box 2.

2. HWR to EBW, 5/7/[43], EBW Box 85.

3. Installments in White's "Baby" series ran irregularly through volume 5: "Before Baby Came" 2:49 (1/22/27:15); "M'Baby Loves Me" 2:51 (2/5/27:30); "Listen, Baby" 3:32 (9/24/27:20); "Bye Low Baby" 4:4 (3/17/28:25–26); "Baby's First Step" 5:18 (6/22/29:16).

4. For details on the book clubs, see Radway 193, 199–200.

5. HWR to KSW, JCM, WG, "The piece sent in . . . " n.d. [after 11/29], Departments: Policies—1928–1930 (1 of 2), NYer Box 4.

6. NYer to JC, 3/12/28, Cluett, NYer Box 136.

7. "'Fancy, Glendenning—gyved!'" 5:14 (5/25/29:22); "'I want a suit about the color of this dog's hair'" 5:21 (7/13/29:18).

8. Thurber's verse during this period: "Villanelle Of Horatio Street, Manhattan" 3:2 (2/26/27:74); "Street Song" 3:2 (2/26/27:79); "Portrait Of A Lady" 3:8 (4/9/27:99). Two other poems appeared some eighteen months later, in 4:39 (11/17/28), but in the front of the book rather than the back: "Duet" (p. 31) and "Bachelor Burton" (p. 34). The latter was signed "J. T.," presumably to avoid repeating Thurber's name. Also signed "J. T.," a fifth poem, "Bad Boy," ran 5:8 (4/13/29:34), rehearsing some of the same marital conflicts (including the husband's failure to hang up his towels) as the Monroe series.

9. Among the correspondence documenting Thurber's editorial work during this time is a letter to S. J. Perelman, not yet published in the *New Yorker,* rejecting a manuscript as inappropriate for either "Profiles" or "Talk" (5/2/28, Perelman—1928, NYer Box 142). Perelman did not appear in the magazine during volumes 1–5, though he had already begun his career as a humorist. He published a cartoon in *Judge's* 1923 College Wits number while still enrolled at Brown (5/12/23:24), which he left in 1924 without graduating; he joined *Judge's* staff soon thereafter, and began also writing for *College Humor* and *Life* (Perelman xi). Ross initiated efforts to enlist Perelman late in 1930 without much enthusiasm from Katharine White, who granted his comic sensibility but found the humor of *Parlor, Bedlam and Bath* "cheap," particularly in contrast to the "quiet pieces" she preferred by Gibbs, Mosher, and White (KSW to HWR, 11/12/30, Interoffice Memos—1930, NYer Box 151).

10. JGT to CB, 6/27/28, B-BAZ—1928, NYer Box 135.

11. FS to KSA, n.d. [perhaps responding to KSA to FS, 8/22/28], Sullivan—1928, NYer Box 143.

12. KSA to DOS, 5/15/2 and 8/31/28, Stewart—1928, NYer Box 143.

13. KSA to AK, 1/18/29, Kober—1929, NYer Box 147.

14. See, for example, Blair and Hill 421.

15. Eleven installments of the Delphian Society series ran in volumes 4 and 5: "A Safe and Sane Fourth" 3/15/28:79–82; "The Hallowe'en Party" 9/22/28:84–85, "Taking Up Sport" 10/13/28:58–63, "The Coal Fields" 10/20/28:85–88, "The Yule in Retrospect" 12/29/28:40–41, "A New Apparatus" 4/6/29:61–64, "Fun for the Kiddies" 6/1/29:76–78, "Conditions at the Pool" 7/6/29:45–47, "The Cannons Are a Disgrace" 10/19/29:97–98, "Americanization" 11/23/29:73D–74, "Merrie, Merrie, Merrie" 12/7/29:156–57.

In addition, Bruccoli records a twelfth, in volume 6: "Delphian Hits Girls' Cage-Game Foes" 3/8/30:84–86.

16. "The Boss' Present" 4:41 (12/1/28:56–62); John O'Hara, "The House Organ" 5:5 (3/23/29:113–44); "Appreciation" 5:8 (4/13/29:97–98); "The Tournament" 5:16

(6/8/29:81–83); "Convention" 5:17 (6/15/29:80–82); "Mr. Rosenthal" 5:22 (7/20/29:24–25); "The Boss Talks" 5:24 (8/3/29:43–45); "Staff Picture" 5:29 (9/7/29:84–85); "Hallowe'en Party" 5:36 (10/26/29:36); "Getting Ready for 1930" 5:38 (11/9/29:115). Bruccoli identified additional installments running through volume 6 (364).

17. Woman speaker, "Beaux Arts" 5:49 (1/25/30:30); football coach, "Between the Halves" 5:34 (10/12/29:81–83); Clevelander wishing to be an easterner, "Out Of The West" 5:32 (9/28/29:51–52).

18. "Through the Magnifying Glass" ran on Hermann Oelrichs, ill. Ernest Hamlin Baker, 7/9/27:25–26; on George Jean Nathan, ill. Baker, 10/15/27:30–31); on Ralph Barton, ill. Peter Arno, 11/5/27:21–22; on Michael Strange, ill. Baker, 12/3/27:36–38.

19. He signed nothing else in the early *New Yorker,* and does not appear in editorial correspondence.

20. WEF to "Talk" editor, 2/28/28, Farbstein—1928, NYer Box 137.

21. Farbstein—1928, NYer Box 137.

22. Hall's bibliography lists "Parodies of Newspaper Features" as the *New Yorker's* designation (C557).

23. "Our Own Modern English Usage" appeared 1/5/29:22–23; 2/23/29:19–20; 4/13/29:28; 5/4/29:28; 6/22/29:27; 7/20/29:20–21, 8/17/29:25; 11/2/29:27; 12/21/29:31.

24. The Monroe series includes "Tea at Mrs. Armsby's" 4:45 (12/29/28:15); "The 'Wooing' of Mr. Monroe" 5:12 (5/11/29:17–18); "The Monroes Find a Terminal" 5:14 (5/25/29:20–21; "Mr. Monroe Outwits a Bat" 5:17 (6/15/29:17–18); "Mr. Monroe Holds the Fort" 5:41 (11/30/29:24–25); "The Imperturbable Spirit" 5:43 (12/14/29:25–26); "The Middle Years" 5:47 (1/11/30:18–19).

25. Thurber and Althea separated in 1929 (Kinney 1084).

26. HWR to RL, 9/9/29, Lardner—1929–30, NYer Box 6.

27. "Word Rates of Preferred Writers," n.d., Editorial—1930, NYer Box 5.

28. Two exceptions, however, are "Study for a Portrait" and "Portrait of My Brother" (6/22/29:36–38; 9/21/29:45–46).

29. Other Frankforter sketches in script form include "Coiffeur Pour Dames" 5:13 (5/18/29:87–90) and "Something to Read" 5:19 (6/29/29:71–72).

30. WG to EBW, n.d. [1950], EBW Box 83.

31. FD to KSW, 12/12/29, D—General Correspondence—1929, NYer Box 146.

32. ELR to KSA, 10/10/28; KSA to ELR, 10/12/28, Rice—1928, NYer Box 142.

33. E.g., Follies piece, KSA to AK, 1/18/29, Kober—1920, NYer Box 147.

34. KSA to HO, 11/9/29, Ober—1929, NYer Box 147.

Chapter 8: That Other *New Yorker* Humor

1. WCW to KSW, 10/1/30, Williams—1930, NYer Box 153.

2. Widdemer's poems all appeared in early volumes: "Catty Portraits" 10/24/25:37,

"In Praise of Predecessors" 12/5/25:23, "Songs of Tears" 2/12/27:43, "Daily Papers" 5/28/27:19. She also contributed one piece of prose humor, the epistolary "Personal-Touch Department" 10/26/29:112.

Wylie's verse contributions include "Peregrine's Sunday Song" (2/12/27:29), "For A Good Boy/For A Good Girl" (5/28/27:25), "Hughie at the Inn . . .; Mary at the Fair" (11/10/28:25), and two posthumous publications, "Anti-Feminist Song, For My Sister" (2/16/29:22) and "Restoration Love Song" (3/30/29:20). Laura Benét published "Noah's Dove" (5/21/27:21) and "Mouse" (10/12/29:96); Rosemary Carr Benét, "Bon Voyage" (10/2/26:66–67), "Elegy For Janes" (5/25/29:21), "Godiva to Tom" (8/3/29:20), "Reform" (2/15/30:70); Stephen Vincent Benét, "After Attending a Seance" (7/10/26:24); William Rose Benét, "The Narrative of Hard-Boiled Nan: A Theme for the Harpsichord" (10/16/26:68–69), "Communication" (3/10/28:34), "West Street Blues" (3/17/28:28), "The Littérateur" (4/14/28:24), "Visionary" (4/28/28:30). Nancy Hoyt's verse contributions—"At The Costumer's" (2/5/27:31), "Food" (2/5/27:65), "These Vanities" (3/12/27:34)—antedated her work as Dorothy Parker's backup book reviewer.

3. NL to KSW, 12/21/29, L—General Correspondence—1929, NYer Box 147.

4. KSW to NL, 12/24/29, L—General Correspondence—1929, NYer Box 147.

5. JE to KSA, 11/22/28, Embry—1928, NYer Box 137.

6. RBB, form letter, 6/6/30, 1929 Revenue & Pages, NYer Box 3.

7. KSA to JDeM, 5/26/28, DeMiskey—1928, NYer Box 137.

8. HWR to CMB, n.d., B—1928–30, NYer Box 3.

9. NYer to PRR, 7/17/28, Leacock—1928, NYer Box 140.

10. HWR to HB, 1/2/29, B—1928–30, NYer Box 3. Brubaker's column ran unsigned until 1:12 (5/9/25:17).

11. "Word Rates of Preferred Writers," Editorial—1930, NYer Box 5.

12. KSA to WRB, 10/11/28, Benét, NYer Box 135. Wylie received only $68, however, as the magazine kept 20 percent, or $17, to reduce $160 in advances.

13. "Follows an attempt," n.d., Contributors: Correspondence—1925, NYer Box 2.

14. AG to HWR, 4/12/26, Manuscripts: Miscellaneous—1927 (2 of 2), NYer Box 1349.

15. Parody Issue, 11/6/26:3, NYer Box 2.

16. NYer to C, 8/1/25, Form Letters—1925, NYer Box 3.

17. NYer to C, 9/2/25, Form Letters—1925, NYer Box 3.

18. White's "Definitions" series included "Critic" (10/17/25:8), "Commuter" (10/24/25:33), "Corset" (11/7/25:12), "Prude" (11/14/25:27), "Clergyman" (11/14/25:35).

19. John Roach Straton, 1875–1929, of New York City's Calvary Baptist Church, railed in radio and print against the immorality of the twenties (*Encyclopedia of New York City*).

20. The five poets' signed verse totals 280 items, 38.8 percent of the 721 poems by women, and 18.6 percent of the 1,503 items in volumes 2–5.

21. KSA to PE, 9/29/28, Thomas—1928, NYer Box 143.

22. Originally titled "What Price Gas: A Guide for Automobilists," Fishback, NYer Box 1348.

23. EBW to KSA, n.d. P-Q—1929, NYer Box 147.

24. KSA to NH, 11/30/28, Hoyt—1928, NYer Box 139.

25. CHK to HWR, 11/14/27, Knapp—1927, NYer Box 3.

26. "Word Rates of Preferred Writers," Editorial—1930, NYer Box 5.

27. KSW to CHK, 12/13/29, Knapp—1929, NYer Box 147.

28. Margaret DeSilver to NYer, [Jan. 1929?], D—General Correspondence—1929, NYer Box 146.

29. KSA to NL, 1/3/29, L—General Correspondence—1929, NYer Box 147.

30. HWG to KSA, 4/14/28, Gleason—1928, NYer Box 138.

31. KSA to HWG, 5/25/28, Gleason—1928, NYer Box 138.

32. KSA to HWG, 8/18/28 and 9/6/28, Gleason—1928, NYer Box 138.

33. KSA to PC, 6/16/28, Cummings—1928, NYer Box 136.

34. WRB to HWR, 8/28/30; HWR to WRB, 8/27/30, Benét—1930, NYer Box 3.

Appendix

1. Identified in Benchley's notebook RB 21–229.

2. KSA to PGW, 4/16/28, NYer Box 144.

3. Flanner—1928, NYer Box 138.

Works Cited

ABC News. "Drawing Laughter: The Cartoonists of *The New Yorker.*" Transcript of television program. Producer Dora Militaro. Host and interviewer Ted Koppel. *Nightline,* 1997. Online: http:// wwwabcnews.come/onair/nightline/html_files/transcripts/ntl1212. html.

Adams, James Truslow. *The Tempo of Modern Life.* New York: Albert and Charles Boni, Inc., 1931.

"Alajálov, Constantin." *1942. Current Biography.*

Amory, Cleveland, and Frederic Bradlee, eds. *Vanity Fair: Selections from America's Most Memorable Magazine, a Cavalcade of the 1920s and 1930s.* Picture ed. Katharine Tweed. New York: Viking P, 1960.

Angell, Roger. "'Congratulations! It's a Baby.'" Onward and Upward with the Arts. *New Yorker,* Dec. 15, 1997: 132–39.

Armitage, Shelley. *John Held, Jr.: Illustrator of the Jazz Age.* Syracuse, N.Y.: Syracuse U P, 1987.

Auden, W. H. "The Adult Voice of America." Rev. of *The New Yorker 25th Anniversary Album* (British edition) (Hamish Hamilton, 1952), unpaginated clipping, EBW Box 147.

Bagdikian, Ben H. *The Media Monopoly.* 5th ed. Boston: Beacon P, 1997.

———. "The Wrong Kind of Readers: The Fall and Rise of *The New Yorker.*" *Progressive* 47.5 (May 1983): 52–54.

Baker, Russell. "From Robert Benchley to Andrew Dice Clay." *American Heritage* 44.6 (Oct. 1993): 105–8.

"Baird Leonard Dies; Author and Critic." Obituary. *New York Times,* Jan. 24, 1941: 17, col. 4.

Becker, Stephen. *Comic Art in America: A Social History of the Funnies, the Political Cartoons, Magazine Humor, Sporting Cartoons, and Animated Cartoons.* Intro. by Rube Goldberg. New York: Simon and Schuster, 1959.

Behrman, S. N. "Old Monotonous—II [Robert Emmet Sherwood]." *New Yorker,* June 8, 1940: 23–34.

Benchley, Robert. "All Aboard for Dementia Praecox." Illust. Gropper. *New York American,* June 18, 1934. March of Events Page (Monday). Unpaginated clipping. Folder 1930–1919, Robert Benchley Papers, Billy Rose Theatre Collection, New York Public Library.

Benjamin, Walter. "The Work of Art in the Age of Mechanical Reproduction." Ed. and introd. Hannah Arendt. *Illuminations.* Trans. Harry Zohn. New York: Schocken, 1969. 217–51.

Bier, Jesse. *The Rise and Fall of American Humor.* New York: Holt, Rinehart and Winston, 1968.

Blackbeard, Bill, and Martin Williams, eds. *The Smithsonian Collection of Newspaper Comics.* Foreword by John Canaday. Washington, D.C.: Smithsonian Institution P and Harry N. Abrams, 1977.

Blair, Walter. "'A Man's Voice, Speaking': A Continuum in American Humor." *Veins of Humor.* Ed. Harry Levin. Harvard English Studies 3. Cambridge, Mass.: Harvard U P, 1972. 185–204.

————. *Native American Humor.* 1937. 2nd ed. Scranton, Penn.: Chandler Publishing Company, 1960.

Blair, Walter, and Hamlin Hill. *America's Humor: From Poor Richard to Doonesbury.* New York: Oxford U P, 1978.

Bliven, Bruce. "Flapper Jane." *New Republic* 44 (Sept. 9, 1925): 65–67.

Bruccoli, Matthew J. *The O'Hara Concern: A Biography of John O'Hara.* New York: Random House, 1975.

Bruère, Martha Bensley, and Mary Ritter Beard. *Laughing Their Way: Women's Humor in America.* New York: Macmillan, 1934.

Burke, Kenneth, and Malcolm Cowley. *Selected Correspondence of Kenneth Burke and Malcolm Cowley, 1915–1891.* Ed. Paul Jay. New York: Viking, 1988.

Carmody, Deirdre. "New Yorker's Editor Sees the Future in the Past." *New York Times,* Sept. 24, 1992: B1, 4.

Carson, Tom. "She, Tina." *Village Voice,* July 21, 1998: 47–49.

Cohen, Marilyn. *Reginald Marsh's New York: Paintings, Drawings, Prints and Photographs.* Catalog of exhibition held at the Whitney Museum of American Art, New York, N.Y., June 29–Aug. 24, 1983. New York: Whitney Museum of American Art in association with Dover Publications, 1983.

Corey, Mary F. "Mixed Messages: Representations of Consumption and Anti-Consumption in *The New Yorker* Magazine: 1945–1952." *American Periodicals* 4 (1994): 78–95.

Cornebise, Alfred E. *"The Stars and Stripes": Doughboy Journalism in World War I.* Contributions in Military History 37. Westport, Conn.: Greenwood P, 1984.

Cowley, Malcolm, ed. *After the Genteel Tradition: American Writers, 1910–1930.* Pref. by Harry T. Moore. 1937. Carbondale: Southern Illinois U P, 1964.

Craven, Thomas, ed. *Cartoon Cavalcade.* Assisted by Florence Weiss and Sydney Weiss. New York: Simon and Schuster, 1943.

Davis, Linda H. *Onward and Upward: A Biography of Katharine S. White.* New York: Harper and Row, 1987.

Day, Patrick. "Corey Ford." *American Humorists, 1800–1950.* Ed. Stanley Trachtenberg. Dictionary of Literary Biography 11. Detroit: Gale Research, 1982. 147–51.

Dell, Floyd. *Love in Greenwich Village.* New York: George H. Doran Company, 1926.

DeVoto, Bernard. "The Lineage of Eustace Tilley." Rev. of *Native American Humor,* ed. and intro. by Walter Blair. *Saturday Review of Literature* 16 (Sept. 25, 1937): 3–4, 20.

Donovan, Josephine. *New England Local Color Literature: A Women's Tradition.* New York: Frederick Ungar, 1983.

Douglas, Ann. *Terrible Honesty: Mongrel Manhattan in the 1920s.* 1995. Rpt. New York: Farrar, Straus and Giroux, 1996.

Douglas, George H. *The Smart Magazines: Fifty Years of Revelry and High Jinks at* Vanity Fair, The New Yorker, Life, Esquire, *and* The Smart Set. Hamden, Conn.: Archon, 1991.

"Downey, Fairfax (Davis)." *1949. Current Biography.* 168–70.

Eastman, Max. *Enjoyment of Laughter.* New York: Simon and Schuster, 1948.

Elledge, Scott. *E. B. White: A Biography.* New York: Norton, 1984.

Elson, Robert T., and Duncan Norton-Taylor, eds. *Time Inc.: The Intimate History of a Publishing Enterprise 1923–1941.* New York: Atheneum, 1968.

Emery, Michael, and Edwin Emery. *The Press and America: An Interpretive History of the Mass Media.* 7th ed. Englewood Cliffs, N.J.: Prentice Hall, 1992.

The Encyclopedia of New York City. New Haven: Yale U P and the New-York Historical Society, 1995.

Erkkila, Betsy. "Frank Sullivan." *American Humorists, 1800–1950.* Ed. Stanley Trachtenberg. Dictionary of Literary Biography 11. Detroit: Gale Research, 1982. 478–85.

Fass, Paula S. *The Damned and the Beautiful: American Youth in the 1920's.* New York: Oxford U P, 1977.

"Fillmore Hyde, Author, Is Dead." Obituary. *New York Times,* Jan. 27, 1970: 43, col. 2.

"Fishback, Margaret." *1941. Current Biography.* 281-83.

Fitzgerald, F. Scott. *F. Scott Fitzgerald: A Life in Letters.* New York: Simon and Schuster, Touchstone Books, 1994.

Flanner, Janet. *Paris Was Yesterday, 1925–1939.* Ed. Irving Drutman. New York: Viking P, 1972.

———. Introduction. "The Unique Ross." *Ross, the* New Yorker, *and Me,* by Jane Grant. New York: Reynal and Company, 1968. 7–16.

Folkerts, Jean, Stephen Lacy, and Lucinda Davenport. *The Media in Your Life: An Introduction to Mass Communication.* Boston: Allyn and Bacon, 1998.

Ford, Corey. *The Time of Laughter.* Boston: Little, Brown, 1967.

Gerber, John C. "Mark Twain's Use of the Comic Pose." *PMLA* 77 (June 1962): 297–304.

Gill, Brendan. *Here at the* New Yorker. New York: Random House, 1975.

Grant, Jane. *Ross, the* New Yorker, *and Me.* New York: Reynal and Company, 1968.

Grant, Thomas. "Dorothy Parker." *American Humorists, 1800–1950.* Ed. Stanley Trachtenberg. Dictionary of Literary Biography. 369–82.

———. "Feminist Humor of the 1920s: The 'Little Insurrections' of Florence Guy Seabury." *New Perspectives on Women and Comedy.* Ed. Regina Barreca. Studies in Gender and Culture 5. Philadelphia: Gordon and Breach, 1992. 157–67.

Grauer, Neil A. *Remember Laughter: A Life of James Thurber.* Lincoln: U of Nebraska P, 1995.

Hall, Katherine Romans, comp. *E. B. White: A Bibliographic Catalogue of Printed Materials in the Department of Rare Books, Cornell University Library.* Pref. E. B. White. New York: Garland, 1979.

Hamburger, Philip. *Friends Talking in the Night: Sixty Years of Writing for* The New Yorker. New York: Knopf, 1999.

Harriman, Margaret Case. *The Vicious Circle: The Story of the Algonquin Round Table.* New York: Rinehart and Co., 1951.

Held, John, Jr. *The Works of John Held, Jr.* New York: Ives Washburn, 1931.

Hendin, Josephine. "The *New Yorker* as Cultural Ideal." *Dissent* 29.4 (1982): 450–54.

Herrmann, Dorothy. *With Malice Toward All.* New York: Putnam's, 1982.

"Hokinson, Helen Elna." *Dictionary of American Biography.*

Hoover, Ellison. *Cartoons from* Life. Foreword by Robert Benchley. New York: Simon and Schuster, 1925.

Horn, Maurice, ed. *The World Encyclopedia of Cartoons.* Asst. ed. Richard E. Marschall. 6 vols. New York: Chelsea House, 1981.

Inge, M. Thomas. "The *New Yorker* Cartoon and Graphic Humor." *Comics as Culture.* Jackson: U P of Mississippi, 1990. 109–16.

Ingersoll, Ralph. *"The New Yorker." Fortune* 2.10 (Aug 1934): 72–92, 97–98, 150-52.

Ingersoll, Ralph McAllister. *Point of Departure: An Adventure in Autobiography.* New York: Harcourt, Brace and World, 1961.

James, Henry. "The Middle Years." Ed. Quentin Anderson. *Selected Short Stories.* Rev. ed. New York: Holt, Rinehart and Winston, 1957. 145–66.

Johnson, James Weldon. *Black Manhattan.* 1930. New York: Arno P and the New York Times, 1968.

Kahn, E. J. *About* The New Yorker *and Me.* New York: Putnam, 1979.

Keefer, Truman Frederick. *Wylie, Philip.* Twayne's United States Authors Series 285. Boston: Twayne, 1977.

Kinney, Harrison. *James Thurber: His Life and Times.* New York: Holt, 1995.

Klein, I. "Memories of Milt Gross." *Cartoonist Profiles* 14 (June 1972): 54–57.

Klein, Marcus. *Foreigners: The Making of American Literature, 1900–1940.* Chicago: U of Chicago P, 1981.

Kramer, Dale. *Chicago Renaissance: The Literary Life in the Midwest, 1900–1930.* New York: Appleton-Century, 1966.

———. *Ross and the* New Yorker. Garden City, N.Y.: Doubleday, 1951.

Kroeber, Karl. *Retelling/Rereading: The Fate of Storytelling in Modern Times.* New Brunswick, N.J.: Rutgers U P, 1992.

Kunkel, Thomas. *Genius in Disguise: Harold Ross of the* New Yorker. New York: Random House, 1995.

Lears, Jackson. *Fables of Abundance: A Cultural History of Advertising in America.* New York: Basic, 1994.

Lears, T. J. Jackson. "From Salvation to Self-Realization: Advertising and the Therapeutic Roots of the Consumer Culture, 1880-1930." Ed. richard Wightman Fox. *The Culture of Consumption: Critical Essays in American History, 1880–1980.* New York: Pantheon, 1983. 3-38.

Lee, Judith Yaross. *Garrison Keillor: A Voice of America.* Studies in Popular Culture. Jackson: U P of Mississippi, 1991.

Lorenz, Lee. *The Art of* The New Yorker, *1925–1995.* New York: Knopf, 1995.

———. "Cover Stories: Five From an Era of Extreme Incorrectness." Illustrations by Will Cotton, et al. *New Yorker,* Dec. 15, 1997: 124.

Lott, Eric. *Love and Theft: Blackface Minstrelsy and the American Working Class.* New York: Oxford U P, 1993.

Lupton, Ellen, and J. Abbott Miller. *Design Writing Research: Writing on Graphic Design.* New York: Princeton Architectural P, Kiosk, 1996.

Mahon, Gigi. *The Last Days of* The New Yorker. 1988. Rpt. New York: New American Library, 1989.

Marchand, Roland. *Advertising the American Dream: Making Way for Modernity, 1920–1940.* Berkeley: U of California P, 1985.

McGrath, Charles. "Life and Letters: The Ross Years." *New Yorker,* Feb. 20, 1995: 180–90.

McKelway, St. Clair. "Gossip Writer [Walter Winchell]: II—Upstart Stays Up." *New Yorker,* June 22, 1940: 24–30.

McNutt, James C. "Donald Ogden Stewart." *American Humorists, 1800–1950.* Ed. Stanley Trachtenberg. Dictionary of Literary Biography 11. Detroit: Gale Research, 1982. 466–73.

Meyrowitz, Joshua. *No Sense of Place: The Impact of Electronic Media on Social Behavior.* New York: Oxford U P, 1985.

Miller, Nina. "Making Love Modern: Dorothy Parker and Her Public." *American Literature* 64.4 (Dec. 1992): 764–84.

Mitchell, W. J. T. *Iconology: Image, Text, Ideology.* Chicago: U of Chicago P, 1986.

———. *Picture Theory: Essays on Verbal and Visual Representation.* Chicago: U of Chicago P, 1994.

Moon, Ben L. "City Magazines, Past and Present." *Journalism Quarterly* 47.4 (1970): 711–18.

Mott, Frank Luther. "Fifty Years of *Life:* the Story of a Satirical Weekly." *Journalism Quarterly* 25 (Sept. 1948): 224–32.

MPA [Magazine Publishers of America]. *Magazines Move Millions, One Mind at a Time.* Advertising supplement. Created by Bernice Kanner. *New York Times,* Oct. 20, 1997: MP 1–20.

"A New York Diary." *New Republic* 52.667 (Sept. 14, 1927): 96–98.

New Yorker Magazine. *The Complete Book of Covers from* The New Yorker, *1925–1989.* Foreword by John Updike. New York: Knopf, 1989.

The New Yorker *Out Loud.* 2 cassettes. Mercury, 1998. Cassette recording.

Nickels, Cameron C. *New England Humor: From the Revolutionary War to the Civil War.* Knoxville: U of Tennessee P, 1993.

North, Michael. *The Dialect of Modernism: Race, Language, and Twentieth-Century Literature.* New York: Oxford U P, 1994.

O'Connor, Richard. *Heywood Broun: A Biography.* New York: Putnam's, 1975.

O'Hara, John. "An Open Letter to the *Tiger.*" *Princeton Tiger,* Feb. 14, 1951: 1, 3.

————. *Selected Letters of John O'Hara.* Ed. Matthew J. Bruccoli. New York: Random House, 1978.

Ohmann, Richard. "History and Literary History: The Case of Mass Culture." *Modernity and Mass Culture.* Ed. James Naremore and Patrick Brantlinger. Bloomington: Indiana U P, 1991. 24–41.

————. *Selling Culture: Magazines, Markets, and Class at the Turn of the Century.* London: Verso, 1996.

Ortega y Gasset, José. *The Dehumanization of Art and Other Writings on Art, Culture, and Literature.* 1948. Princeton, N.J.: Princeton U P, 1968.

Pemberton, Murdock. "A Memoir of Three Decades." *Arts,* Oct. 1955: 27–32.

Perelman, S. J. *Don't Tread on Me: The Selected Letters of S. J. Perelman.* Ed. Prudence Crowther. 1987. New York: Penguin, 1988.

Pinck, Dan. "Paging Mr[.] Ross: Old Days at 'The New Yorker.'" *Encounter* (London, England) 69 (June 1987): 5–11.

Pinsker, Sanford. "Arthur Kober." *American Humorists, 1800–1950.* Ed. Stanley Trachtenberg. Dictionary of Literary Biography 11. Detroit: Gale Research, 1982. 237–41.

————. "On or About December 1910: When Human Character—and American Humor—Changed." *Critical Essays on American Humor.* Ed. William Bedford Clark and W. Craig Turner. Boston: G. K. Hall and Co., 1984. 184–99.

Platt, Susan Noyes. *Modernism in the 1920s: Interpretations of Modern Art in New York from Expressionism to Constructivism.* Studies in the Fine Arts: Criticism 17. Ann Arbor, Mich.: UMI Research P, 1985.

Pogrebin, Robin. "Staff Writer Named Editor at New Yorker." *New York Times,* July 14, 1998: C1, 6.

————. "The Year of the Pointing Fingers at The New Yorker." *New York Times,* Feb. 16, 1998: C1, 6.

Radway, Janice A. *A Feeling for Books: The Book-of-the-Month Club, Literary Taste, and Middle-Class Desire.* Chapel Hill: U of North Carolina P, 1997.

"Rea, Gardner." *1946. Current Biography.* 499–501.

Richter, Harvey, ed. *Best College Humor: The First Collection from the American College Humorous Magazines.* Intro. by H. C. Witwer. Reading, Penn.: Handy Book Corp., 1920.

"R. I." [Obituary of Rea Irvin]. *New Yorker* 48.16 (June 10, 1972): 132.

Rood, Karen L. "Janet Flanner." *American Writers in Paris, 1920–1939.* Ed. Karen Lane Rood. Foreword by Malcolm Cowley. Dictionary of Literary Biography 4. Detroit: Gale Research, 1980. 151–61.

Ross, Lillian. *Takes: Stories from "The Talk of the Town."* New York: Congdon and Weed, Inc., 1983.

Rovit, Earl. "Modernism and Three Magazines: An Editorial Revolution." *Sewanee Review* 93 (Fall 1985): 540–53.

Rutledge, J. H., and P. B. Bart. "Urbanity, Inc." *Wall Street Journal,* June 30, 1958: 1, 6.

Sasowsky, Norman. *The Prints of Reginald Marsh.* Intro. by Lloyd Goodrich. New York: Clarkson N. Potter, 1976.

Seldes, Gilbert. "The Newspaper Colyumists." *Vanity Fair* 21.1 (Sept 1923): 46, 86.

Shaw, Vivian. "The Cuckoo School of Humour in America." *Vanity Fair* 22.3 (May 1924): 16, 98.

Slade, Joseph W. *Pornography and Sexual Representation: A Reference Guide.* Westport, Conn.: Greenwood, in press.

Sloan, William David, James G. Stovall, and James D. Startt, eds. *The Media in America: A History.* 2nd ed. Scottsdale, Ariz.: Publishing Horizons, Inc., 1993.

Sloane, David E. E. *American Humor Magazines and Comic Periodicals.* New York: Greenwood, 1987.

Solomon, Eric. "Robert Benchley." *American Humorists, 1800–1950.* Ed. Stanley Trachtenberg. Dictionary of Literary Biography 11. Detroit: Gale Research, Bruccoli Clark, 1982. 22–37.

Stahl, Sandra K. D. "Personal Experience Stories." *Handbook of American Folklore.* Ed. Richard M. Dorson. Bloomington: Indiana U P, 1983. 268–76.

Steiner, Wendy. *Pictures of Romance: Form Against Context in Painting and Literature.* Chicago: U of Chicago P, 1988.

Sterling, Christopher H., and John M. Kittross. *Stay Tuned: A Concise History of American Broadcasting.* 2nd ed. Belmont, Calif.: Wadworth Publishing Company, 1990.

Stewart, Donald Ogden. *By a Stroke of Luck! An Autobiography.* New York: Paddington P, 1975.

Swords, Betty. "Why Women Cartoonists Are Rare, and Why That's Important." *New Perspectives on Women and Comedy.* Ed. Regina Barreca. Studies in Gender and Culture 5. Philadelphia: Gordon and Breach, 1992. 65–84.

Tatham, David. "Introduction." *Art Artists and Museums.* Exhibition catalog. Works selected by David Tatham, catalog by Domenic J. Iacono. Syracuse, N.Y.: Syracuse U Art Collections, 1980.

Terrie, Philip G. "Arthur Guiterman." *American Humorists, 1800–1950.* Ed. Stanley Trachtenberg. Dictionary of Literary Biography 11. Detroit: Gale Research, 1982. 165–68.

Thorpe, T. B. "The Big Bear of Arkansas." *Spirit of the Times* 11.37 (Mar. 27, 1841).

Thurber, James. "E. B. W." *Saturday Review of Literature* 18 (Oct. 15, 1938): 8–9.

———. *The Years with Ross.* 1959. New York: Ballantine, 1975.

Todd, Ellen Wiley. *The "New Woman" Revised: Painting and Gender Politics on Fourteenth Street.* Berkeley: U of California P, 1993.

Toombs, Sarah. "S. J. Perelman: A Bibliography of Short Essays, 1932–1979." *Studies in American Humor* n.s. 3.1 (Spring 1984): 83–98.

Toth, Emily. "A Laughter of Their Own: Women's Humor in the United States." *Critical Essays on American Humor.* Ed. William Bedford Clark and W. Craig Turner. Boston: G. K. Hall and Co., 1984. 199–215.

Updike, John. "Books: Witty Dotty." Rev. of *Dorothy Parker: What Fresh Hell Is This?* by Marion Meade. *New Yorker,* Apr. 25, 1988: 109–12.

Van Doren, Carl. "Day In and Day Out: Adams, Morley, Marquis, and Broun: Manhattan Wits." Illus. Harry Turner. *Century Magazine* 107 (Dec. 1923): 308–15.

Veron, Enid, ed. *Humor in America: An Anthology.* New York: Harcourt Brace Jovanovich, 1976.

Walker, Nancy. "The Remarkably Constant Reader: Dorothy Parker as Book Reviewer." *Studies in American Humor* n.s. 3.4 (1997): 1–14.

Walker, Nancy A. "'Talking Back to the Culture: Contemporary Women's Comic Art." *New Directions in American Humor.* Ed. David E. E. Sloane. U of Alabama P, 1998. 103–17.

———. *A Very Serious Thing: Women's Humor and American Culture.* Minneapolis: U of Minnesota P, 1988.

Walker, Nancy, and Zita Dresner, eds. *Redressing the Balance: American Women's Literary Humor from Colonial Times to the 1980s.* Jackson: U P of Mississippi, 1988.

Ware, Caroline F. *Greenwich Village, 1920–1930: A Comment on American Civilization in the Post-War Years.* 1935. New York: Harper Colophon Books, Harper and Row, 1965.

Warren, James. "Sunday Watch: Audacity at The New Yorker." *Chicago Tribune,* June 20, 1993: Tempo (Section 5) 2.

"We Thank You All Very, Very Much for a Very Very VERY Happy Birthday." Advertisement. *New York Post,* Feb. 18, 1927: n.p. [archival clipping].

Weales, Gerald. "Taking Cover." Rev. of *The Complete Book of Covers from "The New Yorker," 1925–1989. Gettysburg Review* 4.3 (Summer 1991): 498–510.

Weaver, Leah. "The Feminine Condition." *Inks* 1.3 (Nov. 1994): 8–17.

White, E. B. *Letters of E.B. White.* New York: Harper and Row, 1976.

Williams, Raymond. "When Was Modernism?" *Art in Modern Culture: An Anthology of Critical Texts.* Ed. Francis Frascina and Jonathan Harris. 1989. New York: Icon Editions, HarperCollins, 1992. 23–27.

Williamson, Juanita V., and Virginia M. Burke, eds. *A Various Language: Perspectives on American Dialects.* 1926. New York: Holt, Rinehart and Winston, 1971.

Wilson, Edmund. *The Twenties: From Notebooks and Diaries of the Period.* Ed. Leon Edel. New York: Farrar, Straus and Giroux, 1975.

Yank Talk: A Review of A.E.F. Humor, Trench and Billet. Paris: Lafayette cie, 1918.

Yates, Norris W. *The American Humorist: Conscience of the Twentieth Century.* Ames: Iowa State U P, 1964.

Index